THE LIFE OF FRANCESCO GUICCIARDINI

FRANCESCO GUICCIARDINI
Oil on wood portrait by Giuliano Bugiardini
*(Yale University Art Gallery, the Rabinowitz Collection, gift of
Hannah D. and Louis M. Rabinowitz.)*

THE LIFE OF FRANCESCO GUICCIARDINI

by

ROBERTO RIDOLFI

Translated from the Italian by

CECIL GRAYSON

Routledge and Kegan Paul

LONDON

Originally published in Italy as
VITA DI FRANCESCO GUICCIARDINI
Copyright 1960 by Angelo Belardetti Editore, Rome

First published in Great Britain 1967
by Routledge & Kegan Paul Limited
Broadway House, 68–74 Carter Lane
London, E.C.4

Printed in Great Britain by
Cox & Wyman Limited
London, Fakenham and Reading

English Translation
© *Routledge & Kegan Paul Ltd 1967*

CONTENTS

CONTENTS

TRANSLATOR'S NOTE

For this English edition of Guicciardini's Life the author has
revised and brought up to date, especially in the notes and
bibliography, the text of the original Italian edition published
in 1960.

C. G.

PREFACE

I WOULD have liked during my lifetime to write at least one book which did not need a preface, that is, which did not need justifying. This might be the one, at long last, for no one can deny that a biography of Guicciardini is needed. On Machiavelli, before I wrote that almost too popular Life, there were the weighty works of Villari and Tommasini, full of faults if you like but also full of learning. On Guicciardini there were only the few and meagre biographical pages in Benoist's monograph and the all-too-numerous pages of Zanoni, who compiled an enormous book to tell us practically nothing and tell it badly. In our own day Otetea's work certainly has its merits, but quite apart from the fact that too many documents escaped his notice, how could we be satisfied with a monograph on Guicciardini where there is merely a passing reference to the *Ricordi* and the *Storia d'Italia* is not even mentioned?

Anyone undertaking this work was therefore justified in advance, and I more than anyone perhaps, having worked for so many years on the papers of that great writer, discovered his unpublished works, gathered a great harvest of documents and received the kind and authoritative encouragement that I have shamelessly described in a recent work.

If that had not been enough, there would have been the words with which Emilio Cecchi closed his review of Machiavelli's Life to which I have just referred.

All the same, I shall not be able to seize even this last chance, or overcome that 'guilt complex' which weighs upon me every time I am about to add further printed matter to the already far too great quantity flooding the world, in which the little that is valuable is lost. I must in fact justify myself for having decided to write this book after having sworn in public and in private for so many years that I would never write it. I will not here give all my reasons for going back on my word, because there are things one cannot or should not say. I cannot get out of it with a joke to the effect that 'evil too often prevails over good'. To explain the motives of this unexpected capitulation I would have to go back to my reasons for not writing the book, given by me in *Memorie di uno studioso*. But above all the overt reasons why I was unwilling to undertake this work there was another which I did not express: that I have never managed to like Guicciardini, though he is possibly the intellect I most admire.

Thus I was quite unable to make up my mind to write his Life, having always thought, and having recently written, things like this: 'Love and affinities help one to understand, and to look into oneself is always helpful. If a constitution of the republic of letters were promulgated (awful thought), it should compel biographers to portray only men in some way similar or congenial to themselves: so many insincere or lukewarm books would be avoided. Let Villari's *Machiavelli* be a lesson to us all.'

The interesting thing is that my lack of human sympathy for Guicciardini, having held me back for so long, was what finally made up my mind. Having studied and loved the biographical genre since childhood, I wished in this last experiment to test the truth of my affirmations. It is a bold attempt as will be seen. If it succeeds, so much the better; if it does not, I shall at least have the meagre comfort of being confirmed in my former belief.

In this Life, where for the first time are collected my well-known Guicciardini discoveries, from the *Cose fiorentine* to the Commentaries on his service as Lieutenant, there is more new material than I suppose has been published in this century on any other of our major classical authors. This book will lack the human warmth which pleased the public in my *Machiavelli*; the biographer as well as the subject will lack cordiality. In any case as I have always tried to identify myself with the men whose portraits I have chosen to draw, a certain detachment seems to me to fit the character, and were he able to offer an opinion, the wishes of Guicciardini himself.

La Baronta,
   13 July 1959   R.R.

Finally, at the end of these long labours, my thoughts return to Paolo Guicciardini and to my kind Roman editor Angelo Belardetti. With deep feeling I write their names in these pages which for so long they hoped for and did not live to see.

Chapter I

UNDER THE SIGN OF POLITICS:
THE SCHOOL OF HIS ANCESTORS:
THE SCHOOL OF BOOKS

◇◇

I
N EVERYONE's writings, conversation and thoughts the name of
Guicciardini is linked with Machiavelli or is immediately associated
with him. Now Machiavelli's biographer embarks upon Guicciardini.

Born within a few years of one another in the same city, both
Florentines by origin and in spirit, both historians and politicians, they
were so different in character, in education, in condition, that one might
think a parallel could only be drawn of their dissimilarities and contrasts.
Eminence was practically the only thing their intellects had in common. In the words of Cellini one might say that of men like them,
there could be only one at a time in the world. Yet Florence within the
narrow bounds of her walls had two of them together.

These first pages will enable us to consider the contrasting background and education which went to make them different, and how
even the few years which divided them in age contributed to that
result. The differences of nature and mind we shall consider further on
when we have more material for doing so, and we could not discuss
those aspects at all before observing the conditions which surely influenced both character and intellect. On the other hand it may suffice
for the time being to remember the brief comparison I drew in the Life

of Machiavelli, with which this book, at least in the intention of the author, should almost form a single unity. Nor is it because of any unhealthy literary itch that the timeworn comparison tempts me: at a certain point it will appear quite clearly that Machiavelli can help us to understand Guicciardini.

The Guicciardini family, of whom Francesco wrote that he had sought the origins in vain,[1] seem, according to the documents recently published and illustrated, to have been descended originally not from Poppiano in Val di Pesa as Verino says, but from Mugello where they were wealthy landowners in the twelfth or perhaps even as early as the eleventh century.[2] It seems certain that they were related to if not directly descended from the local feudal lords the Suavizzi, a connection that sent into ecstasies a seventeenth-century genealogist like Gamurrini. But the family was never known as one of the aristocratic ones of the republic, and I prefer to start with what is certain, that is, those country properties which formed the basis of their early fortunes in the city. Those were times when the lure of the city and of 'quick profits' led those whom the Florentines called 'nobili selvatici', nobles from the wilderness, to settle one after another in the city. Whether or not the Guicciardini were among those, in the earliest days they were known, and ranked, as 'good plebeians', as the saying went. Francesco himself says so.[3] Up to this point the origins of the Guicciardini seem no different from those of the Machiavelli.

The differences begin later. Early set on the road to civic honours the Guicciardini obtained the Gonfalonierato di Giustizia in 1302, barely ten years after the founding of that supreme office. They held it again repeatedly; only five Florentine families held it more often than they, and among those five we find, besides the dominant Medici, the Salviati, the Strozzi and the Ridolfi, all sooner or later connected with the Medici. Forty-four times they sat in the Signoria as Priors.

In spite of all this, the Guicciardini, from the time of those early honours, remained for nearly eighty years in a moderate state of wealth and position, just like the Machiavelli, until, becoming richer they also became more influential. This process began with Luigi Guicciardini who was gonfalonier at the time of the Ciompi rebellion when 'in the space of two or three days his house was burnt down, he was removed from office, driven from the city and raised to knighthood by the same people'.[4]

The prime mover if not the author of that tumult was Salvestro de'

Medici who then, without realizing it, laid the foundations of the future greatness of his family. When that greatness was firmly established with the final victory and return of Cosimo de' Medici, *pater patriae*, in 1434, it could be said that the greatness of the Guicciardini was founded simultaneously. For one of them, Piero, Luigi's eldest son was among the principal figures responsible for Cosimo's return.[5] From that time the fortunes of the main branch of the family were firmly linked with those of the triumphant Medici.

Luigi and Iacopo, Piero's sons, won fresh grace and merit with the Medici who were now princes in all but name and certain outward forms. When the Medici state appeared to be in danger, whether out of sincere affection or because they were now too deeply involved to do otherwise, or because they smelt victory, they threw themselves impetuously into its defence 'boldly and without fear'.[6] Thus it was when Luca Pitti tried to bring down Piero de' Medici in 1466, and after the Pazzi Conspiracy when 'Iacopo did more perhaps than any other citizen to maintain Lorenzo's power'.[7] Much new light is thrown on these relationships and also on the politics of the Florentine Republic both at home and abroad by the differences and indeed the contrasts between the unpublished correspondence of Lorenzo and Iacopo, and the parallel exchanges of letters between Iacopo and the Signoria.[8]

So much loyalty, accompanied by a political sense made ever sharper by tradition and exercise, was richly rewarded with a continual and remarkable succession of offices, embassies and commissions. So much so that one can truly say that Piero the son of Luigi, and Luigi and Iacopo the sons of Piero, were inferior to none apart from the Medici themselves in the government of that principality which was ruled with the forms of a republic. I do not think that any other Florentine family was so continuously in power from generation to generation for more than a century from 1434 onwards. Carlo Strozzi wrote that nobility is 'old-established continuing wealth, constantly illustrated by civic virtue'.[9] If this statement be true, and for civic-minded Florence it certainly was so, I do not know any other Florentine family which might claim to be nobler than the Guicciardini at the time of the birth of Francesco.

He was born in Florence in a gloomy house in a street, then called 'di Piazza', which was to take his family name a century later.[10] It was the 6th March 1483 at the fifth hour of the night according to the method of counting time then in use, which meant about 10 p.m. In that age great importance was attached to the moment of birth because of its astrological implications, and astrology was indeed brought to bear on this occasion.

He was the third child of Piero, only son of Iacopo mentioned above. Piero on the other hand, married at eighteen to Simona Gianfigliazzi, had a large family: thirteen sons and daughters of whom eleven survived. The other sons were called Luigi, the eldest, Girolamo the second, Iacopo, and Bongianni. In his daughters Piero 'was not lucky, for three became nuns owing to their deformity'.[11] The other three he married off. Of his wife Simona we know only that she was the daughter of Bongianni Gianfigliazzi 'in his day a well-known citizen'. Piero's famous son, who collected so much information about his relations and wrote at length about his grandmother Guglielmetta Nerli, praising her great qualities with a warmth and affection very unusual in him, did not leave a single loving word about his mother in his Memoirs,[12] but his nature was such that one cannot assume that this meant he was not fond of her.

Florentine histories say a good deal about his father Piero, and not only in the youthful works of his son the historian, who loved him 'more dearly than men commonly love their fathers'.[13] However, in these pages which are more strictly chronological than usual, it will be better to mention these matters further on, since, until the day of Francesco's birth Piero had done nothing but apply himself quietly to his studies. He is said to have been gifted with a political flair hardly less keen than his father's, his uncle's, his grandfather's or his great grandfather's; in fact it was said that 'apart from Giovan Battista Ridolfi there was no one in Florence to equal him for intellect and seriousness'.[14] However he was timid and over scrupulous, and even when older he preferred to attend to his private affairs and his studies of the humanities which were a consolation to him in the changes of government, when an interest in politics would have served him much less well. A Platonist by inclination as well as by the fashion of his day, Marsilio Ficino was his teacher and friend and honoured him in his writings: it was Ficino who held Francesco at the font.[15]

The latter grew up with an immense respect for the study of letters which 'perfect the qualities of the mind'.[16] He also respected philosophers although he felt that when they examined 'the invisible' they talked 'infinite nonsense';[17] but he greatly preferred the study of government. All the praises he wrote of his beloved father appear in his pages

4

shadowed by open regret that he had not engaged more resolutely in politics. However, while awaiting the freedom of adult years, he had to be content to be the godchild of philosophy.

Of his childhood we know only the few facts that he mentioned in his *Ricordanze* and scattered references in his other writings. With the greatest caution we might also mention here a curious document unknown until now: a voluminous horoscope compiled several years later by a person who knew Francesco's past very well indeed if not his future, and he refers to his past year by year, which would be much harder than predicting the future if the author had only astrological information to go on.

On the evidence of this horoscope we hear of certain illnesses which are of small importance to a biography like ours, and some other details, but we would now rather dwell on the more general statement of Guicciardini himself when he tells us that he was 'brought up piously as a child'.[18] There is no doubt that with such a father deeply devoted to Savonarola from the religious point of view though less so in politics, he grew up among those children of the Friar when

'This city seemed a foretaste of paradise'.

Francesco himself tells us in the *Ricordi* of his maturity that his earliest years had known 'no corruption of any kind, no frivolity, no wasted time'.[19]

Piero 'educated his children most diligently', and being inclined as he was to the study of letters and philosophy, he had the boy study 'the humanities'. He learnt Latin from the age of six to twelve without having to go outside his own home, under the guidance of a ser Giovanni della Castellina, preceptor to him and his brothers.[20] One should not underestimate this aristocratic character of his education which was to have a certain influence on his closed and haughty nature. His first studies in the humanities must have been in accordance with the habits and pedagogical rules of the age, and his mature writings do not show signs of particularly long study or great love of ancient authors, with the exception of the historians: especially, after Livy, Xenophon, Thucydides and his beloved Tacitus. We should note what he said about Tacitus and Frontinus: 'One came to light not many years since, and the other's first three books were discovered during my own youth.'[21] A little further on he makes a note albeit for a particular purpose: 'Find out what histories Dante knew.' It would be impossible to say which of these historians, beyond the usual ones which were set before all schoolboys, were read and studied by him in childhood, but even if he did not read all of them, it is certain that his earliest inclinations were formed by these texts, and also the first ambitions of one who was to be called, *par excellence*, 'the man of the histories'.[22]

These were the years during which, in Florence, the young men of noble family frequented the lectures of Politian, and the aristocratic Nerli had the first edition of Homer printed at their own expense. Thus the young Francesco also learnt a little Greek, but he did not go further than the first elements and he forgot it all as he tells us 'within a few years'.[23] For Greek and Latin letters after he left the care of ser Giovanni, it seems that he attended the lectures of Marcello Virgilio Adriani, whose pupil he declares himself in a letter which I had the good fortune to discover, and which is the first of his that we know. At that time or a little later he enjoyed or rather he practised writing humanist letters and even Latin verses.[24] He also attended lectures on logic but soon gave this up with his other humanist studies and turned to the study of law.[25]

He was barely sixteen and already ambition and an irresistible longing for power gnawed at his young heart. His adolescence itself 'without any frivolity or wasted time' tells us a great deal, when we stop to think of it, about his secret thoughts. In the youthful companies and associations which he frequented (and with a father like his they must, as I have said, have been those of the Friar) he had no other wish than to dominate the others, to lead them, to have a following, placing himself at the head of little bands and societies, so much so that his restless and ambitious nature caused him to be nicknamed Alcibiades.[26] The horoscope, though it was written before his character had fully developed, describes him as a 'lover of nobility, honours and great things'.

For such a nature, as he himself admits in the *Ricordanze*, the obscure fame of letters could hardly be attractive. Francesco therefore chose the study of law, which as an education and an investment seemed to him a better means to that end which he now saw clearly before him. One author who wrote, though all too briefly, about his legal studies, states that it was his legal vocation which made of Guicciardini a man of action.[27] I would prefer to reverse that statement, and say that it was his imperious vocation for action which caused him to study law, though no one would seek to deny the influence on the politician and the writer of his legal education.

Therefore in November 1498 at the age of fifteen he began to study civil law in Florence, where the University had moved because of the rebellion in Pisa, and for the whole of that academic year he attended the lectures of messer Iacopo Modesti da Prato. In the new year too, beginning in November 1499, he continued to attend the former's lectures, but in the evening: in the morning he heard messer Ormanozzo Deti until Lent, then when Deti went over to common law Guicciardini went to his successor messer Francesco Pepi.[28] Of this period (10th May 1500) there is a Latin letter from Francesco which shows him after the delightful Easter holidays at grips with his authors Titius and Sempronius under the guidance of Pepi.[29]

Things were just the same in the following academic year until Pepi went as ambassador to Rome in February 1501 and Giovan Vittorio Soderini took his place. Francesco then went to him in the morning for civil law and in the afternoon to the celebrated Filippo Decio for canon law. All this changed suddenly on the 19th March 1501 (in the *Ricordanze* he puts 1500 but the date there is written in the Florentine style) when he suddenly left the University of Florence and transferred to the one at Ferrara.

In fact his worthy father with his usual wisdom had already considered sending him to study outside Florence where he might get on with fewer distractions and temptations, although that remarkable son of his appeared to have very few temptations. Even then he appeared to deserve that expression of praise (if it really is one) which a few years later was to be uttered by the famous General of the Order of Camaldoli Pietro Delfin: 'young in years, already old in gravity and demeanour'.[30] However, the recent misfortunes of the Republic with which we will deal briefly, led Piero in his great prudence to anticipate or rather precipitate half-way through the year the carrying out of the decision he had already taken. In that way he sought to prepare for his family and himself a peaceful refuge, and in the meantime sent to safety a large sum of money together with the son on whom he already placed most reliance. Between what he gave him on his departure and other sums sent on subsequent occasions, it was two thousand ducats in all.

Francesco therefore moved to Ferrara, a quiet city and cheap to live in, which must have been welcome to the Guicciardini parsimony. That University was of small merit, as the salaries it paid were low,[31] but among the other teachers he could hear the lectures of one Giovanni Sadoleto at that time quite a famous civil lawyer, now better remembered as the father of the famous humanist. Guicciardini however was a critical pupil, and in November 1502 'because the University of Ferrara did not satisfy him' he left it for the more glorious and famous one of Padua.

There he again found messer Filippo Decio who had left his chair at Florence, and for that and the following year he actually took lodgings with his old master. Until Easter he heard the lectures of messer Carlo Ruini and messer Cristoforo Alberizio of Padua in civil law, then 'because his lectures did not please him' (I said he was a difficult pupil to please) he went for the rest of the year to common law with Filippo Decio. And thus he continued through the academic year until the end of October 1504.

In that year Francesco reached a crossroads which was to decide his future life. His uncle Rinieri fell dangerously ill and died the following February. This was the bastard son of Luigi Guicciardini, and he had been Archdeacon of Florence and Bishop of Cortona, so that Francesco now had the chance of obtaining the reversion of his ecclesiastical benefices which bore an income of 1,500 ducats. At the thought of all this the young man's greed and ambition were kindled. However, as he confesses in the *Ricordanze*, it was not the idea of the rich benefices 'to fatten oneself with a large income as most other priests do' which tempted him, but because he felt that the noble origins of his family, his father's reputation, his own age intellect and studies, were 'a foundation on which to make oneself great in the church and offered hope of one day becoming a cardinal;[32] at least he did not say he wanted to be Pope. Such was Francesco Guicciardini even at that early age. He did not regret the sacrifice of all his other ambitions, he did not recoil from entering the ranks of those whom he was later to call 'wicked priests', he had no objection to approaching sacred things and making himself God's minister without a vocation. For him the vocation of greatness was enough.

Luckily his father was a man of quite a different stamp and on that good soil the word of Girolamo Savonarola had fallen as a fertile seed. The great friar had so often cried out: 'do not make your son a priest', and then: 'O Clergy . . . I tell you the time will come and that soon, when people will say: happy the family where none bears the tonsure',[33] and so the good and pious Piero 'preferred to lose a great present benefit and the chance of having one of his sons a great man, rather than burden his conscience with a son who was a priest only out of greed for greatness and riches.' On his part the son, recalling this veto four years

8

later, owns that he agreed to it 'as best he might', that is, with all the regret and dissatisfaction which these words convey.[34]

He returned therefore from such unsettling thoughts, to the peace of his normal studies. All the rest of the university year until July 1505, still in Padua, he attended the lectures of Girolamo Botticella in civil law in the morning and Carlo Ruini in the afternoon.[35] After that he returned to Florence where he was at once appointed by the Signoria to lecture in the University on Civil Institutions at a yearly salary of twenty-five *fiorini di studio*, which were worth about sixteen gold florins: not much gold among the laurel leaves. His rival candidates for this post were, besides Giovan Battista Gamberelli, 'one of the oldest senior doctors in Florence, but not very good in his subject',[36] that Iacopo Modesti of Prato who had been his first teacher in the University of Florence. This has caused him to be reproached with ingratitude by a modern author. He took his doctorate on the 15th November in the Chapter of San Lorenzo before the College of the Pisan University, not *in utroque*, in both, but only in civil law 'to avoid the expense of $12\frac{1}{2}$ ducats',[37] as he felt it of little importance to have an additional degree in canon law. And that morning he gave his lecture.

At this point Francesco, who had now become 'messere', notes in his *Ricordanze* in the most commercial manner: 'I calculate that Piero my father has spent on my studies, from the day when I began to study until now, part on books and part for the time when I was away from home, and part for the doctorate which cost 26 ducats, more than 500 gold ducats.'[38] His legal studies had a considerable influence on his development and the course of his life: even the doctorate helped him along the way he had chosen. No sum of money that he or his father had to debit in their accounts either as brokers or in their trade as silk merchants or spent on their property, ever came back to the credit pages showing greater profits than this one.

9

Chapter 2

UNDER THE SIGN OF POLITICS:
FIRST IMPRESSIONS

<figure>◇◇◇</figure>

FRANCESCO was born when the Florentine Republic had been dominated by the Medici for fifty years. Lorenzo had been in power thirteen years, and his nature, his genius, his very enemies in the Pazzi conspiracy had combined to make him ever more tyrannical under the outward forms of constitutional government. Finally when the Magnifico took away from the Seventy the power to elect the Signoria and gave it to a committee of seventeen citizens of whom he was one, and the others his own strongest supporters (1490), he had made himself prince in all but name.

Guicciardini himself, a judge above suspicion, remarked in later days that 'the Medici State was grievous to the majority of the citizens',[1] less so, however, in those early years and while Lorenzo was alive, since the city, no longer remembering the democratic State and grown early accustomed to the government of the few, cared little which family governed it as long as the civic forms and ancient republican framework were preserved – which Lorenzo was always extremely careful to do. The domination of the Medici was specially welcome to the humblest elements of society which did not desire political power but bread, circuses, and justice, and to that section of the nobles which had struggled to achieve the Medici victory or had gladly agreed to follow the victor's chariot.

We have described briefly the place of the Guicciardini among the principal supporters of the Medici. Only Luigi, the son of Piero, had in his last years cooled off towards Lorenzo. After having laboured so hard for him, Luigi had thought to control him, whereas in fact Lorenzo was a man quite capable of governing himself.[2] Iacopo on the other hand succeeded in preserving his good will and confidence, so that it was said he was, after Lorenzo (a long way after), the first citizen of Florence. Iacopo died in 1490. Francesco, who was then eight years old, was, in his memoirs written at the age of twenty-eight, unusually fulsome in his praise of this grandfather so fortunately endowed by nature and by fate.[3]

Iacopo was one of the Seventeen created for the purpose of usurping the State. When he died, his son Piero took his father's place, having also inherited a large measure of Lorenzo's good will. Hence it was a time when he might have risen to power, if his own timidity and his character as we have described it, quiet, withdrawn and studious, had not led him to refuse rather than to accept the offices which were offered him.

When the Magnifico died, it at first did not seem likely to bring about a change in the fortunes of Piero Guicciardini, because the other Piero, Lorenzo's son, showed some affection for him. So much so that he immediately sent him as ambassador to Milan, where for a year he struggled in vain to mitigate the growing enmity between the Duke and the new master of Florence. The latter who had inherited only his father's power but not his wisdom or any other quality, daily helped to dig his own grave. While alienating within the city the support even of the most faithful citizens, abroad he made an enemy not only of Lodovico il Moro but, against all the traditions of Florentine politics, of Charles VIII of France who was preparing at that very time to invade Italy. Piero was driven out by the popular rising on the 9th November 1494. The same day the Republic lost Pisa. At the head of his army, victorious without ever having done battle, Charles drew near to Florence, he was at the gates. He entered the city with the attitude and intentions of a conqueror on the 17th November, and among the crowds which lined the way to see the pomp of that entry must have been a boy of eleven, Francesco Guicciardini.

That was Savonarola's great hour. The Friar who had already dared to oppose Lorenzo and cry out from the pulpit of the Cathedral in Florence against his usurpation of power, and against the corruption of morals encouraged by him, had by the saintliness of his life, the fascination of a new style of eloquence, his fearful threats and prophecies which had proved true, acquired favour among the lower classes and subsequently also with the nobility and the educated, even among the very Medici courtiers. Florence owed to him, after Piero was ejected, a more tolerable agreement with Charles VIII, the pacification of civil hatreds which had threatened to end in bloodshed after the bloodless revolution, and the constitution of the popular government, the best the city had ever had.

The ruin of the Medici seemed likely to involve that of the Guicciardini family, compromised as few others were with the banished usurpers. Although thanks to the Friar's efforts no revenge was exacted either in blood, property or banishments, the loss of power in government must have seemed inevitable, and as Machiavelli said, 'if you have not the political power in this country you will not find a dog to bark at you'. Yet Piero, who was popular by reason of his kind and gentle nature, who had refused at the time of the Medici all the offices he possibly could, though belonging to the party which the people then commonly called *Bigi,* was so successful in toning down his political colour that far from being persecuted he was actually elected one of the Ten in the popular government. Two years later, his attitude unchanged, he refused an embassy to the Emperor.

Certainly he was helped to remain afloat by the fact that, being a deeply religious man, he had been among the early followers of Fra Girolamo, who now had control of the State. But with him too he acted according to his nature. He was not a party man or likely to take sides with excessive passion on any issue. We know that he was a God-fearing man, but also afraid of other men, and he would never have gone down armed into the streets to defend his prophet like that Giovan Battista Ridolfi, his equal in wisdom and reputation. Savonarola often had occasion to urge him on, always without success, 'for he was lukewarm in his support of the great work'.[4]

When it suited certain outside powers such as the Borgia Pope and the Moor, no less than certain citizens within, to silence that terrible voice, Piero bore himself in such a manner as to cause not the slightest displeasure to the Friar's triumphant enemies. The day of the attack on the convent of San Marco, he, like other leading *piagnoni,* kept his house full of armed men, but they were for his own defence, not for that of the unarmed prophet. On the contrary, when he found in his wallet a paper electing him to one of those offices he usually declined, and seeing things going badly, he mounted his horse in haste to go and extricate himself from this compromising situation.[5] On the 23rd May 1498 Girolamo Savonarola was burned in the Piazza della Signoria, and at that time Francesco was proposing to enter the University of Florence, yet something of the faith, and sincere, albeit timid, affection that Piero had entertained for the Friar, the crumbs of the bread the good father had broken at his table, we will one day find again in the attitude and in the works of his great son.

Savonarola's death brought about no changes in the form of government he had fought for. It made very little difference, and that for a short time only, in the men who administered it. Before two years had passed the most passionate *piagnoni* were again seen in the highest offices of the State. We find that Piero Guicciardini, just as after the last change of government, had lost nothing by the Friar's fall. Yet these years were among the most troubled and dangerous the Republic had ever known. On that occasion the high priest did not pay the blood money to those who had handed over an innocent victim to him; the Florentines did not receive their thirty pieces of silver. If they wanted to retake Pisa they must exhaust themselves in a long war, bear vast expense, betrayals, humiliations, decline of power, must become abject before foreign powers and their own subjects.

In 1501 came the enterprises of Valentino which were quite the opposite of a reward for their betrayal. Instead of paying the Florentines, the Pope's son came up to the very gates and had them pay a ransom in cash. While his sword hung over them, the Florentines were on the verge of losing Pistoia and actually lost Arezzo. The rich lands of Valdichiana rebelled one after the other (August 1500–August 1502). In these disasters, in that final downfall of the nation, the most influential citizens, fearing the people's jealousy and seeing the general ruin, refused offices and embassies. This was done not only by Piero Guicciardini (who was at that moment finding a place of safety for his son Francesco and his money) but also by the most courageous such as Giovan Battista Ridolfi.[6]

And yet in that extreme state of dejection the noble city found itself again and revived. A Signoria led by Alamanno Salviati, a man of great good sense and courage, free, straightforward, impetuous, again restored the government's authority, and with its authority the government was again able immediately to find the money that was needed, and courage and strength. Their lands were recaptured, the disorders of the dominion were put down, then all minds turned to solve the city's internal disorders. The first institution to be cured by thorough reform was that of the Signoria, where too often men of little worth held office. Further, since they only did so for two months, they would have been able to accomplish little, however capable they might be. Thus they came to elect a gonfalonier for life who was, because of his general popularity and the support given him by Alamanno Salviati, the saviour of the Republic, the good though mediocre Piero Soderini. He entered into office on 1st November 1502, certainly an excellent pilot for the renovated galleon of the Republic while the good weather held. At the time the only clouds threatening navigation were the war in Pisa and the expeditions of Valentino. To the latter had been sent the still obscure head of the second chancery, Niccolò Machiavelli, which gave him the opportunity to be present at the revenge taken by the Duke on Vitellozzo, Oliverotto and the Orsini, and as a result to write some of his most famous pages. To relieve Machiavelli in this most difficult embassy, Piero Guicciardini had been elected, but as he was not the sort of man to appreciate Valentino, he as usual refused.

A popular proverb said death was an old ally of the Florentines. And on this occasion by removing Pope Alexander death removed some of the city's worst worries; but one cannot say that the Republic gained much by the election of Julius II. There was still the Pisan war to make sailing hazardous and a certain amount of discord in the crew's quarters. For the Gonfalonier sought favour with the people and governed somewhat despotically, taking his authority from the least qualified citizens; and now he was constantly at odds with men like Giovan Battista Ridolfi and Alamanno Salviati, although the latter had been active in securing his election.

In these wrangles Piero behaved with all the discretion and prudence we would expect, careful to offend no one, and although by class and conviction on the side of Alamanno and Giovan Battista, yet he did not oppose the Gonfalonier as violently as they; in fact Alamanno's vehemence displeased him. Francesco thought his father's timidity and coolness excessive. Yet he too, though much more spirited and driven by ambition, was later to show that he had learnt much in the way of caution, prudence and realism in that virtuous school.

Perhaps the occasion when Piero most firmly opposed Soderini was when the introduction of the militia, Machiavelli's invention, was being debated. This was indeed something which would appear too new and bold to a man of his character. His son was one day to follow Piero's example in this matter. There was also very lively opposition, among many other occasions, when an embassy was to be sent to the emperor (1507). The Gonfalonier would have liked to send Machiavelli who was altogether his own man, while the opposition managed to send first Francesco Vettori, then to get elected men with greater authority, Alamanno Salviati and Piero Guicciardini. But the Gonfalonier, knowing that one was his enemy and the other loyal rather to the city than to himself, managed in the end to win the fight and Machiavelli went.[7]

Thus Machiavelli's affairs had to some extent come to connect or merely to coincide with Guicciardini's. There was a better opportunity in autumn 1509 when Machiavelli was sent to Mantua on a mission connected with the Emperor's descent into Italy, and there met Luigi Guicciardini. This meeting, with the gossip and exchange of letters which followed on it, improved his acquaintance with Luigi but brought him no closer to the younger and greater brother Francesco, who barely mentions him in his private letters of that time.[8]

In any case since they have now been brought together at least in these pages, it seems opportune to take up the parallel mentioned at at the beginning of this book. Although at this point we have neither the opportunity nor the intention of drawing a parallel or developing it, we seem better able to see what, beside temperament, separated these two men: the status and fortune of their families which placed Niccolò among the lower classes and Francesco among the optimates, and the circumstances which, added to other more special ones and perhaps their natural sympathies, placed one devotedly on the side of Soderini, the other wholeheartedly with his aristocratic opponents.

Even the fourteen years' difference in their ages seem more considerable in such an epoch as that, of change and transition, especially when one considers the special conditions of the city and their personal fortunes. Those few years enabled Niccolò to feel something of the former life of Florence still living in the squares, in the stores, in the wine shops or within the walls of his own home. Francesco belongs to another age. Furthermore, the man of the people was old enough to be employed in government at the very moment when the Medici had been driven out and the Republic had regained its freedom. His political education had been acquired in those exciting and passionate years. Francesco on the other hand, at the time of that expulsion which certainly could not please his family, was only twelve years old and concerned only with his studies, in pursuit of which he then spent five years away from home. When he returned, political rivalry meant the continual bitter encounters between the popular party led by the Gonfalonier (whose secretary, Niccolò, was sneered at by men of Francesco's class as being Soderini's puppet) and the party of 'respectable men', to whom Guicciardini belonged by birth and character. After a few years Guicciardini was again to be away from Florence for a long time, and on his return a still broader and deeper chasm was to divide these two great citizens.

Luigi Guicciardini has brought us to Machiavelli. Machiavelli brings us back to Luigi whom he met in Mantua where the latter had gone to see his brother Iacopo who was ill. This meeting has given us not only the Secretary's famous letter on the incident which happened to him in Verona 'for lack of a wife', but perhaps also the poem in *terza rima* dedicated to Luigi himself. Therefore it would seem to be time to introduce Francesco's brothers, of whom it was said 'each of them would be almost worthy of an individual study';[9] we will deal with them in a few words. Leaving aside Girolamo, entirely absorbed in money-making, and the retiring Bongianni (the most like his father) withdrawn into the peace of the country and the consolations of philosophy,[10] and putting off until another time some remarks about Iacopo,[11] all we now need to discuss now is Luigi himself.

Of him it was written – imprudently – that it was hard to know where to place him 'whether beside or even above, but never below his illustrious brother, raised by circumstances and character to a fame so much greater than his'. I am sorry such a silly remark should have come from the pen of one who was my teacher in the study of archive material.[12] In fact all Luigi possessed in greater degree than Francesco were certain faults, such as arrogance which Francesco showed to all and Luigi only to his inferiors, the harshness and pitiless rigour which became in Luigi actual and ugly cruelty, when he enjoyed, in his petty positions of authority, inventing and trying out on prisoners being put to the question, new methods of torture.[13] In politics though more subservient to his masters than Francesco was, he came into unsuccessful competition with him.[14] He also tried to compete with him in works of intellect but without success. A wordy author of dialogues and other writings,[15] he was more educated in letters than Francesco, but far inferior as a writer. As a good Florentine and like Francesco, when choosing between *res* and *verba* he chose in life real things, but in literature he was satisfied or had to be with mere words.

Francesco much preferred his gentle brother Iacopo, a *piagnone* and a republican, and virtually attributed his father's death or at least the unhappiness of that beloved man's last days 'to some emotion or distress he suffered on account of disorders and debts incurred by his eldest son Luigi'.[16]

In short, Luigi turns out very unattractive in his actions and writings, nor can one think of him without finding very appropriate (apart from the degree of relationship and the doctorate) what was written of his son Niccolò, who resembled him in his pretensions, in his mediocrity, and in other respects, and who, according to the historian Varchi, 'deluding himself that it sufficed to be a doctor and a Guicciardini, vainly aspired to the greatness of messer Francesco his uncle'.[17]

Chapter 3

UNDER THE SIGN OF POLITICS: MARRIAGE: FIRST WRITINGS

THESE, therefore, were the origins and the youth of Francesco. This was his family and these the principal events which took place in the city and in his father's house from the day he was born until he took his doctorate on returning from his years of study in Ferrara and Padua. The doctorate, which was much respected in those happy days when doctors were few, opened up the path to honours and office, which now only his youth prevented him from attaining. While waiting for this last obstacle to be removed, he dedicated himself to advocacy. In this, his training, his intelligence and natural disposition brought him early success,[1] acquiring a good practice among institutions and private citizens.[2] In short, as he was soon to write with his usual lucidity in the *Ricordanze*, he set himself to build up a reputation in Florence.[3] Practising as a lawyer, in fact, was a means not an end, and to that end only all his thoughts tended.

For no other reason, and thinking of nothing else, he 'addressed himself' as he records, to obtain as his wife Maria Salviati, the daughter of Alamanno who with his cousin Iacopo led the struggle against Soderini and had a great following in the city. Francesco 'being much attracted to such things', as he confesses in the *Ricordanze*,[4] made up his mind to have Salviati as father-in-law at all costs. That was all that mattered to him, this is the only point he mentions in his memoirs, not his wife's beauty or qualities or money, although he did not usually despise money.

He set his mind to this project, indeed he set his heart on it 'although I might then have found a much larger dowry, and the daughter of a noble house', and although this alliance did not please his father – partly because of the dowry which was smaller than he wished, partly because he disliked the very thing that attracted his son, the factious and too energetic role of the Salviati in the Republic and their continual attacks on the Gonfalonier. However, Francesco was so obstinate and importunate that in the end the match was made 'with Piero's consent though he agreed only with difficulty'. The difficulty was such that his dutiful son, more than a year later wrote in the pages of his diary: 'I cannot help feeling some scruples and doubt whether I may have offended God, particularly having a father such as mine.'[5]

The match with Salviati's daughter, concluded on the 4th January 1507, was made public only on the 22nd May 1508, on which day he went for the first time to see his affianced bride.[6] The marriage was celebrated on the 2nd November, 'secretly to avoid noise and publicity'. His wife came to his house 'at evening in darkness on horseback without lights'. The dowry was, according to the agreement, two thousand florins and two hundred in kind. But as we said, Francesco took no account of this, though he regarded his wordly goods as of great importance, feeling that five or six hundred more ducats in the dowry 'would not make or mar him'.[7] Proud words and very characteristic of him. Three years earlier he wished to espouse the Church, not for love of God but not out of avarice either. Now he married Maria Salviati, not because he loved her but not from greed. Then as now he was moved only by his desire for a great position.

Properly considered, in choosing Maria Salviati he was also making another choice, or rather making it publicly, having already made it in his heart long before. Being by his own confession ambitious and restless, he could have joined the majority party, as men of his stamp often do. The party of the majority was also then the party in power, that of the Gonfalonier. He too was a noble, whose natural inclination and also his ambition and method of ruling caused him to stand with the people or the middle classes. In marrying a Salviati out of political calculation Francesco on the other hand showed that he stood with those great citizens who opposed the Gonfalonier. He had chosen the party of the men fewer in number, greater in position and ability. This marriage of party, like the other, was to be indissoluble for him.

He was biding his time, as we said, and not as a mere metaphor; he was waiting for his thirtieth birthday which would make him eligible for the councils of the Republic, for offices, for embassies. As early as January 1509 his name was put forward and voted on for an embassy to Lucca of minor importance. The fruit was not yet ripe, but his relatives and his father-in-law's partisans were preparing the ground for him. Thus, to put him forward, they sought some minor appointments such as entertaining foreign ambassadors. For his part the young man supported the Salviati and other opponents of the Gonfalonier in meetings, discussions, private arguments, since he could not yet do so in the Palazzo, and would have played his part more vigorously had he not been restrained by his always prudent father.[8]

At that moment when the Florentines had at last retaken Pisa on the 9th June 1509 to the everlasting credit of Alamanno Salviati who was commissioner there, Francesco went there at once, and remained some days basking in his father-in-law's glory.[9] He returned again in January 1510 when Alamanno was seriously ill with the disease from which he was soon to die. Francesco was grieved 'beyond measure', confessing in a long and warm eulogy in the *Ricordanze* that he had not in all his life felt anything so keenly. Some part of this was due to the hopes he had had 'of so great a father-in-law' (and he does not forget to say so on this occasion), 'the great capital' he counted on for his ambitious plans while he waited for the last few months of his junior status to run out.[10]

In the meantime he was working with the greatest energy as a lawyer. He was most successful in this, and the career appeared to be made for him. As for some time he had wanted to go and 'live near the Palazzo della Podestà, as is the custom of the other doctors', he had taken up residence in a house in via San Procolo given him for his use by the Salviati according to the provisions of the dowry.[11] His clientele increased constantly with religious communities, confraternities, friaries, private persons. He showed no reluctance though honour and earnings were small, and some of those appointments brought in only candles or 'a goose and a ducat'. He refused no one, took on anything, for, as he remarked on listing his appointment as lawyer to the friars of San Donato in Scopeto which brought him in 'a pair of capons per year' and no more, 'everything should be judged at its own value'.[12]

He was also doing something else which earned neither pairs of capons nor geese nor candle ends, but rather led him to consume many of those ends earned by advocacy. Of this period indeed are his first attempts as a writer which began with his marriage. The *Ricordanze* which have been our main source until now and which will take us yet a little further, differ little from similar writings left by other Florentines of his class, and then only by certain bald and frank admissions. In the *Memorie di Famiglia* as they were entitled by posterity, also plainly written in everyday language, we find already, with striking instances of his impassive objectivity and critical acumen, a fine mastery in certain portraits sketched with a sure hand.

Of the same period, as we discover from internal and external evidence, is his major youthful work the *Storia fiorentina*. The idea and the impulse to write it must have come to him during the composition of the *Memorie* mentioned above, which caused him to search out many documents and histories. It remained at the time, and in subsequent centuries, entirely unknown, and was published a mere century ago.[13] On its appearance it occasioned great astonishment and some people thought quite wrongly that from certain points of view this unripe fruit was better than the achievements of his maturer years. Certainly one is astonished in this work by such precocious maturity, depth, dispassionate judgement, the careful search not only for facts but for the causes of events and their hidden motives, and his keen insight into character. In short, if this is not final perfection, yet all Guicciardini is there present, and there already appear, even more amazing and revealing at that early age, the clear signs of his characteristic pessimism.

The Ciompi riot begins the narrative, a point chosen (if not for the pleasure of beginning with the name of Luigi Guicciardini, Gonfalonier) for historical reasons and perhaps even more for political ones, since in these pages, written in a partisan spirit during the struggles for power of the optimates, there is always present the memory of the benefits conferred in former times on the Florentine Republic by the rule of 'wise and reputable men'. The first half century is dealt with in a single page of the autograph, up to the exile and return of Cosimo *pater patriae*. The next twenty years are recalled with hardly less brevity up to the peace of Lodi, after which the historian promises to give a more detailed account 'because from that time onwards no one has written histories'.[14] With these words which are true if one considers not only the solemn humanist writing of Bruni and Poggio, but also some others more popular in approach, the writer states the importance and seriousness of a work undertaken without literary ambitions.

Yet even after that year (1454) and after these promises, the narrative continues very thin and bare in the form of a summary of events up to the death of Piero di Cosimo and the rule of Lorenzo. Then, coming to the period for which he had most help from the papers of his family archives and the reminiscences of members of his family, the account becomes very detailed, particularly from the year 1494, relating now the events in Florence within the historian's memory. After that it proceeds slowly year by year. Thus two-thirds of the whole book in the form in which it has come down to us, are devoted to the account of only fifteen years.

Notwithstanding the many and just praises earned by the *Storia fiorentina*, I consider that this continual altering of proportion and perspective leads inevitably to a certain disproportion, rendered more noticeable and tiresome by the lack of any divisions, and hence of suitable breaks between periods treated with different criteria;[15] even the division into short chapters, rather than 'roughly into books', praised by Fueter, is entirely arbitrary and the work of modern editors.[16] Such a disproportion is reflected, if I am not mistaken, in the style which has been so highly and so justly praised. Indeed though here and there some rather commonplace turns of phrase seem out of harmony with the nobility of the narrative and of the author, even though the text is sometimes bogged down in details, these youthful commentaries might be described, like Caesar's, as *nudi recti et venusti*. Written without pretensions and without any attempt at elegance, they have the natural style, the simplicity and the energy common to all Florentine authors of that time who were content to write as they spoke; with this difference, that the good homespun of Guicciardini's prose is always further supported by the thread of a vigorous line of thought. Certainly it would be useless to seek in it, in thought or in form, any of Machiavelli's soaring flights.

The work was probably begun in 1508, and from one precise reference we know for certain that on the 23rd February 1509 he had got to the end of what in the most recent edition is Chapter XXI, where the narrative reaches the year 1502. The historian was therefore writing those pages at a time when the recapture of Pisa was imminent, upon which he broke off.

During the next two years the young doctor's practice grew, his public work increased in quantity if not in importance, his private affairs were complicated by the birth of a daughter who was the first to survive; hence it is not surprising if the writing of the

History went more slowly. He had indeed to interrupt it for his visit to the captured city in summer 1509, and then again if not finally in January 1510, when he returned there to visit his father-in-law who was ill. The latter shortly afterwards died, leaving him lamenting among the ruins of the hopes he had built on him. Writing was always for him, during periods of 'idleness', a study and an exercise to prepare himself for affairs. Now the time for affairs had come, and sooner than he had expected.

The Council of Eighty had elected him ambassador to the Catholic Monarchs of Spain: an embassy not purely formal but of absolutely vital importance at a time of the utmost danger for the Republic. Nor was he to share this important task with another as often happened. Young as he was, he had to go alone – indeed he was not yet qualified for office by age. This was an election such as had not been made within living memory, a signal honour. So there came about what he had hoped for in his restless adolescence and written in his secret pages: not to run after the appointments and great prizes he desired but so to prepare himself and act, that appointments and business would pursue him. Meanwhile this first legation he had not intrigued or canvassed for, as other young men had done, to their discredit; and not only had he obtained it against all reason before the official time, but he actually had some thoughts of refusing it.[17]

He was worried by the distance involved – very formidable for those times, the inconvenience of so long a journey in the cold season, the fear of not making much money out of it (he was to receive three gold ducats a day plus a gift of two hundred, later increased by another hundred), and of losing his normal earnings from his practice. Not that he placed such considerations of greed and reluctance before his political ambitions, but as he liked to have honours pursue him rather than have to pursue them, he thought his 'position might be more firmly established by staying in Florence another two or three years'. He did not place in the balance – or at least he did not think it worth recording with the other reasons for and against in the *Ricordanze* – the young wife whom he was leaving pregnant. He left behind no children, since he had just lost his first born Simona at the age of two, 'who had been ill about 18 months and suffered from a kind of consumption'.[18] Finally, having weighed everything up, following his father's wise advice, and counselled perhaps no less by his own secret impatience, he accepted.[19]

He did not leave at once, in fact his departure continued doubtful and in suspense until mid-January, as were the minds of those who were sending him. For the free Florentine Republic the twelfth hour was approaching, the struggle between Julius II and the King of France was now a hand to hand fight. Having lost Bologna, beaten by temporal forces, and his spiritual arms weakened by the *concilium* which had been called against him and at the very moment when he seemed in total defeat, that formidable Pope struck a master-blow against the enemy by forming an alliance, made public on the 3rd October, with the King of Spain, in fact Ferdinand the Catholic, King of Aragon. By means of these foreign arms he who had so loudly announced his intentions of driving the foreigners out of Italy, proposed to confront the King of France his former ally and to punish the Florentines guilty of remaining perpetually faithful to their ill-starred love for the crown of France, and of having given hospitality though unwillingly and grudgingly to the *concilium* at Pisa.

The city no longer knew where to turn. France her ally was implored to make peace with the Pope or at least not to drag Florence with her into a war in which she would suffer the first and heaviest blows. She pleaded with the Pope, who was increasingly hostile, trying to make him understand her circumstances and the treaties by which she was bound, offering him her mediation. And beside the Pope, beside the Venetians those jealous and malign cousins, there now appeared the King of Aragon whose troops were entering near-by Romagna.

To those external ills was added internal decay, the city being more than ever plagued with discord and contentiousness. There were the enemies of the Gonfalonier ever more importunate and bold. There were the enemies of expenditure whom no nation ever found itself short of, least of all the Florentines. There were the friends of the Medici again raising their heads, since after the death of the 'brutish' Piero, the kindness and tact of his brothers were reviving around the sons of Lorenzo the Magnificent their former popularity. The *palleschi* were glad of the rage of Julius II, who was saying openly that he proposed to change the government of Florence. The Gonfalonier following the traditional inclination of his people, their interests, and his own, would have liked to declare himself openly and fight for France; the enemies of expense, and not they alone, would have liked to remain neutral, as though neutrality were possible or helpful in such a situation.

In so much disunity every measure became extremely difficult, everything was uncertain and in suspense. The decision to send an ambassador to the King of Aragon, opposed by Soderini as it might offend France, and favoured by his enemies the optimates who had chosen one of themselves as ambassador in the person of Guicciardini,[20] was debated at length in the Council of Eighty and then long deferred by the efforts of the Gonfalonier who in these constant duels with his enemies often got the upper hand. Finally when he could no longer delay the ambassador's departure, he took his revenge in the instructions, seeking to water down still further the wine already watered when the subject was debated in the Council, so that Guicciardini, as he himself was to observe with some bitterness, 'was not given instructions capable of mitigating in any way the enmity of the allies'.[21]

Briefly and in substance these instructions commanded him, according to the ancient custom of the Florentine Republic in cases of doubt and disagreement in the Councils, to listen intently, gather as much information as possible, and not to commit himself in any way whatsoever, to speak in general terms, to take as they said 'the benefit of time'. In this case such a benefit was promoted all too well by the great distances involved, for between the sending of letters and the receipt of an answer, there could never elapse less than two long months and often much more.

The essence of those instructions was in fact 'to endeavour to find out how His Majesty plans to proceed in the affairs of Italy and Bologna particularly since . . . this army which is now here, left Naples two months ago with all the reputation and understanding that it would regard as its enemies all the friends of its opponents',[22] hence also the Florentines. These (and this is the good bit), having been allied with the King of Aragon in the past, sought urgently to have from him 'that number of troops which his obligations require', giving orders to his officers in Italy to furnish them with aid for all their needs. In short he ought to assist them against himself with a force to oppose his own forces. Of course these were mere words, just as the King was all action.

Since on the question of observing that article of the alliance, the King had up to that time replied through his agents, when approached by the Republic, that it should be understood that his promised assistance could not be given against the Church, the instructions required the new ambassador – who in these matters as a good doctor and professor of law ought to be quite in his element – to refute the fallacy of such an interpretation and demand the faithful carrying out of the terms of their treaty.[23] Alas, not even on this occasion were arms to give way to the gown.

Guicciardini's instructions were written in the name of the Gonfalonier and the Signoria, but in fact it was the Ten who administered the foreign policy of the Republic, 'and thus ambassadors went on their departure to the said magistrates for their instructions'.[24] At this time their secretary was, as is well known, Machiavelli, who in this capacity, but still more so as the Gonfalonier's right-hand man, must certainly have had a hand in the drafting of that document, and if I am not mistaken, I think I sense his presence here and there – in the form of course, for as regards the substance, he was obliged to do what his master wanted. All the same (as we now know) Guicciardini 'on his departure, went for instructions' to Machiavelli.

Chapter 4

THE SPANISH EMBASSY UNDER
THE POPULAR GOVERNMENT

<><><><><><><><><><><><><><><><><><><><><><><><><><><><><><><><>

H E LEFT on the 29th January 1512. We do not know who
accompanied him, but probably, to put it in the manner of
Berni:

With a swarm of beasts and men.[1]

For he proceeded in an easy and stately manner as befitted his looks
and character, very different from those wild rides of Machiavelli on
post horses with few companions, which we have seen him undertake
when he was sent beyond the Alps with less ceremony. Guicciardini left
a diary of the journey, which remained unpublished even after the
publication of his *Opere inedite*, and was discovered not many years
ago by the author of this present volume.[2] Our progress, however,
being more urgent than that of the new ambassador, does not allow us
to accompany him step by step in these pages.

Through the rich lands of Lucca, in which the greed of the Florentines at that moment was beginning to be felt (and as a good Florentine
Francesco does not spare his neighbours certain pointed observations in
the *Diary*), he came to Lunigiana, to the castles of the Malaspina who
were so numerous 'that if the seed of marquesses were to be exhausted in
Italy, it could be revived through them'.[3]

He reached Pontremoli and crossed the Appenines, and then through
Borgo San Donnino (where he arrived after an interval of seven days,
while Machiavelli had done it in less than three), Piacenza, Tortona,

27

Alessandria, Asti, Moncalieri, Susa, he reached the foot of Mongenèvre which he crossed on the 14th February. For five days he rode through the mountains, and it was not a pleasant ride through wild strange uncultivated places with much snow and poor lodgings in small places scornfully described in the Diary as 'miserable hamlets', except for Briançon and Ambrun, 'which might do as a castle, but to call it a city is a joke'.[4] Finally on the 19th at the hour of vespers near Le Buis he saw 'olive trees' again, which 'he had not seen between Montgenèvre and this place.'[5] And when he saw them at evening, the Florentine must have been touched, to have noted such a thing in so dry a narrative.

He got to Avignon on the 21st February having been twenty-four days on the road. On one occasion Machiavelli had taken only six days to reach Lyons. There Guicciardini stopped three whole days, 'to rest the horses', he notes, but adds at once: 'and also we were encouraged by the carnival'. Thus he had an opportunity to see the city as well as the festivities, and to give a fairly detailed account of it. He admires its walls, the bridge over the Rhône, and the Papal palace, 'which is of marvellous size and has great walls, although bit by bit it is falling down and being ruined by the evil nature of the priests, who wish to consume and profit and not to put anything into it'.[6] He profited from this long stay by writing to the Ten what little news he had picked up in France. To his brother Luigi he wrote on more general matters; about Avignon, where the carnival madness raged, he wrote it was 'indeed a city where one might have a good time'.[7]

When Lent began they took up their journey and came to Nîmes and Montpellier; this was after the governor of Villeneuve on the Rhône had refused them passage on account of a command of the King that no one should be allowed to travel from Italy to Spain. The embassy might have ended there if Francesco had not managed to get round the prohibition by showing a letter from the French ambassador in Florence to his opposite number in Spain. Arriving at Narbonne and crossing the frontier at Salces on the 2nd March, he reached Barcelona safe and sound on the 7th, certainly not very cheerfully, through forests infested with brigands. After the danger was past, it gave him the opportunity to dwell at some length in the Diary on 'the activity of these bandoliers as they call them'. At Barcelona which he compared to Florence, he took another rest day, and another at Zaragoza capital of the Kingdom of Aragon. Thence he came on the 20th March to Logroño, and on the 23rd to Burgos where the court was, having delayed for some days so that his lodging could be prepared, finally entering the city 'met by a large number of mounted men and many of the principal nobles'.[8]

The following day he had a ceremonial audience with the King, and simply explained in general terms his commission and received in return kind but general words. They got down to details only on the 1st April, and then the King, always so virtuous in words, said to him in substance: that he had made great efforts but in vain to compose the quarrel between the Pope and the King of France. He had no desire for the property of others, but that all should enjoy their own in peace. He had sent his troops into Romagna because as a Catholic King he was obliged to help the Church in the matter of the schismatic *concilium* (as he described it) and in the recapture of his territory. His armies were in no way to disturb Florence as long as the Florentines did not support the French in the matter of the *concilium* or the usurpation of Bologna. Apart from that he was ready to help the city in fulfilment of the treaty.

Such kind words accompanied with 'friendly gestures', the King's affability, the honours received, delighted Guicciardini and filled him with great hopes, especially as he did not yet realize how great a distance lay between words accompanied by 'friendly gestures' and the inner thoughts of the Aragonese King. For the rest the famous secretary Miguel Perez de Almazan went to call on him, merely repeated the royal words, adding that it was enough for the Florentines to remain neutral; they did not wish to compel them to abandon their friendship with France.[9] If this were not enough, the same things were repeated to him several times, indeed the King assured him that he had written to the Viceroy of Naples who commanded that army in Romagna of which the Florentines were so suspicious, to defend the city with his troops 'as he would the Kingdom of Naples'.[10]

Thus the new ambassador felt he had begun his first embassy quite well and that things were going better than one could have hoped. The honours he received, which were a speciality of that court, and the King's kindness, consoled him for the strangeness of the place and people, the discomfort of the lodgings, which his Florentine taste found hard to bear. He was more disturbed by the lack of letters from Florence – with the discouraging certainty that any news he sent or was sent to him, would not be less than a month on the way, and any question he put would not receive a reply within two months. And this at the height of a war, with the changing events of arms and politics, making him feel still more the lack of instructions within which he might have had room for manoeuvre.

The Ten with whom he had to deal and to whom he had written a few letters of small importance during the journey, had not troubled in the meantime to inform him what the Pope, the French, and the Spanish army were doing in their vicinity. At court they inquired if he had news, and hearing that he had none, they were surprised. He wrote bitterly to his brother: 'they will think it a miracle when I do get news.'[11] He felt marooned. The Council had disputed over sending him, and the Ten were satisfied to have pleased those who wanted to send him and for him to keep the King in a good mood as best he might with soothing words. On his part Guicciardini being the man he was, though lacking 'all the instruments with which to serve well',[12] yet tried to serve as well as he could, in the role of a good and diligent ambassador. He reported to the Ten, who had not written to him, the information he had picked up at court and what was visible all around him – all warlike preparations: the provision of money, of victuals, news of the English army embarking to carry the war into France. In a letter of the 15th April sent on the 21st, he wrote that as the Spanish ambassador had been recalled from the French court, the French ambassador at the Spanish court had departed too. An unmistakable sign of war, although the King, when the French ambassador came to take leave, had spoken of peace.

However, while Guicciardini was writing this, in Italy the opposing armies had already met some days earlier in the pitched battle of Ravenna on the 11th April. This was a great victory for the French though a Pyrrhic one, for they lost many men including their captain Gaston de Foix, while the Spanish infantry emerged intact from the slaughter. Meanwhile France triumphed and so did the Florentine government. The Ten remembering at long last that they had an ambassador in Spain, gave him the first news on the 15th April,[13] and this was also the first letter they had written to him since his departure, nearly three months before. Subsequently they informed him in more detail of the victory and in such terms that Guicciardini was to complain to his brother Luigi, 'that Machiavelli wrote of these matters with prejudice particularly over the number of the slain, diminishing them on one side and increasing them on the other.'[14] But even the private accounts he received from his own family must have seemed biased to him, compared with those circulating in the Spanish court, which in turn would have seemed prejudiced to the Florentines for, from the beginning of the world battles have always been differently described by the winners and the losers.

The Ten, informing Guicciardini of the victory at Ravenna, instructed him to offer their condolences to the King, telling him how sorry they were – they were exultant – and how kindly they had received in their territory the fleeing Spaniards. But this letter of the 15th April arrived only on the 16th May, while the first news of the defeat had reached the King on the last day of April with the usual speed of bad news. He bore it well 'saying that such chances are common in war'.[15] Perhaps that great dissembler was just pretending; perhaps he was too, when he announced his decision, taken as a result of those reverses, to send the Grand Captain to Italy to take revenge.

Guicciardini therefore had to hear the news of a victory so fortunate for the government which sent him, from the King himself, a fortnight before receiving news of it from his own government. For that fortnight he had to manage on his own and he did the best he could, but he relieved his feelings in complaints to his brothers. 'I have been well received here and up till now have been highly respected, but to keep that respect I would have needed one of two things – either instructions to negotiate something, so that it should not appear that I had been sent here for mere shadows, or at least daily information of what is going on at home.'[16]

The fault (and we have insisted almost too much on this point) was not Soderini's who had sent him unwillingly, and still less Machiavelli's who often wrote the letters. The fault lay in the quarrels and factions which divided the city so that the parties blocked one another's actions in turn according to the changing circumstances of war and politics. What was thought in Florence of Guicciardini's embassy is shown clearly in these words written to him by his brother Iacopo: 'your expedition is spoken of differently according to the turn of events. At the beginning when Brescia rebelled it was regarded as a very good thing. Since the French retook Brescia the embassy has been condemned with those who brought it about, and since they defeated the Spanish much more so . . . Now it is no longer mentioned, as though you had ceased to exist.'[17] This must have given him a lot of satisfaction.

He had not, however, ceased to exist, even though lost and abandoned in that distant land of Spain, and he did his best to prove it. The King asked him if after their victory the French had requested Florence to declare for them, to which he replied ingeniously that as they had made such a demand before victory, he thought it likely they would have been much more urgent on the point afterwards, but that he thought they would have received the same answer, 'unless, through the French victory, the situation had become such that necessity was more powerful than their own wishes'.[18]

Not necessity but the joy of that victory, pride in finding themselves on the winning side, moved the Florentines to make a fresh pact with the victors, regarding the King of Spain as being rendered harmless. He however bore his defeat with courage, and while his English allies were disembarking at Fontarabia on Spain's frontier with France, he sought to encourage the depressed Julius II and to revive the war in Italy. There, after that Pyrrhic victory, the fortunes of the French declined rapidly, so that the Florentines were more frightened than ever. Piero Guicciardini wrote to his son the ambassador that the new treaty had been made 'when the King of France was victorious and perhaps if it were to be done again they would not be in such a hurry'.[19]

Nevertheless it was done and there seemed no other remedy in that sudden reversal of fortune but to make another treaty with the other side. This Machiavellian expedient was first suggested to Guicciardini by his father before it was proposed by Machiavelli on behalf of the Ten.[20] However the letter from the Ten which finally offered the ambassador this means of approaching the King, reached him only on the 21st July and in the meantime much had happened. In Italy the Pope had quite revived, the fortunes of the French had declined daily, until having lost all Lombardy they shut themselves up in Asti. Beyond the Alps the English who had disembarked at Fontarabia were raiding France, and the troops of the King of Aragon were massing on the borders of Upper Navarre which was a kind of enclave of French territory inside Spain.

In the evil hour when Guicciardini had to communicate to the King that untimely league with France, and try to justify it, the King showed his displeasure in word and gesture but with his usual dissimulation he added: 'Since the thing is done there is no more to be said.'

Indeed there was no more to be said; he was preparing for action, commanding his viceroy (as was already openly said at court) to move against Florence to change its government.[21] The Machiavellian anti-dote of a league with Spain was therefore somewhat belated. However, counting the days with hindsight one can see that it might still have worked if the medicine had been taken with prompt decision. Instead the ambassador had to present himself to the King with this last remedy hedged around with all kinds of reserves. And when the King said to him: 'Ambassador . . . have you, when we come down to facts, any power to conclude a treaty?', he had as usual to say that he would have to write and refer back. The King replied: 'It would take too long to wait for an answer: I will write to the Viceroy . . . and give him authority to conclude . . .' But in Italy in the Viceroy's camp, the papal Legate at his side was the hardly disinterested Cardinal de' Medici, and things were seen in a different light. Thus the last chance was lost.

South of the Alps events pursued their fatal course. Lorenzo Pucci, Papal nuncio and datary, had already come to Florence with the Spanish ambassador demanding that they should contribute to the League against France. This was even harder to swallow for the Florentines than the new treaty to be made with Spain to balance the one with France. When the Florentines delayed, taking, as usual, the benefit of time, the council of the League discussed what should be done with them. The enmity of Julius II was clear but the plans of the King of Aragon were doubtful.

At that moment indeed the King was showing displeasure at the Pope's immoderate ambitions. Having sent for Guicciardini on the 19th August he told him that the Pope wanted to change the government of Florence without reason, showing thus that he wished to dominate all Italy. He protested that this attitude did not please him and added 'that it was his intention that the city and its present government should be preserved at all costs and that he proposed to support and defend it against all comers'.[23] The young ambassador again allowed himself to be charmed, writing to Piero his father: 'These last reports of the demented actions of the Pope . . . have quite reassured me, because Spain would be extremely sorry to see the Pope's power increase . . . [the King] has seen the truth of what I have always said, that to stir up our state would result only in making a government to please the Pope. And in short I think he is today well disposed, and he has spoken to me very kindly of the city and the Gonfalonier who has cause to be grateful to me, for I have made far greater efforts than I have described in the letters to the office.' And he then adds: 'I do not think he will believe it, nor do I care, for I have acted in the belief that in these present times any disturbance would be the ruin of the city.'[24]

These curious words (which are written in cypher in the autograph and deceitfully omitted, i.e., without warning, by the first editor of the letter, who had not been able to read them) are a contribution of extra-ordinary importance to our knowledge of Guicciardini the man, blindingly clear evidence against certain calumnies, of his loyalty to the government which had sent him, of his love of country which led him to defend a faction and a man whom he hated.

They are also further proof that he had once again allowed himself to be deceived by the old Spanish fox. He was to admit as much in the great work which was the consolation of his later years, where, going back to those conversations, he recognized that the King wished just as much as the Pope did to change the government of Florence 'although in speaking to the Florentine ambassador', that is himself, 'he used words very different from the truth'.[25]

The facts show us that on that very day, the 26th August, on which the ambassador sent off his trustful letter, the Spanish army under the Viceroy's orders, still accompanied by Cardinal Giovanni de' Medici, camped at Calenzano virtually under the city walls. Within the city and backed with such military arguments, an ambassador of that King who in Spain had spoken to Guicciardini in the pious terms here reported, was instructing the Florentines to depose the Gonfalonier, reinstate the Medici and pay out a certain sum of money. What followed is well known to everyone and it will be enough simply to sketch the events into the background of our portrait.

These exorbitant demands of the Spanish viceroy were bravely re-jected by the Council; but after the enemy had taken Prato and sacked it, all they found heart to do in Florence was to persuade the Gonfalonier to go away, and then elect a committee of twenty citizens with full authority to reorganize the government and negotiate with the Viceroy. Piero Guicciardini was one of those Twenty, but he refused on account of ill health. Such a refusal should not have surprised anyone by this time; the surprise is simply that on this occasion his illness was genuine. In the meantime the Medici entered Florence as private citizens.

The first to remember to inform messer Francesco in the midst of all these upheavals was his brother Iacopo. In a letter written on the 3rd and dispatched on the 4th September he told him what had happened. The city's future still seemed doubtful but not without some glimmer of hope for the people's republic: 'There were many who, seeing the Gonfalonier depart and the Medici return, were convinced that the Council was finished and that the power was to be with the Medici as it used to be, but as it has turned out differently up to the present they have regained vigour because they have seen the Twenty keep the Council safe and the form of the government is not altered. And Giovan Battista Ridolfi showed himself to be the leader and all reputation has accrued to him, and indeed he is the first among us and has revealed a wise and patriotic spirit. . . . The Twenty have discussed making a gonfalonier for three years with very limited authority.'[26]

When the Ten in turn decided to inform their ambassador in Spain of these great changes, which was not before the 8th September, things were still at about the same stage. In their letter one may still feel the hand of the chancery *ante res perditas*, where Machiavelli still held his post. The letter speaks of the deposed Gonfalonier without condemnation, rather seeming to regret him. From certain words used to excuse him, one can see the bitterness for the King's double dealing: 'We cannot persuade ourselves nor ever will that he planned such an outcome.'[27] But in another letter that the Ten wrote to the ambassador barely a fortnight later on the 24th September, the tune has already changed. All the blame is laid on 'the one who is no longer here', that is Soderini, guilty at having opposed the universal desire which naturally (just fancy!) had been to return under the yoke of the Medici. They did not want the ambassador to complain to the King of the violence done them and the sack of Prato, but he was virtually to thank him for having done no worse.[28] This change of tune should not surprise us when we think of the much greater changes taking place in Florence about that time. First Giovan Battista Ridolfi had been elected Gonfalonier for little more than a year; later the square and the palace were occupied by armed men and the bells were rung for a Parliament, and a new reform had been instituted by which the Medici had again become masters of the city just as before their eviction.

These great new events were to reach far off Spain in their own good time, though many were to be lost on the way. In the meantime Guicciardini, lost in the wilderness and still uninformed of the course of events, was still on the 17th September writing officially to the Ten and privately to his father that the King, displeased with the ways and nature of the Pope, wished to ally himself with the city.[29] Although thus deceived by that master of deceit, Guicciardini's acumen reasserts itself in the *Discorso del modo di ordinare il governo di Firenze*.[30]

In this Discourse the faults of the popular government are analysed, and he would like to preserve substantially Savonarola's Great Council and the Gonfalonier for life or for a long period, but he would slightly blunt the peak of the pyramid by curtailing the authority Soderini had assumed and giving greater limiting power to men of quality. His own Optimates in fact! He adds many detailed provisions for the administration of justice, finance, etc. He sets above all else the formation of a national militia: Machiavelli's great idea which Guicciardini was later to reject, but always for practical or circumstantial reasons. Full of good sense even if without great brilliance of thought or style, the work begins with a forecast which was really extraordinary at such a moment, that 'it would not be long before the city lost its freedom and its government if indeed God did not come to its assistance'. At the foot is the date: 'Finished on the 27th August in Logroño.' Three days later this forecast was proved true.

Chapter 5

THE SPANISH EMBASSY UNDER
THE MEDICI GOVERNMENT

G UICCIARDINI only heard the news of the great changes in
Florence on the 25th September, and it would really have been
a miracle if he had been informed by his own people. As usual
he had to hear it from the King who that day had received letters
announcing the sack of Prato, the deposition of the Gonfalonier and the
capitulation of the Republic. With a wonderfully brassy countenance
'and no mention of the conversations they had had in the past' (in the
course of which, with just as bold a face, he had asserted the exact
opposite) the King told Guicciardini it had been done, 'because he and
the other princes of the League had supposed that the Gonfalonier of
Florence was so committed to the French cause, and furthermore was
so powerful in the city, that while he held that office they could not feel
secure.'[1] When he felt the earth shake under his feet and heard that a
new heaven and a new earth had been created in his native land, the
poor ambassador had to do the best he could, and he seems to have
managed quite well.

He had the first news from Florence the following day, but privately
in the letter sent by his brother Iacopo we have already mentioned.
Then no more letters for a whole interminable month, and it does not
require much imagination to realize how he must have felt during that
time. To fulfil his obligations he wrote every now and then to the Ten,
though from them he received not a whisper. His monologue acquaints

D   37

them with events in his part of the world. The Aragonese fox had occupied that part of the Kingdom of Navarre which lay on this side of the Pyrenees, using on Spanish soil and for his own purposes the English troops which had come to help him carry the war into France. Then when he showed some signs of wishing to move into France, the English complained of the time wasted 'in serving his own ends', and prepared to return to their own island. The King did not wish to embark on that war without them, and perhaps not with them either.

For Guicciardini, though outwardly impassive, it was torture. 'You can imagine how I have been on the rack,' he wrote disconsolately to his brother Luigi on the 26th October.[2] Up to that day he had had only the news sent by Iacopo. All he knew in addition from certain confused and delayed messages received from Genoa, was that in Florence the bells had rung for a Parliament, a new Balìa had been chosen, and Giovan Battista Ridolfi had been elected Gonfalonier. Were then the optimates in power? But why the Parliament and why the Balìa? As the Medici could not be satisfied to remain private citizens, there must have been or there soon would be another revolution. Would it be peaceful like the last, or violent? And what had happened to his family and particularly to his father who was seriously ill? And what about his wife Maria? And a little daughter born after his departure and bearing the name of the little girl who had died? He wrote to Luigi: 'It cuts me to the heart not to be there with you.'

Only at the beginning of November did he hear from his brother Iacopo of the new *coup d'état* which had again placed the city in the hands of the Medici. He did not love them then or later on when all his fortunes hung on theirs. He cannot therefore have been very pleased by the information which increased a hundredfold his hunger for news. Desperately he insisted with Luigi: 'I would like you to write to me often and in detail of everything that is going on inside and out, for the Ten keep me as dry as they can. Knowing the course of public events helps me so much in my work here that without such information I am a fish out of water. Hearing about our private affairs helps me to peace of mind, which you must understand I need, and the lack of such information would be enough to make me unwilling to stay here. . . . Thus I beg you to write to me and especially tell me who after the Medici seems to be influential in the government.'[3] In those words is all Guicciardini, with his ambitions and his inward passion, fretting and champing at the bit.

At last, in mid-November, a letter came from the Ten, the first since the change of government! It was the one we saw departing on the 24th September with news of the Parliament and the Medici return to power. The letter of 8th September had been lost on the way, others of the 1st and 12th September, which they said they had sent, must have been lost actually under the pen of the secretaries as no trace of them remains even in the registers and minute books. Apart from the summer when it was so hot in Tuscany with that Spanish army at their backs, the Ten certainly did not give themselves much trouble writing to Guicciardini. The letter of the 24th September was a solitary one, and for six weeks they seemed to have forgotten that they had an ambassador at the court of Spain.

It is true that the substance of his embassy had dwindled; and this was the main reason the Ten offered for their strange silence on the 12th November when he heard from them again. As the purpose for which the embassy had been created no longer existed, the ambassador no longer had anything to negotiate about. He wrote to Luigi: 'We have little to do here and little to write about, and if it were not for the local custom of hearing Mass with the King on feast days I think I might sometimes be a month without speaking to him, so that now I am beginning to be bored by my stay here.'[4] And apart from the King he had no conversations with the other Spaniards which he could find interesting.

Thus the embassy became simply an exchange of news: the Ten wrote to Guicciardini on Italian events: Maximilian Sforza had become Duke of Milan and a fresh league had been concluded between the Pope and the Emperor. Francesco wrote to them of the small progress made in the war at the foot of the Pyrenees where the King of Aragon, satisfied with his acquisition of Navarre, would have been glad to stop; while the French, with such a heavy burden on their backs, were disinclined to follow suit. But it was hardly worth while keeping a Francesco Guicciardini in Spain simply to exchange news, and on the 10th November he wrote asking to be allowed to return.[5] He did not know that the day before, the government had chosen Giovanni Corsi as ambassador to replace him. He was at that time one of the Signori, but would be ready to leave as soon as his term of office came to an end.[6]

It seemed as though for once their thoughts had coincided. Indeed, though it may surprise that request and permission came at one and the same time, it should surprise even more that the Ten's decision had delayed so long. The Medici, after the people's government had been extinguished by means of the King's forces, should in all reason have sent him at once a new ambassador, and would certainly have done so if they had had less faith in the former one because of his family and his own qualities.

Indeed they might well rely on him. Their victory and his ambition were a sufficient pledge of his fidelity. A pledge more valuable than the loyalty of his forefathers was his own father, who had welcomed the newcomers and been gladly received by them. We have already mentioned in passing that Francesco did not love the Medici, nor could a man of his stamp really like being subject to those to whom in the free competition of a free republic he would always have risen superior by his own talents. And yet in his private letters he shows himself already devoted to the new masters. He was soon to bring a more important proof of this by writing to Giuliano de' Medici, then to the young Lorenzo, Piero's son, and finally to the chancellor Niccolò Michelozzi who on the dismissal of Machiavelli had succeeded as secretary to the Ten. He would not have condescended to write first to Machiavelli, but he did not mind writing first to the lesser man 'in officio amoris et diligentiae', merely because he was on the winning side.[7]

Shortly after, he had good reason to be confirmed in this attitude when on the death of Julius II on the 26th February 1513, Cardinal Giovanni de' Medici became Pope under the name of Leo X. Thus the Medici good fortune multiplied. Luck had come home to the palace in Via Larga. Piero Guicciardini was one of those who went in a solemn delegation to honour that election, which strengthened the chains binding the city, but also filled her with boundless hopes. This time he took good care not to refuse, indeed he had the honour of himself delivering the oration. Francesco too from his distant post wrote a letter to the Pope full of joy and devotion.[8] Of course he longed for his native land and his father, and wanted to see his wife again and the daughter newly born to him, although he never mentions these two in his private letters. But if the biographer has at all learnt to read between the lines and in Guicciardini's heart, he was moved above all by a strong desire to try what the favour of the Medici princes could do for him, to try his luck.

Because of this his sojourn in those far-off lands was more irksome. In his impatience he wrote to his brother Luigi: 'This is a country to wear anyone out with its many discomforts, and where you may spend a lot and enjoy very little. Conversations here are not on a very high level, for they are not naturally fond of strangers, and if it were not for the wisdom and great kindness of the King, and the great honour he shows to the ambassadors which creates respect in the others, people like us would have a hard time here.'[9] The discomforts of his stay were increased by the trouble he had with his secretary Bernardo, brought to court three times, 'once for gambling, twice for whoring', involved in debts and all kinds of wickedness, until the poor ambassador decided to send him back to Florence, not without a nagging suspicion that he would have further trouble with him and would be 'at the mercy of his lies and follies' because of the influence that pearl of secretaries boasted he enjoyed with the Medici.[10]

Thus he urgently and unsuccessfully requests his recall, but his successor's departure is constantly delayed and there is no way of discovering why. 'Thus it is willed where will and power are one,' that is, no longer in the Palazzo dei Signori where Piero vainly uses his authority to try and find out something about the matter, but in the Medici palace. These delays are certainly not instigated by Corsi who is impatient to be off, and like a good old-fashioned humanist and rhetorician has even got his speech ready and goes around reading it to his friends. When they write to tell Francesco this, one can imagine how funny he finds it: 'Those are goods in little demand here; in fact, in common parlance, when they want to say that someone is crazy they say: "madder than a scholar"; so you can see how they value letters.'[11]

In fact there was nothing more he could do but have patience. While he stayed he endeavoured to make himself useful and enhance the reputation he had built up during his embassy. He watched and listened, thought over intently what he heard and saw at that court. Thus he was able to give the Ten early notice that there was something new in the air. This was the secret negotiation of a treaty between the Kings of France and Aragon. Guicciardini confirmed this on the 3rd March when it was half concluded. In Italy, where the hands of the French were freed now the burden of the other war was removed, it was a thunderbolt. Imagination ran riot and provided a theme for Machiavelli to write on, now confined to his hermit refuge at Sant' Andrea.

These letters from Guicciardini to the Ten are both worthy of him and entirely characteristic: serious, substantial, acute without any attempt to be subtle, without any of the liveliness and brilliance which dazzle us in Machiavelli's letters. He prefers to give us a careful account of the facts rather than pass judgement on them or offer forecasts. When he does offer an opinion (as he was begged to do by the Ten), he does it in his own way and according to his own temperament, as one who prefers to tread solid ground rather than walk the clouds. During the latter part of his embassy he writes at greater length to the Medici and to Iacopo Salviati his brother-in-law and a very powerful adviser of the Pope. In this he was following those forefathers of his who told Lorenzo more than they told the officers of government.

However, we prefer his private letters to the official ones, for they lack something of that sustained gravity and are written in a more domestic and pleasing style where something of his normally impenetrable character can be glimpsed. These letters too are full of information. In one he gives Luigi an account 'of the navigation to the West Indies as they call it here where many years ago Columbus discovered a number of islands . . . and later they also discovered the mainland'.[12] Then suddenly he would be seized with impatience, it maddened him to have to stay there far from the scene of action where his fortunes would be decided. He complained to his brother: 'Since I left Florence all kinds of things have happened there and everything is changed and new so that I could not have been away at a time when I would have more greatly desired to know all about what was happening at home . . .'; and yet because of the indifference of the magistrates and his own family, 'if it were not for the information I have had . . . from our merchants here whom I have had to pursue to get news, I would know less of Florence than of the Indies'; and of the latter he gave details in this particular letter.[13]

The peace concluded in the war beyond the Pyrenees, where only the King of England still offered any threat, diminished the material and importance of those bulletins which, as we have said, had become the ambassador's main function and occupation.[14] All that was left for him to do was to offer the King shameful thanks and fidelity on behalf of the city. I cannot say whether Guicciardini felt these were rather undignified, certainly he thought them inopportune. On this subject he had written to his father, as he could not say it to the Ten: 'I think it a good thing for the city to remain friendly to this King, but I do not know if it is proper to throw oneself so entirely into his arms. . . . You will be esteemed the less by him and others; and you should not suppose that your showing him friendship and loyalty will enable you to rely on his help when you need it except solely in so far as his own interests might require it. Anyone who supposed anything else, could be deceived, because here they pursue their own ends without any other considerations at all.'[15]

Holding this opinion of the Spanish (who ought not at least in this respect to have displeased the ambassador who himself resembled them) Guicciardini watched them suspiciously, reporting to the Ten and to Salviati a great coming and going of messengers and envoys in strange guise hurrying to and fro between the courts of France and Spain. There was fighting in Italy, while on this side of the mountains an Augustan peace reigned. The truce had been arranged because these people liked to have peace at home and war at a distance. Francesco, as an Italian, would have liked the same thing only the other way round, war over there and peace here, but a balanced peace not a Spanish peace, 'since we fought the French to free Italy not to change masters'.[16]

He would therefore have been glad to see the power of France decline, but not so much that the Spanish had not to guard against her.[17] Instead France had regained almost the whole of Lombardy in consequence of the truce and then lost it again with equal celerity, and was now attacked on her own territory by the English and the Emperor. In the meantime the Fox of Aragon was enjoying the newly acquired lands of Navarre, happy for others to fight the French and perhaps quite willing to do so himself but on other people's territory and at other people's expense. Keeping a watch on these movements was Guicciardini's principal occupation during the last days of his mission.

This was now really drawing to a close. His successor, after so many delays and setbacks which are, as we have said, the best tribute to the esteem in which Guicciardini the people's ambassador was held by the Medici government, took ship on the 7th or 8th September at Savona and disembarked at Barcelona on the 18th, reaching Valladolid on the 12th October. On the 25th Guicciardini had his last audience of the King and his successor his first, and they wrote jointly to the Ten. Two or three days later Guicciardini took his way home through Bayonne, Toulouse and Lyons, having spent a little less than twenty months on Spanish soil. He had stayed in Burgos, Logroño, Valladolid, and Medina del Campo, besides Barcelona, Zaragoza and other places called at on his journey, and once he had spent a few days at Salamanca for his own pleasure. However, he did not want to go on to Madrid where the

43

King was bound when he had his last audience. He had had enough of Spain.

On his return journey he was, as he writes, very cheerful and well satisfied: 'I was fortunate in this legation because . . . I was in excellent health all the time, I had a good reception and enjoyed the King's good opinion and had a good reputation there. In Florence while the popular government lasted, my letters and efforts gave great satisfaction, and no less so when the government was changed on the return of the Medici to Florence. . . . On my departure the King made me a present of silver to the value of 500 gold ducats, so that counting everything I made a good profit.'[18] Among the items to be included was a sum of a thousand florins carefully put by during the twenty-three months of the legation.[19]

Counting everything, Guicciardini had gained other things in Spain as well. Besides the reputation he had earned at home, a good basis for future earnings, besides the money earned and the gift of silver, there were two years spent outside the circle of the city walls, outside the boundary of the Alps, in a nation which had just achieved its unity, and which according to his far-sighted prediction was moving to a higher destiny along the Ocean ways first opened to them by Columbus.

Among his gains was the experience he had had of a royal court, of a King with the highest mastery of statecraft, who one may say applied on a large scale and with fewer scruples that doctrine of utility for which Guicciardini will be criticized when he follows it in a small way. That King, like Guicciardini, circumspect and parsimonious, sagacious and dissimulating, who with few troops and not much money had won the recent war and increased his territory, made a deep impression on the young ambassador. His *Ricordi* among other things, bear witness to it, where he was to distil the quintessence of his thought; not a few of them refer to his Spanish experiences.[20]

Rosini, who produced a bad edition of some of the documents relating to the Spanish legation actually blamed this embassy, with no due consideration, for everything that was thought immoral in Guicciardini's actions and in his writings;[21] just like Machiavelli, who was supposed to have learnt at the school of Caesar Borgia, during a mission which has become all too well known, the arts which inappropriately bear his name. Less positively Gino Capponi affirms that Guicciardini did not have a very virtuous example in Spain;[22] quite so, but he had no need to go so far to learn the elements.

Nor had he in Spain studied only the arts properly described as political. He writes to his brother Luigi: 'I am glad to have been here in this time of war and to have seen the preparations for it and the characteristics of their militia, of which we have seen so much that one may calculate very nearly what the power of this kingdom is.'[23] This too was a not unappreciable item in his baggage. Then one must take into account certain large files of papers filled with his angular and rather heavy writing which he bore away packed up with the royal silver on mule-back.

In Guicciardini's life, as we will see more clearly as we turn these pages, *otia*, idleness, and *negotia*, affairs, are clearly divided into shorter or longer periods. We shall see that his productivity as a writer flourishes almost exclusively during leisure and dries up during times devoted to affairs. The Spanish legation is only superficially an exception to this rule, because for the reasons we mentioned while narrating it Guicciardini had more idleness than business. Therefore, it is right to count among his gains the progress he made in his vocation and his practice of writing.

We have already mentioned the discourse on the popular government in Florence written before the revolution, with its almost prophetic opening. Another discourse on the Medici government which followed, is certainly much later, and if it were not for the lack of any reference to the election of Leo X (however this is only an argument *ab silentio*), I would regard it as written actually after his return from Spain.[24] On the other hand, in Spain and in May 1512 he wrote the discourse on the state of Italy after the battle of Ravenna.[25] At the same time or just after, he wrote the two discourses for and against the arrival in Italy of the Grand Captain,[26] dialectical exercises of a kind which he always enjoyed. In January 1513 he wrote another about the great changes which had taken place after that battle, at the beginning of which he wrote the following words, which may serve as an introduction and foreword to all those Spanish writings: 'The desire to know, the interest aroused by these events are so great that one cannot refrain from writing something about it, particularly since, having much leisure during my embassy to the Catholic King, this exercise can only prove useful and pleasant.'[27] An exercise to occupy idleness and satisfy the 'desire for knowledge', the desire to see more clearly into things and into the writer's own mind by seeking cause and effect in human actions, this is what most of Guicciardini's writings are, beginning with these Iberian ones.

45

Finally we must mention the most important and the most Iberian of them all: the *Relazione di Spagna*.[28] Villari criticized this rather harshly, judging it to be lacking in general ideas and deep concepts, too analytical, fragmentary, disjointed, which according to him is the fault 'of the form of the *Relazione* itself, which is broken up into disconnected paragraphs'.[29] This is one of Villari's usual simple-minded efforts, as the separate paragraphs are the work of the first editor. In spite of what Villari says, this piece of writing seems to me, lucid, perspicacious, and acute, and with the exception of a few pages of the first History, the best thing written by Guicciardini up to that time. His portrait of the Spanish and their background, if one removes a few of those rather crude strokes of colour which one can always expect in descriptions of foreign lands and peoples, is very fine and lifelike;[30] one can already see in it the master hand of the *Storia d'Italia*. The prose too is Guicciardini's best, before he adopted for his masterpiece the composite and grandiose style which is his alone. It was inevitable that Villari should compare that *Relazione* with Machiavelli's and that the latter should come off the better. Guicciardini is an acute observer, shrewd, sound, free from prejudices in his impassive coldness; and these seem the most desirable qualities for this kind of writing. Of course with Machiavelli, an artist and an idealist, this sort of material also bears the stamp of his own genius. If I had lived in those times, I would have gone to Machiavelli for brilliant intuitions into the future, but I would have wished to learn of past and present events from Guicciardini.

Chapter 6

TROUBLES IN FLORENCE

<><><><><><><><><><><><><><><><><><><><><><><><><><><><><><><><><><>

MESSER FRANCESCO'S return journey was made in short stages and so slowly that at the beginning of the New Year he had only got as far as Piacenza. Once again his slow and solemn progress, so well suited to his looks and character, reminds us by contrast of Machiavelli and helps us the better to imagine the differences between two such dissimilar natures. He rode easily through the great misty plain recalling past good fortunes and anticipating those to come. In a few days he would have crossed the mountains which were the outer defences of Florence; on the other side of the mountains he would see the olive trees again. On the way out he had been moved to see them again after all the stones and snow, but this time the olives marked the return to his native land. Then in the distance he would catch sight of a small forest of towers and spires dominated by the great dome. There were the streets and squares where he had grown up, there was his home and his father.

He loved him 'most dearly', as we said. Such a word, very unusual in him, so cold or at any rate so reserved, is the one he uses in the secret pages of his memoirs to tell us, or rather to confess to himself how much he loved him: 'more dearly than men commonly love their fathers'.[1] Thus he was returning 'with a great desire' for his dear father, kind, affectionate, refined, and adorned by his studies, and he 'expected to have more joy and pleasure of his company than ever before'.[2] So he thought, and not without reason: Piero was not yet old; Guicciardini himself had now reached maturity. Besides his age, his

47

greater status and honourable efforts had drawn him closer to his father, lessened his fearful respect, while his love had increased and to his former feelings would have been added affectionate friendship.

Instead, as they were passing through Piacenza, they gave him a letter which told him that his father had died in the night of 20–21st December.[3] The blow fell 'without any preparation or warning', since he had had no news of any illness. He wrote further in the *Ricordanze*: 'I was coming home with honour, with good health, with material profit, and very happy, but it pleased God to set grief in the other balance.'[4]

He had to resign himself to God's will philosophically but also with religious resignation, 'considering with what goodness my father had lived and died'.[5] Thus one of the first tasks on his return was the division of the patrimony. After setting aside the daughters' dowries, each of the five brothers got about 4,000 florins between cash, assets and property.[6] In land Francesco received the farm of Massa in Poppiano, 'a country property which has been ours for a thousand years', and another in Lucignano, holding in common with his brothers the houses in Florence and in the country.[7] Their father had left them something else as well to share equally, although Francesco's circumstances enabled him to derive greatest benefit from it: an excellent social position and a great reputation among his fellow citizens.

Piero's character had been such that he had no enemies in Florence. He had never been willing to make himself head of a party and had never offended or hurt anyone. He came of a family always most loyal to the Medici and always greatly favoured by them. After the Medici fell in 1494, we saw him very acceptable to the popular government promoted by Savonarola, and then to those who burned the Friar. Finally when the people's government fell and the Medici returned, he had been kindly received by them and placed in the highest positions in the State, from the first committee of fifty-five citizens to the more restricted one of seventeen after the creation of Pope Leo. This committee should have taken power on the 17th March, but as Piero had died before then his place was given, not without the displeasure of Luigi the eldest brother, to the third son, Francesco, and it was a further item in his inheritance.

After his return he had again taken up his law practice with a greater number of clients because of his enhanced reputation after the mission to Spain.[8] This improved still further when offices began to come his way in great numbers. He was made one of the Eight in the same year 1514, and the following year he was made one of the Signori. He had thus reached the pinnacle of ambition, although the Medici had meantime blunted and lowered it a good deal. The rewards were equal to his ambition, but I would not like to swear that Francesco really enjoyed it as much as he had hoped. For this reason.

The election of Leo X had not failed of course to bring about great changes in the affairs of Florence. On the one hand it had reinforced the Medici government with the power of the papacy and also with a thousand private hopes it had kindled in the hearts of the Florentines, healing in most of them the displeasure of having lost their freedom. On the other hand the Medici desire and means to make themselves absolute masters had increased. Giuliano by his own nature and the teaching he had received from his father, might perhaps have continued to govern kindly and pleasantly as he had begun, but having gone to Rome after the election of Leo and become Gonfalonier of the Church, he now was ambitious for a greater princely state. At first he was actually thinking of the Kingdom of Naples, though later this ambition waned. Thus the twenty-year-old Lorenzo was sent to govern Florence; in him the character of Piero his father could not be without effect, nor the fresh infusion of Orsini blood; all the same, during the first months he behaved correctly.

When he found everything was in Lorenzo's hands, Guicciardini had hastened to send him, before leaving Spain, a very flattering letter in which the obsequious adulation and offers of so eminent a man to his adolescent master are really disagreeable. However, he had not too many prejudices in this respect, and the results showed he was right, because on his return those obsequious words bore fruit. Another letter also bore fruit, this time to Cardinal Giulio de' Medici who was all powerful and all important with Pope Leo. He wrote it on his return from Spain, and now the Cardinal presents him to Lorenzo as 'the man he is, a friend of our House and of great ability', recommending him to 'love and esteem him, for he deserves all honour'.[9] Certainly there were qualities there, but this assistance, added to his father's merits, caused them to be better recognised. No wonder he was thereupon honoured and employed as we have seen and as his *Ricordanze* permit one to observe even better.[10]

However, shortly afterwards Lorenzo went to Rome himself to dip, as all were doing, in that well which, according to a happy image of Ariosto, was the liberality of Leo X. The city remained in the hands of

49

Iacopo Salviati and Piero Ridolfi, the Pope's brothers-in-law, and Francesco like everyone else had to go to them to discover his masters' wishes.[11] The Medici were intervening excessively even in civil litigation, and Guicciardini, professing law, had to exercise all his skill not to run on any rocks. Once, thinking the cause he defended a just one, and Lorenzo having signified that he supported the opposing side, he wrote him a quite dignified letter to explain his client's good reasons; it is a pity that he should have ended it with these less dignified words: 'If I hear that Your Magnificence thinks otherwise, I will do as you wish.'[12] If he wanted to stay afloat in those waters, there was nothing else he could say or do, but he was the sort of man, inwardly, whatever he seemed outwardly, to whom things of this kind must have caused the deepest displeasure. Indeed he was to unburden himself in one of those lucid accounts written for himself alone in which he discusses the way the Medici ought to act to make their government secure, hateful as they were to the majority of citizens.[13]

A worse case, which nearly became an affair of state, was that of Antonio Gualterotti. In the failure of a certain merchant company the said Antonio was accused of having used some thousands of florins to the detriment of his creditors. Public opinion was on his side, the Medici against him. The case went before the Signoria and they, thinking like everyone else, did not heed the warnings from Rome. There were some who added fuel to the flames, the more so since the city's faith in French arms was then revived, and the enemies of the Medici were beginning to raise their heads and criticize them.[14] *Inde irae*.

Luckily for him, Francesco was appearing for the parties against Gualterotti,[15] but that did not prevent some all-out Medici supporters from misrepresenting him as having bribed his brother Iacopo, who had a seat on the Signoria which was guilty of having returned a judgement against the will of the real masters. The innocence of Francesco appears obvious to anyone reading the letters he was writing at this time to his brother Luigi.[16] None the less, the unfortunate Iacopo had to go to Rome to justify himself, and Francesco did not lack his share of ill luck when in May 1515 Lorenzo returned from Rome.

The latter, tired of having to behave so circumspectly in Florence after spending all those months around the skirts of the Pope, had at last succeeded in obtaining from the Pope greater authority and a higher title and degree. The title was that of Captain General of the Republic, promptly allowed him by the magistrates, as soon as asked; his authority was up to a certain point left to his discretion. He returned therefore, changed within and without. Without, having dropped his civil habits and manners, he no longer took account of his relatives such as his uncles Iacopo Salviati and Piero Ridolfi. The latter in particular, though he hid his feeling out of fear of the Pope, he could not forgive for having married two daughters, one after the other, to the lord of Piombino, thus preventing him from taking over that small state. He surrounded himself with young men like courtiers whose leader was Filippo Strozzi, and with men not very decently behaved such as Francesco Vettori; in fact he began to retrace his father's footsteps.

Nor could such behaviour please Guicciardini who saw the government of Florence drawing ever farther away from that model which he favoured: a state in which the most noble and most wise, the optimates in fact, should have, if not the greater part, at least a decent share. The worst was when he saw that because he had been calumnied as having favoured Gualterotti in that notorious case, Lorenzo was now suspicious of him and no longer esteemed him as before. So much so that when the young prince elected a council of citizens to meet, no longer in the public places of government but in his own home, Francesco was excluded from it. He did not rest until he could get into that private council, and regain the prince's lost favours with the intercession of Matteo Strozzi and with a frank explanation in which he spoke earnestly to Lorenzo, showing him that he was wrong to suspect him and doubt his loyalty.[17]

At that very time he wrote the Discourse of which we have spoken,[18] where he examines the conditions necessary to maintain the city for the Medici, who had become ever more onerous to the city because of the changed style of the young prince. The things proposed there, are full of wisdom and correspond in fact to his former inclinations and present desires: in substance the Medici should have made friends of, and bound to themselves men of quality and ability by using and compromising them. They should have had more civil manners 'after the manner of the old Lorenzo', and give up their suspicions of the best citizens. Guicciardini was here pleading his own interests, but also those of the whole city. He added, alluding to the young Lorenzo's suspicions recently experienced by him: 'It is clear that they hold this opinion and it is mortal to us, because it does not allow them to consult, to be open, to be friendly to us, but always to be on their guard and with reserve.'[19]

With these words he put his finger on a sore point of the Medici government, but the remedies he suggested for it were suitable for healing the sore places of his own mind too. To win the minds of the citizens with benefits and gratitude, 'which may be effective in minds which are not entirely made of iron' (nor was his own on this subject); 'in everything their private interest would move them, which is the mistress which moves all men. . . . These are no longer the ancient times of the Romans and the Greeks, nor of those generous spirits entirely aspiring to glory; there is no one in Florence who loves liberty and popular government so much that, if he is given under another system a greater part and better conditions than he expects to have in that, will not turn to it wholeheartedly'.[20] The man who wrote this was not a poet nor a hero, nor one of those 'generous spirits': he was simply a mind which did not like leaving the solid ground of reality; he applied an extremely lucid mind to the conditions of his times, and looking into himself as into a mirror, saw human nature as it is.

It would be difficult to say whether he imparted to Lorenzo anything of such counsels after writing them in his secret books, but I will conjecture that he did not, even diluted with all the discretion in the world.[21] At all events he must have known better than we do, from his own experience, what we know from the evidence of Filippo Strozzi, that Lorenzo thought it the 'greatest shame and infamy to allow oneself to be governed by others', and 'himself believed so little in wise and good counsels, that it was almost impossible that he should not ruin himself and all others who were or thought themselves his supporters and friends'.[22] Not much satisfaction for a man like Guicciardini to be his counsellor. That is why I have said, not only on the basis of what has been glimpsed of his character but also because of a certain bitter tone caught in his own words,[23] that he did not find in the honours of his native land all the pleasure he had hoped for.

Meanwhile around him scenes and actors were changing briskly. Louis XII died on the first day of that year 1515; Francis I had succeeded him on the throne of France and shown immediately that he wished to revive the honour of French arms, throwing into the war the ardour of his youth and his generous nature. The battlefield must as usual be Italy, and he was busy augmenting with men and provisions the army his predecessor had amassed to cross the Alps. That formidable engine of war had caused Leo to tremble, so much so that his counsellors had even sought the advice of the suspect and unpopular Machiavelli. In a most brilliant letter he had suggested they should align themselves with the French.[24] Instead of which, Leo, moved by various appetites, not so much his own as of his insatiable relatives, and exercised by contrary fears and suspicions, in the end, though doubtfully, adhered to the League the King of Aragon, the Emperor and the Swiss had renewed among themselves in mid-February.

If the Pope was still unresolved, torn between two opinions, even after this decision, in Florence feelings were similarly divided. The supporters of the popular government raised their heads again, hoping for a French victory which would have revived their cause. The supporters of the Medici government feared what the others hoped, and among them was Francesco Guicciardini for the special reasons he gave in the Discourse we quoted. To give himself courage he wrote to his brother Luigi: 'If the French do not win, we are safe; if they win, I cannot believe that the Pope will fail to come to an understanding with them.'[25] One cannot say that so much faith in the arts of Pope Leo was ill-founded. This does not mean that in addition to the thoughts he had for his mother and his wife, both at that time seriously ill,[26] his letters do not allow one to perceive some preoccupation for the Medici fortunes in Florence, to which his were now joined.

His worries grew apace as the doubtful outcome of the war drew near; it having been decided that the Pope would come in with his own army and that of the Florentines, of which Lorenzo de' Medici was to be Captain General, and Cardinal Giulio de' Medici papal Legate. The Swiss boasted that they would stop the French army now on the move, on the mountain passes. Francesco always firmly asserted that they would not succeed and the outcome showed he was right; so after the event he was able at least to enjoy that meagre satisfaction.[27] He wrote to his brother with increasing pessimism: 'The Legate and the Magnifico, although they planned to go to Piacenza, cannot in reason at this point go beyond Bologna, and if they do, I shall say that God wants to punish us.'[28] And another day: 'Short of a miracle, the King has won in the Milan expedition and we, i.e., the Pope, have made two mistakes: the first in coming out against him, the other, having decided to declare against him, in doing so with such delay that our forces and his (the Pope's) could not be ready in time.'[29] In fact it was clear to Guicciardini that France would win the war, as Machiavelli had forecast as early as December; but Machiavelli was entirely for the popular government and the French, while it seems a great virtue in Guicciardini, who for many reasons was inclined to the Spanish side, not to have allowed himself to be blinded by prejudice.

By now he was again in the good graces of the young master of Florence, even though luckily he was denied those greater favours, though of a worse nature, allowed to Filippo Strozzi and Francesco Vettori. He was able to note in the *Ricordanze*: 'And as things were a good deal unsettled because of the coming of the French, to whom the Pope and the people here declared themselves hostile, and as Lorenzo was to go personally with our troops and those of the Church into Lombardy, and for this reason wanted to leave a Signoria here whom he could trust, I was made one of the Signori for September and October.'[30] Shortly before, he had had other employment of minor importance, as that of meeting first the Cardinal Legate who was going to the war in Lombardy, then madama Filiberta of Savoy who was coming to be married to Giuliano de' Medici.[31]

The two armies were already facing one another at a distance. The French were at Novara, the forces of the King of Aragon, of the Pope and the Florentines, were still on the south side of the Po, and one could hardly say which of the three was least anxious to cross it. 'The Legate is at Bologna and the Magnifico at Parma, whence they are in continual negotiation with France',[32] that is, with the enemy; a fine way indeed of preparing oneself to fight. On the 11th September the Swiss were at Milan, the French at Marignano, the Spanish at Piacenza. Lorenzo de' Medici was also in Piacenza, but when he finally prepared to cross the Po with the troops of Florence, her commissioner, who was his great friend Francesco Vettori, came to him to say that the city did not want its men to fight the King of France. Vettori boasted of this salutary intervention in his *Sommario*[33], as if anyone could believe that he would take upon himself such an authority with his master if they had not agreed upon it beforehand.

As a result of this comedy within the tragedy of war, the French having shortly afterwards defeated the Swiss at Marignano with great loss of life, the Pope remained under the stigma of having taken up arms against the victor, but not, however, of having used them. Thus immune from the mortal sin, in order to be forgiven for the venial one, he prepared to make a pilgrimage to Bologna where he was to meet the victorious young king. There he solemnly ratified the agreement which had been concluded in the meantime, 'with conditions' (Guicciardini noted in a letter to his brother Luigi) 'which I do not know, if we had won, if we should have such good ones'.[34] The arts and luck of Pope Leo were more powerful than his arms. He got out of it with the restitution of Parma and Piacenza, and with the promise that he would restore or rather sell Modena and Reggio to the Duke of Ferrara. He never minded making promises.

That pilgrimage was in the month of November, and messer Francesco took part in the embassy sent to the frontiers of the Republic to honour and accompany to Florence the Florentine Pope, while the city prepared to receive him with unexampled pomp. For the occasion Piero Ridolfi, recently bereaved of his wife the lovely Contessina, the Pope's favourite sister, had been elected Gonfalonier.[35] And because on that triumphal entry the Gonfalonier among so many other scarlet and peacock robes wore 'a gown of black satin lined with sable', not minding that 'in such an office and on such a day mourning should be suspended',[36] he caused scandal and was criticized by the people, but not, surely, by His Holiness his brother-in-law.

Guicciardini did not accompany the Pope on leaving Florentine territory as he had done on his arrival. He did not go to Bologna for the meeting of Leo and Francis, but composed a discourse addressed to both, one of his favourite rhetorical exercises. This was more rhetorical than previous ones, if the author could imagine in it that the Pope and the Most Christian Monarch were meeting not to negotiate on Milan, Parma and Piacenza, on Modena and Reggio and Urbino, but on no less a matter than the liberation of Jerusalem and the Holy Sepulchre. This must have seemed so far fetched even to himself while writing it, that he left his discourse half finished; and after starting it anew in Latin (most unusual for him), and vainly trying to excite his enthusiasm and imagination with resounding phrases and hemistiches, he even broke into Italian verse. It is only three terzine and the beginning of another, but the phenomenon of a Guicciardini writing verse is so extraordinary that, merely to indicate its existence, it was worth recalling this draft discourse: it is a most singular document among his literary fancies.[37]

After the celebrations at Bologna, Leo returned to rejoice more quietly in Florence where he remained nearly two months. 'Let us enjoy the papacy since God has given it us', he is supposed to have said one day; and he must have enjoyed being Pope in his own city among the Florentines. The King of Aragon died at that very time; the Florentines regarded it as a special dispensation, and felt almost that it was bestowed by that Pope who was among them and in whose train fortune and prosperity followed. For the rest the city had from this sojourn more inconvenience and expense than gain, even if many citizens obtained special benefits from the liberality of Leo. Our Francesco received the title of consistorial lawyer.[38]

When the Pope left, things in Florence remained in their usual state under Lorenzo whose ambitions were ever increasing. On the 17th March the death of his uncle Giuliano removed a rival and the only thing preventing him from making himself Duke of Urbino, ousting Francesco della Rovere. This enterprise, as easy as it was ephemeral, was executed by him in the month of May almost entirely at the expense of the Florentines. But if the Florentines disliked the expense as usual, they liked still less being ruled by one with the title and ever increasingly the manners of a duke.[39] Nor could it have pleased Guicciardini very much, who was not even one of those nearest him; and then what pleasure could a man like him take in the honours and offices of a city where they were given only for show, and where one had to go to the Duke to know who was right and who was wrong in a case at law?

He must therefore have felt himself blessed when that Spring, 'having neither sought nor asked it, they sent him to govern Modena: for this office all conspired, those of Rome and those of Florence – and in particular madonna Alfonsina',[40] the ambitious and intriguing mother of Lorenzo de' Medici. When Francesco received the first news of his sudden good fortune we do not exactly know. A papal brief nominating him, bears the date 5th April 1516, and (it has not been observed before) the office conferred on him is that of commissioner, and no other is given either on the outside of the act or within;[41] on the other hand Guicciardini left only on the 26th June and as Governor.[42] The second thoughts and manoeuvres between Rome and Florence we know nothing of; we only know that during that interval the job improved. The day Guicciardini mounted his horse on his way to Romagna, he might have written in the book of his succinct *Ricordanze*, and we in any case write it here in this book of his life: *Incipit vita nova.*

Chapter 7

THE HOROSCOPE:
A PORTRAIT

<><><><><><><><><><><><><><><><><><><><><><><><><><><><><><><><><><><><>

'IF YOU had seen messer Francesco in Romagna . . . with a houseful of tapestries, silver and servants, with power over the entire province, which apart from the Pope, who left everything absolutely to him, knew no authority above him; with a guard around him of more than a hundred pikemen, with halbardiers and other mounted guards; if you had seen him go through the streets of the city always surrounded by hundreds of men, never riding out with less than a hundred or a hundred and fifty horse, smothered in "lordships", in titles, in "most illustrious", you would never recognize him as your fellow citizen, your fellow man; but considering the greatness of his affairs, his unbounded authority, his vast power and importance, his court and his magnificence, you would have thought him nothing less than a duke . . . Now, in gestures, preoccupations, desires, in all his actions he no longer resembled in any way a private person. Already his speech, his manners, his haughtiness, his desire to be understood and obeyed at a sign, were no different from what is found in a man who has been and always lived a prince. . . .'[1]

These words which portray him to life, are Guicciardini's own, and although he puts them in the mouth of an imaginary accuser, he then gives them substance with complacency in an equally imaginary defence.[2] One could not, therefore, wish for a more authentic self-portrait than this, which has until now been overlooked by scholarship.

Those details, so sharp and brilliant against the background of the picture, can represent to us as no imaginary description or other information could, what sort of life Guicciardini led and what was his demeanour in his governorship of Romagna, so different from Florentine ways. These were a life and manners which doubtless suited the dignity of the office, indeed were used by him as instruments in the art of government; but there seems to me no doubt that some of these were particularly well suited to his own character and that he boasted about it slightly. Certainly later on the long continuous habit of so great an authority and power, could not be without effect on a nature already haughty, authoritarian and imperious.

Let us allow him to tell us more of these governorships. 'Imagine great cities, abundant, rich, full of nobility, full of counts and barons, where the rulers have huge ordinary and extraordinary emoluments, where their authority is immense, not subjected to any law or rule, and entirely at their own discretion. The Pope being far off and occupied with much greater affairs, his subjects can only have recourse to him at vast expense and with great difficulty, and very little likelihood of success, so they think it a lesser evil to bear the injuries done them by their governors than to seek a remedy, losing time and money and further provoking those who are in a position to damage them. Hence the Governor both is and seems master of the city.'[3]

In the complacent detail of that portrait everything is true, but one thing is particularly evident: 'the huge ordinary emoluments' (the extraordinary ones we shall mention when they occur); because at the outset Guicciardini received, as Governor of Modena alone, that is before the limits of his jurisdiction and his salary were extended, the handsome sum of a hundred gold ducats a month: as much as Piero Soderini had in his time as life gonfalonier of the Florentine Republic. Such therefore was the office, such the authority, the honour, the reward it brought with it. And being so, it is not difficult to imagine that together they drew behind them a fine train of clients, obsequiousness and adulation.

A piece of evidence unknown up to now, is the horoscope which has already been mentioned and which was composed on that very occasion. It would be of no moment if it were a horoscope like so many others consisting of one or two pages of writing or a thin volume containing the usual more or less commonplace prognostications. But this is an actual quarto volume of hundreds of pages, where the whole life, past and future, the nature and actions of Guicciardini are examined. The book is elegantly bound in brown morocco, tooled, with chiselled and gilded edges. A luxury object, even though the writing, since it is autograph, is not always either clear or beautiful. The author may have been the prince of astrologers, but not, I would say of calligraphers. Although the book bears among other ornaments a tasteless dedication, one does not find in it (or in any other part of the work) the name of the author nor of the person whose birth is in question, nor any date.[4] The date of compilation, however, may be gathered from the text, where in Chapter XVIII, *De dispositione annorum*, under the thirty-fifth year of Guicciardini's age, which according to the anonymous astrologer's calculation is in fact 1516, the text passes from the past to the future tense.[5] Under the previous year (which, in Florentine style, ended on the 24th March 1516) it is stated how even then 'an honourable movement began to bring you wealth and office in a very alarming and difficult position, and thus you attracted some envy and trouble'.[6] From this we have confirmation of what could have been deduced from that brief of nomination, that is, that the decision to make Francesco governor of Modena was not such a sudden one, and perhaps did not come as such a surprise as the *Ricordanze* would have us believe.

We shall see all in good time what he foretold of the future (and some fine things indeed), but meanwhile one thing is quite certain: this mysterious astrologer was well informed on the past of messer Francesco Guicciardini. At a certain point in his development declaring the need to narrate '[things] past to support those of the future', he admits with an ingenuousness which might also conceal a sly irony, that it was much easier for him to contemplate the former.[7] To give an example, it cannot have cost him much labour to give the date of Guicciardini's father's death, a recent event well known to every Florentine,[8] but it is something to have 'guessed,' strengthening his harmless mystification with a 'perhaps',[9] the now distant and certainly unmemorable date of the death of Rinieri Guicciardini ('and perhaps one of your relatives died'). Leaving out the childish ailments which it would have been ridiculous to describe to the person who had suffered them if they were not true, to us it seems more illuminating where he accurately quotes particulars which must have been well known to only very few of his nearest relatives, such as: 'at the beginning of the thirtieth year . . . danger from assassins and alarms on the roads':[10] the alarm he felt in the woods of Catalonia 'on account of the bandoleros' on the way to his

Spanish embassy. Nor is this all: the curiosity of so strange a document is enhanced by the notes which Guicciardini, inquisitive as to his future, added in his own hand, though unfortunately only to decipher the astrological signs.

Messer Francesco was a believer in the 'airy spirits', in prophecies which he recognized as due to 'hidden powers of nature, or rather of that Power which moves everything'.[11] He expressed his disbelief of astrologers in the *Ricordi*: 'they do not know what they say, they are right only by chance'.[12] Yet later, while writing the *Cose fiorentine*, he noted in the margins: 'Consult the astrologers for the moment of origin and the rebuilding of Florence';[13] and when the question arose of the foundation of the fortress of Florence, he was to advise half humorously to take astrology into consideration: 'Certainly it would be good to choose propitious times for doing such things, particularly since four or six days more or less at the beginning would not matter at all. . . . . I am more afraid of earthly astrology than of the celestial kind, but when both are in agreement it is all the worse.'[14] Perhaps he too may have thought there were more things in heaven and earth than our philosophy dreams of, and so he went on annotating and leafing his way through the voluminous horoscope.

The biographer, trying as he does to see into Guicciardini's thoughts and life, cannot avoid doing likewise. We are not much interested in the matters of the future, those subsequent to the compiling of the horoscope, since we have better information on them. We might possibly take account of the influence which certain predictions favourable or otherwise might have had on Guicciardini's feelings as he read and annotated, hesitating between doubt and belief. Perhaps when he was to see some of them come true, his belief may not have been strengthened or his doubts diminished; he must have gone on believing, as he says in the *Ricordi*, that astrologers 'are right only by chance', and that they utter 'among a hundred lies one truth'.[15] Now, however, that all the things in the horoscope are past, it will not be surprising if we seek in it those things told us by the anonymous author because he had seen and known them, rather than those he attempted to foretell.

Meanwhile, because no one will be willing to judge him so foolish as to believe more in astrological lights than in his own eyes, the horoscope gives us material to complete the well known portrait by Bugiardini, painted, if we are to believe Vasari, twenty years or so later. This portrait, according to the testimony of those who knew him in his lifetime, 'was a good likeness and was much approved'.[16] In any case, where comparison is possible, it is not unlike the portrait traced by the astrologer when messer Francesco was in his thirty-fourth year, and at this age already set in outlook and appearance.

Francesco Guicciardini was, then, tall and 'rather fat than otherwise', though not excessively so; he had a broad face, fair skin, black eyes, round and somewhat prominent, dark hair thick and curly, a high forehead, long sharp nose, a grave gait: 'incessu potius testudineo', as the anonymous author so expressively puts it.[17]

In his nature he was 'phlegmatic mixed with a sharp temper', and somewhat melancholy; he is shown as a lover of nobility, honours and great affairs; proud, 'all for himself', 'very confident in himself and his own opinion and judgement'; reserved yet friendly with other men, courteous towards women, prompt to serve but 'with a reward in view', ready to please but not to 'give himself much trouble'; brave, constant, tenacious to such a degree that our astrologer does not hesitate to use on this occasion, a vivid popular expression: *formica di sorbo* [proverbially the ant which infests the rowan tree will not come out when the tree is shaken – a sticker. *Trans.*]. With no less truth he calls him a 'secretive man'. Of a reserved nature, he knew better how to hide his deepest feelings and suffer silently than to relieve them by sharing them with others.

In an age not noted for decency he was regarded as of virtuous and sober habits. 'Much inclined to lechery with women,' nevertheless, 'he would not give effect to all his desires from considerations of honour.' *Si non caste tamen caute*! Our anonymous author who insists in various places on this point, will describe him as frequenting whores, and we have evidence of this elsewhere. This peccadillo was natural to a man of his temperament, and with his reserved nature, even 'considering honour'; nor was it dishonourable for anyone in that century to consort with 'decent courtesans'. When in Spain on his thirtieth birthday he wrote himself a pious and severe admonishment reproving 'a life and habits unworthy of a man brought up to virtue and piety from a child', and such that it was impossible 'to persist in it without great shame at least in one's conscience';[18] in that contrite moment such associations must have had no little part. This tendency to lechery to which he was undoubtedly led by temperament, (and this is confirmed by a medical opinion recently come to light [18a]), he inherited from his great-grandfather Piero, 'lecherous and a powerful womanizer', and from his grandfather Iacopo whom, physically, he so closely resembled.[19]

I do not think that he accused himself so strongly of any other failings in that exhortation (certainly unusual in him and to be taken well into account in judging him), except perhaps for a certain lukewarmness in religious matters in contrast to his passionate cupidity for earthly honours: he admonishes himself in this wise: 'You must make the same efforts in divine and spiritual affairs so that God in His Grace may give you that share in paradise which you yourself desire in the world'. Religion met in him with conflict and disharmony, but was at the same time deeply rooted in his father's teaching and the *piagnone* tradition, even though sometimes buffeted by a powerful genius or withered by pessimism, owing to the extreme corruption into which the Church had fallen.[20] Then the despairing maxims of the *Ricordi* came from his heart, but if one compares them with so many other things he wrote which we record without comment in these pages, it is clear that one cannot judge Guicciardini's religion by those maxims alone.[21]

'Avid for wealth, yet never willing to acquire ill-gotten gains,' he was parsimonious without meanness. I believe the poor astrologer sought in vain to advise him – thinking perhaps of the reward expected for his astrological labours – to show a munificent and liberal spirit. Many of the qualities here described seem just like those which are to be read in the face portrayed by Bugiardini, or which are glimpsed while reading the author's pages and in the events of his life. Certain other aspects, which have come to light only in our own times when the figure of the historian and the politician has finally appeared to us in its entirety, it is surprising to find described so acutely in the pages of this anonymous author at a time when Guicciardini was still obscure and *in minoribus*: among other things when he describes him as 'an acute man, an investigator of things'.

Such a portrait, which we partly see and in part feel to be so like the man himself, does honour to the natural perspicacity of this unusual astrologer. Nor could I say if one should attribute to uncommon or astrological lights a prognostication which may perhaps seem less startling than others of his, but which considering the date will seem anything but obvious. This is when he predicts that Guicciardini 'will rise to a position never attained by any of your forefathers'.[22]

But it would really be too indiscreet to expect from the prescience of one who knew how to examine so acutely if not the stars, the spirit and the intellect of the great Florentine, to prejudge his work as an author, which then was hardly beginning. For in his lifetime this work, not only in his period, but in maturer years, was entirely unknown, and the greater part of it has come to light only in modern times. It is a good deal for our astrologer to have perceived back in the year 1516 that the man whose birth he was scrutinizing would delight 'in matters of the mind and similar disciplines'.[23]

He enjoyed them, we have seen, in the solitude of his study; for his own pleasure only and to clarify his thoughts he liked to marshal his ideas in opposing armies and make them do combat; in works and opuscules during periods of idleness, and in brief writings during busy times. 'An investigator', as with prodigious divination the astrologer describes him; in historical writings and political researches he endeavoured to find the ultimate causes and reasons of human actions and decisions, but recoiled from those which seemed to him 'vain excogitations', and from everything not practical or real.

His study was more hidden than Machiavelli's, and while he lived, nothing came from it to be printed or even published in manuscript. In that secrecy the author opened his mind, always securely shut away, and disclosed his thoughts to himself. The curial robes he put on when he entered there, were not so different from what he wore every day; and little inclined as he was to treat shadows as things of substance, he did not converse with those phantoms 'of the ancients' to which Machiavelli dedicated himself so wholeheartedly. He liked instead to deal with living men, with real and present affairs, he examined opposing views, weighed reasons for and against, dissected, revealed and scrutinized actions and thoughts as though he were anatomizing them. In the past he sought only what one of his old Florentines had called 'the truth of things that were certain', and if, more unwillingly, he fixed his eyes on the future, he, who was not, like the great Secretary, a passionate man, an artist, a poet, a prophet, did so not in sudden flashes of intuition but in the cold steady light of sound reasoning. Such was Guicciardini.

Chapter 8

GOVERNOR OF MODENA

MODENA had been held by the House of Este by imperial investiture until it was taken from them by Julius II. It was ceded almost immediately by Julius to the Emperor Maximilian, who, being always short of money, gave it in pawn to Pope Leo for 40,000 ducats; a pledge given without any intention of ever redeeming it. Bought with the moneys of the Church, it was not only the greatness of the Church which had persuaded Leo into this bargain, but also the desire to aggrandize his brother Giuliano to whom indeed he planned to give it, to hold in perpetuity. After the battle of Marignano, when he had to make terms with the victors, he had to promise to return Modena to Alfonso d'Este. How he meant to keep that promise, even after Giuliano was dead, was shown by sending Francesco Guicciardini as governor with express instructions to restore order and peace to that city 'torn by internal discord and civic hatred'.[1]

The papal brief did not exaggerate in describing the condition of Modena and its territory in such dark and bloody colours. It had changed hands four times in six years, and was just as though it had had no ruler at all. The factions, which had their origin in family feuds and personal enmities, sad heritage of this area, had left it torn and bloodied. Now, taking advantage of the political situation, they wanted to play a greater game, and ranged themselves for or against the new master.

Among the great feudal powers the Rangoni family was divided against itself. Count Guido, called the Tall, stood for the House of Este; for the Church stood Count Gherardo and Contessa Bianca, who was a Bentivoglio and devoted to the Medici: the latter's son, too, called the Small though in fact he was larger than his namesake, always campaigned on the ecclesiastical side, but his impetuous and rash temperament rendered him somewhat suspect at that time. Among the other great families, the Tassoni were for the Church; the Carandini and the Foiani against. Passionate 'ducheschi' (Duke's men), that is, followers of the Este family, were certain powerful princes in the surrounding country, such as Count Giovanni Boiardo di Scandiano and Contessa Diana de' Contrari who actually was an Este: their castles and their men were at the service of the Duke of Ferrara, and almost all the hill area of the State of Modena was for him.[2]

Private rancour, hatred, and desires for revenge smouldered under the ashes of past conflagrations, and it was enough for a small fire to flare up for the whole area to burst into flames, for destruction, violence and looting to break out. The population of the city was more inclined towards the Church which would mulct them less heavily, yet this was, in Guicciardini's words, support 'after the fashion of the people', not to be relied on in dire need or extreme danger. In such conditions the town could be lost whenever an insurrection, deliberately provoked or not, caused the streets to run with blood while an Este army appeared before its walls.

In the month of May the celebrated Cardinal Bernardo Dovizi da Bibbiena had been there; as pontifical legate to Maximilian during one of his inglorious expeditions to Italy, he had stopped in those parts under the pretext of a cold until the inevitable imperial retreat. He then went to Modena, where by the Pope's authority and his own skill he managed to conclude a solemn peace between the two factions.[3] Indeed, while he was there no agitation of any kind arose. Arms were laid down, pacts were observed, the outlaws kept their distance. The cardinal left on the 16th May, the following day a man was killed and the town was again filled with the usual trouble-makers.[4]

But now the disciplinarian was on his way. Guicciardini had left Florence on the 26th June, as we said: a few days later than he intended, so that at Rome they thought he had arrived when he had not yet departed.[5] He reached Modena on the 29th, and the entry was in his own style, and such as to acquaint all with the character and intentions of the new Governor. Knowing that they were preparing to receive him with the usual ceremonies and solemnity, he entered the city unannounced at daybreak. When the principal citizens and not a few lesser ones came to

65

the palace to do him honour, to promise to observe the stipulated peace and ask that justice be maintained, he 'let them understand well' that he wanted obedience, and that as for justice they would be surfeited with it. He said 'no means whatever would be spared to achieve that end'.[6] The same day the heralds cried Guicciardini's first severe ordinances. The factious, the outlaws disappeared, so did all arms: he even conveyed to the soldiers of Count Guido the Small, captain of the Church party, whom he had seen moving in armed bands through the streets, that he would not suffer such behaviour.

Only twenty-four hours after his arrival he had already dealt with his own bodyguard, the city gaol and the policing of the country area where disorder was greatest, but Guicciardini proposed to restore it to order, 'thrashing any who are reluctant'. He had also looked into the revenue, *nervus rerum*, and had never seen anything in such confusion. Besides the actual financial loss there was also the disrepute into which it brought the government, for most of the taxes were not collected, and the few that were, were stolen by the officials, whose accounts had not been examined within living memory. Therefore, it was necessary to provide for the levying of taxes, to check their collection, dismiss thieving and corrupt officials and provide a good treasurer. Nor in so brief a space of time had he studied only ways of increasing the revenue; he was already thinking how to limit expenditure, having noticed certain superfluous offices. On all these matters he reported in detail to the Duke Lorenzo de' Medici,[7] who had not the investiture of the province like Giuliano, but it was just the same as though he had; Guicciardini recognized the office as received from him, and from him was hoping for a yet greater one.

In short those in Florence and Rome who had sent him, could already begin to congratulate themselves, and he too could feel a certain pleasure in those first actions. He was confident that in time, with unfailing diligence and rigorous firmness, he could make real and stable that pacification which at present he judged to be superficial and unstable. He had no illusions indeed about his subjects' feelings, and wrote to Lorenzo: 'I find their spirits all so rebellious and full of suspicion, and I believe also ill disposed, that at any slightest opportunity they would revert to their former condition.'[8] Not for nothing did he end the first letter sent from Modena to his brother Luigi with a request seldom found in his letters: to tell madonna Simona, their mother, to have prayers offered for him.[9]

He needed it. Though he had for the present driven them from the city, or forced them into hiding, there was still the scum of assassins, thieves, and hired bullies to be dealt with. That plague had to be cured. He would have liked, out of humanity, to distinguish the natural delinquents from those who had erred 'because of the inveterate infection of the parties and universal decay of the city . . . which has been so long without justice or government'; but he realized that if he had wanted to proceed with some distinction and tolerate for any reason a single offence against the law, a single act of disobedience, a single outlaw, he would lose his 'reputation for severity' and the name he had gained at once through impartial justice. It was difficult to allow special pardons without damaging that reputation, and a general amnesty did not appeal to him. Since it was necessary, he proceeded with a prompt and merciless rigour. He had one Carlotto del Fante arrested, 'a most ferocious man of great fame and following among the bravos of all these factions', though a follower of those Rangoni who supported the Church, and after a trial lasting only two days, fearing 'that there might come some letter from Rome to prevent the execution of justice', he had him decapitated.[10]

There was an even more difficult matter requiring more caution and delicacy in handling, not for personal reasons, for he was not a timid man, but because it disturbed the political wasps' nest and because at every step one might expect difficulties from Florence or Rome: this was the question of the privileges of the nobles. Some of these, according to the nobles, were ancient or recent imperial concessions; some had been confirmed by the new masters so that the holders should not regret the former ones; some they had usurped on their own account, taking advantage of the general confusion.

Guicciardini's superiors in Florence and Rome had a weakness for these great vassals, since they wished to keep their friends and not embitter their enemies. On the other hand liberties of such a kind and so extensive, seemed intolerable to the juridical mind and the equanimity of the new Governor in his desire for order. However, the nobles brandished vast numbers of imperial diplomas, genuine or false, valid or out of date, and he, like a good jurist, pursued the elucidation of the formulas of those more or less ancient acts. He was most perplexed on one occasion when Gherardo and Guido ('Grosso') de' Rangoni unfolded before his eyes certain opinions elucubrated with learning by his old teacher Carlo Ruini. He noted that 'although, all things considered, it rather demands the approval of the Court, nevertheless there are many clauses in it which render the case somewhat doubtful'.[11]

This was not at all events a matter to be settled boldly or hastily until he had come to a decision on the authenticity of the privileges, and the nerve of his superiors. In certain cases he preferred to request a decision from them, before the lordlings could approach higher authority directly, to the detriment of his own dignity. He had therefore to navigate with care, balancing firmness with a certain toleration. Thus one day when the agents of madonna Diana de' Contrari seemed disposed to give in to the formidable Governor, he, 'so as not to go beyond his proper authority', was not willing to go so far and risk having to withdraw later, and resolved the difficulty saying 'that for love of madonna Diana, who is said to be a beautiful lady, he was willing to be patient for a few days'.[12] Our astrologer was quite right to say that messer Francesco was courteous to women.

Indeed there was a certain connection between this sore matter of the feudatory lords and the criminal classes. Guicciardini had been in Modena only a few days when contessa Rangoni complained to him about a murderer under arrest, protesting that the man was her vassal and that her privileges were not being observed.[13] Later when he had Carlotto beheaded, who was a follower of Count Guido ('Piccolo'), the latter made a great fuss, insisting that the truce had been broken, as though the governor had punished the man not for his crimes but at the instigation of the opposing faction. He raised bands of armed ruffians, threatened to do and say all kinds of things, and protested that he would take his case direct to Florence and Rome.[14]

In fact it was Roman weakness, rather than the outbursts of those people, which alarmed Guicciardini. If in Rome they gave way to a single one of them, the fortress he had built for himself to safeguard his authority, would have collapsed like a house of cards. He wrote of the vassals to Lorenzo de' Medici: 'For some time they have wielded such authority in this province that it seems very hard for them to be made to give it up; and if they were to be successful even in only one of these complaints they carry to Your Excellency, I warrant you they would become so bold that my work would be at an end.'[15]

Extremely jealous of his prerogatives and his independence, he would not tolerate them being usurped either by the secret paths of personal favours or by open and legitimate means. From the outset he had asked to have the prerogative of pardon, and when he heard that it had been given him but in a brief addressed to the Governor of Bologna, being the Vice-Legate and an ecclesiastic, 'as it was not customary for such commissions to be given to laymen', considering the facts and rights of the matter he wrote a strong protest to Lorenzo: 'Such a commission directed to the Governor of Bologna or to anyone else but myself, will immediately destroy my strength and my reputation here, where I have attained great prestige and reputation among all men, through which I have enjoyed, up till now, respect and obedience; whereas such treatment as this will cause me to become a cypher, and all these gentlemen and citizens will be amazed that I am held in so little account. . . . Your Excellency is my master and I am here as your representative, and have come here, as you know, only to serve you. I beg you to consider my honour.'[16] He won: victory was sealed by the papal brief of 22nd July addressed to him.[17]

Conflict flared up immediately over the right of appeal. There existed the custom that appeals were made to the Governor of Bologna who could decide to judge them himself or send them back to the courts at Modena. But when he sent some to Guicciardini, the latter refused to accept them, 'it not seeming honourable to act as delegate in another's name in cases under his own jurisdiction'. On this occasion too the Vice-Legate could see that the new Governor of Modena was a hard nut, or as our astrologer said, 'the ant in the rowan tree'.[18]

In short, he asserted himself no less towards those set above him than to those below, nor, authoritarian and greedy for power though he was, did he act thus merely out of greed or desire for authority, but to strengthen the power of his position. To his reputation for inflexibility he soon added that of being incorruptible. Madonna Diana de' Contrari, seeing she would not succeed in the matter of the privileges, offered him one day more than he earned in a year, but the formidable Governor did not merely refuse, he hastened to inform Duke Lorenzo.[19]

Thus if he did not earn their love (of which Guicciardini gathered a meagre harvest in life and death), he gained such a reputation with his subjects that discipline and order in the city and a good part of the area round very shortly became exemplary, the envy of neighbouring provinces. Even the public revenues were restored under Rosso Ridolfi, the new treasurer sent him from Florence. Messer Francesco had been in office only two months, when reporting that he had somewhat suppressed his rebellious vassals, he wrote those words which might be used as epigraph to his work as Governor: 'Count Guido and all the rest have swallowed the medicine and reduced themselves to their proper limits; and thus when justice is done everyone in the end settles down and order is restored.'[20]

To achieve this, he was by nature and education just the man they needed. Gino Capponi recognizes that the success Guicciardini had as Governor is partly due to his profession as lawyer, 'as this consists in seeking within the complex of human affairs their relationship to the high and immutable principle of law, which is accompanied as a natural extension by the idea of duty; that is why real jurists, when they are set to govern, always bring with them something at once more elevated and more practical'.[21]

Once the city had been settled and cleared of its disorders, Guicciardini's first thought was to clean and beautify it. After men, the stones: a cleansing which was the confirmation of and finishing touch to the other purification. He wrote to his brother Luigi: 'Since we lack other tasks, we have turned to having the town cleaned and paved and put in order, so that where it used to be like a pigsty, particularly in winter, it will now be comfortable to live in.'[22] And to Duke Lorenzo: 'This city ... with the works we plan, will seem quite a different place, which besides being decorative will get greater reputation, and the entire population could not be better pleased.'[23]

The miracles he had worked in Modena encouraged him to ask also for the neighbouring city of Reggio. From a somewhat obscure reference (which has hitherto gone unnoticed) we gather that he had sought it soon after his arrival in Modena.[24] He had then been given encouragement, and since, as the months went by, this produced nothing, he began to be 'very anxious'. Unburdening himself to his brother Luigi, he did not fail to enumerate to him the reasons which moved him in desiring that other governorship. Above all, if he had it, 'both honour and wealth would be increased'; then the two districts would be governed 'better and with greater reputation and ease and less expense'; finally the inhabitants of Reggio, seeing what he had done in Modena and being dissatisfied with Giovanni Gozzadini their Governor, 'would be extremely pleased'.[25]

But it did not do much good to write these things and others to his brother. At a certain point, losing patience, he began to bombard Rome and Florence with a persistence surprising in one who had boasted that these appointments had sought him out; though this may well be true, it is clear that at the beginning he applied the spurs to make sure they pursued him faster. Thus in a letter of the 4th December 1516 he reminds Goro Gheri, minister of Duke Lorenzo, of his ambition; on the 12th hearing that madonna Alfonsina and Lorenzo himself were favourable, he urges Gheri to keep on reminding them, 'for in Rome there are all kinds of affairs, and thus it is necessary to keep reminding them of one's own';[26] on the 18th he sets him a good example returning again to the charge: he thanks him for the 'almost certain' hopes he had given him, and for his own part offers more certain ones that he will do better than Gozzadini, adding not very generously: 'and it will not be too difficult . . . for if you knew the quarter part of it, you would think them very strange and ugly things, and the conclusion is that there everything is done by money'.[27] After which, he does not fail to offer the final bait: if those cities were to be made over, as it was said, to the Duke or madonna Alfonsina, they ought to be pleased for someone to be governing them who knew how to make them profitable!

I do not know if this final argument was more effective than the others. The fact is that on the 27th December, while from Modena the applicant was reiterating his plea,[28] the longed for brief was at last written. In the elegant chancery hand and rotund Latin of Sadoleto it expressed the highest praise for the government exercised until then by Guicciardini, together with hopes that he would show the same qualities in the government of Reggio.[29] This was 'as regards honour'; 'as for income' the 'usual salary' mentioned in the brief, was to carry Guicciardini's monthly stipend to 160 ducats.[30]

Meanwhile Guicciardini knew nothing about it: honour and income were long to remain a dead letter in the polished phrases of that parchment, because the brief was not then dispatched. Held up at first by the usual delays in the chanceries, it was later impeded by the desperate resistance of Gozzadini who was in Rome defending his own honour and income, if not actually as Guicciardini suspected, using golden arguments.[31] Whatever the obstacle was, it would soon have been overcome by the pressing insistence of the applicant with his masters in Florence and Rome, if something had not intervened which gave them quite different matters to think about in both cities, and also removed Guicciardini's desire to insist.

The year 1517 had barely begun. On the 12th January Guicciardini dispatched a messenger to the Duke Lorenzo to notify him that a Spanish army was moving out of Verona and was already on the way; on the 15th he followed this with the information that those troops, seven thousand foot and one thousand horse, were preparing to cross the Po 'with the intention of attacking here, at Bologna, and wherever they may'. The following day it was learnt that the dispossessed Duke of Urbino, Francesco Maria della Rovere, was with them. A thunderbolt out of a clear sky, just when disrupted Italy seemed at last to have attained a moment of peace. Reggio might be the first church possession to be attacked. There were things to think about other than changing its Governor.

At Modena Guicciardini, regarding this 'as a very grave situation which one could not resist', protested strongly to Gheri at having been left without military defence of any kind. 'From what I can see, you have thought only of saving Bologna, and here you have left us unprotected to see if we can work miracles; and undoubtedly you might have done something, without weakening the other places you have provided for, not to leave us thus at the mercy of the enemy.' Without losing heart he takes what measures he can: locks up suspect citizens, recruits trustworthy men, lays in food, constructs some defensive works. But time is short, artillery is limited, the city walls are weak, the moats nearly all filled in. It is necessary to rely on the people – though without feeling too sure of them – without whom all would be lost. This briefly is the Governor's cheerless report, ending however, in a typically virile manner: 'Since fate has brought me here, I shall not fail in my honour and duty, and the results will show it. Would that others had not failed me.'[32]

It was not yet known where that flood would strike, and there was a great flying to and fro of messengers and warnings. In Rome they held their breath, but even more so at Modena where the enemy was on top of them. 'They are near here, about thirty or thirty-five miles away, and if they wanted to come this way they could be here at once', Guicciardini writes on the 19th; and the following day; 'A man has just arrived from Finale . . . and he tells me that at that hour the enemy quartermasters had arrived to arrange billets, so they might easily come on here.' On the 22nd there was still uncertainty, but the day after he could breathe again: the army had moved off towards Butrio. The storm was going to break over Urbino.

And there it was more than a hailstorm. After a few days the capital fell into the hands of the former duke, and the usurper Lorenzo de' Medici was gravely injured by an arquebus. A few days later he had lost the whole duchy. But the story of that war does not belong in these pages. What should be mentioned are the many tribulations which Guicciardini suffered in consequence of it, particularly as the result of a large number of foreign troops in his territory; indeed the 'friendly' forces behaved no better than the enemy ones. There was moreover the fear lest the victorious army return in their direction 'with the favour of victory'. He wrote in jest: 'Here we are like Mahomet's tomb which hangs in the air without support of any kind.'[33] But Guicciardini had too many worries and problems of this kind in his lifetime for them all to find a place in the book of his life.

He had other preoccupations at that time, of a different nature. Duke Lorenzo's wound, which made Guicciardini's 'hair stand on end', was followed by an illness of madonna Alfonsina. These were his tutelary saints, and he could not help groaning: 'It would be a terrible blow ... for my personal interests.'[34] Already his 'personal interests' had suffered somewhat from the war in Urbino, in relation to the business of Reggio. 'This war has ruined me personally', he lamented to his brother Luigi,[35] when he realized it was not the right moment to mention it to his Medici masters. But when he got to know of the famous brief which had now been ready more than three months, he comments bitterly: 'Since these troubles started, they have been as unwilling to offend Gozzadini as though he were the first cardinal in the court. It annoys me that it should be known at Rome and there (in Florence) and at Reggio, and here it is public knowledge, although I have always denied it, so that besides the loss I have also the humiliation of it. We shall be patient and think about returning home; for if I see this I shall be clear for ever.'[36]

Fate helped him. At Reggio the leader of the Bebbi had been murdered on Easter Monday by the leader of the opposing faction Vincenzo Scaioli. Guicciardini had immediately drawn an unfavourable conclusion for his own affairs. 'Lo how often human judgement errs!' According to him, Gozzadini still at Rome *sub judice*, would in this crisis be sent back to Reggio and the dear brief torn up.[37] Indeed Gozzadini was sent back to Reggio, but that return which should have been his resurrection, was instead the end of him, and not metaphorically. For on the morning of the 28th June the Bebbi, who had vainly awaited justice from him for the killing of their leader, murdered him in the Duomo during mass. Thus the field was clear and the way opened for the brief of nomination. In fact while Reggio was abandoned to destruction and looting, the alarm felt in Rome for that city was so great that they sent their brief by the swiftest means. It left on the 30th June, the very day the news from Reggio arrived, and on the morning of the 3rd July it was in Guicciardini's hands. He, however, with his customary phlegm sent credentials as apostolic commissioner to the very capable Rosso Ridolfi who was on the spot, and decided to set off himself only after an interval of four days.

While he was still in doubt whether he would ever have that so greatly longed for governorship, and, disappointed 'in honour and money', had decided to go home though most unwillingly, he had written these words: 'It displeases me greatly because I am losing an opportunity the like of which may never offer again in my lifetime.'[38] It was true. If in that disappointment he had left the government of Romagna, his life would have taken another course. Now beyond this fork in the road there lies before him a long straight run: one which leads first to Reggio, now covered with the blood of factions.

Chapter 9

GOVERNOR OF MODENA
AND REGGIO

‹‹

THE city of Reggio, formerly a possession of the Dukes of Ferrara like Modena, had also been added to the states of the church by Julius II. Unlike Modena it had not been taken by armed force but had surrendered to the Pope as the lesser evil, and since then had not changed hands. The fate of the two cities was again identical when Leo X retook Modena from the Emperor and also when he had to promise Francis I to restore both to the House of Este. This promise was honoured no more for Reggio than for Modena, nor indeed, any more than Leo X's promises usually were.

This circumstance might lead one to suppose that Reggio was easier to govern than Modena, yet in fact the opposite was true. In Reggio too the Duke of Ferrara had his supporters, either from old affection for him or hatred of the ecclesiastical government, stirred up by the turbulent factions. There were no great nobles as at Modena, but only small ones, or rather citizens more powerful and richer than the rest, but its divisions were no fewer and no less inflamed for that. Those had been neglected and had worsened under the inefficient government of poor Gozzadini, who had fallen at last into the pit he had dug for himself.

Of the opposing factions the Bebbi stood for the Duke of Ferrara while the Scaioli and their adherents supported the ecclesiastical government. It was natural, therefore, that these last should have been favoured by the former governor, but he had gone beyond what was reasonable and did not trouble to make a show of impartiality. Vincenzo Scaioli, author of the ugly crime of Easter Monday, should have been prosecuted and sentenced with all rigour, and might then have been allowed to enjoy life in Rome or elsewhere. Guicciardini would have done so. Instead his predecessor started a half-hearted trial for form's sake, and then took no action,[1] defying justice all too shamelessly and exasperating those who had no further need to be exasperated. The day Gozzadini was hacked to pieces and the days following, more than a hundred people were killed and there was endless pillage and destruction.

When on the 7th July the new Governor arrived, the storm had passed over. Only the marks of it remained on things and people. Once Matteo Strozzi arrived with a large company of soldiers, calm was restored. The Bebbi more or less sated with blood and plunder had made off, frightened by the soldiers and their own excesses, and influenced also by a subtle arrangement made by Guicciardini, Rosso Ridolfi and Girolamo Moroni before the brief of nomination arrived. The Bebbi were to depart with their women, children and possessions, with an assurance that the Scaioli outlaws would not be allowed back to take their revenge on them. To this end the severe Governor had gone so far as to write to his 'most dear' Vincenzo Scaioli a honeyed letter, in which he declared that he 'bore him affection for his good qualities' and because he knew him to be 'a good supporter of the Church'.[2] That honey was soon to be turned to vinegar.

Having given the unhappy city the benefit of this first respite he set to work to doctor its ills. He was not a gentle practitioner, as we know, and would not allow sores to suppurate. Strong remedies were the ones he preferred. The hated Bebbi, for whom he had made it easy to depart, at a time when his superiors would have liked to arrest them, he banished as rebels, ordered the confiscation of their property, set a price on their head and other pleasantries. He also demanded at once that Rome should give him strong support against those who sheltered these gentlemen; threatening with the loss of their fiefs those who were vassals of the Church, and with severe censure those under other jurisdiction. He demanded further sanctions against those who received goods looted during the troubles. In particular he would have liked to do something against the counts of Nuvolara: 'people who deserve thrashing', he wrote. And as a weapon, he requested *in primis et ante omnia* that his guard should be increased and a more energetic captain sent to command it, as the one he had seemed to him 'a shadow of a man rather than one fitted for such employment'.[3]

Having struck a blow on one side, he could now turn to the other. Guicciardini, unlike his predecessor, knew that people cannot be governed without a semblance of justice. The Bebbi had to be punished severely, being the authors of such excesses, but the Scaioli who had sown 'the bad seed' with the Easter Monday murder should not be let off either. His masters in Florence and even more so those in Rome would have thought merely that the Scaioli were their friends and the others declared enemies of the government, and Guicciardini agreed, but he could not go beyond certain limits and openly defy justice. Once again the conscience and training of the man of law went hand in hand with the art of the Governor.

In fact between the anvil of his biased superiors and the hammer of those enraged factions, he had greater difficulties in Reggio than in his first government. There was no easy task either in the country districts, as we see from the accounts in his letters: 'Things . . . could not be in worse disorder; it is like a wild orgy. It all arises from the fact that everything was sold for money. I am thinking how to reorganize, for if I am not mistaken they are in a worse state than Modena was and the area round,'[4] i.e., before the arrival of the scourge. This comparison with Modena and his experience there, recurred to him frequently: 'If in the affairs of Modena, where the heads of parties are of some noble consequence, I have not showed favour except when forced to by needs of state, I shall do so all the less here where the leaders are private citizens and need not be taken much account of.'[5]

The difficulty was that more or less 'forced to by needs of state' those in Rome did take account of them, and – worse still – they took account not only of the Scaioli and their main adherents in the city such as the Zoboli. In the country outside was Domenico di Amorotto, a certified double-dyed villain and gallows-bird, who, seeing which side his bread was buttered on and becoming more ecclesiastical than the Pope, had acquired (and perhaps not merely metaphorically) the good graces of the previous governor, and had even become his secular arm. With the Governor's support he had obtained from His Holiness the fortress of Carpineti, a very strong position in the mountains of Reggio, and thence he swooped down to murder, burn, destroy, and in particular to plunder the enemies of Holy Church.

After having been the previous Governor's instrument to hold and in some sense to rule the troubled hills of Reggio,[6] this Domenico at once became Guicciardini's *bête noire* (nor could it have been otherwise). Tirelessly he insisted and repeated that he could do nothing of value if that scandal were not removed. Once he wrote to Cardinal de' Medici: 'So many are the killings, rapines and other wicked deeds which this man daily commits from the shelter of that fortress, that to me it seems a tyranny to be compared with many of the ancient ones we read about; and it is with such infamy and displeasure to God and man that it far outweighs in my opinion the fact that he is considered a supporter of the Church. Nor do I believe that it is to the honour of Holy See to lend favour to such men.'[7]

But to remove the scandal it was necessary to remove Domenico from that fortress, and although Guicciardini wore himself out in insisting on it, in Rome they did not seem to hear him. Nor did they hear any better when Domenico, with the Scaioli and Zoboli and a small band of armed men actually attempted a raid on the city, coming up to the walls one night, 'proposing to execute a sack and ruin worse than the last'. Having a few hours' warning of the affair, the Governor's prompt vigilance was able to foil the plan;[8] but it became all the more difficult for him to govern. Indeed it was much harder after that armed attempt to show any decent favour 'in the interest of the state'; rather he had to please and cultivate the good will of the Bebbi faction, his government's enemies, to gain their support against those factious friends.[9]

He had so longed for that office, but for two years after his happy time at Modena it brought him nothing but trouble and bitterness. He was living nearly all the time in Reggio where the need was greatest, and in the citadel for his greater safety, as he was not anxious to meet the same end as his predecessor. But in that hot weather he had poor lodging there and bad air, so that he fell ill for a long time 'with two fevers', from the end of July to the middle of September, thus adding the troubles and difficulties of illness to those of his work, which he never ceased attending to with his usual assiduity.[10]

Dealing with his superiors had become more difficult for him since the beginning of the war of Urbino. Duke Lorenzo, removed first by military affairs and then by his grave injury, no longer took so much interest in the papal states, and Cardinal Giulio de' Medici, the son of old Giuliano, had taken up the reins instead. Lorenzo was what he was, and as we have briefly attempted to portray him, but he was a man used to command and to government, used to military discipline and justice.

With his soldierly manners Guicciardini was more at ease than with the subtle and irresolute behaviour of the Cardinal.

It is true that in mid-September that ill-omened war ended, not indeed by virtue of papal arms, but by the efforts of the Catholic and Most Christian monarchs to relieve the Pope of that burden (as though to justify their titles). Though the war ended, nothing was changed, for Lorenzo went off to France, whence, having feasted and celebrated at length, he returned with the bride destined to him by that King. On his way home he came through Modena, and it goes without saying that Guicciardini made tremendous efforts to give a worthy reception to one he expected soon to have as his master again. He had to entertain and accommodate a great crowd of followers with two hundred horses and forty mules. The Curators of the city, poor things, understanding that they were to provide all with a subsidy from the town council of only fifty ducats, refused the charge, adding 'quod nollunt intrare in hoc labirintum cum tam paucis pecuniis'. They should not have done so, and above all they ought not to have written in those terms to the haughty Governor. He replied among other things that 'the letter would not deserve an answer, for if I required you to honour His Excellency the Duke, I did so more for your honour than for his, for His Excellency is of such quality that he has no need to be honoured by you, but it becomes you and it is your duty to honour him . . . But I am not surprised by such letters in view of the fact that a few days since, I had another letter from you of a most peculiar kind, for I believe when you write to governors you think you are writing to your stable boys'.[11]

Of course after that everything went perfectly and Lorenzo was duly honoured; but the young duke now had before him only the celebrations in Florence and his joyful reception in Rome, then six long months of illness and death. So that at this point the author and perhaps the reader of these pages sees him withdrawn, almost foreseeing his destiny, as in Michelangelo's marble figure. And Guicciardini, passing finally from military to ecclesiastical hands, will now have to deal with the Cardinal whether he likes it or not.

Henceforth having followed him step by step to Modena and Reggio we know what was his daily round of business and cares in these governments, and how he dealt with them. On that 'long road' which we have seen him set out at the end of the last chapter, the biographer can now hasten his steps. It will be enough to describe briefly his principal tasks or the most difficult ones that he had to deal with at this period.

The worst was still the factions, and still the greatest difficulties came from the 'ecclesiastical' faction of the Scaioli who were absolutely determined to punish the Bebbi, while Guicciardini was determined that he was the only one who was going to mete out punishment in the lands he governed. Without ignoring the wishes expressed or tacit of his superiors, but without giving them undue weight, he continued to act according to what was just. He concluded the trial of Vincenzo Scaioli, condemning him to banishment and confiscation of property. Before publishing his sentence he asked for the Cardinal's views, reminding him however that 'impunity for past offences is an incitement to future ones'.[12]

Nor did the opposing faction of the Bebbi fail to give the Governor some trouble just to keep him in practice and lest he might become completely devoted to them in consequence of the activities of their enemies. Early in July that year 1518, suspecting something, he had three of them arrested, two being priests; interrogated by torture, and a plot being discovered to open one of the city gates to the exiles of their faction, he had them beheaded.[13] At the end of August he had information of another attempt to take Reggio with the assistance of the Duke of Ferrara, but nothing came of this *coup de main*. There was only an armed raid on the possessions of the Zoboli and Boiardo's castle of Scandiano with the object of killing Vincenzo Scaioli who had taken refuge there. The raiders killed and robbed, but Vincenzo escaped. The Governor was obliged to punish this crime too.

However, neither these nor any others could be punished or forestalled while bandits and factions found a hospitable refuge in neighbouring castles and small states. The thunderbolts Guicciardini had requested when he took office had all remained in the Roman heavens. He received some help from Rome only when the castles were fiefs of the Church and their wardens were not supporters of the Church, as occurred with the castle of Vignola of Diana de' Contrari which he was given powers to take by assault, though later he was able to take it peacefully without other arms than a papal brief.[14]

Things obviously were more difficult with the feudatories who were not dependent on the Church; worse still with those who supported the Duke of Ferrara. One was Count Federigo Gonzaga da Bozzolo, who had taken in the raiders and the proceeds of their raid on the territory of Scandiano. Guicciardini had an exchange of harsh words with an agent of the Count. But all things were not rosy for the Governor even as regards the small states friendly to the Church, like those near by of Carpi and Mirandola. Carpi was the little principality of Count Alberto Pio, much loved by Pope Leo for his talents, since the Count was a great patron of arts and letters and a man of letters himself, and loved even better perhaps for his implacable hatred of the Duke of Ferrara. This papal favour, which often became partiality, was the cause of no little trouble and displeasure to Guicciardini. Thus it was when the rich lands of San Felice were detached from the territory of Modena and given to Pio with Leo's usual generosity and facility. As a result 'all the inhabitants fell into indescribable despair', and were on the verge of rebellion, 'wailing and crying out . . . with violent words, saying they would resist with arms'.[15] Instead they had to bear the Pope's will patiently. It was also necessary to take account of papal partiality when the lords of Carpi proposed to move their produce from their Modenese territories without the Governor's permission. And as we shall see, from that quarter came worries yet more tiresome with regard to his dear 'private interests'.

Mirandola, a fortress battered by high tides in the storms of Italian politics, was devastated within by the appalling family feuds of those who held it, which at that time had also spread to their neighbours and relations at Concordia (the name could scarce be more ironical!) and gave the ruler of Modena no little trouble on the borders, and a good deal of cause for correspondence. At that time the new master of Mirandola was Count Giovan Francesco Pico, nephew of the famous Pico, in whose footsteps he followed though at a distance. Like him devout, like him a philosopher and eclectic, but far inferior in intellect and much more 'lettered' in the bad sense of the word. Guicciardini with all the respect we have heard him profess for letters, had little for men of letters and still less for philosophers. To him, that Count Giovan Francesco, greatly favoured in Florence and Rome, seemed 'a man who deserved little respect'. On one occasion the Count, having been asked not to shelter a man from the district of Modena, who, from Mirandola, had raided and pillaged on the borders, refused 'with a thousand fine philosophical reasons'. So Guicciardini relates humorously: 'I, who do not profess philosophy, had to be patient.'[16] And he had to be patient when the Count obtained from Rome certain extraordinary favours, and Guicciardini was informed of them by Alfonsina his mistress and patron; yet he replied: 'I shall do what Your Worship wants, if Count Giovan Francesco will be satisfied with the results and does not try to dispute the matter philosophically.'[17]

How dangerous it was to overlook anyone who enjoyed the favour of the Roman court, he was able to see even better in two civil actions brought in Rome by one Ercole Sadoleto and the Cappelli his relatives, against the Colombo family, all being citizens of Modena. These Cappelli, in another case they brought in Modena, had committed perjury and been condemned. It seemed quite an ordinary affair, but its special interest was that it touched, if only indirectly, the family of Iacopo Sadoleto, of whom it is hard to say whether he was more beloved by the Pope as his secretary or for his Ciceronian Latin. Cardinal de' Medici wrote to the Governor that 'His Holiness had been very upset',[18] the affair having been reported to him with all kinds of distortions; the Governor, full of bitterness, unburdened himself to Gheri: 'In Rome they have given so much attention to this affair with Sadoleto, that if I had massacred an entire population I do not believe they would have said so much, and all of it against reason.'[19]

Pope Leo may really have had a wish for a more manageable and Ciceronian Governor, or it may only have been a round of words and vain hopes, but at that time the rumour spread that the Pope had given the government of Modena and Reggio to his beloved Alberto Pio. With suppressed indignation Guicciardini wrote at once to Cardinal de' Medici and to Alfonsina asking, if this were true, 'to be allowed to return to Florence as soon as possible'.[20] If there were really anything, the intriguing and aggressive Alfonsina who had placed Guicciardini where he was, made enough fuss in Rome to avert the danger. When he got over this, and it was not the only thing, in the late autumn of 1518 he was ill again for a long time with the same fevers. Ill as he was, he had to get his brother Iacopo to help him in the work of government.[21]

His tribulations continued in 1519. Early in February two of the Zoboli, who were partisans of the Scaioli, murdered in church and during mass, as was now the custom, two of the opposing faction. The Zoboli fled in time, but four of their accomplices, the principal of whom was one Count Alessandro da Sessa, were caught in the Governor's net, and he did not fail to inflict prompt and pitiless justice, so that that mob should 'remember and be more careful in such matters in the future'. Nor did Cardinal de' Medici fail to make his usual last moment bid to save the Count, ordering the sentence to be delayed for eight or ten days, but Guicciardini's answer was the usual one: justice had already been done.[22]

If he could always have done things in his own way! Meanwhile, however, he was still unsuccessful in getting from Rome the help he needed to drive out the exiles from those castles outside his territory, and even in his own domain he could not dislodge that Domenico di Amorotto from his fortress at Carpineti. After the Zoboli outrage he again vainly asked the Cardinal for such powers, but it went unheeded. Before twenty days had passed, other exiles murdered the mayor of Finale. Blood continued to flow without respite in the lands of turbulent Romagna.

Intrepid though he was, Guicciardini must sometimes have feared for his life as well as for his work. Light is thrown on this, as well as by the prayers requested of his mother, by the strange letter of a monk whom he had approached to find out – more clearly than in the famous horoscope – what the future held for him, and whether he had not better leave his dangerous post. This monk – I do not know whether he was 'endowed with a prophetic spirit' (but it seems that a nun was who spoke through him) – replied on the 2nd April that 'the hearts of the enemy had been somewhat softened, and in particular one had been removed who beset him terribly'; and he added: 'When peace is made ... your enemies will be quiet.Now you are in less danger.... Be gentle with your subjects, for many were angry with you for using such haughty words, and imputing to them things which were not true. There is no reason for you to go now, and you will succeed with honour in your government ...'[23] I do not believe Machiavelli would ever have occasioned the writing of such a letter; it needed Guicciardini, who was fearful and devout for all his scepticism.

Not, however, that he needed such suggestions to cultivate diligently that peace to which the good friar referred. For some time, ever since he had the Count of Sessa in his grasp, he had been industriously weaving the threads without losing heart if his labour, patient and unremitting, was interrupted now and then by all that tangle of rancour and hatred. In the end his perseverance and perhaps universal exhaustion conquered. On the 14th July he was able to announce with triumph to Cardinal de' Medici that on that very day a treaty of universal peace had been concluded and stipulated between the opposing factions of Reggio.[24]

He took advantage of this to ask the Cardinal in the same letter for permission to go to Florence 'for twelve or fifteen days' in order to regain his health; he would leave his brother Iacopo in his place, who, 'because he had already been there six months at different times' during his illnesses, had had good practice in government and knowledge of all its transactions.[25] It was true about his health, for he had been attacked by the usual fevers which had left him but a short time before; but between him and his brother there was a little plot. The Governor's intention was to stop at home, where he had not set foot for three years,[26] far more than 'twelve or fifteen days', but if he had revealed this, they would have sent someone other than his brother to take his place and there was already someone eager for this juicy morsel.[27] As it was, all went well. The Cardinal replied expressing his pleasure at the peace that had been made and gladly giving him the permission he sought to go to Florence. The Cardinal, who had himself been in Florence for the last two months, would be glad to see him and hear all the details from him.[28]

To tell the truth, Guicciardini was just as pleased to be seeing the Cardinal. Besides his desire to recuperate in his native air, to see his home again, his daughters, his wife,[29] that must have been one of the main reasons drawing him to Florence. For, as Duke Lorenzo had died on the 4th May, a few days later a papal brief had informed Guicciardini that in future he would be under the orders of Cardinal Giulio de' Medici.[30] Alfonsina's power was small once her son was dead. It is not difficult to imagine, therefore, that Guicciardini needed to put his affairs on a different footing, to reach an understanding with his new master, to know him better and become better known by him, to win him over, 'speaking to him vigorously' as he had once done to regain Lorenzo's favour. As then, he was armed with intellect, address, honesty, his upright character, and resolution. And in addition he had in his favour those three years of exemplary government culminating in the peace of Reggio.[31]

Chapter 10

POPE LEO'S LAST ADVENTURE

I N FLORENCE, to which Guicciardini had now returned, the people were giving voice to their resentment, long stored up against the dead Duke. It was said that his princely ambitions had grown since his return from France and that he meant to make his power absolute. Francesco Vettori, his courtier, counsellor, and friend, 'had a hue and cry after him, worse than when the wolf is sighted'.[1] In the Florentine manner it was only an outburst of hard words, but often even words leave their mark. Then there were the facts: that is, the disorders in financial and other matters left behind by the Duke's mismanagement.

Cardinal Giulio de' Medici, sent at once by Pope Leo to take over the government of the city, was doing everything possible to cure these ills, doing exactly the opposite of what Lorenzo used to do. Easy and pleasant in audiences, he listened kindly to everyone's opinions and advice, indeed he invited them, and not only on particular subjects but also on the general organization of the State. Parsimonious to the point of seeming mean, he brought order into the administration of the treasury, and limited expenditure. Thus he achieved the conquest of the sensitive hearts of his fellow citizens, who very much enjoyed the excessive magnificence of Lorenzo but only if they did not have to pay for it out of their own pockets.

There is no doubt, and the correspondence bears witness to it, that Guicciardini had at that time long and frank conversations with the Cardinal. We know him well enough now, and need not be surprised if he succeeded in winning his confidence. Perhaps at this very moment there began what became in time a mutual feeling of trust, esteem, and affection. The Cardinal must have asked his opinion at length about the affairs of Florence, as he did with everyone, but he could not help hearing about those of Reggio, including some things which he would really have preferred not to hear, and which, indeed, he had pretended not to notice when Guicciardini had written about them from Reggio. Marvellous to say, he began to show signs of understanding even when Guicciardini spoke to him about punishing that ruffian Domenico di Amorotto. It seemed to him that such punishment must weaken too greatly the Church party, but Guicciardini would have been satisfied with chasing him out of his castle. Indeed during his long stay in Florence from 24th July to 2nd October 1520[2] (not twelve or fifteen days!) he at last succeeded in having the fortress at Carpineti exchanged for that at Buscello near Modena.[3]

It is true that, after he had returned to his government, the thing got bogged down again, and he vainly reminded the Cardinal of it in his letters. It was different when he could speak directly to him, but from afar the Cardinal would not hear. The affairs of Reggio were so quiet that this was almost the only sore point with which the Governor had to deal. There were small things like the usual incursions of the Pio clan of Carpi, against which, however, he had obtained a papal brief while in Florence, which enabled him to force them to restore their booty, even by force.[4]

At the beginning of 1520 he had to deal with the moves ordered by the Pope against Ferrara. A large section of the wall along the Po having fallen down, he planned to have something besides water enter through the breach. It was to be a flood of 2,000 foot soldiers collected by Alessandro Fregoso, bishop of Ventimiglia, with the pretext that they were to be used against Genoa, while Sigismondo Santi, chancellor of Alberto Pio of Carpi, was collecting boats to transport them.[5]

Guicciardini was involved in this business only indirectly 'only in the matter of the boats'. Unused to acting simply as an assistant, he stuck fast punctiliously, offering a thousand reasons, to this role which did not suit him; and writing of it to Santi, he protested that he wanted to share the benefits as well as the disadvantages, 'because . . . as I shall gain little or no advantage from success in this affair, it seems reasonable that those who have authority to commit me should make their requirements so precise and clear that I have only to carry them out and not to interpret them, so that whatever happens I shall incur as little blame as praise. Hence you will not be surprised if, not content with what you have written, I ask for some more exact statement, for I wish only to execute and not to interpret . . . And because I know that if it is not successful, everyone who has been involved will say what they like and try to throw off the responsibility, therefore before I enter into this affair I wish to make my position quite clear, and what may happen if it becomes known that I did those things, which I do not refuse on my own account but I bring it to your attention, because what I am known to have done will be attributed to others. You understand the whole affair, and I have written clearly and distinctly to obtain a clear and distinct reply, and hence you will write to me definitely whether or not I have to take these measures, and I will obey you as I do my masters with that loyalty and diligence which is my habit in their affairs, for that is my duty by virtue of your credentials. I wish to advise you that I have kept a copy of this letter to protect myself, feeling that it is a case of such importance one cannot be too cautious.'[6]

The expedition was abortive from the first, showing that Guicciardini's doubts and caution had not been without reason. In July he again brought up the subject of Amorotto and the place to be given him in exchange in order to eject him from Carpineti: 'Every day we have so many and such grievous complaints of him, and under his protection so many and such serious excesses are committed, that it would be the greatest service to God to set it right.'[7] In fact he dealt with it himself, but he had to go to Florence again. He went for that and other reasons, besides wishing to spend the hottest period of the year in healthier air and to make the acquaintance of two further twin daughters born meanwhile, Lisabetta and Maddalena, fruits of his previous year's holiday. Perhaps he was also attracted by the hope of further fruits of this kind, but male ones, for the lack of sons was his great sorrow. Those hopes were disappointed, but the trip on the 23rd July 1520 enabled him to win the contest with Domenico.

He was assisted by fresh disorders at Reggio. Count Gaspare di Roio revealed to Iacopo Guicciardini, who had now taken the title of Vice-Governor, a plot arranged by Roberto Messori with other members of the ecclesiastical party, in which Domenico was also implicated, to raid Reggio and put their enemies to fire and the sword.[8] One should not suppose that Francesco at this news flew back to Reggio to make sure, purge the disease, lay hands on the conspirators, and avert the danger. If he had returned then, a few heads would have rolled, he would have written letters and written again, but Domenico would have remained to plan further crimes in his inaccessible nest. All would have gone on as before. He could only win that game in Florence.

Indeed there came from Florence the Cardinal's letter enjoining Domenico to leave the fortress and withdraw to Bologna, where, however, after so much murder, arson and rapine, there awaited him not the gallows or prison, but an honourable post in the city guard. Meanwhile, as the ruffian turned out to be innocent of this particular piece of wickedness, the Vice-Governor felt some scruple about sending the fatal letter to Domenico, but then he overcame it and wrote to the Governor his brother: 'Knowing what his life is and how you hate him, I decided to send it . . . My belief is that Domenico will refuse to obey but that he will come to Florence.'[9] He would have gone to Florence if he had not known that Guicciardini was there.

When Domenico received the letter, he called his brother Vitale to read it to him, but he had not read half before he began to shake his head violently and bellow: 'God's blood, I will not do it! They will take my life sooner. Over my dead body! I know whence this comes: it is that traitor Francesco Guicciardini who is the cause of this. Traitor! . . . I wanted to go to Florence, but then I heard he was there and I would not go where he would have had me arrested. Very well. They want to believe what my enemies say about me. And what the devil do they think? That when they have taken the fortress from me, my hands will be tied? Blood of the Virgin! I will do worse and I will have means to do it. . . . The Governor has kept me here like a monk and a friar, I have put up with a thousand outrages, and still it has not been enough. And when I came into his presence, he shouted at me and turned his back, and he has never looked kindly on me. . . . I shall not restore the fort for anything: they need not think it, and if they take it they must take my life. . . .'[10]

After saying and doing all kinds of wild things, having provisioned the castle for a long siege, filled it with crossbowmen, walled up the gate, leaving access only by one window, he finally gave in to the persuasion of his friend the Governor of Bologna who had been called in by Guicciardini, and then commanded by the Cardinal at Guicciardini's request. But Guicciardini, his battle won, returned to Reggio at the beginning of October,[11] and early in December Domenico returned to the fortress. Although this was held by a warden with an adequate force Domenico entered through a tunnel he had prepared and concealed before leaving. As though this were not enough, he added insult to his offence, since when he entered the castle, he forced the warden to write in the Governor's name to some of his enemies to bring them there, and when they arrived he took them prisoner. He did likewise with four soldiers whom Guicciardini, still unaware of this coup, sent there to reinforce the guard; one of them he had thrown off the tower.[12]

Thus the measure was overflowing. The Vice-Legate and Governor of Bologna, although he had a weakness for Domenico, sent reinforcements of soldiers and artillery to recapture the fortress, but at the same time he did his best to help the ruffian, getting others to intervene so that he might come out with life and liberty.[13] Hence Guicciardini's just indignation expressed in a splendid letter to the Vice-Legate, which ends with these words: 'It grieves me exceedingly, for it has been too great a loss of honour for our master on account of such a wretch. I do not speak of my own honour, for where that of His Holiness is involved, mine should not be considered, but Your Excellency should think, what if something of that kind happened in your states, what would you feel? And I was not born in the backwoods but in so great a city and of so great a family, and also have lived in such a manner, that you ought to understand that I too value my honour.'[14]

Meanwhile Domenico had taken refuge in Bologna where he was kindly received by the Governor[15] who, to give him at least that satisfaction, continued to occupy the fortress of Carpineti himself, despite his colleague. This called for renewed and more violent protests by Guicciardini to the Cardinal: 'I beg you to order that it shall be placed in my hands and that the Governor of Bologna shall not interfere in my government as I do not interfere in his.' And in another letter after recapitulating the crimes committed by Domenico: 'I have used in Reggio every kind of severity, confiscated goods, cut off heads, pulled down houses, but I have never been able to put an end to his violence. What does Your most Reverend Lordship think will happen when so serious a crime is seen to be remitted? . . . All the good done in these years will be destroyed for love of that ruffian.'[16]

The affair had now gone so far that there could be no doubt of the Cardinal's reply. Domenico was banished, his house and those of his accomplices razed to the ground. This done and having presented himself repenting and contrite before the Governor at Reggio, the latter gave him absolution after so much penance, and actually interceded for him with the Cardinal as long as he would promise never to set foot in the lands of Reggio again.[17] Thus, fortunately for Guicciardini and for ourselves, a curtain falls on the last act but one of this tragicomedy.

But at that moment the Governor had quite other negotiations in hand. It was a question of taking something quite different from a mere fort! The Pope with his ambition to capture Ferrara was still looking for a means of taking it by surprise. The attack by river having failed, he welcomed the offer of a German captain of the ducal guard who was to open the gate of Castel Tialto to him, showing he loved ducats better than the Duke. Unlike the last time, Guicciardini took part in the whole plan having discussed it at length with the Cardinal at Florence and 'given lively encouragement to his master'.[18] It is a fact that we find him involved in these manoeuvres from early autumn in the year 1520, and then with greater activity between February and May the following year. I would not like to say that he welcomed such shady machinations, but if there was anything distasteful to him in this, it was certainly not the prospect of playing a low trick on the Este, especially since he had knowledge of a plot by Cardinal Ippolito d'Este to murder him.[19] Poor messer Francesco! After the factions and the outlaws, a cardinal now was out for his blood, and one of Ariosto's 'generous Herculean family'.

Not that he placed blind faith in men of such doubtful loyalty or thought he might not be betrayed by a traitor, but contrary to what is said by Otetea who did not know many of the documents,[20] he thought it worth risking. He discussed it at the outset with Giberti and Schönberg, who took turns to hold the keys to the Cardinal's heart. He wrote to the former: 'The importance of the thing, were it to succeed, is such in all respects that it deserves to be attempted even if we have not complete certainty, the more so since these things by their nature, when they have to be obtained in such a manner, and cannot be regarded as certain, render it necessary to run the risk.'[21]

He worked on these secret manoeuvres, particularly, as we said, from February 1521 after the arrival of the protonotary Uberto da Gambara, watching the negotiations with the Este captain, and dealing with the troops who were to enter Ferrara. Among them was Count Guido Rangoni who was already counting on rich spoils. One day waxing enthusiastic in conversation, he even counted up the artillery he would be able to sell to the Pope, when Guicciardini, 'laughing heartily', replied 'that would be going too far to leave His Holiness only the walls'.[22] On this occasion too, a collaborator, if not the prime mover, was Sigismodo Santi, chancellor of Count Alberto Pio of Carpi.[23]

This broth was boiling hard, indeed the lid was nearly rising off the pot when in mid-May Niccolò Machiavelli came to Modena, sent on a pointless mission to the chapter of minor friars then being held in Carpi. He stopped that evening, the night and part of the following day, being most kindly received and entertained by Guicciardini. Nature had made these two men very different and fortune had still further divided and set them apart, as I have explained in Machiavelli's Life, and have already mentioned here. There is nothing to show that until that very day there had ever been any friendship or acquaintance between them. However, besides the fascination of his intellect, Machiavelli shone with a human warmth which broke the ice with Guicciardini; and meanwhile he had read Machiavelli's *Discourses* as certain words written by him at this period indicate.[24] When beneath the robes, everyday or curial, there is good human material, a moment may suffice to bring understanding and liking. On that occasion a few hours spent together in a foreign place were enough for these two great fellow citizens; each found in the other something of Florence and longed to be back there.

If we cannot know their conversation at that time, we know the letters which were the continuation of those talks, when Machiavelli had left Modena for his mission to the friars. It would not seem appropriate to say much about them here, having said a great deal in Machiavelli's biography.[25] This interlude has more importance for his life than for Guicciardini's, and at that time it meant more to the unoccupied man of San Casciano than to the very busy Governor. All we are interested in, is to note the warmth, the confidence, the merry cordiality of this correspondence, so unusual in that it brightens up Guicciardini's otherwise sombre collection of letters.

If it was Machiavelli's idea to make a joke out of the rapid exchange of letters, with their fat envelopes and the desperate haste of the messengers, which were to mystify the friars and the host Guicciardini had found him, the latter at once took up the jest and developed it. Do we not remember what the grave and severe Governor wrote to his new friend? 'I am sending you in all haste this archer whom I have told must

travel with all speed, it being a most important matter, so he comes
without his shirt touching his bottom; and I doubt not that, what with
his galloping and what he will tell the bystanders, everyone will think
you a most important person, and your business much more vital than
anything to do with friars. And so that the nature of my plump letter
may convince your host, I have put in certain messages which have
come from Zürich which you may make use of, either by showing
them, or by holding them in your hand, whichever you judge more
expedient'.[26] And Machiavelli in return: 'I can tell you that the smoke
rose high in the sky, for between the breathlessness of the messenger and
the size of your packet of letters, there is no one in this house or in this
neighbourhood who is not filled with wonder; and so as not to appear
ungrateful to messer Gismondo, I showed him those agreements
between the Swiss and the King. He thought it was very important. I
told him of the Emperor's illness and the estates he wanted to buy in
France, and he was agape with wonder. But I really think that in spite of
all this he wonders whether he has not been had, because he feels
doubtful and cannot understand why such immense letters have to be
sent to these Arabian deserts where there is nothing but friars. . . .'[27]

There was a side to the jest which escaped Machiavelli and must have
made Guicciardini smile to himself. The Gismondo whom he and his
friend were mystifying, was none other than Sigismondo Santi, the
inspirer of the secret moves against Ferrara. Perhaps at the beginning he
may have believed that the negotiations for which they had sent from
Florence so great a man were really more than just the affairs of friars.
If such were involved, he may have thought, as Guicciardini wrote to
the dominican Schönberg on the subject of this conspiracy, 'that the
friars have a genius for this kind of negotiation'. A little of the joke
within a joke was at Machiavelli's expense, because the clever chancellor
of Alberto Pio was not so slow as to allow himself to be deceived more
than once by those extravagant missives. For that reason he was right to
show some reserve, and he hit the mark when at last he said to his guest:
'I believe that the Governor is making fun of both of us.'[28]

With all his perspicacity Machiavelli could not see this other aspect of
the joke, because his friend was not a man to reveal so jealously guarded
a secret, not even on his way home, when leaving the Republic of Clogs
he returned to Modena where Guicciardini (as he wrote affectionately)
was waiting for him 'with the greatest longing', and where he, finally,
cocking a snook at those who had sent him, stopped for a few days to

enjoy the Governor's 'fine meals and glorious beds', after those he had had at Carpi.

The plots against Ferrara were broken off as the Duke had got wind of them. In any case it was no longer a moment for plotting but for open war. With the young Charles V who had recently and formidably combined the forces of Flanders, of Spain and of the Empire, Leo had on the 8th May concluded an alliance under which Charles pledged himself to give the Pope Parma and Piacenza as well as helping him to take the long-desired Ferrara. In fact it was only a few months since the Pope had made an alliance with Charles's natural enemy Francis I of France with the object of removing the Kingdom of Naples from Charles; however, we should not be surprised at this since the previous year on the same date he had negotiated one treaty with Charles whilst signing another with Francis.[29] Leo X was like that.

This was the serious one. While the two new allies attempt a *coup de main* to remove Genoa from its subjection to France, the Pope weaves plots to do the same at Milan using as his tool that prince of plotters Girolamo Morone. He was to come with a large number of Milanese exiles to Reggio, whence the attempt was to be made. Guicciardini was sent from Rome ten thousand ducats 'with orders to give them to Morone to collect troops in secret for the event which Guicciardini was to support but in secret'.[30] However, the expedition against Genoa having failed, and the exiles having come to Reggio not secretly as was planned, but openly, M. de Lescun who was called in Italy 'lo Scudo', and took the place of his brother M. de Lautrec in the government of Milan, came to Parma with the intention of presenting himself the following day, the 24th June, at the gates of Reggio. Our Governor having warning of this, caused Guido Rangoni to come over from Modena by night with his cavalry, and had brought in as many as possible of those soldiers recruited by Morone and ordered that at the ringing of a bell the people should hasten to man the walls.

'Lo Scudo' came with four hundred lances, followed at a distance by fifteen hundred foot soldiers, and demanded to speak to the Governor. They agreed that the latter would go into the ravelin of the Parma gate, and that the Frenchman would meet him there, one guaranteeing the other. At this point Lescun began to complain of the gathering of Milanese exiles in Reggio, and Guicciardini that a French army should without warning have entered Church lands. While they were talking, a sudden tumult arose at another gate where the French had attempted an entry, and crossbows were fired from the walls at the men around 'Scudo'; whereupon the few gentlemen who had accompanied him into the ravelin, fled without a thought for their master. He, 'filled with terror', began to cry out that he had been betrayed and trapped, and could not decide whether to stand or flee. Then 'the Governor took him by the hand and encouraged him to trust and follow him, and brought him into the ravelin', while the French men at arms, believing he had been taken prisoner, fled on the spot. But Guicciardini, because he had given his word and to avoid compromising the Pope, would not keep him, and having shown him that the disorder had arisen from his own men, let him go.[31]

I wanted to relate this incident in detail because Guicciardini in his *History* dwells lovingly on it, and because his account has given rise to some well-known criticism and counter-criticism. Ranke, comparing it with a letter from Guicciardini to Cardinal de' Medici, condemned it as boastful and fictitious, but he was greatly mistaken as in other similar cases, not for the reasons offered as an excuse by Villari, but much more simply because the great German historian, like the Italian later, was unaware of another letter written by Guicciardini to the Cardinal the same day, which confirms exactly what is said in the *History*.[32]

The expedition of the French to the gates of Reggio gave the Pope a pretext for great complaints, showing that he had been forced by it to conclude the league with Charles, though in fact it had been in existence some time. While he made great warlike preparations and while the papal army was being got together under the command of Prospero Colonna, on the 10th July Guicciardini went to Bologna to see to the necessary measures.[33] There, two days later he received his appointment 'as commissioner general of the army, but with very great powers, far beyond those usually vested in commissioners', since he held, if not the military command, 'supreme power to command all the forces of the Church, and the Marquis of Mantua in particular'.[34] The honour therefore was very great, the financial benefit was a stipend of two hundred ducats a month.[35] To these two hundred ducats he still adds the hundred and sixty of the governorships of Reggio and Modena, but he leaves a hundred and twenty to his brother Iacopo who, as usual, is to take his place while he prepares to go to war. From the 29th July onward, all his letters are dated from the field.[36]

The papal army having joined up with the Spanish at San Lazzaro, and then augmented at San Martino by German and Swiss foot soldiers, it seemed that now nothing was lacking, and they could lay hands on their swords and set fire to the gunpowder. Instead there were delays because of differences of opinion and ambitious jealousy between Colonna and the Marquess of Pescara who commanded the papal army. These rivalries had begun before the arrival of the Marquess, and our commissioner had with great difficulty pacified Colonna who refused to share his command.[37] Thus time was wasted, which at the beginning of wars is often the best ammunition. More would have been wasted if Guicciardini 'had not urged them with strong words, showing how damaging it was to the Pope that they should proceed so slowly, and that there could no longer be any excuse to justify such delays'. After this they decided with enthusiasm to lay siege to Parma, held for the French by Federigo da Bozzolo; 'those who the day before had said the opposite, now said that they could expect victory.'[38]

Vain hopes. Those delays and long waits had given the enemy time to make provision, and the city was so strengthened and provided with troops that after twelve days' siege, because of the advance of the French army commanded by Lautrec, the captains decided that it was probably profitless and not without danger to remain. When Guicciardini was asked his opinion he replied that a withdrawal would greatly perturb His Holiness, 'but that the point of this decision lay in the truth or not of their premisses, hence they should consider better the state of the army, weighing which was greater, danger or hope of victory'.[39] Prospero and the Marquess, at last in agreement, replied that all military considerations counselled retreat; the commissioner, who was not a professional soldier, did not dare to oppose commanders of such authority. All the same, before the artillery was moved, he again attempted to persuade Colonna to stay. The latter would have been willing to discuss the subject again in council if the proud Spaniard had not refused to reconsider a decision already taken. Thus the siege was raised that very day with some dishonour, the armies returning to their billets at San Lazzaro.[40]

It was then decided to try Milan, carrying the war beyond the Po where the armies in those rich and as yet untouched lands would be able to maintain themselves more easily. They passed the river on the first day of October and besieged Casalmaggiore, and Cardinal de' Medici went there the same night as legate. Bearing with him 'almost the same authority which the Pope in person would have enjoyed', he stood above the rival powers of Colonna and Pescara.

His arrival was therefore of great assistance to the venture, and also to Guicciardini himself in several ways. Their daily companionship in military lodgings, brought Guicciardini even closer to the Cardinal on whom his future fortunes were so greatly to depend. Perhaps the long discussions he had with him, always bearing on the form to be fixed for the Florentine government, gave him the desire to write about this subject, though in a manner which would not have pleased the Cardinal. The *Dialogo del reggimento di Firenze* (Dialogue on the government of Florence) belongs in fact to this period. He wrote it (whether it was begun then or shortly before) in the field during his leisure time which had increased.[41] Indeed the presence of the Legate relieved him of all but the ordinary functions of a commissioner[42], lifting a heavy burden from him and absolving his biographer from the obligation to follow more than summarily that campaign.

On that subject, therefore, a few words will suffice. When thanks to Colonna's military skill the papal army had crossed the Adda almost under the noses of the French guarding it, Lautrec hastened to take refuge in Milan. But the capital of Lombardy too, in that sudden reversal of fortune, fell at once into the hands of the allies, assisted by the neglect of the enemy and the good will of the citizens. Lodi and Pavia did likewise; on the other bank of the Po Piacenza and Parma surrendered almost simultaneously to the Church.

The taking of Milan filled Pope Leo with unbounded joy. Since the day of his election to the papacy no one had seen him exult and triumph in such a manner. As such exultation seemed excessive and his reasons for undertaking that enterprise dubious, some very recondite and peculiar motives were attributed to him. Perhaps all that moved this most authentic son of Lorenzo the Magnificent was the desire to outdo his predecessor, to leave the Church greater, and to make a greater mark on the age, which in fact took its name from him.

In the villa of Magliana, where on the 24th November he received the great news, his people celebrated with bonfires that victory which set Italy on the way to a long, painful servitude. But who, that evening, would have thought so? The Pope, filled with childish joy, spent part of the night between a fire in the chimney-piece in front of which he sat, and the windows open on the green where his people were rejoicing, and the great bonfires blazed up joyfully in the damp night air of the Roman countryside.

A slight fever the following day was judged by the doctors to be unimportant,[43] but in fact within four days Leo died, at the very crest of his success. A little before his death they brought him news of the taking of Piacenza and Parma: when he had made up his mind to war, he had told Cardinal de' Medici that to have those cities he would gladly give his life.

Chapter 11

THE DEFENCE OF PARMA:
GUICCIARDINI AS GOVERNOR
UNDER ADRIAN VI

THAT first day of December, which was Pope Leo's last, Guicciardini was at Parma. The news had come on the 28th November that the French had left the city, and Cardinal de' Medici had sent him from Milan to hold it in the name of the Pope until the election of a governor, who, in fact, was to be Guicciardini himself; yet another government to add to those of Modena and Reggio, a further honour and more money. But the Commissioner had been there three days, when, instead of the brief of nomination, there arrived news that the Pope was dead.[1]

That bolt from the blue destroyed the victory, halted the victors and broke up their armies. It would have been difficult to obtain from the sacred college the prompt decisions and allocations necessary to defend the places lately acquired for the Church or even those which had been theirs longer. Everything depended on the ability and resource of the men on the spot. The difficulties in Parma were greater than anywhere else, without arms, without munitions and the walls breached by papal cannon in the recent siege. Guicciardini remained there without much cheer.

Cardinal de' Medici gave him some encouragement on his way through, travelling in haste to Rome for the funeral and the conclave.

He told him he thought that the new Pope would soon be elected, that while his brother Iacopo would look after Reggio, Guido Rangoni would keep watch on Modena, so that all he had to think of was Parma. Since that city was hard to defend, particularly on account of the French troops holding Cremona near by, the imperial troops would surround them so that they could not move. Furthermore, he would send a thousand Swiss foot out of those in Piacenza, whither in the meantime the Marquess of Mantua was to return with all the army of the Church which had been at Milan. Bologna was well guarded by the troops of Vitelli; in Modena, besides the men of Count Guido, there were two thousand Swiss who offered greater security to near-by Parma. If all these measures had been taken, there was no need to fear.

Instead everything went wrong. The conclave was very slow in reaching a decision; the imperial army avoided troubling the French in Cremona, and the papal army remained idle in Milan, though it should have moved to Piacenza. The Swiss assigned to the defence of Parma refused to move out of Piacenza. Furthermore, Parma could not feel any protection from the vicinity of Modena since the Swiss guarding that city had moved on to protect Bologna, left without defences by Vitelli who had gone to oppose Francesco Maria della Rovere who was now on his way to attempt to retake the duchy of Urbino.

All these difficulties were so many opportunities for the French and their allies to retake Parma, and from there to overturn all the papal states. Urged to take advantage of the circumstances by Federigo da Bozzolo, who was well aware of the city's weakness and knew it to lack armaments since he had removed them himself when he was in control, the French planned to move against the city with a large army. In Parma there were only seven hundred Italian troops under the command of Francesco Salomone, and fifty men at arms. The people supported the Church, but were not warlike; rather they were frightened and intimidated by the harsh treatment suffered under the French occupation.

The Commissioner, even before that flood could come down from the Po had taken the few precautions that he could: he had taken possession of three pieces of artillery which the governor of Bologna was sending to San Secondo, he had munitions and a thousand pikes sent from Reggio, and he had made some attempt to arm the citizens. While he was seeing to these extemporary measures, news came that the enemy was crossing the Po; Guicciardini had arms distributed, the city surrounded by lookouts and the walls manned. He decided, in the face of contrary advice, to abandon that part of the city called Codiponte beyond the Parma river as it was too difficult to defend. The evacuation of Codiponte was being carried out in haste when the enemy came in sight and a trumpeter of Federigo da Bozzolo presented himself under the walls to demand surrender.

Guicciardini had him brought in, and told him, mingling with firmness some Florentine humour: 'Tell your masters that if they asked me for anything that was mine, I would give it to them gladly, but since they ask for something which has been placed in my care by others, I cannot dispose of it. In particular tell Signor Federigo that as he was kind enough to abandon Codiponte three months ago when we came to besiege Parma, I too, wishing to do no less, have gladly left it for him. I hope that he in turn will not allow me to outdo him in courtesy, and as we did not take the city from him when we came to the walls, he will not now try to take it from us.'

The rest of that day and the following night the enemy made no move, but in the besieged city there was little rest between alarm cries and ringing bells. Guicciardini on horseback hastened wherever there was trouble, restoring order and encouraging the defenders. They had greater need for encouragement the following day when the besiegers were reinforced with more troops. The city was surrounded by five thousand foot soldiers, five hundred light horse, four hundred French lances – which means not less than another twelve hundred men. In artillery they had only two falconets unsuitable for breaching the walls. They had no heavy cannon because of the difficulty of carrying them across the rivers in flood and through the seasonal mud.

When the besieged saw the numbers of the enemy, there were none who were not afraid. The Council met, and the Elders all agreed to surrender and they all went to the Commissioner to get his assent, promising they would not capitulate without safe-conduct for him, his soldiers, artillery and possessions. The commissioner objected, minimizing the number of assailants, showing it was nearly impossible to take the city without heavy artillery and that defence was possible.

While he endeavoured to persuade them and make his will prevail over all theirs, a dispute arose and a far greater danger: the papal troops were rioting and demanding their pay. There was no money and only the city could give any, but how to get money for the war from a people which had decided to surrender? Nevertheless the commissioner did his best to persuade them to disburse at least half the pay, and skilfully insinuated that as they wanted to capitulate, that payment would prove their devotion to the Pope and would gain his pardon for the cowardice of the surrender.

He got the money, but his troubles were not at an end because the troops refused half pay. They wanted the impossible, full pay. Rioting, they moved to one of the gates to depart, leaving the walls undefended. Amid the general confusion the Elders reproached Guicciardini with refusing to surrender even when he had no soldiers, but he exclaimed: 'Until the troops have gone out of the city you cannot say that I am left without men.' He hastened after them, and on horseback, and deploying all his powers he harangued, he exhorted, and he stopped them. They were persuaded to stay.

The Elders and all the citizens were less convinced because of their great fear of being sacked and put to the sword, nor did they fail to implore and importune him to condescend to capitulate at last. As each enemy herald appeared to demand surrender, the drama was renewed. If the Commissioner would not allow the herald within the walls the citizens wished to send envoys to the enemy, to assure them that it was the Commissioner and not they, who rejected him. The citizens' unwillingness aroused the resentment of the soldiers who had no wish to fight an enemy with treachery at their backs. Thus the night passed with the same alarms as the previous one, but with greater tumult and fear.

Towards midnight Guicciardini, now fearing the worst, wrote a letter in cipher to his brother Iacopo with orders to decipher it at once and send copies to Florence and Rome. He wanted the present situation of the enemy and the city to be known, and it is clear that the city frightened him more than the enemy. In particular he wanted Florence and Rome to have what was virtually his spiritual testament. 'As fate has brought me to a place where my life and fortune are in such danger, I shall at least save my honour. . . . I have been in Lombardy all these years with the reputation everyone knows; the end may be unhappy but at least I shall not allow it to be dishonourable.'[2]

At one moment he sought to give courage to the populace maddened with fear. Calling together the Elders he endeavoured to convince them that all the coming and going of trumpeters was a sign of enemy weakness. Furthermore as they had no artillery to break down the walls, women even could prevent them taking it by assault, and the assistance he had asked for from Piacenza and Modena was sure to come. Even if the danger were as great as they supposed it to be, he would have no less to fear than they. He proved all this with many efficacious reasons which might indeed persuade them if fear did not persuade them more. Finally, as their importunity increased, he told them plainly 'with words and expressions most vigorous' that he would never surrender; that he was not strong enough to coerce them, but instead of the assent they were trying to extort from him, only for their own justification, as it was all he could do, he would give them a splendid testimonial as rebels and traitors.

Meanwhile with these disputes and altercations daylight had come and the enemy were preparing to advance to the walls. The Commissioner then went into the main square to take charge, but he still had with him the Elders imploring him at least to send out heralds, one for him and one for them, to make sure of the enemy numbers, Guicciardini insisting that there were three thousand and the others saying that there were five thousand, as indeed there were. They urged that defence would be impossible against such numbers. But he stood firm and passed the time in subtle tergiversation: assailed as he was from all sides, he was waiting to be freed by the enemy assault. Indeed when they heard the besiegers advancing against the walls the wrangling ceased, as now 'it was necessary to think of defending themselves rather than capitulating'. He spoke a few words reminding them of the fate awaiting cities taken by force, turned his horse and left them there on those words, which the circumstances rendered all the more convincing.

The first attack was very strong, between Porta Nuova and Porta San Michele; others followed at several points but always between these two gates which were manned by the papal troops. At first only a few citizens came to their aid, then warming up and seeing things going well the defenders increased in numbers and energy, and even the women came to carry munitions, stones, and food. The Commissioner was in the main square on horseback to deal with any disorder or emergency with prompt counter-measures.

The battle lasted four long hours without diminishing in force, and still at the same place except for a minor assault towards Codiponte. After which the enemy, with many dead and a very large number of wounded, all tired and having lost confidence in victory, withdrew, leaving under the walls ladders, arms, and even a few arquebusses.

Federigo da Bozzolo had then to sustain the indignation of his enraged troops and of Marcantonio Colonna who reproached him with having deceived him, representing as easy an enterprise which turned out to be so difficult. The following morning, humiliated and inglorious they departed. Thus Parma was saved.[3]

Indeed Federigo had not deceived anyone. The enterprise had become difficult only because garrisoning the weak and ill-supplied city, besides the few soldiers and the unwarlike citizens he had left behind, there was the spirit and mind of a Guicciardini. He left us an account of this defence written for himself alone, which he judged to be his most honourable enterprise up till that time. It is a work complacent yet truthful, as he always was in every word and in all that he wrote, without elaboration, without even the art of a deliberate simplicity. Tempted again by the parallel which often suggests itself, we might say that, if Machiavelli had been in his place, Parma might not have been so well defended, but his account of it would have consoled us.

The reverse inflicted by Guicciardini on the French greatly weakened their cause in Lombardy and was extremely salutary for the cities of papal Romagna. The enemy, however, though discouraged, were still close and the Commissioner had no money to pay the garrison, nor could he squeeze any more out of the empty purses of the citizens, who to pay them up to now had pawned the public and private silver plate, and melted down the crosses and communion cups. As the Holy See was vacant and the once all powerful Cardinal de' Medici could now do little, Guicciardini had written to the Sacred College on the 22nd December and he wrote again on the 5th and 8th January of the new year 1522 with expressions ever more pressing and anxious. Giving notice of the preparations which he heard the French were making, their army being only ten miles distant, he admonished the reverend cardinals thus: 'They should remember that men's spirit and good will is very important but only when accompanied by material necessities and not otherwise, and that the people quickly abandon those by whom they see themselves abandoned.'[4] But what he needed did not come, not even a reply of any kind.

Things were unchanged after the election of the new Pope on the 9th January, the cardinals' votes having brought in the Fleming Adrian Florent, to the general consternation of Italy and even of those who had voted for him. As Adrian was then in distant Spain, the administration of the Church still remained for many months in the hands of the

Sacred College, disunited and discordant, pulled in different directions by national or private interests. In any case the College could have done little even had it wished to, since the unbounded prodigality of the dead Pope had emptied the treasury, left infinite debts, mortgaged the jewels and all the precious objects of the Papal treasure, whence it was said facetiously that other papacies had ended with the death of the Pope, but Leo's would be continued during his successors'.

Thus Guicciardini's anxiety turned to despair, and after other vain appeals, in mid-January he begged Cardinal de' Medici to do all he could to enable him to 'return home and the sooner the better'. On the 18th, losing patience, he threatened to leave without permission 'and turn his back on those places which he could no longer either guard or defend'. He would have been quite justified, having done his whole duty 'and something more'. But at last the Cardinal wrote to him asking him to remain, and he did so; perhaps he desired nothing better than such a request.[5]

He had not yet drunk the lees of that bitter cup. He was confident that the new Pope would confirm him in his old governments of Modena and Reggio where he had done wonders, adding Parma as a reward, which he had saved even more miraculously. For the time being, the reward was quite a different one. One black day there arrived patents from the Sacred College bestowing the custody of Modena on Guido Rangoni, and that of Reggio on Alberto Pio, giving each of them authority over the revenues and enjoining the Governor to obey them. Shortly after, the same humiliation fell upon him in Parma, which was given to Federico Gonzaga Marquess of Mantua. Guicciardini, who was not a man to accept such arrangements even had there not been old quarrels between him and those two men, again asked the Cardinal for permission to leave, more insistently, and with a shaft of bitter irony: 'If the provision in the manner in which it has been made and in which it will be carried out has been well contrived or not, I would not like to say . . . but if more difficulties arise, the result will show whether it has been medicine or poison.'[6]

Meanwhile it was added poison for him. And he stayed there draining it to the last drop, for if he was unwilling to stay, he was no less unwilling to go; thus, after also seeking permission to leave from the Sacred College, he gave way to another measure of kind words from Cardinal de' Medici. He relieved his feelings in an acid letter written to the papal secretary Paolo d'Arezzo who had written to the Medici Cardinal certain amusing reflections on the Governor's umbrage: 'It is all very well for you in Rome to say that you do nothing but spend vigils and labours in your assiduous attempts to preserve (as we see the results) the State of the Holy See. . . . The advice pleases me, particularly the bit about drawing the salary to fill one's purse, and I would like it better still if you, Sipontino, Nigrino and the rest of the Academy of Marignano were here spending your time and money playing cards; although I think you would have to pay with money outside your salary because the patents are written so cleverly that Count Guido has publicly ordered the treasurer of Modena not to pay me any salary.'[7]

He settled therefore for 'drawing his salary', even if only on credit, which was Paolo d'Arezzo's advice as a good courtier, without worrying about anything else; and that period of leisure gave him time to finish and correct the first draft of the *Reggimento di Firenze*.[8]

Resigned to be content with the money, for 'honour' he stood firm on the fortress of Reggio; he would put up with anything, but he would never cede that last bulwark of his authority to Alberto Pio or his brother Lionello who was standing in for him. Also refusing to share it with anyone else, he alleged reasons of security which hardly concealed the tremblings of his exacerbated pride.[9] Imagine his feelings on hearing that Pio, not satisfied with the ample patents he had obtained for Reggio, was asking to have them rephrased so as to have all the government in his own hands! The dispossessed Governor protested strongly to his Cardinal, complaining that he had been retained when he had asked to go, whereas it would have been more honourable to leave voluntarily than to see himself driven out and made ridiculous 'by those farcical patents'. Nor was he afraid to remind him: 'Your Excellency also has some obligation to support me, having been (if you will forgive me for saying so) the sole cause of my having remained here with so much trouble and danger.'[10]

Danger apart, he had really had so many troubles in the past that they may even have depressed the reader of these pages. But while in Modena and Reggio almost nothing remained for him to do but debit his salaries to the Apostolic Chamber, in Parma someone was doing his best to enliven his retirement. On the Ides of March he was deserted by Salomone's troops because they had received no pay; only two hundred men remained, and some of them were leaving; a few days later there remained only seventy. In the month of June, as Giovanni de' Medici had entered Church territory with his bands to resolve by force the disputes between the lordlings of San Secondo, the Governor of Bologna expressed his indignation with Guicciardini for not driving him out: 'With seventy men?' he replied. In August those very troops of Salomone who had moved out of Parma, occupied by a surprise attack the Castle of Soragna in the territory of Parma in support of the Meli Lupi who had been ousted from the place by the Sacred Rota.[11]

Finally among all these clouds the sun shone again, though a pale autumnal one. Early in October, after he had had to cede even that last bulwark, the fortress of Reggio, agreeing to let his lieutenant share it with Pio's, finally Rangoni and Pio removed themselves from the scene. Guicciardini revived; he would have liked to take possession again of his governments of Modena and Reggio which seemed to him a good basis for the future. He was confident in fact that the new Pope would be willing to confirm him in them, and sent to Rome his own agent the Modenese Cesare Colombo to look after his interests and promote them, making capital especially of Cardinal de' Medici and the Auditore di Camera who was the Archbishop of Cosenza, Giovanni Ruffo, whom he had known at the Spanish court.

It was a fine and honourable thing for the Governor to have an agent at the papal court, so much so that he eventually made it a permanent arrangement.[12] Meanwhile he had given him permission to negotiate the restoration of the citadel of Reggio, which Alberto Pio, after abandoning the city, protested he would not evacuate until the Holy See's debts to him were settled. As for reconfirming him as Governor, Guicciardini was no longer satisfied with the two former cities but he also wanted Parma, which as Commissioner he had held in so laudable a manner. If he saw any coldness in these matters he would ask leave to go, for although as usual those posts 'brought honour and profit', he yet did not wish to beg for them.[13]

Not beg, perhaps, but haggle a bit. Informed that the Pope was giving Modena to someone else and Parma and Reggio to him, he wrote that he disliked the thought but would accept 'if he were to be given two hundred ducats a month as governor of Reggio, as is given for Parma, Modena and Piacenza'; he would certainly not stay with the old salary of a hundred and sixty ducats. So much for the ordinary pay; for the extras he would be satisfied with an increase from sixty to a hundred ducats on the proceeds from criminal cases.[14] On All Saints he writes: 'My wish would be to have all these three governments, and this is what my honour requires.'[15] Yet, notwithstanding many protests to the contrary, he had a great desire to remain even with worse conditions.

He was torn between honour and money, both so dear to him. At one point it seemed that honour had the advantage; so, on 5th November, he drafted a brusque letter to the Pope asking leave to go; but hardly had he composed it when he joyfully wrote in the correspondence register: *Non missa quia mutata sunt omnia* [not sent, as everything has changed]. Indeed all was changed, for at that moment he had received a papal brief confirming him in the government of Modena.[16] That was one city! Tearing up his irate letter to the Pope, he wrote in cheerful vein to his agent at Rome: 'If I could have one like it for Reggio, it would be all the better',[17] and to obtain it he got the Reggians to petition the Pope. On the 14th November, meanwhile, nearly a year later, he returned glorious and triumphant to the scene of his very first governorship 'to the greatest joy of the city' and was gladly received by Count Guido who had buried his old resentments.[18] There almost at once he received another papal brief which confirmed him in all three governments; on the 26th November he entered Reggio, received with great ceremony and festivity, and with the title 'Padre della Patria'.[19]

It was not long before his fortunes suffered a reverse. For the government of Modena had really been given to one Andrea di Crusciano with a papal brief, before it was given to him. The former, unable to stand comparison with Guicciardini either in merit or in powerful support, had to give way. Then Guicciardini, barely a month after the brief of appointment, had to cede Parma to Tommaso Campeggi Bishop of Feltre, who had been after it for some time.

Parma, however, without being in any way solicited by him, would not bear in silence such an injustice and insult to one who had defended and saved the city from the foreigner, almost in spite of itself. Furthermore, perhaps without any love for him, they had learned to respect the justice and rectitude of that man whom a chronicler of the period describes as severe of countenance and prompt to anger, who trusted few and had no friends, who seldom appeared at public dinners and festivities, and then only briefly, who went about (as we have heard him say himself) *magnam secum semper peditum equitumque catervam habens* [always accompanied by a large band of foot and horse].[20]

The citizens of Parma therefore sent an ambassador to Rome for the

express purpose of asking that the city should be given only to Guicciardini, whose merits they praised in their official letters, and first and foremost the famous defence. With the utmost firmness they refused to
receive the Bishop of Feltre or the brief appointing him, giving way
only before a threat of excommunication, and a promise of the 'barbarian' Pope in his rough Latin: *Infra mensem habebitis Guizardinum*
[within a month you will have Guicciardini].[21]

The Pope's promise would not be kept. This loss and insult meanwhile caused Guicciardini to brood again on thoughts of departure. He
wanted to go, not however before he had got the better of Alberto Pio
and forced him out of the coveted citadel of Reggio: another wound to
his pride and also, one must say, to papal authority and to common
sense. There is the splendid letter he wrote to Sigismondo Santi (the
man he played the joke on with Machiavelli) on his difficult relationship
with Pio – a very fine letter, and typical of Guicciardini. I would quote
it at length if I were not afraid of the biography becoming an anthology.
It is all Guicciardini, even the way in which he replies to the very
cultured secretary at a certain point with careless disdain: 'I do not
understand what you write in this part about the fable of the frog and
the mouse';[22] perhaps he did not in fact remember it. Come, messer
Francesco, what about Aesop's fables!

In that letter, as Santi had told him that Alberto's enmity was no
help to him, Guicciardini replied: 'I am not so arrogant or so unaware
of my own station that I think, if friendship and enmity exist only *inter
pares*, that this word fits me, for I well know the distance of degree
which separates us.' If it was not enmity, call it what you like, but there
was bad blood between the two for some time past, and not long after,
the lord of Carpi, like Ippolito d'Este earlier, was actually to attempt the
assassination of Guicciardini.[23] Meanwhile, besides occupying the fort
to the great disgust of Guicciardini, he also handed over the ill-famed
fort of Carpineti to the still worse famed Domenico di Amorotto who
had been expelled from it two years earlier with such difficulty.

During the recent war, as there was a great need of men like him, the
latter had not only had the ban lifted from him, but the Vice-Governor,
Iacopo Guicciardini, unknown to his brother had actually made him
commissioner of the Reggio hills;[24] and when the war was over, he had
continued to make war for his own profit and pleasure. Everything went
well for him until the return to Reggio of Francesco Guicciardini who
was made of different stuff from his brother, and who, having written

to the Pope on this subject several times, obtained from him on the 22nd December a very effective brief. To render it harmless there came a week later the gift of that damned fort to Domenico by Alberto Pio.[25] That this was done on purpose and merely to annoy the hated Governor seems more than probable, it seems certain. Certain it is that Alberto Pio could not have inflicted a greater displeasure on the Governor.

Another blow, in fact, to his pride. And the wound inflicted by Parma was reopened at that very time, for, though it had been newly vacated by the election of the Bishop of Feltre as Nuncio in Venice, the promise made by Pope Adrian to the city ended there. First Campeggi was allowed to leave his brother Antonio as Vice-Governor, in spite of the protests of the inhabitants, then the place was given to Mattia Ugoni, Bishop of Famagusta.[26] Guicciardini poured out his resentment in a letter to the Pope on the 13th January 1523. Finally on the 23rd March, losing hope and patience, he wrote abruptly asking that a substitute should be found for him, and leave given him to return home 'because of certain necessities which have arisen'. He presumed this permission would be easily forthcoming as he wittily observed to his new patron Giovanni Ruffo, 'as there are incomparably more governors than governments'.[27] And he told his brother Luigi that he was determined to remove from there in any case, and that would be 'at the latest within a month'.[28] This time he meant it.

To cut matters short, he allows Ruffo, the Pope and others, apart from the faithful Colombo, to understand that the necessities which had arisen were family or private concerns. However, that public affairs were the real difficulty, he admitted to Archbishop Ruffo a few days later when his anger had somewhat cooled: 'To speak frankly, I will not deny that I was extremely angry about the government of Parma.'[29] Private matters touched public ones only in this: that over a long period the governments of Modena and Reggio were not enough for him for the reason he wrote not long before to his agent: 'If I stay here, I cannot avoid bringing my wife and in so doing my expenses are increased.'[30] It seems that he was not very keen to bring her, but 'there was nothing for it'; and he had to give way to that poor woman who had seen him twice in seven years.

This worry could not however be so pressing if then, having been enjoined by Ruffo to remain, as he had been the year before by Cardinal de' Medici, he did not even need to be asked twice. To put a good face on it he wrote to Colombo and others that he was remaining because at

Florence there was plague. If the plague had been at Modena, he would still have stayed on. Apart from honour and profit, used to the kind of life and authority we have seen, it would have been hard for him to readapt himself to Florentine egalitarianism. Yet he was sincere in writing to his agent that if the citadel of Reggio were not returned to him he would go back to Florence, plague or no plague.[31]

While 'the affairs of government are going on quietly and in the normal way',[32] there are still the two vexed questions as material for the Governor's letters: the citadel and Domenico di Amorotto, 'rusticus tam facinorosus'. He writes, he insists, because it is his duty, but his rigour seems somewhat modified. Of the affairs of Parma he writes to his agent: 'It is a subject not in season, therefore let it go.'[33] And on Domenico he writes: 'If you find great difficulty over the question of the fort, let it go, for in any case it is bound to be settled by some other means.'[34] It was a true prophecy. It was settled in fact by Domenico's death on one of his expeditions. So the curtain fell on the last act of that long tragi-comedy.

The comedy of the citadel also had an end. Alberto Pio, after refusing to receive from the Governor's envoys a papal brief requiring him to hand it over, was later compelled to give it up to an apostolic commissioner who restored it to the triumphant Governor. Only a short time after, it was seen how valuable had been Guicciardini's persistence in demanding its restitution. In fact Alberto Pio and his brother Lionello who had had their territory of Carpi confiscated in the recent war as supporters of the French cause, were preparing a secret attack. Guicciardini, who was capable of hearing the grass grow, got word of it. While on the 1st September the Pio faction occupied Carpi with four hundred men, evicting the Spanish garrison, he was informing the Pope of an attempt by them to take Reggio from the Church. If he had not made such a fuss to get the fortress back, the city would have been lost. Meanwhile he moved to Modena to be where the threat was strongest. From there he wrote words which may seem arrogant but which are simply true: 'If things get worse, I could not be here and at Reggio simultaneously, and things would be worse in whichever town I was not.'[35]

A few days later Renzo da Ceri, who as is well known was an Orsini, went to reinforce the garrison at Carpi, and was raising troops and patrolling the roads to intercept letters and money which might be sent from Rome. Guicciardini sent almost daily warnings to the Pope of the threat from Carpi, without receiving any answer, 'a fact which really is enough to make anyone despair', he noted complaining to his agent;[36] and on another day referring to something else, but still on the subject of the attitudes of the authorities in Rome: 'As for all this, I do not mind them getting it all wrong, as they do so many things, because the worst they can do is dismiss me, which from several points of view would be a blessing rather than a punishment. Nor do I wish to justify myself against all the briefs and insults that have been written, because I see that one cannot satisfy these ignorant and suspicious minds whose judgement I respect very little. I have decided whilst I am here, to govern things according to what seems to be the best interests of the cities and the country and my honour, and if it does not please them they have the remedy in their own hands. . . . And I write you all this without cipher because I would like our master and everyone else to know it.'[37]

In vain Guicciardini wrote to the Pope and hoped for an answer. Adrian VI could not reply for the simple reason that he was *in extremis*. Thus the painful history of the vacant See began again, and war returned to the border cities. On the 16th September news was received of the Pope's death and that the French had crossed the Ticino. If Rome, which after the carnival of Leo X had suffered lenten fare under Adrian, greeted his death with unbelievable joy and facetiously gave public thanks to his doctor, at Modena the Governor was certainly not saddened by it. Danger and hard work lay ahead of him. Those governments of his, which had only just been confirmed after so many vicissitudes, were again to be uncertain and doubtful. But apart from the fact that it relieved him of the labour of writing letters in his un-Ciceronian Latin to a 'barbarian' Pope who did not speak Italian, the event inspired him with great hope. Thus the same day he wrote: 'I heard with greater displeasure of the crossing of the Ticino by the French than of the death of His Holiness.'[38] This was Francesco Guicciardini's funeral oration for Adrian VI.

Chapter 12

THE TRIBULATIONS OF THE VACANT SEE UNTIL THE ELECTION OF CLEMENT VII

<><><><><><><><><><><><><><><><><><><><><><><><><><><><><><><><><><><><><><><><>

A T THE beginning of his brief tenure, so unhappy in its consequences to himself and to others, Adrian had showed a neutrality which was as honourable as it was difficult for one who had been Charles V's tutor. He was supported in this attitude by Cardinal Soderini, who was for the French, and the first of the Italians to enjoy Adrian's confidence, but when the 'imperial' Cardinal de' Medici took his place the Pope began to lean towards Spain, that is towards the Empire in the person of his former pupil, with whom he finally joined in a league, together with the King of England and others including the Florentine Republic under the leadership of that same Cardinal de' Medici. Against this overwhelmingly powerful confederation, the King of France, alone, 'with unconquered spirit', was about to enter Italy at the head of a very large army, when the treachery of the Duke of Bourbon was discovered and he was obliged to remain on the other side of the Alps with a good part of his army, and to entrust Admiral Bonnivet with the expedition which thus lost force and impetus. Moving on Milan which was unprotected, the French could have taken it without difficulty if they had not wasted three days on the Ticino; they crossed the river on receiving news of the Pope's death, but finding the city in arms they were content to besiege rather than assault it. This siege, which was not destined to give them back Milan, caused Bonnivet to lose an easy opportunity of taking some other city belonging to the Church.

But Guicciardini who had feared to see him cross the Po after the Ticino, had not much time for rejoicing, for after Adrian's death the Duke of Ferrara too was on the move. He had an old account to settle with the Apostolic See, which after despoiling him of so many lands had tried every means, while Leo was alive, of removing his last possession. As he came out, according to his motto, *ex ore leonis* [from the mouth of the lion, Leo], the usual disruption caused by the vacant See gave him a good opportunity to settle that debt, or at least to take something on account. His chances were improved by the occupation of Carpi which was a hostile sword in the flank of the Church states. Indeed while he was getting his forces together, his first care was to reach an understanding with the occupiers.

Again as in the last vacancy of the See it was Guicciardini who had to sustain the attack and almost without defences. Modena's walls were weak and old, unable to stand against bombardment, and the artillery of the Duke of Ferrara was famous. To defend that city which was of the first importance, and possibly Reggio and Rubiera too, there were in all nine hundred Italian troops, to which could be added the cavalry of Count Guido Rangoni and a thousand foot which the imperials had given the Count to attempt the recapture of Carpi. The population was supposed to be loyal to the church, but this time it was not to be the loathed foreign soldiery which came beneath their walls but the arms and ensigns of the house of Este 'in these parts loved by some and feared by all'. There was no artillery in the city, not a single ducat in the funds. All our Governor could dispose of was his indomitable spirit, his intellect, his pride, and ink to write to his superiors about the things he needed.

Heaven knows he did not spare these resources. He wrote to the Governor of Bologna to send him artillery, pointing out that Modena was the defence of Bologna, but it was hard to talk about outer defences to one who did not look beyond his own walls. He even wrote to Florence for money;[1] he wrote to hurry on the arrival of one thousand five hundred Spanish foot soldiers being sent from Rome; he wrote above all to the Sacred College and to Cardinal de' Medici, letters which grew more and more agitated and frequent. The only result of all this writing was, for the time being, the arrival of the Spanish troops which, after 'torturing him [with suspense] for several days',[2] entered Modena when the Duke was only five miles distant.

No other help appeared, no money to pay the few soldiers he had; indeed to send his urgent letters to Rome he sometimes had to get the Governor of Bologna to pay the posts. We already know that Guicciardini's resolution spared no one, but in writing to the Sacred College, his words grew more resolute as his anger increased: 'We shall not fail to do our duty and all that may be done, and if there is some disaster, no one can be blamed but Your Most Reverend Lordships who not only have failed to send any assistance in money or troops, but have not even sent us the smallest reply',[3] 'just as though these cities belonged to the Turk', as he commented in a letter to the Florentine magistrates. He promised Cardinal de' Medici that he would do his duty to the end, but only for his own honour's sake, 'since, as for the College, I should be glad to see them lose Rome'.[4]

He could not defend two cities with those few troops. To divide them would have meant losing both. He therefore decided to defend Modena which was the larger, and nearer the other cities of the Church. It would also defend Bologna and allow hope for assistance from her. At Reggio he kept only five hundred soldiers, being sure they would suffice to defend, not the city, but at least the citadel, which might be a good means of recapturing the city after losing it. He also sent a letter to the Elders urging them with powerful arguments to engage a further three hundred men: 'I do not want to discuss which is better, to be under the dominion of the Church or of the Duke of Ferrara, for you yourselves, considering the conditions of both times, can be the best judges of that. But I remind you that if the Duke should enter any of these cities, it would bring them a perpetual disturbance and affliction; for, whoever is Pope will think of nothing but regaining his property, which cannot happen without the gravest danger to the country.'[5] These were good reasons, but they did not find ears to hear them, so the defences of Reggio remained as they were. To hold Modena with Count Guido and his men there were a thousand Italian foot, those providential Spanish troops, and what counts most, himself, Guicciardini. Truly, as he had written many days earlier, 'that place would be worst off where [he] could not be'.

The Duke came with his army up to Modena on the 28th September; making a wide circuit round the walls of that city which had belonged to him, he made his camp a mile away. If the city were taken, Guicciardini knew what awaited him, since the Duke had an account to settel with him too. In that grave hour, therefore, having made his final arrangements for the city, he thought of his family far away. He called a notary and bestowed on his daughters certain property in Mugello recently bought by proxy, and unseen;[6] a gift which seemed rather like a last bequest, and was indeed partly so. Then he wrote to the Governor of Bologna a quiet and confident letter which yet concluded: 'Dubius est eventus belli' [The outcome of the war is uncertain].[7] It was thought that when night fell the enemy would bring up his artillery, and all night they kept armed watch; instead at dawn the army moved on towards Reggio.

The Governor, advising the Sacred College of this at that very hour, drew a pessimistic forecast: 'I am convinced that he will take it without opposition. . . . Thus through no fault or neglect of mine, the Apostolic See will have lost a noble and beautiful city . . . It is sufficient excuse for me that I have so repeatedly begged and importuned the College. God's mercy in heaven do the rest, for the ears are closed of those, who representing him on earth, allow the Church patrimony to be dispersed and the inheritance of the Holy Apostles.'[8]

He was easily proved right. It was enough for the Duke to present himself before the walls of Reggio and the city capitulated at once. There remained the famous citadel, which being very strong could have been defended for a long time, not without difficulty and danger to those occupying the city. Instead, because of the warden's cowardice, it surrendered at the first cannon shots, and this at least was contrary to all Guicciardini's expectations, for though he had not a high opinion of mankind, he occasionally failed to conceive that they could fall so far short of his own quality.

All that remained for him to do was to advise the Sacred College of the loss of 'that noble and beautiful city abandoned to the enemy as though it were a miserable castle . . . God forgive those who were the cause.' One city less for the Church, one government less for him; and warning those most reverend gentlemen that perhaps Modena's time had come, he concluded nobly: 'We shall do our duty. I call it duty in respect to our honour, not because we are under any obligation to our superiors. Totally abandoned by them we are not obliged to take greater account of their interests than they themselves do.'[9]

The saving of Modena had been those Spanish soldiers which, added so opportunely to the other defences, had caused the Duke to judge the grapes not quite ripe. They might ripen, however, when the soldiers had gone, and they would certainly go if the Governor could not find some means of paying them. He wrote repeatedly to the Sacred College to send the money quickly in God's name. Instead they sent a penal monitory to the Duke of Ferrara; it cost little and was worth even less. And Guicciardini replied at once: 'This measure pleases me, but I would be much more pleased if money were sent';[10] then, with greater sarcasm, 'if all they send is paper, we shall try to defend ourselves with that'.[11]

Papers turned out to be a poor defence. The monitory letter was conveyed to the Duke while he was at the walls of Rubiera, and as an immediate receipt to the Sacred College he started to bombard the place with his cannon. Still, he would not have taken it so easily if as usual the weakness and faithlessness of the defenders had not come to his assistance. Thus in a cowardly manner was stripped off another of the brave conquests of Pope Julius, who at that period must have turned repeatedly in his temporary grave while awaiting the sepulchre whose completion by Michelangelo was also threatened by Julius's successors.

However, the lesson of events taught the Sacred College better than Guicciardini's contemptuous words. Money began to come from Rome and Florence, even the Governor of Bologna made a move, Bishop Averoldi, who with extraordinary obtuseness had never been willing to listen to Guicciardini's warnings. He had never sent a ducat nor a gun nor a soldier, and in the end he sent four cannon. But after the pay of the Spanish troops, that of the Italians fell due, then the light horse, and each time Guicciardini's anxiety, sufferings and desperate appeals were renewed. The people, inspired by their intrepid master, behaved as he would not have dared to hope. The Modenese, having listened to 'a short speech' of his, gave five thousand ducats.[12] Count Guido, who after the old resentments healed, had arrived at a cordial and loyal understanding with the Governor,[13] even though there were still owing to him by the Apostolic See the moneys lent during the last vacancy, pawned his last pieces of plate to pay the soldiers. But time ran on, pay ran on, and pay days followed one another, and meanwhile the Duke, in conquered Rubiera, knowing the nature of the soldiery, like an old fox was waiting for the fine grape that was Modena to ripen. This would have happened without fail if the election of the new Pontiff had been delayed.

The cardinals had now been locked in conclave for nearly two months. Giulio de' Medici stood above all the others in greatness and in the size of his following, and he was determined this time not to give way again to other people's obstinacy because of long-drawn-out proceedings, since he regarded as definitely in his favour the votes of fifteen cardinals. Against him were the cardinals who supported the French, and notwithstanding the open favour shown him by the Duke of Sessa, the Imperial ambassador, even some of the Imperial party. Among these and more bitter than the others was Cardinal Pompeo Colonna, his worst enemy. Indeed the usual Romanizing letterati recalled another war fought out in the City between another Julius and another Pompey. The length of the conclave, unheard of in living memory, caused great scandal; the danger for the states of the Church was extremely grave.

After the loss of Reggio and Rubiera, Modena, till then preserved by the will, the vigilant care, the firmness of Guicciardini and Rangoni, suddenly found itself betrayed, sold to the enemy by that very League to which it adhered as a city of the Church. Prospero Colonna, unable to obtain money from Rome while the See was vacant, got the Duke of Ferrara to promise him fifty thousand ducats if he recaptured Modena by his agency, and with his authority as Captain General of the League ordered the Spanish troops and Count Guido to move out and come to Milan, which meant handing over the city to the Duke. Yet again Guicciardini saved the city. Having a hint of Colonna's intentions from Rangoni, and penetrating it with all his intelligence, so that he soon understood the whole intrigue, he revealed it to the Sacred College and Cardinal de' Medici in particular, so that the Duke of Sessa, though fully informed and consenting, was forced to disown so black a betrayal of the confederate Church, and to write at once to the Spanish troops and the Count that they should not abandon the defence of Modena, no matter what contrary orders they received. These letters arrived a few hours before the orders sent by Prospero Colonna. Anyone wishing to understand with what timeliness and address Guicciardini conducted this affair, should read, rather than his own History, the letters he was daily writing in his minute books.[14]

But that defence which did not involve the clash of arms like that of Parma, and yet was no less arduous, nor less praiseworthy, could not go on indefinitely against friend and enemy alike. 'Now I am so exhausted that I can do no more',[15] he wrote on the 12th November to the Governor of Bologna; and some days before to Cesare Colombo, referring to the implacable obstinacy of Cardinal de' Medici (*his* cardinal!) who was fighting another battle in conclave: 'His election would not help me much, when I had gambled away my money and my life.'[16]

Instead, life and property safe, the election was of great value to him. For after fifty days in conclave, finally, like last time, Julius overcame Pompey. On the 19th November, the very same date on which two years earlier he had entered Milan victoriously, Cardinal de' Medici was elected Pope with the name Clement VII. Guicciardini's pleasure is not expressed in any letter, but it is not difficult to imagine it. It was not only a Florentine, it was, as I said, '*his* own Cardinal'; unlike Leo X, he had had with him a long intimacy and constant association; he was *his* Pope.

As soon as 'this blessed news' was received (these are the only words which allow one to glimpse his exultation), we find him building up his fine castles in the air, not without informing his agent at the court of Rome. Now he would like something better than governorships, which he shows he is 'really weary of' (and he had good reason), but if there had to be governments he would accept nothing less than the usual ones, Parma, Modena and Reggio. Reggio, of course, they no longer held. Then, in that first moment of jubilation, a thousand mingled hopes smile on him: he would like something, as he wrote, 'that would put a few thousand ducats in [his] purse'; and because 'the papacy is like a sea', he vaguely glimpses in that immensity 'many saleable treasuries, banks, offices and castles, with which a layman too might be endowed'. Of all these things he cannot yet say 'either what or how or when to negotiate'; one thing alone he sees quite clear and definite: 'When you congratulate His Holiness, you can tell him that I hope to be able to give up practising as a lawyer.'[17]

His uncertainty continued during subsequent days; not knowing what to ask the Pope for, or in what way the Pope wished to make use of him, he awaited on tenterhooks some good news from Colombo. Meanwhile he was again hankering after the three governments with which he could have contented himself only if he had not to serve a Legate. Certainly he could have made better terms if he had gone to Rome, and yet he refused the very honourable opportunity of going there as ambassador of the Florentine republic. 'I do not think of such vanities,' he replied to those who suggested it to him.[18]

Finally on the 25th December several letters from Cesare Colombo finally brought him the Pope's Christmas present: he was to have the Presidency of Romagna. A princely gift, but Guicciardini, not realizing at first what it meant, seemed not to value it greatly: 'I do not know what this position in Romagna is, and whether in taking it I go forwards or back, I mean in honour and income.'[19] Indeed, so great was his diffidence, and one would almost say his disappointment over the new post, that while charging his agent with asking what the President's ordinary salary was to be, he entrusted him with a delicate inquiry whether he would be allowed to return to Florence, reviving an old solution planned in the days of Pope Leo when there was a question of giving him, in exchange for the governments of Modena and Reggio, an income of five or six hundred ducats a year.[20] It would have been a loss for messer Francesco's purse, but he would have had in compensation leisure and his own home.

He had promised to come to some decision within four or five days on maturer deliberation; instead New Year 1524 found him even more irresolute. As he had lately been asked to choose between the governments of Modena and Reggio alone (when the Duke returns it) or the Presidency, he, without rejecting the Presidency until he could know more about its status and income, showed himself rather inclined towards the city governorships, 'feeling that it was more to his honour to be present at the taking of Reggio since he had been present at its loss'[21]: an account to settle, in short, with the man who had attacked the city, and perhaps with some of its citizens. But returning to the eternal question, he did not wish to be under a Legate, 'for [he wrote] a superior will not fail to find a way, indirectly, to cause me or anyone standing in for me such annoyance that we will go away of our own accord'. Therefore, if there was to be a Legate he would prefer the Presidency, there too on condition that he would not have any superior other than the Pope. Further, he had been told that the Presidency of Romagna would bear a salary of only one hundred ducats a month, and that seemed to him 'a bad beginning'.[22]

However, while preoccupied with such cautious considerations of honour and profit, entirely characteristic of his temperament, having understood that the Presidency carried with it very large extraordinary payments, he wrote at once to his agent to make sure; then the following day, without waiting for an answer, he instructed him to accept, as long as, between ordinary and extraordinary it amounted to three thousand ducats a year.[23] Finally without even sleeping on it, that same evening he dispatched another letter to Colombo, by a special messenger at his own expense (and he asked him to note this), to say that he accepted the office in any case 'as it seemed more honourable than this one [of Modena], and believing that, as for profit, the Pope would not have given it [him] if it had not been suitable'.[24]

Having taken the decision, his only thought is to hasten to Rome to discuss the matter in detail with the Pope. He is dying to leave these governments, and now he can do so without regret as they no longer run any danger. He is no longer afraid of the Duke who had divided them, as it seems more likely that it is he who should be afraid of the Pope. From afar he already longs for his new office, and is filled with jealousy when he hears that in the meantime they plan to send a commissioner there. 'Should this happen [he writes at once], it would not be to my honour and it would spoil the position with regard to profit.'[25] And four days later: 'It would be a shame and a loss to me if that affair were not left entirely to me.'[26] This henceforth has become the crucial point: 'All the reputation I can derive from going to Romagna depends on my going there now while the province is in disorder; and if the credit were to go to others, I do not know to what purpose I should go there.'[27]

He could no longer hang back. He wanted to go, and had instead to wait for his brother Iacopo to make up his mind whether he would or would not come to take his place. Finally, cutting short all these delays, on the 19th March he took the road to Rome with a worthy following of about ten men.[28] How things went at Rome with the Pope we do not know; one must again imagine it, conjecturing from the results. To mention only the money, the President's ordinary salary, though it counted for little by comparison with the extraordinary emoluments, was as an exception raised for Guicciardini from a hundred to a hundred and sixty ducats; the relevant papal brief to the treasurer of Romagna bears the date 8th April 1524.[29]

As this date also suggests, the President's visit to Rome cannot have been brief; that to Florence which followed it, was shorter, where we find him at the beginning of May,[30] as he did not even have time to go and see what the villa at Finocchieto was like. That was the property in Mugello lately bought by proxy with the great sums amassed in the governing of cities and armies.[31] On the 3rd May he set off for Romagna, on the 6th he was in Forli, where he began to take up his new office. From this, 'with regard to the money', he was to draw more than four thousand ducats a year, something like three hundred and fifty a month.[32]

Thus he could satisfy the desire expressed as soon as Pope Clement was elected: 'to put a few thousand ducats in [my] purse'. He had put in a good many since he had been in those posts. But if he filled his purse, his files as an author remained nearly empty, where for seven years almost nothing was added to his youthful works and the few things written in the intervals of the Spanish legation. Nothing was written in the following five years except the draft for the *Reggimento di Firenze*, dashed off in the military lodgings of Lombardy, nothing in those unproductive governments of Romagna. Up to now his might seem the life of a man of government not without letters, rather than that of a great author.

It is true that in the first three-quarters of his life Machiavelli had written even less. But for him, who was above all things a writer, the 'continual reading of ancient things' might have been enough, even without the 'long experience of modern things'. Guicciardini, with a less rich imagination, less warmth of feeling, not gifted for pure speculation, was above all a man of business and such he always remained, even in his study. Greater affairs will make him a greater writer.

Chapter 13

THE PRESIDENCY OF ROMAGNA

❖❖❖

'MAGISTRATUS VIRUM OSTENDIT.' The truth of this old saying, that appealed to Guicciardini, was illustrated by himself; and also its opposite in the case of this Presidency, for in his hands it not only received a higher salary, but the man himself determined the importance of the office. With an old title in new boundaries it was called 'Presidency of the Exarchate of Ravenna and the province of Romagna'. It was therefore of Romagna properly so called, with jurisdiction over the cities of Ravenna, Imola, Faenza, Forlì, Cesena and Rimini, besides the smaller places of which Lugo was at that moment occupied by the Duke of Ferrara.[1] The governors were dependent on the President who, according to his nature, and unlike his predecessor, ruled them with a rod of iron.

The province, which was proverbially the most factious in Italy, was split by the parties of the Guelphs and Ghibellines, preserving from their ancient namesakes only the name, the enmity, and the tendency of the first to support France, traditional weapon of the Guelphs, and of the second to support the Empire. These had the advantage in Forlì and Ravenna, the others in Cesena, Imola and Rimini. The city and district of Faenza were quieter. There is no room in these pages to describe the sedition, destruction and atrocities committed before Guicciardini's time, as for example when they played football in the public square of Forlì with the heads of the slain. We shall not give much space either to the less remarkable outrages committed during his own time, and we shall only give briefly some events in his administration which can add nothing to the portrait of these pages, for Guicciardini as President of Romagna differed in no way from Guicciardini Governor of Modena and Reggio. Nor unfortunately was the behaviour of his superiors altered.

Indeed he had barely left Rome where he had come to a complete understanding with the Pope, and for these few days was enjoying being at home before taking up his office, when he heard that a papal *motu proprio* allowed safe conduct to all the outlaws of Romagna who had submitted to the ban. Losing no time, he wrote to the datary Matteo Giberti to beg His Holiness not to let people extort such acts of clemency from him before he (Guicciardini) had been able to see and report on the situation.[2] Reaching Forlì, he was able to see the harm done by that *motu proprio* and to complain of it more vigorously. 'All Romagna, that is those who wish to live decently, of whom there are indeed a few, have been awaiting my arrival like the Messiah. . . . Now in this safe-conduct everyone is lost, and only rogues are pleased by it, which is not much to His Holiness's honour, and I am defeated here.'[3]

Thus was repeated the painful story of the conflicts which had so greatly tormented and hindered him in his governments, particularly in the early years. He wanted to restore the authority of the state and impose respect for law by a rigorous administration of justice, but this salutary work was perpetually interrupted by the Roman Court, some-times too easy going, sometimes factious, sometimes bestowing more or less disinterested favours. In the Presidency the worst moment was to be when the immutable justice of Guicciardini struck at the Ghibellines, particularly those of Forlì, of all the cities of Romagna the most tur-bulent and the worst infected by that plague, since Cristoforo Numai, Cardinal of Aracoeli and their great patron, was a Ghibelline and a native of Forlì. It was he who had obtained those safe conducts, it was he again who assaulted the Pope's sensitive ears with complaints of the rigours of the new President, accusing him of taking sides with the Guelphs. The truth was that he struck at the Guelphs no less than the Ghibellines. He wrote to Rome: 'Believe me, if you had a Guelph cardinal from Romagna there, His Holiness would have no less trouble from his complaints than he has from the other one.'[4]

After his first month as President he was able to report: 'In the first degree of crimes committed by those factions are those who went *armata manu* to the houses of their enemies to murder them and sack and burn. . . . In the second degree I place those who, hearing the tumult, ran together with their arms, and they too *ex post facto* gave themselves up to robbery and other wickedness. . . . It is my plan to proceed vigorously against those who are in the first degree, doing them through legal proceedings all possible harm that one reasonably can: that is, condemning, confiscating, and declaring peace and truces broken.' With delinquents of the second degree, as there were too many of them, he proposes to use a certain clemency, punishing them with fines. But it seems wrong to him to exercise clemency through a general safe conduct, for, 'besides the fact that one's reputation is damaged, it confuses the first category with the second'. He adds that many things would have been cleared up already if he had been able to 'act vigorously from the first and if there had not been the hope given them by these accursed safe conducts'.[5]

All these and many other things he wrote in a letter sent to his agent with orders to show it to the Pope. The latter must have read there among other things these words: 'It will be unworthy of His Holiness, it will also be far removed from the hopes of all those in this province who wish to live decently, and of those who hoped that as His Beatitude had so well administered the affairs of the Church while he was *in minoribus*, he would do much better now that he is in that See.'[6] These words anticipate right from the first months of the papacy with a quite Guicciardinian frankness, the posthumous judgement of Francesco Vettori on Pope Clement. 'He went to a great deal of trouble to develop from a great and respected Cardinal into a small and little respected Pope.'[7]

The awesome President went on writing those terrible letters which, without fail and on his instructions, ended up being read by the Pope. 'I came to this province, torn by strife, with the intention and hope of reorganizing it and I have made no small beginning, having immediately on my arrival reduced it to the greatest terror and obedience ever known. . . . Let them allow me then, in the devil's name, to govern this place since they have sent me there, and by God's grace they shall see that I will reduce it to a condition where severity and mercy may be used fairly and without disorder resulting. And if they do wish to ruin it, I shall not fail to write the truth boldly to His Holiness.'[8]

Meanwhile from Forlì, following his 'pastoral' visit (a shepherd with a big stick or even an axe), he had gone on to Ravenna which was also Ghibelline, and led by the Rasponi Ghibellines, powerful and factious; 'the others are quieter folk, yet dyed with the same ink'.[9] Then he had moved to Imola where the parties were more evenly balanced, although the Guelphs were in a majority, their leader being Guido Vaina. From there he wrote: 'I try to do all I can not to seem partial for I am not, and so that those who have done nothing wrong may be reassured.'[10] Another day he reports that he 'has begun to take action against Guelphs and Ghibellines'.[11] He acted thus everywhere and not just at Imola; but even this impartiality did not satisfy the Cardinal of Aracoeli, who, to quote a facetious expression of Guicciardini's, would have liked to 'dress up Saint Peter in Ghibelline stockings'.[12]

At that time the worst scandal, the greatest infamy for the authority of the state and those representing it was the problem of Bertinoro. There at the heart of the province, almost at the gates of Forlì, about forty of the most factious Ghibellines of Romagna had dug themselves in, defying not only the President's gaols but also his troops. Not that the President lacked courage to take the town by force, but he could not do so without the Pope's permission, and the commissioner in Bertinoro was none other than Antonio Numai, brother of the thundering Cardinal of Aracoeli! Guicciardini had no scruples about telling this commissioner to his face, one day, that he would take those rebels wherever they might be, and would have them hanged, since he respected the Pope and no one else. He said it to him so awesomely that Numai 'remained quite crushed'.[13] In fact the commissioner later told his brother the Cardinal that instead of these general terms, the President had stated the name, surname and title of the person he did not at all respect. The outcry raised by Aracoeli that time really reached to high heaven.

These were bitter days for Guicciardini who once again threatened to return to Florence. He was frustrated; he wrote: 'I cannot do otherwise than curse every day a thousand times the hour in which I came to this province, and surely if His Holiness wished it to be governed in this manner, he should have sent someone else.'[14] If, like his friend, Niccolò Machiavelli, he had had Dante's poem often in his hand and always in his heart, who knows how often he might at that time have quoted 'Oh Bertinoro, che non fuggi via?' (Oh Bertinoro, why do you not fly away?). But he had little familiarity with Dante as we shall see further on, and not because Dante was a Ghibelline and precursor of Aracoeli, but because he was a poet.

Finally there came from Rome permission to proceed *armata manu*, requested with great secrecy, and conceded with equal secrecy so that nothing might leak out to Aracoeli. For Guicciardini it was like wedding bells. He collected four hundred good soldiers between those of his own guard and others brought in from Florentine territory, and they took Bertinoro by surprise entering by a gate opened at daybreak. Some of those factious exiles fled, but a good few fell into the net of the President, who had promised them in advance 'that they would not be safe under the cloak of the friars'.[15] Among the prisoners the most important was one Manfredi Maldente, one of the three whose safety Aracoeli had got the Pope to promise unconditionally. But Guicciardini took him, tried him summarily, and had his head off before the capture of Bertinoro was known in Rome. Further, as a punishment and so that this game could not be played again, he had destroyed and thrown down a good piece of the castle walls. 'An action,' he wrote triumphantly, 'more honourable and salutary than any ever before achieved by any President of Romagna.'[16]

That time the thunder came after the deluge and the hail: it could not have come before. It must have been louder in the ears of the poor Pope than in far off Romagna. Guicciardini wrote: 'I am sorry that His Holiness should have this trouble, and I can only blame his own weak attitude, which merely encourages the insolence of Aracoeli: I cannot suggest any other remedy than that he should remember he is Pope, and that with one word he could remove for ever that pest.'[17] Some days later, as Aracoeli was persisting in his attacks he wrote: 'I see that His Holiness takes too much account of him, and I cannot fight cardinals; therefore, if this game goes on, I shall ask leave to go.'[18] In fact the game went on for some time. For those Ghibellines of Bertinoro the Cardinal's commissioner brother and two ambassadors from the town went to Rome. Announcing in advance that they would have told them 'some fine things' to say, Guicciardini noted with scorn: 'I too would be quite brave enough to get my peasants in Poppiano to say anything I liked.'[19]

Luckily for him he had at that moment something to distract his attention from these tiresome difficulties. There were preparations to be made for an expedition to recapture Lugo from the Duke of Ferrara, and it was in his nature to enjoy such preparations. He collected fifteen hundred to two thousand soldiers near Faenza, almost all brought in from Florentine territory. He did not want any more so as not to make a great stir. With these troops and a few falconets, the army was to set off towards Lugo in darkness, and the same night a great culverin and a medium-sized one were to move from the fortresses of Cesena and Ravenna. The cavalry of Count Guido Rangoni had set out already. But at the last moment a messenger from the Pope brought the order to stop.

Meanwhile Guicciardini continued to move from one city to another to give satisfaction to the population, see things with his own eyes and cause the governors to pay more attention to their duties.[20] From Imola he had moved to Faenza and from there returned to Imola going on the 1st October to Forlì. In mid-October he was at Cesena where to his annoyance and loss of prestige he had to lodge with the friars, 'very uncomfortable and dishonourable', because in the presidential palace it was raining in everywhere. In Faenza, a quieter and more comfortable city, he had his daughters and his wife; she, however, during the four months she was there had been ill 'with a low continuous fever caused . . . according to the doctors by an ill disposition of melancholy humours . . . arising out of her troubles in past years'.[21] The poor woman was paying the price usually paid by the wives of great men. Perhaps Machiavelli's Marietta, whose husband was less courteous and reliable, but good company, may have enjoyed amid the storms, some better days than the grave and reserved Guicciardini's Maria ever knew.

Guicciardini, because of his wife's long illness, now asked leave to take her home to Florence, 'if she got worse or if some important consultation were necessary'; but, thank God, there was no need. On the contrary, instead of staying with her in her illness at Faenza, he spent a good deal of the winter between Ravenna, where those Rasponi were giving him trouble, Rimini, Cesena and Imola.[22] He returned to Faenza and his wife on the 1st February 1525. There on the last day but one of that month, the great news reached him which moved Italy and all the Christian world. The imperial troops besieged in Pavia had inflicted a memorable defeat on the King of France who had been besieging them for three months, the flower of French nobility had been destroyed and the King's own person captured.

The last joust of Leo, the betrayal of Bourbon, the ill-conducted expedition of Bonnivet, the ill-luck and carelessness of the French, the energy and incredible good fortune of Charles V, had together brought a great and glorious king to ruin. The second Medici pope had conducted himself with the same tortuous ambiguity as the first, but what in Leo was astuteness, was in Clement irresolute and ill-fated timidity.

When Bonnivet's army 'went up in smoke', and the imperial forces had retaken Lombardy and carried the war into French territory, he had sought in vain to restrain them. When the French returned to the rescue and recaptured Milan in one of the usual sudden reverses of fortune, Clement began to incline in their direction and concluded with the King certain terms which were half an alliance and must have seemed like a betrayal to Charles. Thus, after the rout of Pavia, he could not find anything better to pacify the victor than to negotiate a new alliance with him which was signed on the 1st April of that year 1525. The agreement was that the Pope and the Emperor pledged themselves to defend the duchy of Milan given to Francesco Sforza 'under the shadow of Caesar'. The Emperor undertook to defend the States of the Church and return Reggio, and moreover, under the Medici, to defend the Florentine Republic – which had to bear that affront and pay the expenses of it, giving Caesar a hundred thousand ducats. In Romagna the great imperial victory at Pavia and the imprisonment of the French King caused the Ghibellines to raise their heads again, and foremost among them the notorious Antonio Numai 'more imperial than the eagle'.[23] But it was not their joy, or fear of their movements that disturbed the President. Moved by so important an event, he wrote to urge the Pope not to lose courage, 'because it is too much to go into servitude for nothing'.[24] From then on the minor events, the small struggles of the province more and more give way in his letters to that great contest. Held there in that corner of Italy between the mountains and the sea, his mind ranges anxiously over the affairs of all Italy and all Europe. It is not his job, no one asks him to do so, and yet he sends his counsels to Rome,[25] first discreetly, then more and more openly. Hearing of the new alliance with Caesar, he praises it as a lesser evil, as a poison to be used as a medicine, but knowing the nature of the Spaniards, and fearing that sooner or later it will be necessary 'either to succumb entirely, or break with them', he advises the Pope 'to take it for granted that there must one day be enmity, and on that basis he should not fail to make all the provisions which can be made day by day'. He ends with an apology: 'His Holiness must forgive me if I write of what does not concern my office, because it should be attributed rather to affection than to presumption.'[26] But he ordered Colombo in a separate message to watch the Pope while he read this letter, and inform him 'in detail of all his words and gestures'.

The affairs of the Presidency were proceeding as usual and by now had begun to bore him, so much so that without being driven to it as on other occasions by disappointments or injured pride, he was again talking of going home, leaving in his place his brother Iacopo to earn for them both those fine thousands of ducats.[27] One preoccupation which recurs persistently in his letters during the Easter season, was that of obtaining absolution for all the ecclesiastical persons whom he had interrogated, tortured, decapitated, with a lavishness only a papal officer could permit himself. There were enough of them to cause the excommunication of all the republics and princedoms of Italy. But 'every Easter' his confessors raised difficulties, and, most surprisingly, even when specially approached by Colombo, the grand penitentiary Lorenzo Pucci was reluctant too; he was nicknamed Cardinale Santi-quattro, and once had been so very generous with those ill-famed indulgences. Therefore Guicciardini had to approach the Pope, and to this subject he the *piagnone* returned with a persistence which I do not think Machiavelli the *arrabbiato* would have shown.[28] Naturally such scruples did not prevent him beheading yet another friar at this very moment.

Lupus in fabula. Machiavelli was at Faenza when the friar's head fell, and with it the same night there fell so much water from the sky that Romagna was flooded although it was July, and more than thirty houses in Cesena collapsed in ruins; 'so that the ordinary folk, the peasants and the women were more frightened by one dead friar than by an entire live convent'.[29] We seem to hear the fine jests of messer Niccolò sitting up late with the President, over the affair of the women and the friars. But the reasons which had brought him into Romagna were not jokes, even if they finished with one.

He had not been brought there either by his friendship with Guicciardini, although that friendship had not lessened since the days of Carpi and Modena, nor can it be measured by what has remained of their correspondence. In four years, one small letter. But from that we gather that Guicciardini had charged Machiavelli with certain rural commissions for his farms in Poppiano; and certainly he would not have turned suddenly to his friend in such a matter, if there had not been some regular exchange of letters between them. In reply Machiavelli told him about the *Istorie fiorentine* (Florentine Histories) which he was writing 'for florins', commissioned by Pope Clement when he was cardinal; and he added: 'I would pay ten soldi, I won't say more, to have you here and show you the point I have reached, for as I come to certain details I need to hear your opinion whether I err by raising or lowering their importance too much.'30

Machiavelli had written this the year before on the last day but one of August, when he had been busy finishing the work, and in June 1525 he had gone to Rome to present it to the Pope. The latter, struggling in a sea of troubles, his bark tossed by his own lack of resolution, was asking everyone's opinion, and he also sought that of the great political writer. That new alliance with the Emperor gave clear signs that it boded ill, as Guicciardini had forecast, and it was clear that that friendship would not last long. On the other hand the Pope did not know where to turn, being without soldiers and without money to provide any.

But Machiavelli had a remedy all ready. Was he not the inventor or at least the reviver of the Militia? And although his creation, tender and immature as it was, had not survived the test at Prato, what if His Holiness were to arm his subjects in Romagna, more warlike, alas, than the peaceful Tuscan peasants? The Pope liked the idea (not surprisingly since he liked any advice), and it also appealed to his counsellors Iacopo Salviati and Niccolò Schönberg. He therefore sent Machiavelli to the President of Romagna, bearing a very enthusiastic brief, which said, among other things: 'It is a great matter and on it may depend the safety both of the States of the Church and of all Italy, and virtually of all Christianity.' As I wrote in the Life of Machiavelli, it remained to be seen whether such warmth, and whatever the bearer might contribute of his own, would thaw the President's coldness, or whether they would be frozen off by him.31

Informed in due course by his faithful agent, Guicciardini, as a practical man, even before the arrival of Machiavelli and the brief, had immediately found the clue to the affair: 'Ask on my behalf to what ends the Pope plans this; for if he intends it as a remedy for present dangers, it is a measure which cannot come in time.'32 And I remarked in that other biography that Machiavelli looked far ahead, Guicciardini close at hand, while the Pope according to his custom could not decide whether to look near or far. That is what happened. Having read the brief and heard the peroration of the bearer, Guicciardini set his prose against his friend's poetry. Writing of it on the 22nd June, he did not deny the greatness and the nobility of the idea, 'which if it could be brought to the desired end, there is no doubt that it would be one of the most useful and praiseworthy works that His Holiness could accomplish'. But then coming to the *quid agendum* (practical applications) he observed that there were lacking in the people of Romagna those presuppositions of Machiavelli: love and fidelity of the subjects, the possibility of extracting from the same province the funds required. Having thus sown doubt in the Pope's vacillating mind, he left the decision to him.[33]

For Machiavelli the stakes were high; it might at last be his opportunity to rise, and at that time he had no other chance available. For Guicciardini it was one more hazard to overcome, and he already had enough of those. The following day, having slept on it, he rewrote his letter in an even more cautious form, and sent it to Colombo with orders to let the Pope read it and as usual to describe in detail 'his actions and words'.[34] Colombo should do the same with Salviati and Schönberg.

To ask Clement for a bold decision was worse than asking him for money, and basically Machiavelli's plan required resolution, courage and money. The President's objections were to do the rest, increase the difficulties and make sure of failure. Thus in Faenza Machiavelli and Guicciardini had a long wait, both of them anxious for opposite reasons. As by the 8th July nothing had been heard of the Papal decision, Guicciardini asked his agent for news. On the 12th he again asked for 'the decision for Machiavelli... for he does not know what to do'.[35] But meanwhile the Pope, pressed by Sadoleto, had replied that he wanted longer to think about it and that Machiavelli should remain at Faenza. He therefore stayed on until making up his own mind before the Pope, he sent to say that he was returning to Florence 'on certain business'; and so ended the great affair of the papal brief.[36]

Machiavelli had to swallow, in addition to his famous pill of aloes, this other bitter pill, but he was accustomed to seeing his dreams shipwrecked on the hard rocks of reality and incomprehension. In any case his friendship with Guicciardini did not suffer, rather it issued strengthened and warmed by that month in constant companionship. Witness is borne to this by their correspondence, which becomes more and more frequent, and a greater intimacy in the tone of the letters. In a letter to his friend who had just left Faenza Guicciardini writes among other things: 'I await your news eagerly ... after your departure Mariscotta spoke of you very honourably and greatly praised your manners and company; this rejoices my heart because I desire all pleasure for you, and I assure you that if you return here, you will be looked upon kindly and perhaps caressed even better.' And Machiavelli in return: 'This morning I received yours in which you told me of Maliscotta's good graces, of which I am prouder than of anything else I have in this world. I should be glad to be remembered to her.'[37] These were jests, but who was this Mariscotta named by both without the title of 'madonna'? Well! we know Machiavelli's habits, and a malicious spirit reminds us of the weakness the grave Guicciardini had for courtesans, on the evidence of those who knew him well.

If the meeting at Modena and the exchange of letters at Carpi had greater importance for Machiavelli than for the eminent Governor, the same was true of Machiavelli's stay at Faenza, and of the correspondence which followed; but it is obvious that something stronger than their differences and inequality of character and fortune unites them in a growing friendship. At last Machiavelli begins to enter Guicciardini's life. Then, reversing what was true in their lifetime, after death this friendship was to honour Guicciardini even more than Machiavelli.

At Faenza Guicciardini had charged his helpful friend with visiting that property of Finocchieto recently bought in Mugello, and another he was planning to buy near Florence. The account he received of them was reassuring: 'I have first to tell you that for three miles round one cannot see anything that pleases: Arabia Petroea is not otherwise. The house cannot be called bad, but I would never call it good, because it lacks the necessary commodities: the rooms are small, the windows are high: it is just like the bottom of a tower. There is a little meadow of a kind in front; all the approaches are steep except for one which is flat for perhaps a hundred yards; and withal it is so buried in the hills that the best view is only half a mile.' He advises him to spend a hundred or so ducats on certain improvements and explains why: 'These fertilizers will be useful for either of two things: first if you want to sell, anyone who came to see it would see something to his liking, and that may bring him to discuss a sale; because in its present state I do not think you would ever sell it except to someone who had not seen it like yourself. If you want to keep it, those fertilizers will enable you to get from the land more wine, which is good here, and not to die of grief when you go to see it. . . .'[38]

Thus stung, to throw off the jest if not the damage, Guicciardini replied with a story in which that same calumnied villa of Finocchieto reproves Machiavelli, used as he is to the easy favours of Barbera, for not having known how to appreciate her shy qualities, suited only to please her own master.[39] Even in this burlesque manner Guicciardini's style is, as always, rather heavy and the humour is not very sparkling. As a writer he can never win a contest with Machiavelli.

These fantasies on the subject of Madonna di Finocchieto must have accompanied or followed very closely another letter which has a really unusual start for our President. Accustomed to stand on his dignity, he now rejects the title of 'illustrious' given him by his friend. 'Most dear Machiavelli . . . I particularly have to tell you that if you honour my superscriptions with "illustrious" I will honour yours with "magnificent", and thus with these reciprocal titles we shall give one another pleasure which will turn to grief when we all, I say all, find ourselves empty handed. So make up your mind about titles, measuring mine according to those you prefer for yourself.'[40]

This short letter of so unaccustomed a style ends, however, brusquely with a concern which must have become habitual with him after Pavia. 'I believe that we are all walking in the dark, but with our hands tied behind our back so that we cannot ward off blows.' The danger of that vast Spanish power hanging over Italy gave him no rest, although by temperament he was not at all inclined to favour the 'mad French'.[41] In September when his agent reported that he had heard from Iacopo Salviati, whose son was nuncio in Spain, of Caesar's excellent intentions towards the Pope, Guicciardini said he was not much convinced by that. Observing that in the past quite contrary signs had been seen, he said: 'Seeing all these proceedings suddenly changed, I fear that what has changed is their manner not their intention. . . . Being in the dark as I am, I may well be mistaken, but I know that ambition for power can do so much that I find it difficult to believe that Caesar, seeing so great an opportunity to grow in might, will throw it away so easily.'[42] 'Being in the dark', he could see much better than those in Rome who were not, and yet wove the threads of a feeble and ambiguous policy. He was to see those threads tangle still further while he went from one city to another of turbulent Romagna, negotiating at the Pope's request, but in his own heart not much convinced, a general peace between the factions.[43]

During his tenure of the Presidency, on which he entered at the age of forty, it seems that Guicciardini's intellect ripens. Age, practice in affairs and experience of men, increased self-knowledge, the fortunate chance of a Pope of whom he can make capital, the gathering clouds of the time, lead his thoughts from a narrow province to broader

K   133

horizons. The character of his new office lays on his shoulders a greater weight of command and relieves him of the daily burden of audiences and minor affairs; he returns, finally, after so many years, to the orderly tranquillity and placid tedium of family life, particularly during the long autumn and winter evenings: it is a fact that he spends more time in his study. Of this period are the 'political discourses' of which we shall speak later on, to which one might add those lucid pages sent to Rome to be shown to the Pope, which are likewise genuine though brief discourses on Italian politics. At this time finally, he concluded and polished the dialogue *Del Reggimento di Firenze*.

We saw this work issuing from the depth of Guicciardini's thought during his enforced leisure in military billets, while Pope Leo's war was stagnating in the plains of Lombardy; then we saw him take it up again in the quieter and longer periods of leisure at Parma when the governments of Modena and Reggio were reduced to a name only.[44] Taking it up again during the Presidency he finished and polished it with a care never before expended on any of his works, yet declaring that he had written it only 'for [his] pleasure and recreation, and with no intention of publishing it'. Nor is it hard to believe that the book was destined to remain for the time being not only unpublished but hidden. For he wrote in it such things about the Medici government, he who owed so much to the Medici, that he felt the need to justify them expressly in the preface which he rewrote several times.[45]

According to this foreword the dialogue was supposed to take place in the year 1494, shortly after Piero's expulsion, between Bernardo del Nero, Piero Capponi, and Paolantonio Soderini, leaders of the *palleschi* (Medici party), of the optimates and of the people's party, and all famous in different ways. The fourth member of this group is Piero Guicciardini, withdrawn and neutral in the book as in real life. He was supposed to have recounted on many occasions and with great satisfaction their conversations to his son, leaving him no other task than that of reporting them. But to investigate the historical reality of a humanistic dialogue is simply a waste of time. Although, according greater credit to Guicciardini as being little infected with any literary disease, we may allow to the simple fiction a kernel of truth, it is too much to believe that the interlocutors were actually those men or that such was the substance of their conversation, particularly as regards Bernardo del Nero in whose clothes the author has dressed himself. Indeed it has a strange effect when one hears the faults and wrongdoings of the Medici and the means of preventing their return, so thoroughly discussed by a man who left his head on the executioner's block because of his support for their return.

The work is divided into two books; in the first, after some general observations, the defects of past governments and those of the popular one recently introduced are discussed; in the second, methods of correcting those defects in a well-organized government. This second book in substance is merely an amplification of the so-called 'Logroño essay' written in Spain in 1513. Starting with well-known classical sources, and drawing inspiration from the living example of the Venetians, the government desired by the author is a mixed one, but a mixed one of a special kind, that is, to the Guicciardinian taste. Leaving the Grand Council at the base and placing at the summit a life gonfalonier, in his government the strength and the virtue are in the middle: in a restricted Senate. With all the ill he speaks of the optimates, following ancient precedent, his is (if I may be allowed the expression) a rather more numerous oligarchy, which would go round within a few families: the usual ones. It is true that he does not hesitate to describe the Venetians' government as a popular one merely because it is extended to all citizens qualified for office, but he does not go into the question of how their selection was arrived at. With all this, the things he suggests are full of good sense and above all practical. From a mind like his one should not expect an abstract treatment reaching out into wider considerations, 'an imaginary government more likely to appear in books than in practice, as Plato's Republic was, perhaps',[46] but the best government that it was possible to introduce at that time and in that city.

This does not mean of course that its author had any illusions about the actuality and practical usefulness of his dialogue; still less that it was for him 'a project of precise and actual reforms . . . to be put into effect at the first opportunity', as one modern scholar believed, to whom Guicciardini studies owe a great deal. It is all the more surprising to see him attribute to Guicciardini thoughts so uncharacteristic.[47]

The book has, on account of its form, a place of its own among those of our author. The style is simple, not solemnly architectured as in his more serious pages, but neither so familiar and colloquial as certain pages of the youthful History. If we follow his work through the corrections, we see that many familiar expressions of Florentine colloquial usage, employed in the first draft,[48] were in fact deleted, without however adopting instead any form of professional rhetoric. But the dialogue lacks liveliness and variety, it unfolds heavily with never an unexpected or a happy turn of phrase to lighten and enliven it.

That Guicciardini himself should have chosen for his treatise this form of dialogue, too literary for him, may cause surprise. A little less perhaps if we think that he began the work only a few months after Machiavelli's dialogues *De re militari*, or the *Art of War*, had come out; these were certainly sent him by his friend on his return from the fine japes enjoyed together in Modena and Carpi. For Guicciardini felt the influence of Machiavelli more than the difference of their intellects and certain very well-known criticisms of Guicciardini might persuade us to think. And we have undoubted proofs of it in this *Reggimento di Firenze*, where some pages savour of a recent study of Machiavelli's *Discourses*; indeed a good deal more than a flavour has remained.[49] Although it sounds like a paradox, in some ways it is true that Guicciardini is the first of the Machiavellians.[50]

Chapter 14

THE LEAGUE OF COGNAC AND
GUICCIARDINI'S WAR

<><><><><><><><><><><><><><><><><><><><><><><><><><><><><><><><><><><>

IT WAS not enough to move in the dark with hands tied behind one's back unable to ward off blows according to Guicciardini's image; they actually had to go out of their way to court disaster. Assured of Caesar's ill intentions by numerous signs, among others by the delay in ratifying the terms of their treaty, Pope Clement was very unhappy. Not knowing what to decide, he took the most desperate course: he let himself be tempted by the devious machinations of Girolamo Morone, chancellor of Duke Francesco Sforza. That supreme inventor of illusions, playing on the jealousy and discontent of the Marquess of Pescara, had encouraged him to betray the Emperor. He was to receive in exchange the Kingdom of Naples. This too was an illusion, but they thought the Kingdom would easily be taken if the Pope, the Venetians, the Duke of Milan and the French, all fearing Spanish power, united in a league of which Pescara himself was to be Captain General. Morone thought he had persuaded Pescara, and perhaps he had. But then the Marquess, having managed his affairs so as to be able to choose whom he might the more profitably betray, chose to betray Morone, and because that was the lesser betrayal, he improved it by the manner he employed to trap the author of the conspiracy. Clement again found himself caught out by the Emperor, nor was it of much avail that he had, beforehand, with the refined duplicity then normal in politics, put him generally on his guard against his captains.

137

The first consequence of the unfortunate intrigue was that it gave the Emperor a pretext to take Milan and all the duchy, all that remained to Sforza being the fortress that he had shut himself up in, and a few others in Lombardy. Guicciardini heard of the arrest of Morone on the 21st or 22nd October, and at first he did not believe it; however, when he was forced to believe, he attributed it 'no less to his own folly and Pescara's astuteness, than to Caesar's luck which daily achieves some miracle'.[1] A few days later, having ruminated further the present and future results of the incident, he writes not without irony for the credulous reports of Cardinal Salviati the Pope's Legate and relative by marriage: 'We must comfort ourselves with the belief that Caesar is as kind as those in Spain report.'[2]

He however does not believe in that kindness, and as usual he sends his opinion to Rome in a letter to be read by the Pope. In the uncertainty of the agreement being negotiated between the French and the Emperor for the liberation of the King, in the certainty of the imperial ambitions, the greatest danger seems to him to be lest Caesar 'should do as he pleases while the others are all lulled to sleep by these negotiations'. He ends: 'And one should avoid this as far as possible, and if it cannot be done by clever means, it should be done in any way possible. Otherwise he will overcome all, not by his overwhelming forces, but, like Cornelius Tacitus, *fatali omnium ignavia* (through the fatal cowardice of all). Yet these are matters of the utmost importance, and between handling them rightly or wrongly may lie the difference between safety and disaster. And they cannot be properly judged by one who is not informed as to the present state of the negotiations in Spain and other places and the dispositions of the potentates . . . And I and others who lack this information, must pray to God that they be well understood, and must approve any decision, for we cannot do otherwise.'[3] But while he was writing these words, in Rome they were already thinking of changing his role from that of resigned spectator to that of one of the principal actors in this tragedy of Italy.

On the 13th October when there were signs that things in Lombardy were taking a turn for the worse, Iacopo Salviati had written to him rather mysteriously, asking if he would be willing to take an 'honourable and remunerative' post at Rome with the Pope. He replied that he would be very glad to, but as the proposal was a general one he gave only a general reply.[4] After, he inquired the details from his agent, requiring him to find out discreetly in what manner the Pope wished to make use of him and, as usual, 'the conditions of honour and re-muneration'. He had so often cursed and threatened to leave the Presi-dency, but now he had the opportunity to leave it and make a good bargain, it had become most dear to him. 'The place I have here is good and honourable, and I would not like to leave it hastily, particularly *transeundo ad novum vitae genus* [changing to a new kind of life].'[5]

At first he could gather little about the honour and the money, and that little cannot have pleased him, for he replied 'curtly' to Giberti who had written something about it to him, and he at once ordered Colombo to break off the discussion and speak of it no more unless the subject were brought up by others. But on the 24th November, as the Pope himself had mentioned it, Francesco Guicciardini began to discuss the deal again. In a letter written so that it might be read at the Court he also mentioned his 'private interest': 'I wish His Holiness to know that one of the reasons why I have been willing to stay out of Florence was to get away from the servitude of law books, and I would find it hard to return to it particularly now I have been away from them for so many years, so that if His Holiness planned to use me in that profession, besides the fact that I am most averse from it, I am sure that I would not satisfy him or my own aspirations.' He would not like, either, that if he went to Rome, the Pope should then send him elsewhere for a long time, and this on account of his wife who had been reduced, on account of her husband's continual absence in past years, 'to an indisposition of melancholy humours so that she has been at death's door'; and he adds: 'Now when she is hardly well again, if I again made her unhappy, I would kill her without any doubt, with great reproach from her family. This scruple may seem absurd, and I myself would in other times have laughed at anyone who felt it in matters of importance. Now these are my circumstances, and although I am sorry, I must take account for myself of what I would have despised in another.'

The sore point of his wife, because of the expense involved in having her with him, brings him to the subject of money, which he mentions in general terms in the letter which is to be shown at Rome. The terms are written on a separate sheet for his agent alone. Pointing out that he would leave his brother Iacopo in his place, and that even if he went on drawing the salary he would have to leave part of it for him, he fears that what he earns at Rome will not suffice to balance the bargain. 'Seeing how guardedly His Holiness spoke, I suspect that he plans to give me such a scanty provision that I must lose a large part of the income I have at present. . . . You will speak to the Datary and where you may tactfully find an opportunity to test him out on this question of the money, you will do so, but in such a manner that I do not appear to be begging or haggling.'6 To tell the truth he did wish to haggle, but with decorum preserved.

After long delay it was enough for him to know that the Pope had finally decided to 'attempt to escape from Caesar's power', for him to set aside all doubts. As he had done with the Presidency, after long delays he made up his mind all at once. He ordered Colombo to negotiate no longer, and remove any displeasure his parleying might have left. With a generous impulse at last worthy of himself, he wrote: 'The greatest satisfaction my service can receive is to see that His Holiness is determined not to wait for servitude.'7

At once he began again to send to Rome his long chapters on the affairs of Italy, which he had stopped sending since the time when he had decided to drop the discussions on the Roman proposals. Amid the sequence and change of events there is a quite remarkable firmness and coherence in his thought, as it appears in his correspondence and in a fine series of *Discourses on Politics*. Four of these are further examples of those double discourses of his, for and against, which he so much favoured as a dialectical exercise, but particularly in order to consider and weigh up all the aspects of a decision.8 As in his letters, in these debates where he develops his own thought against an opponent (and in these dialogues too the one with the last word is always right), he constantly invokes the Pope's firmness, exhorting him to make himself head of a league which could shake off the Spanish yoke.

Great was his anger therefore when he heard that Clement, delighted to be able to put off a firm decision, had concluded a truce of two months with Herrera, sent to him by Caesar with the object of ruining the projected League. 'His Holiness is beyond all argument because necessity forces him to military action, and one cannot balance the dangers it entails so subtly. Rather, for those in such difficulties, too great prudence becomes imprudence. . . . And if one has to do this, nearly everyone believes that the sooner it begins the better. I do not know if I would say the same if His Holiness decides to make friends with Caesar, for it will never be too late to place oneself in servitude.'9

He wrote this in a letter sent on the 24th December to be read by the Pope and his advisers, in fact a public letter; and in a private one only two days later: 'I do not know what to say *de rebus publicis* [about public affairs] for I have lost my bearings; and also, hearing that everyone cries out against that view which I do not like but which seems to me necessary, *non audeo loqui* [I dare not speak]. If I am not mistaken, we shall all know the evils of peace better when the chance of making war is past . . . Hence *si quid adversi acciderit* [if some adversity befall], we shall not be able to say that sovereignty has been taken from us but that *turpiter sit elapsa de manibus* [it has slipped ignominiously through our fingers].'[10] This private letter was written to one who agreed with him about the evils and the remedies, and this was none other than Machiavelli.

In fact the correspondence between the two great politicians had continued all this while more and more cordial and frequent. Guicciardini had written to his friend with the highest praise for his *Mandragola* and stating his plan to have it put on in Faenza for carnival. His friend wrote him some of those marvellous letters, now to explain certain doubts he had about the comedy, now to relate what he had done or thought of to help him marry off his daughters, now older and more numerous; with them the President's worries had increased, besides his growing disappointment at the lack of a son. Maria had given birth to eight daughters and four had survived – Simona, Lucrezia, Laudomina, Lisabetta;[11] which, with the pernicious contemporary custom of large dowries, meant in all twelve thousand ducats which he had accumulated with great labour, so that all he would have left for himself would be 'eyes to weep with'. Machiavelli suggested that he should put down half the sum himself and have the Pope provide the rest, as Filippo Strozzi did when he married his Marietta to Lorenzo Ridolfi with the enormous dowry of eight thousand ducats.[12] And he sagely advised him to make sacrifices to marry the eldest well, reminding him of the example of Romeo, with these lines from Dante: 'Quattro figlie ebbe e ciascuna regina . . .' [He had four daughters and each one a queen . . .].

These lines were found strangely intriguing by Guicciardini who, as we know, was not very familiar with the poets; and though he was to do Dante honour in one of his Histories, yet it was with little knowledge of him. So he replied to his friend in these odd terms: 'You have had me looking for a Dante all over Romagna to find the fable or tale of Romeo, and in the end I found the text but the commentary was not in it'; and, he added, rather stiff and in character and slightly suspicious of his facetious friend: 'I think it must be one of those tricks you always have up your sleeve.'[13] We have already seen him react in this manner, half suspicious and half indifferent, in one of his replies to Sigismondo Santi who had quoted one of Aesop's fables to him: that unfortunate Sigismondo who had died wretchedly shortly before, murdered by malefactors while on his way to France for the Pope. And he was a man of such intellect and character that he too had managed somewhat to melt messer Francesco, and had enlivened his correspondence.[14]

Guicciardini's correspondence with Machiavelli now rises to greater heights, if that were possible, and it fascinates with its curious mixture of the sacred and the profane, public and private, tragic and comic, constantly passing from the most trivial personal matters to the most general and generous ideas, from the comedy of messer Nicia to the tragedy of Italy. Thus Guicciardini could begin the letter where he writes those memorable words *de rebus publicis* quoted above, with these other words: 'I shall begin by replying to you about the comedy, because it does not seem to me one of the least important things we have on hand, and at least it is an affair which is within our power, so that we are not wasting our time thinking about it.' And Machiavelli in reply, before dissecting Italian politics, talks about the songs he had just composed to be sung between the acts of the comedy, about their music and Barbera who was to sing them.[15] In the first of those songs to be performed before the play, there were lines of flattery for the President:

> *Ancor ci ha qui condutti*
> *il nome di colui che vi governa,*
> *in cui si veggon tutti*
> *i beni accolti in la sembianza eterna*

[We have been drawn here too, by the fame of him who governs you, in whom are visible all the virtues united in the eternal form].

It should not appear strange that Guicciardini, to whom we probably owe the Soncino edition of the *Mandragola*,[16] went on deluding Machiavelli with the prospect of the play's being put on in Romagna, at a time when he had already resolved to go to Rome and take up something quite different from comedies. Before all else he had to keep that secret, and then his going was far from certain; indeed on the 4th January 1526 it seemed quite undecided, so much so that he ordered his agent to speak of it no more, and if anyone spoke to him, 'to listen without getting involved and let nature take its course'.[17]

But on Epiphany day he received in Imola the order to go, and at once he set out for Faenza to prepare for the moving of his family: to

Florence however, not to Rome, as he had set aside his scruples on this score. Perhaps he had made use of them only when he was bargaining over the emoluments. While he is attending to this without haste, indeed 'in style', partly for convenience, according to his nature, and a little 'to make people believe that the departure is for private reasons',[18] he has to think how to get his brother Iacopo – whom he prefers – to substitute for him without arousing the jealousy of his elder brother Luigi who desired the post. Therefore to avoid war breaking out in the family, as well as the one about to come in Europe, he had to have it believed that the Pope had made this appointment. The agreement with Iacopo, who was a good-natured and willing man, was that he would pay Francesco the handsome sum of two thousand gold ducats a year, 'and if between ordinary and extraordinary the revenues of the Presidency should be more than four thousand ducats a year, everything over that should be shared'. All this was recorded in writing and in the first year Francesco received more than two thousand one hundred and twenty ducats, in addition of course to his Roman salary.[19]

In mid-January he was still at Faenza and advising his agent that he would be leaving in five or six days. Four days he would spend at Florence, planning to be at Rome at the end of the month, but not without this reserve: 'The great difficulty of having to move the women is the reason why I could not come before, and as I have to cross the mountains with them, if there is any bad weather it may take even longer; but this you should not tell anyone.'[20] In fact he left Florence for Rome on the 29th January, but the same day, before leaving, he made a new will. If he died without male heirs, his daughters should inherit, his wife having the usufruct of the property in Valdipesa. He left two thousand ducats each to his brothers, and the property in usufruct to his wife; all this with various clauses and dispositions.[21] He reached Rome early in February.

Thus Francesco Guicciardini had become an officer of the Roman court. From Romagna where his governments and the Presidency had shown his quality, in one of the gravest hours for the Papacy and for Italy, the Pope had called him to be his minister and his counsellor. And yet he had all too many counsellors: there was Iacopo Salviati his kinsman, a good Florentine of the old school, severe and economical, more wise than acute. There was Niccolò Schönberg, Archbishop of Capua, and the datary Matteo Giberti, Bishop of Verona, who pulled in opposite directions the already too irresolute Clement, the first, as a good

German, being inclined towards the Empire, the second towards the French. And if the second Medici Pope had not, like the first, a Bibbiena,

'Who would have done better to stay at Torse',[22]

there was no lack at court among those ecclesiastics, of acute minds practised in affairs. Instead he chose this layman, a stranger to the Curia, who had risen by the power of his intellect. If Clement VII had no other merits, at least he did that much.

The greatest monument of Guicciardini's political work in this Roman period, rather than the letters written by him for the Pope, is a fascicule of large format in which, together with drafts of instructions and extracts of documents, he set down discourses composed to clear his own mind, according to his habit, or to make things clearer for the Pope. This fascicule is accompanied by a number of other loose papers containing writings of the same period and on similar subjects. The editor of the *Opere inedite* and later Otetea missed them, and they have therefore remained not only unpublished but unknown. This remarkable group of writings was found by the author of the present biography among the sea of papers used by Guicciardini in compiling the *Storia d'Italia*.[23] It enables us to follow step by step our politician in his Roman activities which had major consequences in European politics, and which yet had only been known up to now by a few letters all dated after the 15th March which came to light during the last century. Before that even less was known. There is no need for surprise since Guicciardini himself, who was not at all averse from the limelight, in his *Storia* cloaked this period in a strange silence.[24]

The first writing in this valuable group, and probably the first of the kind written by Guicciardini after his arrival in Rome, perhaps in mid-February,[25] is one of those I have described as designed to clarify things for himself and the Pope. It is more careful and elaborate in form than was the author's habit in office documents. It should take its place in fact among the other political discourses in a future edition of Guicciardini's works.

Whilst the ambiguity and uncertainty of Pope Clement persist, rendered greater by the uncertainty of the agreement between the Emperor and the French over the freeing of the King, in this first writing the good pilot wishes to 'find his bearings' for so difficult a piece of navigation. But we observe that the owner of the ship frightens him more, because of his pusillanimity, than stormy seas do. This preoccupation runs through from the first to the last lines. He reminds him that once 'the bearing is set' he must 'follow that course without turning back every day with fresh doubts or delaying the execution of what has been decided'. As everything comes back to that key point of the King's imprisonment, he considers whether the French, losing hope of his liberation, might join a league against Caesar, and whether, should they not do so, it were a good thing to make a league without them, or come to an agreement with Caesar. Consistent with his ideas ever since Pavia, presupposing the Emperor's intention to subject to himself Italy and the Papacy, rejecting as unworthy of His Holiness any advice to bend his neck to the yoke, and reminding him of the indomitable courage of his predecessor Julius, he urges him to take, though it involves great danger, the path of war: he would have with him the Venetians and the Duke of Ferrara, with whom he begs him to come to an agreement of convenience. Further he would try to involve the King of England, while still attempting to interest the French. His final words are: 'It is bad to make a bad decision but worse not to make any . . . everything is done haphazard, and often today's action is contrary to and ruins yesterday's.'[26]

In another shorter report Guicciardini expresses his opinion on the letters written from Spain from the 20th December onward. The 12th January, date of the last letter received, was two days before the agreement reached between the Emperor and the French. Some conditions of the bargain had leaked out, but the whole affair was still undecided. On the basis of such letters and of those which had come from France, he judges that the agreement would be made 'because, since the Emperor does not propose an alliance to us, nor do the French seek a league, it is a clear sign they both desire it, and the terms of the negotiation are so few that they are sure to resolve their difficulties'.[27] It would have been a severe blow to his warlike proposals, for if the French had wanted to keep the agreement, it deprived him of their assistance. Asking himself what the Pope should do: whether to temporize or seek an agreement with Caesar, he favoured temporizing.

There was no need. The ink of those two reports of Guicciardini's was barely dry when on the 20th February there came the great news of the treaty concluded on the 14th of the previous month at Madrid. The King had obtained his freedom under extremely harsh conditions: to mention only the most inordinate, he was to hand over to the victor Burgundy and other noble lands of France, give as hostages his eldest and second sons, or instead of the second, twelve of the foremost nobles of his kingdom, restore lands and favour to the traitor Bourbon. As soon as the freeing of the King and its conditions were known, there were many who thought that the King would not fulfil them, nor could Guicciardini fail to be among those. With this supposition he wrote an opinion to clarify the situation for the Pope, considering various events which might occur, and concluding that anyway one must be prepared for war with the Emperor, unless he, seeing France, England, Switzerland and nearly the whole of Italy against him, were ready to settle the affairs of Milan and Italy to suit the Pope.[28]

After the King was set free, it had become much more urgent to send to France the ambassador already designated, for they had to make sure whether, as they hoped, the King wanted to repudiate such exorbitant terms signed under duress. If the King were found to be receptive, he should be duly encouraged. Paolo Vettori was chosen, and Guicciardini wrote for him an outline of his instructions as a basis for the papal secretaries' work.[29] Coming from him, they were precise, decisive, unlike certain others which so many ambassadors, himself included, had received from the Florentine republic. Nor do we need to dwell on their contents which reflect his ideas and his previous writings.

While Paolo Vettori prepared to leave, the protonotary Uberto da Gambara was sent to England to induce the King to join the League and use his influence to prevent the King of France observing the agreement. In those feverish last days of February Miguel de Herrera was back in Rome with Charles's final conditions, the same man who on his previous visit last December had caused Pope Clement and his advisers to lose their heads, persuading them to accept the ill-famed truce. But this time Guicciardini was in Rome.

Briefly in his final proposals the Emperor rejected the Pope's terms and made the perpetuation of Francesco Sforza in the duchy of Milan subject to his being innocent of the crime of *lèse-majesté* in Morone's conspiracy. Whether the Duke were guilty or innocent, it was a means of making sure of the duchy for ever, and Guicciardini would never have capitulated on this point. He thought the other conditions could be discussed, if the Emperor were willing. Instead Herrera and the Duke of Sessa had informed him arrogantly that 'it was not in their power to change a single syllable'.[30] 'A method of negotiation,' observed Guicciardini, 'most barbarous indeed.'[31]

But this same 'most barbarous' manner gave him occasion to write again to Spain, temporizing until news should come from France of the King's intentions. Unfortunately, while he was writing in Latin the draft of the texts to be sent to Caesar and the draft of the letter to the Nuncio which was to accompany them, (also autograph in the papers found by me),[32] he received news that Paolo Vettori was kept in Florence by a severe illness which in a few days was to carry him off and not to France. Then Guicciardini had to prepare fresh instructions for Capino da Capo, sent in all haste in his stead, and for Roberto Acciaiuoli, who, chosen as ambassador to the King, was to travel more slowly than the former.[33]

Having done these things, he saw clearly that the chief concern was to hold firm Clement's vacillating spirit. In this fascicule we find memorable pages, so frank and bold that one would not think (and I would not say for certain) they were composed for the eyes of the Pope if they were not written by Guicciardini, who, as we know, never lacked boldness or frankness. Speaking of the great reputation Clement had won as cardinal, governing the affairs of the Church under Pope Leo, of the hopes aroused by this reputation on his election to the papacy, and finally of the disappointments which had followed from it, he gives a marvellous portrait of that timid irresolute character, skimping neither praise nor blame and using where necessary very strong language. He analyses that timidity: 'because we see that these scruples often keep him helpless in affairs and with people where fear is of no avail', and he concludes that it arises from an easy-going attitude which he cannot express otherwise than 'by its plain name ineptitude'. He exhorts him to recapture the reputation he has lost 'acting boldly in something which shows spirit and enthusiasm', as in retaking Reggio, changing the government of Siena, 'playing some trick on Cardinal Colonna', who is reviving ancient enmities with his espousing of the imperial cause. Finally, after his suggestions to the Pope for a general and radical reform of his character, he urges: 'And if nature cannot be forced always and in everything, he should try at least to force it in most things and in those that matter most; if he began to form different habits and enjoy the good results, I am quite sure that it would be harder for him to return to his old ways than it would be now to get used to this new one.'[34]

It was the Ides of March and everything seemed in suspense: in that anxious waiting the destinies of Italy and Europe hung in the balance. Guicciardini, who at Rome held some of the threads, followed in his thoughts and with his letters the road which Capino and Gambara were following on horseback too slowly for his impatience. Restless as he was and wishing to know his opinion, it was he who was busy who wrote first to Machiavelli who had nothing to do and had not written to him for some time; nor do I believe that it was his custom to ask other people's advice. Machiavelli replied with that famous letter in which, speaking of the Emperor and the King, he advises Guicciardini to have Giovanni de' Medici raise a troop of soldiers of fortune; then concluding with one of his disconcerting passages: 'If Barbera turns up there and you could do anything for her, I recommend her to you, for she is in my thoughts far more than the Emperor.'[35] Nor could I say whether it was more for the good of the fortifications of Florence, or to find something to do for that dear friend who was pining for work, and also to give him an opportunity to be with his Barbera, that Guicciardini at once did something for him, having him come to Rome for a few days and persuading the Pope to set up for him the new office of the *Provveditori alle Mura* [Curators of the Walls].[36]

Finally, on the 20th April, letters came from France written on the 29th and 31st March in which Capino said he had found the King and those around him 'determined not to observe the terms and determined to make war'. It gave him new life. Although in Spain, seeing the danger, they had abandoned that 'very barbarous manner of negotiating', and there had arrived 'great proposals, offering safety for the affairs of Italy', the Pope, held firm by his inflexible counsellor, who meanwhile never tired of writing, writing again, admonishing and inciting Capino and Gambara,[37] at once sent to France the order to make a pact. The League was concluded in fact at Cognac on the 22nd May 1526, but at Rome they heard that all difficulties had been overcome by the 17th.[38] The same day Machiavelli prophetically wrote to Guicciardini the fateful words: *liberate diuturna cura Italiam.*[39]

At that time not even the plague daunted Guicciardini, who wrote to his brother Luigi: 'plague has begun to do some damage here but not much . . . I would like you to send me some remedies for before and after, if it should so happen . . . I shall protect myself as far as I can but I do not know how much one can do, as I am forced to work on all this business.'[40] And his work continued, augmented by his Roman responsibilities and those of Lombardy. Days later he wrote: 'I believe that now they are beginning to form an army in Lombardy, the Pope will decide that I should go to take charge.'[41] Indeed Clement had already made up his mind. The title at first was Commissioner General as last time under Leo,[42] but as time goes on the dignity and authority of the post increase. As for money, this time it was left to Guicciardini's discretion, who having been discreet enough not to establish any salary, was given two hundred and forty ducats a month by papal brief,[43] to be added of course to those of the Presidency which his good brother Iacopo kept for him.

The news of the treaty of Cognac reached Rome on the last day of May. But in Rome they had not waited for that information; a good week earlier Guicciardini had written to Bishop Averoldi, Governor of Bologna, and lately designated Nuncio at Venice, the vital member of the League, to inform him of the arrangements already made in advance of the promulgation; and it must have been no small pleasure for him to give instructions 'ex palatio apostolico' (it is merely a detail but in the minute books we find letters dated in this manner, only to the Cardinal)[44] to the man who wanted to regard Guicciardini as a subordinate in the Modena days! The main provisions were these: Count Guido Rangoni was at once to raise six thousand good soldiers and send them on to Piacenza: meanwhile five or six thousand Swiss were to come down from their valleys to relieve the castles of the Milanese which were still held for the dispossessed Duke. These Swiss, offered so opportunely by the warden of the Castle of Mus, who was the Milanese Gian Iacopo Medici, seemed like manna but in fact they turned out to be a snare and a delusion which caused the failure of an enterprise so well begun.

Unfortunately it was only a pious wish, almost as noble as Machiavelli's old dream, to be able to do without these unbearable foreign mercenaries. Guicciardini had to reply to Gambara who wrote to him on the subject some time later: 'What you say about using only Italian troops is generous and worthy of your lordship, and perhaps no less prudent *sed non persuadetis ducibus nostris* [but you will not convince our officers].'[45] It is pleasing that such thoughts should arise in an enterprise from which Guicciardini, and not only he, hoped for the 'safety and glory of Italy'.[46] It is pleasing that he, if only in words – but what words – should have agreed.

Never in those years was a war entered on in Italy with a more willing and cheerful spirit. That spring there was something new in the air. There was already something national about the enterprise, even if the nation had yet to come into being. While the Pope's ratification, on which the King's depended, was galloping furiously towards France, and while Guicciardini, elected by the Pope 'His Lieutenant-General in the army and whole state of the Church with fullest and almost absolute power',[47] prepared to leave Rome to follow and supervise *his* war at close quarters,[48] there were not a few, and they the best, who felt vaguely, even if they could not express it, Machiavelli's invocation: *Liberate diuturna cura Italiam.*

Chapter 15

THE LIEUTENANT-GENERAL

<><><><><><><><><><><><><><><><><><><><><><><><><><><><>

THERE is no doubt that Guicciardini as a good Florentine preferred a magistrate's robes, if not the lawyer's gown, to a suit of
armour. But how gaily we see him, in these first days of June,
riding along the ancient Roman consular road on his way to war.
Meeting a courier on the way, he stopped him, and breaking the seals of
the letters addressed to the papal court he found one in which Guido
Rangoni wrote, among other things, that he would not move outside
the Church States without a commission. Nonsense! Reaching Orvieto a
few hours later, Guicciardini wrote to the Count that 'if he saw a good
opportunity he should not hesitate to move out or even to proceed as
far as Milan', for 'success in war is sometimes the matter of a moment'.
If he had the opportunity to strike at Lodi and Pavia, he should do so
without delay.[1] How easy everything appeared to the Lieutenant at
that optimistic beginning! He wrote in the same style to Count Roberto
Boschetti. Riding faster than usual, he reached Cortona the following
day, June 9th, and found there men recruiting for Vitelli; but calculating
that these men would reach Lombardy too late, he wrote to Rome that
they should give Rangoni authority to take on another two thousand.

In Florence, since it was that city's fate to have to pay up on all
occasions, he made arrangements about money. Parsimonious himself
or actually stingy, he would not permit economies in war, and though
aware that his own purse would suffer no less than others', he decided
with the principal citizens, to impose a levy. With amusing foresight he
advises them to hurry, to do it at once as they would find the citizens

better disposed to pay up in the first flush of enthusiasm, 'for in the beginning hopes are great, as not everyone can see the difficulties which might arise in the course of time';[2] and besides the Florentines hated spending money but were a little better disposed towards regilding the well-loved lilies of France. These matters were dealt with at a meeting held on the 12th in the Medici palace, presided over nominally by the Most Reverend Silvio Passerini, Cardinal of Cortona who governed Florence for the Pope, and was also governor of the two young Medici bastards Ippolito and Alessandro, for whom Florence was destined. But in fact the one who had most say in that committee was Francesco Guicciardini, returned home 'con altra voce omai con altro vello' [with other voice and fleece of other hue]; that is, with sufficient authority to awe and perhaps offend his fellow citizens.

He wrote directly to the Pope of the decisions taken, not without admonishing him: 'I urge Your Holiness to make a sound basis for the provision of money, for an uncertain income would not do for certain expenditure . . . and always to get the money collected in advance, before some reverse can occur, which may always happen in a war. These citizens show themselves really very well disposed to do anything they can, and they will be even readier if they are confident that the other half of the expenditure will come from Rome at the right moment, so that the city is seen not to be doing more than its share.'[3] Poor Florentines! The burden of such a war, half for them and half for the Church? If Rome kept faith, they would be very lucky.

Taking up his journey again, on the 13th he met on the way don Ugo da Moncada, that damned don Ugo, sent by Caesar to intrigue in France and then in Rome. From Loiano, on the 14th, about twenty miles on this side of Bologna, Guicciardini wrote a number of letters about the military preparations. In one to Filonardi, Bishop of Veroli, who was working with the Bishop of Lodi and the warden of the Castle of Mus on that ill-fated levy of Swiss troops, he puts forward the plan to change it for a levy of eight thousand Italian foot. He writes to the datary Giberti, discussing this and other provisions, and accustomed as he was to travel 'in comfort', adds: 'As I am not used to riding post, and knowing that it does not suit me, I have not given up travelling by daily stages, but if I receive news which gives cause for haste, I shall not fail to travel post.'[4] That same evening he was in Bologna, where he only stopped one night to take a little rest and also to send off other letters intended to augment and hasten the preparations. He wrote to Count

Boschetti, bewailing the unreliability of the Swiss, the slowness of the Venetians, the dilatoriness of all 'these delays kill me'.[5]

The following day he was at Modena in company with Giovanni de' Medici who had gone with him from Bologna, and from that time onward they were always together; Guicciardini was always at the side of the man who was to vindicate the honour of Italian arms. He was in Modena on the 15th, in Parma on the 16th, and in every place where he stopped (he had gone through *his* Reggio without a pause, though met and welcomed with all ceremony by the Este commander!), he never tired of writing and writing again, particularly over the long-drawn-out affair of the Swiss, who according to Veroli were always on the point of moving and yet never did so. He wrote to this same Veroli: 'If I wrote to Your Lordship every hour, I would repeat a hundred times every hour how important it is they should move fast.' To Giberti: 'the coming of the Swiss, if I saw it handled by Veroli alone, I would not rely on at all; however, the Venetians have always understood these matters particularly well and believed in them, and we perhaps have believed in them more than in Veroli.'[6] It was a great trial.

On the 17th June he reached Piacenza where the mass of the papal army was gathered. It was now a matter of crossing the Po and joining up with the Venetian army which was coming on at a funeral pace to the great despair of our Lieutenant. To hasten it on and hear what it intended to do, he first sent them his brother Girolamo and then Count Boschetti. His impatience was increased by certain letters he had intercepted in which the imperial commanders, Antonio da Leyva and the Marchese del Vasto, informed the Duke of Sessa and don Ugo da Moncada of their precarious situation in rebellious Milan.[7]

Meanwhile, however, the first disappointments and worries were beginning in this campaign which had begun with such ardour. The despair over the Swiss was not the only thing: from far-off France instead of the support promised under the terms of the League, there came only words; from the near-by towns beyond the Adda the timid delays of the Duke of Urbino, Captain-General of the Venetians, and worse still his obstinacy in negotiating with the allies, promised ill. The Duke stood fast on some cautious plan concerned with the joining of the two armies. Guicciardini wrote with resigned dissatisfaction: 'We shall regard it as a lesser evil to give way to their wishes than to ruin the enterprise by being undecided.'[8]

This time fortune came to the League's assistance, cutting every knot. No thanks to the Duke's military ardour, but because of a plot with those inside who had had enough of the Spaniards, the Venetian army, crossing the Adda, took Lodi without a single shot. Thus that slow irresolute beginning was at once given a hopeful air. As soon as he had the news, the Lieutenant wrote a warm letter of congratulation to the Duke and rejoiced with Giberti: 'We are forced to praise the Venetians and bestow on them as many blessings as I alone have sent them curses during these recent days.'[9]

Besides the importance of the acquisition, besides the reputation the League derived from it, the capture of Lodi broke off at a good point all arguments about the joining of the armies. It was enough for the Papal army to cross the Po, and this it did on the 26th. After that the two armies went to lodge together near Old Lodi, intending to move on to Milan with speed and in good order. Instead the Duke's cautious delays began again, and with them Guicciardini's impatience, who described them to Giberti thus: 'The Duke in various ways has wasted all this day, and will not move tomorrow, and even being pressed to, particularly by the Provveditore [the Venetian Pietro Pesaro] and myself, in which Count Guido supported me well, he requested almost as a favour that he should be allowed to stay tomorrow to organize himself better and reconnoitre the lodgings. It all arises from the fact, according to me, that he does not much want to besiege Milan if the Swiss do not come, being very fearful of the Spanish; and although he does not want to say so, and in fact when I press him on this point he always evades it, yet in his words and actions I think I understand him all too well.'[10]

Yet with leaden feet on the 28th the army moved to Marignano, where it was necessary to wait until the 3rd July, no less, before taking another step forward, to San Donato, half-way between Marignano and Milan; the following day they were at San Martino only three miles from Milan, and there at long last the first five hundred Swiss appeared, just to show people what they looked like. I do not, however, think that it was the magic effect of that sight but rather Guicciardini's continual stimulus which gave the Duke of Urbino the sudden courage of the timid. So much so that on the 7th July, having moved off with his whole army to set up camp half a mile below Milan, when they got to the place arranged for their lodging, he ordered them instead to go on and lay seige to the suburbs of the city thinking he would be able to take them without opposition. Thus the Lieutenant was able to write at least one letter to Rome dating it triumphantly *ex castris contra Mediolanum*.[11]

It was the first and the last. In it he related how the Duke, making a minor attack on the Porta Tosa and the Porta Romana, had not carried it through, although the ladders had been brought up already and the artillery emplaced before the gates. What counted most was to see him warmed up so that one might hope great things of him. This Guicciardini said in his letter, but two hours later he had to add a sad postscript. Hardly had he gone to bed when the Venetian Provveditore came to get him out. Then calling together Rangoni, Vitelli, and Giovanni de' Medici, he announced that the Duke had just told him that he had attempted that assault entirely against his better judgement, giving way to their insistence, he had observed that the Italian infantry had not shown up well, and the army was encamped in such a manner that it could be routed at any moment; on these considerations he had decided that they must withdraw. It was true indeed that he had given way to the Lieutenant's insistence, but it was also true that he had expected to take the suburbs with ease, and the resolution of the defenders had given him a great fright.

This sudden change of plan and hasty flight astonished the papal commanders who could not see that the danger was so great, and it astonished Guicciardini still more. He said at once that he wanted to discuss it with the Duke, and when he went to him, he saw that the baggage and the artillery were moving and that he had been informed of a decision already taken, indeed that was already being acted on. Strong words were exchanged, but by now they were useless. The finest thing was, when they reached San Martino where the Duke had said he would stop, the Lieutenant saw 'the ranks of men continue onwards' (i.e., back!). Commenting on this with surprise to the Duke, the latter replied that he thought the lodgings at Marignano were safer and more comfortable. As Guicciardini insisted that the troops should stop there, so that their retreat might seem less shameful and those besieged in the castle should not lose heart, high words became angry ones. The Duke replied: 'when my masters want the leadership of this expedition to be in other hands than mine, I shall be very pleased, and I shall obey everybody gladly, but until they give it to someone else, I wish to control all the movements of the war myself.' The Lieutenant having replied that no one wished to deny him the power of command, but that he himself wished to be able to express his opinion, the Duke replied: 'If I am to command, I want us to go to Marignano.'[12] All Guicciardini could do was take his revenge in the *History*, where he remarks that the Duke had rearranged the famous saying as *veni, vidi, fugi* [I came, I saw, I ran away].

In fact Francesco della Rovere was only Captain-General of the Venetians, nor had he until then laid claim to the title of Captain-General of the League, but as there was no one in the papal army superior to him or equal in age, degree, rank, or experience, if he were not supreme commander in name, he was so in fact, while the Pope's Lieutenant could not even balance his authority against that of a Captain-General of the papal forces. What endangered a victory which had seemed certain, more than the defection of the King of France and the failure of the Swiss to help, were the poor organization of command and the weakness of the man exercising it.

These things, foreseen or glimpsed before crossing the Po, seemed very clear to Guicciardini after the hasty retreat from the camp by Milan. His confidence was beset with worries; he knew now that, as had happened at Lodi, they had to depend not on the Duke but on luck, and luck had not joined the 'Holy League' at Cognac, it had remained allied with Caesar. He also knew that, whatever happened, he would not have the role he had hoped for in that enterprise to which he had given the best of his mind and spirit. He had thought to lead it as he had done up to Piacenza and in some sense up to Milan, and instead he was going to be dragged along with it. Our pages which have followed him step by step up to this point may now pass over some of the detail.

We must not leave out a matter which has no significance for the expedition but is not without importance for the subject of our biography: with Guicciardini, who very probably had been instrumental in bringing him there, his friend Niccolò Machiavelli was now at the camp of the League. The date of his arrival I have already given in his *Life*, thereby correcting other biographers.[13] What he was doing there is better explained by one of Guicciardini's letters lately come to light: 'Machiavelli is here. He had come to reorganize this militia, but seeing how corrupt it is, he is not confident they will do him credit. He will stay to laugh at human error since he cannot remedy it.'[14] A stroke of the pen which is as good as a portrait; and in it there is, if I am not mistaken, a touch of affectionate admiration.

One who laughs at human error, being unable to correct it: that is indeed Machiavelli! He must have made game of it with Guicciardini as in his letters of previous years. There was no lack of time to do so while the war languished, and the necessary material abounded as never before. The days which followed the retreat were full of regrets, complaints and remonstrance. Guicciardini's correspondence is full of them. But not for that do his usual encouragements and incitements slacken. They are received by papal ambassadors in Venice, in France, in England, and by Capino, urged to raise more Swiss. He sends to Rome to keep up the Pope's enthusiasm, who sees the enterprise once judged easy and rapid becoming long and difficult; to Florence to reproach his brothers alarmed by the levy decided during his last stay in Florence. He encourages them, he exhorts them to do their duty as citizens, in these words which do honour to a man who has been accused of avarice and too much love for his own interests: 'I am surprised that you and the others are as annoyed as you say in your letters, for the need for which the war was started has brought us to a situation where, if we do not help ourselves in this way, we shall have nothing left to call our own. In fact times are hard, and I feel that everyone ought to help one another willingly and not regret spending for safety a sum much smaller than in other times we spent for ambition.'[15]

He could do no more than write and write and try to infuse into all his own faith, his nerve, and his manly vigour. There was nothing else to be done, for the Duke of Urbino, after the dreadful fright he had had, was protesting that he would not return to Milan if he was not given two armies, each of them equal to the entire joint enemy forces, and in each there must be not less than five thousand Swiss, in all ten thousand.

But there were five thousand already which had come in several instalments; thus the excuse under which the Duke had withdrawn turtlewise, had partly collapsed. It was felt to be more than ever urgent to relieve the castle of Milan and free Sforza, who was an important part of Guicciardini's plan to liberate Italy from the Spanish and French; and as the castle had been reduced to extremity, as witnessed three hundred soldiers, women and children sent out for lack of provisions, the Duke at last consented to attempt or pretend to attempt to rescue him. He could hardly have refused without infamy after the arrival of the Swiss and after the weakness of the enemy trenches around the castle had been sufficiently demonstrated by the three hundred who had got through them without difficulty.

With his usual slowness the Duke led the army to Casaretto two miles from Milan, instead of up to the walls as had been agreed in council.[16]

Having done this he did no more, except hold further councils where it was delightful to hear him discuss the art of war just like a book. In one of these councils the Duke found himself reproached with his cowardice by one of the Swiss captains. In the meantime while they were consulting, Sforza and his men in the castle, supported by nothing but signals and epistolary comfort sent off by Guicciardini, capitulated on the 24th July so as not to die of hunger. Great was the Lieutenant's displeasure, great the relief of the Duke, according to whom the surrender of the castle was all to the good as it finally removed the danger that they might do something rash in attempting to relieve it.

As it had been after the retreat, so after this fine success, discontent and recrimination could not fail to accompany discouragement. As on the first occasion, Guicciardini sent to Rome a detailed account of all the Duke's actions, which in the light of news received from Milan were tinged with an even more sinister colour. The first time when he attacked the suburbs, the defenders had already loaded up their baggage trains, intending to depart in the night, if they had not been so hastily forestalled by the attackers. The second time they had known the condition of the trenches to be such that the enemy could not have defended them. The trouble was therefore either incompetence or treachery; the remedies must rest on an appraisal of the fidelity and ability of the Duke: 'If he is incapable or has aims other than our own, it is madness to depend on him . . . ; if he is capable of this responsibility, the enterprise is so important that not to ruin it we must drink this bitter cup.'[17]

Poor messer Francesco! The bitterest part of the cup was for him. He wrote to Gambara in England: 'I am well in myself. . . . I am full of titles and authority *in ceteris*, with very little or no satisfaction of mind, and to put it in a word, for a hundred thousand reasons I bless every day the memory of [signor] Prospero: think how I must feel!'[18] In Colonna's time too he had had a good deal to put up with!

After the words that had passed between them, he had become morose with the Duke, and the Duke, either for this reason or a bad conscience or other disagreements, 'sought to ascertain with diligence' whether the Lieutenant was dissatisfied with him and wrote to the Pope to complain.[19] Such a preoccupation must have been very troublesome to him since he had got it into his head that he wanted to be made Captain-General of the ecclesiastical army too, which was something it would have been reasonable to ask for after a victory, not after the fine affair at Milan. Because of this undue ambition, ill will and unease grew in the 'most fortunate' (as the formula said) or rather most unhappy camp of the League.

The affairs of this force were going from bad to worse and not only in those watery Lombard plains. Two days after the surrender of the castle a few hundred foot, issuing forth from Siena, defeated and plundered the army which Clement VII had sent to besiege the city and to change its Ghibelline government, while in Rome itself the Pope was besieged by the Colonna Ghibellines. Almost in despair, and because the expenses were growing apace as time went on, the Pope in vain urged the Kings of France and England to keep their promises. To help him out of his difficulties though unwillingly, he also sought to negotiate with the hated Duke of Ferrara. In these moves we find Guicciardini involved, who from the first had always urged an agreement with the Duke as a necessary basis to the enterprise, and so Guicciardini, whose death had once been planned by an Este assassin, found the Duke offering him the title of 'count', a substantial sum of money, and the marriage of one of his daughters. They were well informed at the court of Ferrara of the thoughts which most plagued the Lieutenant. The latter at once sent on to Rome the Duke's letter accompanied with these proud and bitter words: 'I do not care about being a "count", nor do I rely on ever spending his money; the offer for my daughter might persuade me, since the Pope has been so helpful about them.'[20]

At last the Duke of Urbino, graciously recognizing that the army's honour had somewhat declined and that they could not do worse than do nothing, decided to take Cremona. He may have been moved more by his ambition for the title than by the honour of the army, but also the continual urgings of Guicciardini and the Venetian Provveditore bore their share in that decision, whence Guicciardini boasted: 'If it were not for us two, they would not be sending a force to Cremona.'[21] However, this expedition too, commanded at first by Malatesta Baglioni, was ill led, with delays and indecision. The defences were attacked by the artillery, but without success; but fate lent a hand to the assailants by bringing down fifty yards of the walls without anyone touching them. Yet Malatesta was slow to take advantage of it, and when in the end he did, those within had made such repairs that it was not effective. Then the Duke of Urbino arrived with a good part of the army; on that occasion too he did not conquer, but at least he did not flee.

Guicciardini had remained at the camp at Casaretto with the army of the Church, where he had plenty to do to keep the peace between Giovanni de' Medici and Guido Rangoni, and to make sure that the money for the soldiers' pay did not fatten the captains instead of their companies. This scrupulous rigour accompanied with his characteristic severity did not fail to create hatred and danger. On one of those days, having discovered some fraud during an investigation and having arrested the culprits immediately, he was confronted by their commander who laid hands on his sword.

But while he was occupied in governing the army that had been placed in his care, and which was idly wasting time and pay in those marshes, he did not lose sight of the general progress of the war and that other army which was spending its time no less idly under the walls of Cremona. Seeing things drawn out longer than seemed reasonable, he sent Machiavelli there (who, willing as ever, acted as his commissioner, his envoy and even as his secretary)[22] to see, judge and consult with the Venetian Provveditore and the Duke, who was as bold in argument as he was timid in battle. He was to persuade them to leave that enterprise for an attempt on Genoa, if he could see no hope of rapid success there.

Cremona capitulated on the 23rd September, but the news of that negotiated victory, which somewhat revived the League, reached the camp simultaneously with another piece of news which overthrew it entirely. In Rome Pope Clement, betrayed by the diabolical Ugo Moncada and by Cardinal Colonna, after a sudden onslaught had barely managed to take refuge in Castel Sant'Angelo, and had, in exchange for his freedom, concluded a four months' truce with his oppressors, agreeing to withdraw his army beyond the Po. When he heard this, it almost broke Guicciardini's heart.

At first he temporized, hoping that the Pope might change his mind and refuse to honour these conditions agreed to under duress. As he wrote at once to Rome, it was a treaty which it would be shameful to observe, not to break, as the Pope was under a much greater obligation to keep faith with the treaty voluntarily arrived at with his allies, than with one imposed on him by force and with a sacrilegious insult, by his enemies in defiance of another treaty which they had failed to observe. He wrote to Giberti: 'I shall sooner make up my mind to abandon Rome and Italy if fate so wills it, than to live in Rome in the manner His Holiness will have to live there if he continues on the road you wrote to me about this evening. *Tu ne cede malis . . .*'[23]

Then he temporized so as not to leave the camp by Milan empty until the return of those who had taken Cremona and who were dawdling as usual. He negotiated to this end with Bourbon and the other Spanish commanders; offering with great dexterity various excuses for his delays, he worked miracles; but in the end he had to obey, not without having arranged with the allies so that the least possible harm might come to the enterprise. On the 9th October he was at Piacenza which he had left with such great hopes less than four months before. And then full of bitterness and dejection he wrote: 'I am done with being lieutenant or coachman.'[24]

Chapter 16

THE LIEUTENANT-GENERAL
DURING THE 'TRUCE'

❖❖

HAVING written those angry words, he attended more closely than ever to his office of Lieutenant, more than ever he multiplied exhortations, solicitations, efforts to revive the enterprise, even though it was a labour of Sisyphus to repair single-handed such a ruin. He had left as many men as possible beyond the Po. Giovanni de' Medici also remained, nominally paid by King Francis but in fact by the Pope. Anything successful and energetic in that war had been done by him. Under him he had four thousand Italian foot, human material despised by the Duke of Urbino. They could not be any better than those given to Rangoni and Vitelli, but drilled, disciplined, led by him, they had been transformed into a force of brave men feared by the famous Spanish veterans. It is not surprising therefore that Guicciardini showed him great favour, placing as many men under him as he could, showing toleration for his intemperate nature, for the violence and the excesses of his youth and his impetuous and ferocious spirit, and compelling the other commanders to tolerate them.

Giovanni therefore had stayed on the far side of the Po, to make his presence felt far more than the Duke of Urbino ever did, or the Marchese di Saluzzo, who represented the tardy and meagre assistance sent at last by the King of France. Giovanni remained, but, dissatisfied with the Pope, he kept asking and threatening to go. The Lieutenant had to write to him to curb his impatience and to Rome to make them understand that to lose him would be to lose the war.[1] In the end the overlordship of Fano was promised him and Giovanni was pacified.

The open favour shown to the Florentine condottiere provoked the resentment and jealousy of Guido Rangoni, who by certain little manoeuvres and using the Provveditore, did his best to make things difficult for the Lieutenant at Rome. But the latter threw off the accusations in a letter which paints a double portrait, from the life, of the two captains: '[Count Guido] has been so weak in counsel, so lacking in intelligence in carrying out any operation at all out of the ordinary, that no captain in this army has been in less reputation than he, and all [the regard] he has kept, has been achieved by means of clysters, that is with artful practices. . . . What fault is it of mine if signor Giovanni trains his troops, and he leaves his to sleep? What fault is it of mine if signor Giovanni, who constantly affronts danger, wishes to give his companies captains who will fight, and who are soldiers, while the other fellow only had men without experience of war . . . being satisfied to have a table full of them and a fine crowd behind him around the camp. Is it my fault if signor Giovanni is constantly with his soldiers, arming, reordering and improving his companies, while the other never sees or thinks of them?'[2]

Thus, after many vicissitudes, the waters were again stormy between Guicciardini and Rangoni. When Machiavelli, returning to Florence as there was nothing more he could do at the camp during the truce, met Count Guido in Modena, the latter asked him: 'Is the Lieutenant still angry?', and Machiavelli, prompt and witty as usual, replied: 'No, because there is no one there to anger him.' Rangoni swore that he would 'go into exile in Egypt' sooner than take a commission in an army where Guicciardini was, but then, in spite of all resentments old and new, he too agreed that his presence in the camp 'had done more good than harm'.[3] *O gran bontà dei cavalieri antiqui!*

Though the affairs of Giovanni de' Medici were settled, the Lieutenant was not idle. He had to encourage the Pope, who was more than ever unhappy since he saw he could not support the expense of that war and could not make up his mind to an election of cardinals, the only means left to him of making money, 'suffering more scruples over selling four hats than over ruining the Papacy and the whole world';[4] there were the indifferent allies to warm up, the army to keep in order, and the method of waging the war to discuss. The damage had been great, and Guicciardini had to strive to make it good.

During those months the threads of the agreement with the Duke of Ferrara had also been picked up. As we know, Guicciardini had advised the Pope to buy his friendship when he had first felt it was necessary to make an enemy of the Emperor. The old hatred for the vassal who resisted being despoiled, and love of Modena and Reggio had made the Pope an unwilling negotiator in prosperous times when the affair would have been easier; finally he was forced by necessity when it was too late.

The Pope had lost a lot of time; his Lieutenant wasted some too. Having received on the 13th November the papal brief which gave him full authority to negotiate and conclude a treaty, he sent on the 17th an envoy with his credentials to Ferrara to prepare his conversations with the Duke, insisting however that he must make sure that Guicciardini's arrival would be acceptable and likely to be fruitful. Indeed he told him to say, if only in jest, that the Lieutenant would think it inconvenient and hardly honourable to go all that way 'in person and then not achieve anything'.[5] The envoy returned on the 20th with his bags full of the good words and kind offers of the Duke, who had told him that he desired that treaty above all things and that 'it would be concluded in one day'. Therefore Guicciardini should come; if he wanted to make use of the Duke's horses and his cities he had only to ask. If necessary he would come in person to accompany him.[6] The affair therefore seemed well advanced if not actually finished, but adding delays to delays the papal plenipotentiary had to put off his departure, because beyond the Po in that icy late November there was something coming other than the wind from the mountains.

During the summer there had been talk of a levy of lansquenets made in the Tirol for the Emperor by George Frundsberg, but there had been too many words without results and few believed in those lansquenets. And now in mid-November the words take shape, becoming ten or twelve thousand foot soldiers gathered at Bolzano and now on the move. On the 20th they were at Castiglione delle Stiviere, on the 22nd at Corriana, and there was no longer any doubt that they intended to cross the Po. To confront this danger which threatened the territories of the Church, the Lieutenant stopped at Parma which he had reached on his way to Ferrara. Then he decided in spite of everything to go on, and on his way a papal courier whom he met on the road to Modena induced him to hurry. But on the 25th, riding between Cento and Ferrara, he saw coming to meet him Iacopo Alvarotto, ducal councillor, who informed him how the Duke had just received from the Emperor the investiture of Modena and Reggio with a promise of a marriage alliance in addition. Guicciardini made bold to say that, as for Modena, Caesar had given him the investiture, but the Pope could give him the city. The minister having persuaded him that it was useless to go, it only remained for him to turn his horse and calculate the days to prove to the Pope and to himself that the failure should not be attributed to his delay.[7] So this card too, which might have decided the game, had passed into the hands of Charles V.

Meanwhile the lansquenets were moving on, they were at Rivalta, at Borgoforte, they were making ready to cross the Po. They were closely followed by Giovanni de' Medici; with a mastiff like him at their heels it would not have been easy for the Germans to cross. But on the 25th, while according to his custom he was fighting more as a common soldier than as a commander, a great cannon ball from a falconet broke his leg, which was amputated three days later with little hope of saving him; that same day the lansquenets crossed the Po. He died on the last day of that gloomy November.

Guicciardini's admiration for the great soldier had been steadily growing from the time when in the shameful retreat from the suburbs of Milan he alone had remained 'until broad daylight, thinking it improper to gain the infamy of fleeing at night instead of the hoped for victory'.[8] This admiration had been increased even more by the way in which he trained and led his infantry, than by his rash courage in those skirmishes with which he alarmed the enemy. Indeed from the very beginning of the war Guicciardini had preached caution to him incessantly, and looking for someone of greater authority to convince him, he had urged the Pope to do so in these words: 'His person is of too great value, and it is clear that the enemy seek his life with great determination: if we lose him, we shall be losing too much.'[9] And now they had lost him he wrote: 'It has pleased God to extinguish so much courage at the time when we most needed it.'[10]

These were not empty words; the lansquenets were encamped at Mirandola, a few miles from Modena, no longer disturbed by anyone. And from Modena the Lieutenant sent letter after letter, ever more pressing and worried, to the papal nuncio in Venice so that orders might be sent to the Duke of Urbino to cross the Po as he had always

said he would and now refused to do. After sending him messages without result, he reminded the Venetians of the obligations undertaken in
the terms of the League, concluding bitterly: 'His Holiness, if the Duke
does not pass, will be able to complain much more of his friends than
of his enemies.'[11] Then, as he saw small hopes from that direction, he
turned to the Marchese di Saluzzo, repeating the same thing: 'We have
the whole world against us and we are all alone. ...'[12] A voice crying in
the wilderness. These angry and anguished cries were to be for weeks
and months his daily lot.

On the 2nd December Machiavelli returned to him, sent by the
agitated Florentines to see what was going to happen after the lansquenets
crossed the river. But as everything was uncertain, the envoy was able
to get little out of that useless mission. He was not able to enjoy his
friend's company for long either, for the following day, the lansquenets
being at Guastalla, he had to ride to Parma to which it was feared the
enemy would turn. With the burden of so many cities to safeguard and
all the papal army to manage, it was perhaps taking too great a risk for a
Lieutenant to go and shut himself up in that threatened city as though to
revive the memory of that other memorable defence. This time he
would have with him the experienced troops of Giovanni de' Medici,
but the enemy army too would be much greater in numbers and
ferocity.

The affair certainly had some very strange aspects. A truce had been
concluded between the imperial forces and the Pope, who to observe it
had withdrawn his army from beyond the Po, giving up the war, and
now the imperials were carrying the war into his territory. If for some
time past truces between the two sides had not been truces *sui generis*,
one might have thought that those lansquenets were only passing
through the lands of the Church, and so Guicciardini pretended to think
in writing to Frundsberg, who replied in a reassuring manner; then,
having written again to complain of the damage done to the country,
Frundsberg's words became 'impertinent' like his actions.[13] From Rome
they kindly gave him permission to drive them out, but they did not
say with what forces, those he had being barely sufficient to hold the
cities.

The Duke of Urbino was not moving, and under various pretexts he
was not allowing the Marchese di Saluzzo to move either, though he
seemed more willing. Then the Lieutenant began to mingle threats with
his anguished appeals, and the most effective one was that he would

persuade the Pope to abandon those who were abandoning him and make an agreement with Caesar; it would not be difficult to persuade him, because Clement VII always kept some thread of agreement either on the distaff or on the skein-winder, and at that very moment he was spinning or winding something with the Viceroy of Naples and the General of the Franciscans. The allies of course could not like being left alone to face Charles V. At last the Marchese di Saluzzo with his men at arms, with four thousand Swiss and three thousand inferior Italian foot soldiers crossed the Po. But Guicciardini long remembered the anxieties of those days, or at least until worse ones came to make him forget them.

The first days of the year 1527 found him in Parma in council with the Marchese, with the Venetian Provveditore, and – wonderful to relate – with the Duke of Urbino, who, however, returned after a few days beyond the Po to Casalmaggiore, where he had left almost the whole of his army. They discussed what should be done in the light of news which had come through of enemy intentions, it having been heard that the lansquenets, giving up the tempting chance of besieging Parma or Piacenza, had decided to join the Spaniards in Lombardy and move on Florence. To tell the truth, the acute Lieutenant had had some suspicions long before receiving this warning, so much so that without saying any-thing to anyone, even the Pope, he had dangerously delayed putting into Piacenza a large garrison, so that that city might act as a lure for Frundsberg, hoping to make him drop his prey as soon as his claws were on it.[14] But when that suspicion had become a certainty, to the usual letters he wrote to Rome, to Venice, to France and elsewhere to waken the sleepers, he often had to add others to the Cardinal of Cortona, who was parsimoniously governing Florence from the Medici palace, exhorting him to fortify the city and lay in stores. Then he wished at all costs to bring to a place of safety his wife Maria with the three elder daughters (the youngest being too small to stand the hard journey), and had them move to Venice.[15]

Meanwhile the lansquenets in those low countries were held up by the rivers in spate and by the delays of the unprovided Spaniards. Their lives would have been yet more wretched if they had been harassed by that army left to idle its time away beyond the Po, or if the Duke of Ferrara, after giving them the artillery by which Giovanni de' Medici had been killed, had not helped them with money and supplies. Thus one could see every day how great Clement's error had been in not making a friend of him as he had been advised to do by those wiser than himself. It is true that the Pope according to his custom had not entirely broken off negotiations with Ferrara, and his Lieutenant was still willing. But since the Duke had received Caesar's investiture, the price had increased and the goods diminished. He wanted Modena at once without handing over a single ducat, in payment no longer of his alliance but of his neutrality; and then could one be sure of his neutrality if he were given Modena? When the Duke took leave of the emissary who had talked to him of the affair, he said to him: 'Commend me to Guicciardini and tell him I am a man of my word.'[16] And Guicciardini, though with more caution, again advised the Pope to conclude an agreement; but in those very days the Duke's ambassador was concluding with the Viceroy of Naples a pact binding him yet more closely with Charles V.

Thus the Germans of Frundsberg and the Spaniards of Bourbon who had also crossed the Po were able to rely heavily on the Duke's assistance, although the Duke provided them better with advice than with money, provisions and munitions – his principal counsel being that they should not waste their time around those cities, but leave the limbs to strike at the heart and the head – respectively Florence and Rome.

From Florence, where popular discontent grew with increased expense and danger, they again sent Machiavelli to find out from the Lieutenant what help the city could expect from a League which was costing so dear. Guicciardini, informed of his coming, was waiting for him at Parma with the greatest impatience, to the point of sending someone to hurry him on as he was travelling more slowly than usual.[17] This urgency was not to hear what his friend was coming to tell him, but on account of the things he wanted him to say to the Duke of Urbino. As the latter had finally made clear his plan for the conduct of the war, which was as usual a plan tinged with prudence and fear, he hoped that Machiavelli would help him to cow the intractable Duke. It may seem strange that with all the authority of his position the Lieutenant should have need of the support of one whom fortune had kept in so lowly a position. But Machiavelli was the envoy of a republic which was making a major contribution to the cost, and also the author of the *Art of War*, a book which, like all the commanders of the time, the Duke must certainly have regarded with respect.

They therefore went together to Casalmaggiore on the 7th February. I do not know what Machiavelli said to him, but the Duke seemed to be irritated by it,[18] perhaps because he hoped he would bring him, together with arguments and urgings, the promise of the longed for restitution of San Leo, given to the Florentines by Leo X to repay them for the expense they underwent in the conquest of Urbino. Lieutenant and envoy returned to the charge the following day but with small profit. The conclusion was this: if the enemy took the Pontremoli road, the Duke would precede them into Tuscany with the whole army, but if they took the Bologna road, only the army of the Church would be before them. The Duke with the Venetian army and the Marchese di Saluzzo with his own would follow.[19]

There was no moving him from this plan or from his camp. Instead Guicciardini and Machiavelli had to move from Parma because the enemy army seemed to be about to move. On the 24th they were at Scandiano, where in other days, as fateful as these for the lands of Italy, Boiardo had written:

> Mentre che io canto, o Dio Redentore,
> vedo la Italia tutta a fiamma e a foco. . . .

(While I sing, O Redeemer, I see all Italy in flames and fire. . . .) On the 27th they were camped with the Papal army near Bologna.

That same day the enemy crossed the Enza, but in the following days they did not make much progress, making camp first on one side of the Panaro and then on the other, held back in that rainy winter by the floods in the rivers and from the sky, demoralized by lack of supplies and money and everything else. While lansquenets and Spaniards were thus bogged down, Guicciardini and Machiavelli were not doing too badly in Bologna. In that city there was Cardinal Innocenzo Cybo, Legate and allied by marriage to the Pope, who as Legate and kinsman wanted to have his say about the war, and hinted that if the army went, he would go too. Irritated, the Lieutenant wrote to Rome that they should not consider him if they wished to please the Cardinal, for he would gladly be rid of the Lieutenantcy and he did not want trouble with the Cardinal who proposed to accompany the army 'not just for the form', but 'to interfere and ruin things'. He gives these reasons: 'In addition to the ordinary work of my charge I am not left so much leisure by the endless imprudence of these French . . . or the difficult nature of the Duke of Urbino, with whom one must always proceed astrolabe in hand, that I have any to spare for this other diversion.'[20]

Among the ordinary 'diversions' of messer Francesco was still that of working with pen and paper and perhaps 'astrolabe in hand' to get the Duke to cross the Po. He had to persuade the Venetians that, Duke or no Duke, they should in God's name send him their troops. With that reinforcement it would be easy to quell an enemy reduced to its present condition. To get out of this situation Bourbon met the Duke of Ferrara on the 5th March, receiving from him, however, only a few victuals, a few sappers, a little money and the usual advice to move on to Florence quickly: in that way he would be rid of them. After which Bourbon sent a messenger to Bologna asking for provisions and a safe conduct to go to Naples. When asked by which road, he replied through Romagna.

But neither that way nor any other could the enemy move. Lacking food, their lodgings are scattered, so that Guicciardini observes with melancholy: 'If we had enough forces here or the kind of leadership which could hem them in, they would not know where to turn. God forgive the Duke of Urbino who insisted on this division of forces.'[21] On the 13th March the Spanish and Germans mutiny; while George Frundsberg is trying to stop the tumult, he is struck down with apoplexy. As though this were not enough, after a few days and just on the eve of Spring there fell so much rain and snow that Guicciardini exclaimed: 'I never saw anything where God's assistance was more clear and more manifest.'[22]

But God helps men who help themselves, and those of the League were indeed doing nothing for themselves. The temporizing Duke was still temporizing. He said that the joining of the two armies was an invention of the Lieutenant's, and that he would not place 'the honour of his cuirass and his sword' in that man's hands.[23] 'That man', therefore, could only eat out his heart every day, but he had courage enough to do what was in his power. Machiavelli, who was still at his side and loved and admired him more and more, portrays him thus on the 30th March: 'The Lieutenant lives in great anguish and reorganizes and remedies everything he can, and God grant he may be able to do enough.'

Then, to complete the work, the Pope took a hand, making in Rome another of those pacts which had brought him into this situation: a truce for eight months, obliging him to pay the famished enemy hordes a certain sum of money and restore the lands of the Kingdom of Naples. The imperials were to remove their armies from the States of the Church. Then the Pope handed over the lands and, untaught by recent experience, dismissed the troops he had gathered near Rome after the insult he had suffered after another similar truce.

Bourbon on the other hand, protesting 'that necessity forced him since he could not make his soldiers obey him', came on with all his army. For this reason the Lieutenant left Bologna with the papal troops, 'for fear the enemy might try to capture the main road into Romagna'. The following day he lodged at Imola; on the 5th April at Forlì, preceding the Imperial army now near Imola. Meanwhile the tragi-comedy continued. The Pope believed the Viceroy who had gone on to stop Bourbon; Guicciardini believed less than the Pope but more than Machiavelli,[24] and wrote to his brother Luigi, just appointed gonfalonier, urging him to come to an agreement with the Viceroy if one were possible and bearable.[25] Meanwhile the allies would no longer help the Pope in the war, since the Pope had made peace without them, while Bourbon went on with the war and continued to advance. In desperation the Lieutenant wrote to the Florentine Eight: 'The French and Venetians . . . are full of confusion and mistrusts; I have no information here, nor do I know in what state things are . . . so I am more confused than anyone else and I have to guess, for I do not know that I ever saw greater wickedness or negligence.'[26]

In those anguished days, during which he saw the war he had wanted and prepared tumbling from ruin to ruin upon his own Florence which he loved more than anything on earth, his only comfort was the presence of Machiavelli. Their love of country, their greatness, their human qualities, both evident and hidden, had at last bridged the distance that nature and fortune had set between them. During those days they were drawn together by a common bond of anxiety and affection which warmed the last days of their friendship. On the 16th April Guicciardini wrote to Florence: 'I have decided with that little understanding which I have of my own, since I have not been helped by others, to send down to Florence all the forces I can dispose of';[27] and Machiavelli in a letter of the same date, in which the same things on peace and war are expressed almost in the same words, suddenly breaks out with this exclamation: 'I love messer Francesco Guicciardini, I love my native land more than my own soul.'[28]

With such fervour and with the few remaining troops, after leaving some to garrison the towns they had passed through, Machiavelli and Guicciardini were coming to succour the city. The latter had written in the last letter which has been quoted here: 'I have never seen any miracles, and I do not know whether I shall begin to see any now.' Instead he must have seen one in those very days: while he was hastening towards Florence, the Duke of Urbino, perhaps coming to life on account of the restitution of San Leo, lately wrested from the Pope by the Lieutenant, was moving south with the Venetian army by long marches.

Francesco reached Florence on the 23rd April. He expected to find the city discontented and turbulent; indeed it seemed practically in revolt. Discontent was nourished by the war which had lasted much longer and cost much more and gone a great deal worse than had been foreseen, with the remarkable result that the enemy was now at their gates. They brooded over the vexation of being kept for the eventual rule of two Medici bastards. For the moment there was the vexation of feeling crushed under the stingy and uncouth government of the Cardinal of Cortona. Governed by a 'subject'! As a remedy and reinforcement the Pope had sent Cardinal Niccolò Ridolfi his cousin, but allied as he was with all those great families who desired liberty, and desiring it himself, his arrival had just the opposite effect of what was hoped for. Lately Cardinal Cybo had arrived from Bologna but he was useless because a stranger and a foreigner. Of the qualities of Cortona, 'who wants to do everything and does not know how to do anything', of the facts and remedies, Guicciardini wrote a full report to Rome on the day after his arrival, ending with the prophecy that the Medici state would soon be ruined if something were not done: 'And if there is to be any remedy, let it be soon for delay is dangerous.'[29] He was a true prophet and sooner than he expected.

The city being full of troops, the young men were demanding arms to defend it against both friend and foe. While on the morning of the 26th April the Piazza de' Signori seethed with impatient youth, a dispute between a soldier and a tradesman caused an uproar. In the tumult, as the Cardinals Cortona, Ridolfi, and Cybo had ridden out together with the two Medici boys and the Lieutenant to meet the Duke of Urbino, the cry was raised that the Medici had fled, and immediately the wilder elements rushed to the palace crying 'People and Liberty!' Excited by that onrush and the sound of those words, many citizens foremost in age and authority hastened there too. The Gonfalonier Luigi Guicciardini, afraid, and finding himself in such good company, at first looked favourably on that movement, then irreverent youth took a hand and forced the Signoria to declare the Medici banished and rebels, and the government restored as it was in Soderini's time.

The news was carried to the Cardinals and the Lieutenant while they were returning in company with the Duke of Urbino and the other captains. When they came into the square, they found the insurgents had shut themselves up in the Palace and were showing signs that they intended to defend it bravely. The Duke of Urbino had already set up his artillery in Vacchereccia to take the city by force with the certain danger that the flower of the citizens would be massacred and the city sacked, when 'Cardinal Ridolfi and messer Francesco Guicciardini for love of their country ... begged signor Federigo da Bozzolo to go into the Palace to discuss terms'.[30] He went and returned to advise taking the Palace by force. But Guicciardini went to him and cleverly persuaded his old adversary at Parma to take a different attitude and return with him to the Palace where he persuaded, not his brother who was already convinced, but all those principal citizens to accept a general pardon. It was a merciful act, but it is not surprising that both sides, instead of being grateful resented his good deed.[31]

After this short-lived revolution and with all the enhanced prestige of having foreseen it, he sent to Rome a long report on the behaviour and incapacity of Cortona, in which we read things of this kind: 'I have seen in the short time I have been here a thousand things like it, and all derive from the ignorance of this eunuch who spends the whole day in idle chatter and neglects important things ... and if he even governed well, it would be something, but the ignorant fellow does with this as with everything else. He does his best to fill himself and everyone else with suspicion, he makes everyone despair and he does not know himself what he is doing.'[32] These words would tell us enough – if we did not know already who the writer was – of his freedom of judgement and also of his great authority with the Pope which made it possible for him to speak in such terms of a cardinal.

Meanwhile, because the enemy was advancing without paying any attention to the truce, Pope Clement, who had woken up a bit, formed a fresh alliance with his allies who were afraid of losing him. Guicciardini was forming another with their ambassadors in Florence. While these things were being done and the commanders of the League were wasting time consulting one another, Bourbon was advancing with incredible speed. Leaving Valdarno on the 26th April while Florence was rioting, leaving his artillery and transport behind, and impeded neither by heavy rains nor by scarcity of victuals, on the 4th May he was at the walls of Rome.

On that day the Duke of Urbino with his whole army was still at Cortona; from Cortona, Guicciardini who was a day ahead of him with the papal troops, had written to the Datary the evening before informing him of the Duke's cautious plans and slow progress: the Duke did not see his way to go to Rome without at least another six thousand Swiss who were then being recruited in happy far-off Switzerland. The Lieutenant commented: 'It is an impossibility to shift him from this position.'[33] And at Rome the following day the enemy attacked on the side of the Borgo. Bourbon was killed by a shot from an arquebus in that first attack, but they were not held up by his death; they were not commanded by him but by the lust for plunder. Pulling down the walls with their bare hands, undeterred by the slaughter of their comrades, after two hours of fighting they forced their way into the city, where all resistance having ceased there began a long unexampled desecration of everything human and divine. The Pope, as on the last occasion, had barely time to shut himself up in Castel Sant' Angelo.

Guicciardini heard of the capture of the Borghi when he was at Città della Pieve, where a further day had been lost, 'because the Swiss wanted to hold a parade'; but he still hoped the Trastevere would hold out. Only on the 10th at the crossing of the Paglia he received the 'most cruel news of Rome'[34] from Rangoni, who alone had hastened on without however managing to get ahead of Bourbon. Guicciardini loved Italy for everything that name then signified: as an Italian and as a Christian; in spite of his just anger and bitter contempt he venerated Rome; he loved that unfortunate Pope, betrayed and outraged like the Christ he represented on earth. One may therefore imagine what his feelings were as he returned along those roads he had travelled the year before with so hopeful a heart, while the desecration of the sacred city continued.

It was spring, as it had been the first time; the season and the places brought back to him one by one the thoughts he had had then, making the contrast more cruel and his bitterness more intense. However many reasons he industriously sought in events and in himself, however much he examined the thoughts and feelings which had moved him, no matter if he found himself innocent, he could not forgive himself for having opened the way to that apocalyptic tragedy. From Montefiascone he came to Orvieto: he wrote to the Eight: 'If they knew all, they would pity me, for every day I die a hundred deaths.'[35] As they went on, there came every day more terrible news of the horrors at Rome. And he, who had grown up among the Friar's children, who had collected in his own hand the Friar's prophecies,[36] must have heard, echoing ceaselessly in his oppressed soul, terrifying in its aptness, the prophecy of Girolamo Savonarola.

Chapter 17

FROM THE LIEUTENANCY TO
FINOCCHIETO

H AVING lost Rome, Clement VII had now only to lose Florence, where Medici rule rested only on papal power. Thus on the 16th May the city achieved without disorder what it had sought in vain with violence twenty days earlier. It was helped by the wisdom of a few great citizens (among them Niccolò Capponi, Filippo Strozzi, Francesco Vettori, supported by Cardinal Ridolfi himself), and the weakness of the Cardinal of Cortona, who understanding what was generally felt, agreed to depart with his two Medici bastards. It is true that subsequently, regretting his action too late, he refused to hand over the fortresses of Pisa and Leghorn. Thus after losing the state for the Medici, he also lost them that little good will they had earned by this more or less free gift of liberty; he had given up the state and all its territories and grudged two forts.

The day this peaceful revolution was carried out in Florence, Francesco Guicciardini, sorely tried though he was by the continual labour over that useless army and tortured by his regrets, wrote from Orvieto to the Florentine magistrates seeking money for the soldiers' pay. Ironically in his ignorance of what had taken place, he used warmer and more heart-felt words than usual in favour of the Pope: 'I beg you to consider it well and believe this conclusion that, if the Pope is not set free, there will be no remedy for the affairs of the city; therefore think how to provide and without delay.'[1] Not knowing that they had already found a remedy and desired nothing less than the Pope's liberty, two days later he again returned to the charge with the Eight and more insistently with the Cardinal of Cortona: 'I fear that you are so intent on guarding the Palace and the public square that you forget everything else; and yet if the poor Pope is lost, these will be valueless and the soul of the body lost.'[2]

That the body now had another soul Guicciardini did not learn until the 21st in a letter from the Eight. In reply he used none of the congratulatory terms which the case should have demanded, instead he closed his cool reply with a demand to be replaced as leader of the troops in Florentine pay. Being with that army as 'the Pope's man', he would remain only until the Castle where the Pope was besieged was either relieved or taken.[3] In the interests of the Pope and of the expedition he made every effort during those days to stimulate the citizens' enthusiasm for the League and prevent the allies from becoming mistrustful of the Florentine change of government. He never forgot either to repeat his demands for money for the soldiers and release from his duties for himself. But with the change of government, the style of his letters too has changed. It is no longer the haughty Lieutenant of the Pope who is master of the city, but a citizen like any other who writes to the magistrates.

In the military field too things were greatly changed for him. Hated by the commanders for his strictness and arrogance, their hatred was no longer, as before, held in check by authority and fear. One of the most insubordinate, the Count of Caiazzo, 'in Roman territory, when he saw the Pope was lost, stopped one morning on the road to kill him [Guicciardini]'.[4] He escaped by a miracle. With the Duke of Urbino too, things had deteriorated after the Pope's downfall. In council he had now to measure and count his words; he relieved his feelings in letters to his friends, he begged that they should be kept secret, as he feared that the Duke, hearing what he said, might play him false.[5]

Indeed it would have been hard to write letters and discuss that war without speaking ill of one who, having done his best from its earliest days to ruin it, was at the end still doing so. After wasting endless time in some capricious diversion, in moving up to the walls of Rome he showed just as much fear as he had at Milan. And yet only a few troops would have sufficed to overcome the enemy within the walls, scattered through the city in search of loot and women. It would have taken very little to relieve the Castle. Instead the Duke, after temporizing with 'a thousand arts and delays, now showing that he wanted to advance and now that it would be madness to do so', demanded, to attack Rome, twenty thousand Italian infantry, a further levy of sixteen thousand Swiss not counting the five thousand he had, and three thousand sappers and a large force of artillery and so on and so forth – all to move against twelve thousand infantry whom their officers were unable to drag away from pillage, gluttony and lechery. Such cowardice appearing incredible, a doubt again arose which Guicciardini had expressed when they camped before Milan: that the Duke wished to take revenge on the second Medici Pope for the war and despoliation inflicted on him by the first.[6] Perhaps truth lay somewhere in between: under that old resentment, love and pity for the unhappy Clement were not powerful enough to change his cowardice into gallant courage.

Meanwhile the Pope remained without relief, his prison became even more tightly closed and without remedy, when the Spaniards and Germans, having looted all the wealth of Rome and despoiled all the Romans, turned their attention to the treasures and persons locked up in the Castle. Having opened attempts at an agreement with the enemy, Clement was temporizing because of the outrageous conditions imposed on him, and a last hope of being rescued by the allied army encamped only a few miles off. But no one worried about him, apart from Guicciardini who wrote to him daily, sending off several copies of each letter in the hope that one might reach him.[7] Guicciardini did not only write to him, he wrote to everyone whose help he could hope for: to the Florentines, who might be moved, not by compassion they did not feel, but by a victory of the League which was in their own interests; to England, to the protonotary Gambara, to rouse in the Pope's defence that King who styled himself Defender of the Faith; to France, to Robert Acciaioli, to move the Most Christian King to rescue the Vicar of Christ, and finally to the King himself.

Indeed he did not only send to the King the heartfelt and pressing letter of the 29th May,[8] he even wrote to him in verse, he who had always had so little to do with the muses! In fact the *Supplicazione d'Italia al Cristianissimo Re Francesco I* was written then, in *terza rima* in the style of the old popular 'laments'.[9] This is a composition with a notable historical and human value, but very little literary merit, except as possibly the most political poem in our literature. Machiavelli, who even when writing in prose is a poet, when he writes in verse, occasionally finds some good lines, but in this *Supplicazione* of Guicciardini's, which is as long as two whole cantos of the *Divine Comedy*, there is not one really good line.

Our pages have shown for the first time that messer Francesco had already written some things in verse, and curiously enough at the end of another invocation to the same King; but the scholars of the last century did not know it, and they must have been so astonished by the sight of Guicciardini turning poet without warning, that they expressed doubts of the authenticity of the *Supplicazione* – which is beyond question – in spite of the authority of contemporary copies, one of them among Guicciardini's own papers.[10] This may seem almost a phenomenon to us, but its very singularity must speak to us of the author's agitation during those days of anguish. Although it may seem more likely that he composed it like so much else, merely to relieve his own feelings, it is not entirely unlikely that he, knowing the King's unrequited love for the Muses, planned to send it to him and perhaps actually did so.

But the succour invoked in prose and verse could not come in time. On the 8th June the unfortunate Pope, seeing that no one would help him and that the army of the League was in fact retreating towards Viterbo, capitulated under the hardest conditions: he handed over to the imperial armies Ostia, Civitavecchia, Parma, Piacenza and Modena; he paid four hundred thousand ducats in several instalments to ransom himself and the cardinals. Meanwhile he remained a prisoner in the Castle until he had paid the first hundred and fifty thousand, after that he was to go to Gaeta or Naples to await the Emperor's will; he gave as hostages seven great personages, among them three prelates and two close relatives: Iacopo Salviati and Lorenzo Ridolfi.

With this capitulation Guicciardini's term as Lieutenant came to an end, that is the shadow of it that remained. Unwilling to stay for any consideration in the field as commissioner for the Florentines, he importuned more than ever the Eight and the Eight's superior. For at that time they had elected gonfalonier for a year Niccolò Capponi, one of the greatest and best men in the city, wise and moderate, though he had been among the principal authors of the eviction of the Medici. Congratulating him on his election, Guicciardini had written that it would be more accurate to congratulate the city. The two men were made to understand each other and did so at once. Guicciardini, bound to the Medici only by that complex of 'private feelings', which also included duty, loyalty, gratitude and affection, agreed with the anti-Medici

Capponi in political ideas, and with regard to their relations with the Pope, they agreed over the means if not the end. Thus he was, as always, sincere in writing to the Gonfalonier: 'I love the popular government and the freedom of the city as well as anyone else can',[11] and he was equally sincere when he wrote to the Pope, barely a fortnight later: 'I desire His Holiness to know, that in spite of the events which have taken place in Florence and anything further which may happen, I am more ready than ever to serve him.'[12] And yet the Pope and his former subjects were now in opposing camps, the one nursing silent rancour, the other showing overt suspicion.

Guicciardini and Capponi, separated in fact by that gulf but united in wisdom, in goodwill, in patriotism, did all they could so that the affairs of the new government should proceed as they had begun: without bloodshed and without hatred. One did his best to moderate the wilder sections of the population, the other, after condemning the mean fraud of the fortresses and having used his influence to have them handed over, endeavoured to reassure his fellow citizens as to the Pope's good intentions towards the new government while reminding Capponi on the Pope's behalf of the necessary and reasonable conditions for that goodwill to be maintained: 'His Holiness begs that you should not work against his interests, for he will always be ready to please the city in so far as he can, and he would not like any suspicion to be aroused that he might do otherwise.'[13] I would not swear that Clement, that great deceiver, was sincere on this occasion. Even at that time the man who had been his Lieutenant but was doing his best to keep faith with the new government, wrote privately to the Gonfalonier: 'It has been said that there is an article in the agreement between His Holiness and the Spaniards which deals with the affairs of Florence . . . I did not wish to write to the Ten so as not to make trouble needlessly, but I thought it well that Your Lordship should know all that I do.'[14]

In short he wished to be a good citizen, and he was also careful not to offend the popular party, to evade the mistrust he could already feel weighing on him. He could speak freely to Capponi: 'I desire all the more to be freed from my office, because should such suspicions begin to arise, my actions would be suspect there, though wrongly so, and any least thing would suffice to bring me down.'[15] Indeed in Florence they were even more anxious to dismiss him than he was to be dismissed, but they did not dare to arouse the suspicions of the League.[16] In the end they wrote that Raffaello Girolami would come to replace him; Girolami arrived on the 25th June, and after presenting him to the captains, Guicciardini returned to Florence.

Varchi writes that he returned from the army with Machiavelli.[17] However, his friend having accompanied him as far as Orvieto, had had to go to Civitavecchia;[18] and as the revolution had then taken place, he returned thence to Florence and died there on the 21st June. Guicciardini, therefore, did not know of his death until his return. The sorrow he must certainly have felt (even though no sign or word has remained) may have been lost among the many troubles which increasingly oppressed him.

After the 'great and perpetual good fortune' he had enjoyed until then, as he laments in his writings,[19] the hour of misfortunes had come for him too. As soon as he returned the pinpricks had begun, then came more painful thrusts.[20] In the city the Optimates were still supreme, led by the moderate Capponi and also supported, as a lesser evil, by the wiser *Palleschi* (Medici supporters), without increasing the power of that party, but rather weakening it by increasing the suspicions of the supporters of liberty; but already the *Popolani* were champing at the bit, for the most fervent of whom the ancient and eloquent name of *Arrabbiati* (lit. Wrathful) had been revived. The Gonfalonier had to reckon with them and so had Guicciardini, often alas literally. In Florence levies and exactions had always been a weapon to use against the enemies of the government. The Medici had been masters at that game, and now their followers were to enjoy the same treatment. The former Lieutenant had barely returned from the army when he was hit by a levy decided on the 11th June, in which 'the friends of the Medici were to pay the greater sums';[21] on the 14th June he was included in the twenty citizens who were to lend the handsome sum of fifteen hundred florins each. In October he was again on the list for another forced loan, and that was not the end of the matter.[22] The fine gold ducats earned in all those years were flowing out of messer Francesco's strong-boxes. And there was worse to come.

When he was with the army he had written to the Pope: 'I shall also be investigated by them, as I am informed, on account of the management of the war.'[23] He was indeed, though his fear and displeasure were worse than the investigation. Accused by public rumour of having grossly defrauded over the money for the soldiers' pay, he had to render an account not only of the ordinary expenses, but also (against all precedent) the extraordinary ones, for which it was not always possible to have receipts.[24] From a diligent inquiry by the first Syndics elected 'to examine the accounts of those who have handled moneys of the Commune', he emerged without stain and without any sanctions;[25] nor was he troubled by those elected afterwards. But his touchy pride, the attitude of his fellow citizens, the hatred and suspicion he felt growing around him, made him fearful for a long time and caused him to prepare his defences.

If this insult offended and wounded him, there was perhaps something which troubled him more sorely, and with bitterness he poured out his feelings in his secret papers: it was finding himself reduced 'from an extreme pinnacle of honours, reputation, and affairs of the greatest importance to the opposite extreme of a life, idle, abject, without public function of any kind'; so that he admitted to himself that he felt ashamed when there passed through Florence some foreign notable who had seen his former eminence and now found him 'without dignity, without occupation, inferior in his own city to the least citizen'.[26] Such were the sorrows he confided to those papers; the more he saw himself humbled and neglected, the more he felt a longing to be 'esteemed and honoured, to keep his reputation fresh, and as it were to be distinguished by his fellow men . . . for one cannot deny that it is a fine and blessed thing to be highly respected by one's fellows, and in no other way does it seem that we can resemble God'.[27]

To emerge from this situation which seemed unbearably shameful and abject, he would have liked to go to Romagna where his brother Iacopo was still substituting for him. He was held up only by the lack of means, as he wrote: 'If I had the means to stay there even for a month, I could hope to arrange things in such a way that the province might be kept faithful to the Apostolic See and the League.'[28] The 'provision' he wanted was the *braccio ordinario*, that is, the minimum armed guard without which he could not have stayed there even in more peaceful times, but the guard could not be maintained without money, and even the source of money had been lost.

Not, however, that he was entirely cut off from public affairs. Now he was working for a meeting at Ravenna or elsewhere of the few cardinals still at liberty, to provide for the needs of the Apostolic See. He discussed this with Ridolfi who had stayed quietly in Florence after the revolution, finding him 'most ready to join with the others', while Cybo would not hear of leaving his sister-in-law and the pleasures of Massa where his stay was pleasant if not very honourable.[29] Now relying on the fact that he was still the Pope's Lieutenant and that others would recognize him as such, he wrote to the Governor of Parma to save the city from the imperials and indeed from an apostolic commissioner who had gone with them charged with seeing the city handed over. The city he had defended with such obstinacy in happier times, was well worth ink and paper. But then he would have gone out to look for work.

Sometimes, however, work came to look for him. One day a letter reached him from none other than M. de Lautrec, who crossing at last into Italy to rescue the Pope, the League, and the honour of France, now informed him of his military plans. It was certainly a great day for him amid all that greyness. If such a personage still sought him out as in the good days, he had not vanished from the memory and the esteem of men! Lautrec had written to him about those plans with the idea certainly that he might inform the Pope. Since he could not, he told Capponi to whom he at once sent the letter (actually the original, asking him to return it) so that he should show it to the members of the government.[30] They should see that the Pope and the League, *his* League, were not quite finished. And neither was he, Guicciardini.

But these were rare glimmers of light in the darkness. The plague, which had been at work for some time in martyred Rome, now began its sad harvest in Florence. For Guicciardini it was a further reason, and more persuasive than the others, to stay away from the city. He had retired to Finocchieto, the villa which was the subject of Machiavelli's jests,[31] and thence he followed wearily, as a spectator ever more divorced from the game, the belated preparations which were being made for the Pope's liberation. That small concilium of cardinals was at last meeting in Parma, since Cybo, Passerini and Ridolfi had rightly refused to go to Avignon, as the Kings of France and England would have liked. There were the early successes of Lautrec at Alessandria, Genoa and Pavia, where the shame of the famous defeat was cruelly avenged; then his dilatory behaviour after crossing the Po on his way to Rome at the earnest request of Cardinals Cybo and Ridolfi. Then came the entry of the Duke of Ferrara into the League, now it was too late, with all the conditions he was bold enough to ask for, including the Church's renunciation of Reggio and Modena.

He saw the mood of the city worsen, he saw the *Arrabbiati* earn their name. Yet, whether out of affection for liberty and the legitimate government or simple prudence, not only had he behaved as a model citizen, but had also shown that he sincerely desired the city to remain free. He had written to Cardinal Salviati, who was as we know a relative of the Pope's: 'I am sure all will be well as long as the city is convinced that His Holiness at no time contemplates changing the present government. And this is what His Holiness affirms, and he should be supported in it by all his friends and servants, for there lies his honour and profit both with God and with the world.'[32] To the protonotary Gambara, he wrote: 'His Holiness's intention is never to change the government in any circumstances, and if he thought otherwise, it would be a very imprudent counsel.'[33]

It is true that he had written this in July, and since then much water had flown under the bridges of the Arno, water ever more turbulent and dangerous. Things had gone worse for Capponi, for the Optimates, for himself; so much so that, having in August bought a fine property at Santa Margherita a Montici with a great house,[34] very useful to him since he had previously given up the big house in the city in favour of his brother Girolamo,[35] in September he bestowed it upon his four daughters, 'seeing everything in danger, partly because of world affairs, partly because of the humour of Florence'.[36] Further misfortune struck at him through his daughters, for Lucrezia died aged thirteen. And on the 22nd October the unhappy father wrote to his brother Luigi: 'Tomorrow I shall return to Florence where I expect Maria, but with little happiness because we have lost our Lucrezia. . . . How unexpected a misfortune!'[37]

At Finocchieto he had found the background which best suited his melancholy. We are reminded of Machiavelli's description: 'For three miles around nothing can be seen that pleases. . . . The rooms are small, the windows high: it is just like the bottom of a tower . . . and withal it is so buried in the hills that the best view is no more than half a mile.' Buried among those hills and in his grief, he found all his consolation, in his gloomy tower, in paper and ink. Indeed the first thing he writes is a *Consolatoria*,[38] which is just what it should be, issuing from his pen, a quintessence of Guicciardini's spirit.

In this unique piece of prose the writer begins by acknowledging that religion and philosophy would administer most efficacious remedies to him who would cure troubles much greater than his own, but as he lacks the courage to adopt them, he has to take a 'less elevated' consolation in practical comforts 'according to the nature of men and the world', that is, the consolations brought him by his cool reasonings. The things which pain him, the causes of his 'intense grief', are the same ones we have mentioned above: loss of honours and money, a great compassion for the miserable fate of the Pope his benefactor, the mistrust and hatred in which he is held by his fellow citizens, the calumny that he had stolen the money for the soldiers' pay, and allowed them to make up for it with theft, violence and rape; his remorse at having advised the Pope to enter that accursed war from which all his own troubles and those of the Pope and Italy had stemmed.

But here at last are the consolations. Even in those years he describes as happy, he has always regarded honours and earnings as transitory things, because they are dependent on the life of a Pope. And then his sorrow at the Pope's misfortune would not be such as to keep him 'in that great and continual unhappiness' which he feels, and which 'in the course of a few weeks would diminish, for where sorrow arises only from compassion or affection in the one who grieves and there is no foundation of self-interest . . . it easily disappears of its own accord'.[39] The ill-fame acquired with his fellow citizens, being based on an utterly false calumny, can in no way perturb him. Finally, he must not be tormented with remorse for that war (here is the sore point), for reason shows him that he advised what reason demanded, nor should any wise man be condemned for an outcome contrary to his judgement, 'otherwise the counsellors of princes would be subjected to too hard conditions, if they were obliged to bring into their counsels not only human arguments and considerations, but also either astrologers' opinions or prognostications of spirits or prophecies of friars'.[40] The prophecy of Girolamo Savonarola still weighed upon his mind.

Therefore with these practical reasonings he comforts himself at least on paper; making a virtue of necessity he forces himself to adapt to that life of idleness, which was such a novelty for him. On other occasions when he was all greatness and business, he noted in his papers that all have words of praise for idleness and tranquillity, but in fact they prefer to labour in affairs as long as they can, for honour and profit.[41] Now that this maxim has turned against him in misfortune, it has an ironical sound. But those same papers supply another maxim in which he once admitted having sought in affairs honour and profit, and having achieved it beyond his greatest hopes, had not found in them the satisfaction he had expected.[42] He now tests this maxim too, like the first, and concludes that, having tried affairs, the time had come to try idleness. Lucky for him if in this he may acquire as great a fame as he did in the other: in the comedy of life those who act one part well are worthy of applause, and all the more so if they can act two very different parts well. Better still in his own words: 'If in that character you have represented up till now you have earned the highest praise, there will be even higher praise from those who judge you to have done exceedingly well in two different characters.'[43] A work of this kind was bound to contain some kind of rhetorical ornament, but the sorrowful lamentations which the memory of 'great and perpetual felicity' enjoyed in the past, and the contemplation of present unhappiness, wring from that closed, hard, proud man, that cold reasoner, are both sincere and pathetic.[44]

Reasonings can convince but not console, and those of the *Consolatoria* had not the power to calm Guicciardini's tormented spirit. As an exercise if not as a preparation for the reality, he imagined that he had been called by popular hatred before the court of the *Quarantia* (Forty) lately set up for State cases, and he composed a very long *Oratio accusatoria*, attributed to an imaginary accuser,[45] in reply to which he also began a *Defensoria*, but he did not finish it.[46]

A noted historian of our literature finds these two exercises 'unexpected'.[47] I would not call them that, because the essence of them is typical of Guicciardini. Even more so is their form, which is again that of double and contradictory discourse where two opposing theses are discussed with impartial rigour. Such antitheses, which had passed from the Sophists to Thucyidides, to Livy and to the humanists, were extremely dear to Guicciardini.[48] His taste for them and the habit of composing them may have grown out of legal exercises, and this, together with his strong inclination towards dialectics, caused them in his hands to return somewhat to their Sophist origins. But it is true also that he used them according to his own genius to dissect human actions and thought, and therefore in his hands they did not remain mere empty exercises.

That he greatly enjoyed these double discourses, is seen by the frequent use he made of them throughout his life in the treatment of the most diverse subjects, and from his persistence and pleasure in composing them, which is clear from the minute elaboration of the text. The *Accusatoria* especially is more elaborate (the *Defensoria* slightly less so), not only on account of an infinite number of corrections, but also in substantial rewriting which renders it, as is written in the margin of the autograph, *causa stili melius ordinata* [better ordered for the style], whilst the *Consolatoria*, written straight off and corrected in a desultory manner, is certainly not well ordered.

It cannot surprise us if rhetoric, to which our cold realist sometimes gives way more than Machiavelli the poet does, finds in the oratorical style of these two addresses a more fruitful ground than in the *Consolatoria*. The substance of this is also partly common to the *Accusatoria*, where the most debated crime is still the war and its consequences; but then the whole of Guicciardini's life is passed through a fine sieve, from his restless adolescence to the famous 'Friday revolt'. This is turbid matter which the scholar must in his turn sift with caution, nor can one take as accurate everything that the imaginary accuser cooks up over the fires of polemic and rhetoric. But it seems to me that certain very special and circumstantial things would never have occurred to Guicciardini if he had not found them in some recess of his memory or his soul: from his adolescent anxieties to the quite recent desire to return to Lombardy as Lieutenant 'to show himself *in excelsis* to those people whom he had governed for so many years';[49] and then, coming to the time of the unhappy idleness, those dreams at night 'full of nothing but guards, messengers, governments, armies, noblemen'.[50] Thus up to a point Toffanin is quite right when he sees throughout these pages 'a tremor of obsessive ambition'.[51]

The most atrocious crime, though not the most recent, is kept for the last, and it is of having driven the Pope to that ruinous war. 'Because of you Hungary has fallen a prey to the infidel, because of you Rome was put to the sack with such cruelty, such universal ruin . . . , because of you heretics command the holy places, because of you they have thrown the relics to the dogs. You are the plague, the fire, the ruin of the whole world.'[52] Thus all thoughts bring him back to that melancholy abyss. In the Guicciardini of the *Consolatoria* and the *Accusatoria*, just as in his refuge in Mugello, 'all the exits lead downhill'.

Chapter 18

THE 'IDLENESS' OF S. MARGHERITA A MONTICI: THE 'COSE FIORENTINE' AND THE 'RICORDI'

WITH cooler autumn weather the plague eased off. Every day still, twenty or thirty people died, but there was hope that the first winter winds from the mountains would end it all. Guicciardini, therefore, began to think of moving nearer to Florence to the villa bought recently near Santa Margherita a Montici. He had enough of the hermit melancholy of Finocchieto which, in spite of his humourless defence of it, seemed to him also a 'strange place to live':[1] he was afraid, if he had to stay there, of 'dying of melancholy' according to Machiavelli's forecast.

In the villa of Santa Margherita, before he bought it, someone had died of the plague, but during those recent months he had diligently seen to having it all 'cleaned and fumigated' several times; then, like the prudent man he was, he had sent three families one after the other to live there, and had also had several people sleep in the plague victim's room as a test before having it closed.[2] Such things may seem hardly charitable, but in those days were commonplace. In any case, though we are indeed all equal before God, the life of those peasants cannot be regarded as equal in value to that of the first modern historian, who had not yet written his masterpiece. Having taken these precautions, on the 1st December he left the 'gloomy tower' to go with all his family into the new and more attractive dwelling.

188

At the very same time the Pope too was being freed from his prison. Under the safeguard of the treaty but also taught by past experience he left the Castle in disguise and took refuge in Orvieto, where he immediately regained, with liberty, his power, authority and a good part of his former reputation. All the same one cannot believe that Guicciardini ever had the slightest desire to go to join the man who had raised him so high and might so easily restore him to his former good fortune. After the change of government in Florence, nothing can have worried him more than the prospect of having to choose one day between his country and the man to whom he was bound by gratitude, interest and affection. The Pope's liberation brought him nearer to that parting of the ways, but if he had had to choose then, even while he felt offended by the popular state, he would still have chosen his country. He not only revered Florence, he loved her with a proud and filial love, and also with a less pure feeling, composed of all the affections and private interests which bound him to the city. If he had then gone to shelter in the shadow of the Pope, that great shadow which was already beginning to threaten the budding freedom of Florence, he would have given fresh cause for suspicion and harmed himself and the city.

For besides his private interests, or at least so mixed and confused with them that they could not easily be separated, he had the certainty that his wisdom could have helped the Republic much more than those courageous but inexperienced young men. He had no share at all in the government, though greater than any of them, nor any seat other than that in the Great Council, where one found, to put it crudely, even the dogs and the swine, and yet he attended there to do his duty as a citizen even though he could not enter the Palace without being regarded with suspicion, or avoided.[3] However, the Gonfalonier Capponi, disregarding the distrust and hatred he drew down on himself, often called him into the restricted councils or alone into his own room.[4] Florence and the little which might yet be saved of its liberties had no other hope than the wisdom of these two men. Capponi knew it and wished to strengthen the ties between them, giving Guicciardini's daughter Simona in marriage to his eldest son Piero.[5] Guicciardini knew this too, and to support the work of the Gonfalonier for his country he had abandoned his beloved Pope. Or perhaps he thought he could also help the Pope by helping his country.

Meanwhile, being used to great employment, he had to fill that huge void, and occupy his leisure. He had had enough of consolatory, accusatory, defensory letters. He had left those melancholy thoughts on the melancholy slopes of Finocchieto. One cannot exchange the bare mountains for the Florentine hills, created by nature and man together as a work of art, without also a change of ideas. With a new year, a new house, a new life, he sets to work on a new book. In the *Consolatoria* he had exhorted himself to seek 'high esteem' in a time of idleness through 'letters and knowledge of the history of events'. For anyone who possessed these two, no enterprise was then regarded as so worthy and exalted as to write the history of one's own nation, and he was fortunate in being a native of Florence. On Leonardo Bruni, first and greatest of all, on Poggio Bracciolini, on Bartolomeo Scala, the city had bestowed singular honours for their labours. Lately Niccolò Machiavelli had risen somewhat above misfortune and oblivion as a result of having continued the historiographical traditions of the Florentine chancellors. Francesco Guicciardini, having diligently examined their histories with that acumen of his which opened up and flayed like an anatomist's knife, felt capable of writing a history which should be better than any of them. It might win over his fellow citizens, overcome the cruelty which excluded him from government.

His could not be a history full of vain, high-sounding words, influenced by classical models like the works of the humanist chancellors, nor written to discover or prove brilliant theories like those of his unhappy friend. The history he had written as a young man contained little more than the facts which he remembered himself, and the form was unliterary and unpretentious, so he did not regard it highly. The work of his maturity was to be something quite different. For the form he would follow the models of antiquity, but for the narration of facts which he wanted to make very detailed, for often human actions spring from the smallest seeds, he was already thinking of a method quite new, all his own, extraordinarily modern. Before him, caring only for literary elegance, for eloquence, historians used only a few sources, regardless of whether they were good or bad. He would collect and compare and weigh up all those he could find. Never before had sources been used in such a way. Modern historical criticism takes its first steps in these *Cose fiorentine*, as I called them when I first discovered and published them.[6]

To compose this new work, the first perhaps that he may have thought to publish, he therefore adopted a method he had never used before. He writes in thick notebooks of very large format leaving unusually wide margins in which he notes doubts, judgements, discrepancies of sources, facts to be added or corrected. Some of these are real critical notes in which we find him using extracts, mostly indicated by abbreviations as we would do today, from Villani, Malespini (this, however, is a source he rejects as soon as he has tried it, without waiting for the nineteenth-century German critics), Marchionne Stefani, Leonardo Bruni, Poggio, Gino and Neri Capponi, Domenico Buoninsegni, Goro Dati, Niccolò Machiavelli; then the non-Florentine historians: Piccolomini, Biondo, Platina, Sabellico and even Froissart. It is an apparatus of sources extraordinarily varied and abundant for those times, largely consisting of unpublished texts. He makes use of all these authors exercising his alert critical judgement as a modern historian might do. On Marchionne Stefani he notes in the margin: 'Note that *M* [which is the sign he gives him] is a very faithful chronicler of the events of those times, I mean of events outside Florence . . . but for internal affairs he is partisan.' Then, not satisfied with these historians, we find him looking for contemporary sources: the *Commissioni* of Rinaldo degli Albizzi, which he (and not Ammirato as was believed until recently) is the first historian to use, and those, still unpublished, of Michele Castellani, and a great mass of papers drawn from his own domestic archives.[7]

With this method of writing history he was obliged to begin at a time not too far distant which could provide him with reliable and abundant sources. He therefore begins in the year 1375 with the war against Gregory XI, called the War of the Eight Saints, in which the economic and social seeds were sown which led three years later to the Revolt of the Ciompi. It is a fascinating starting point, and it is hard to say whether it was chosen by foresight or a strange coincidence at a time when the danger of another war between the Florentines and the Pope was still distant. He prefaced the narration with 'a kind of brief summary' (yet it occupies the whole of the first book), where with great acuity and always with remarkable modernity he deals in various chapters with the origins, the factions, the population, the city boundary and its other circumstances.

He wanted the architecture and style of such a work to be of a nobility and magnificence suited to it. If we compare it with his youthful *History* the difference of purpose and the greater seriousness of the author are clear from the difference of the form. He returned – after Machiavelli's unique attempt – to the classical annalistic form with all

its faults and all its advantages. The classical orations gave him a good
opportunity to indulge his taste for speeches on opposing sides. Indeed
at one point these discourses take over and the narrative in the end
seems only a supporting framework. At another moment he writes out
the speeches only, in anticipation of the narrative. Characteristically,
however, these orations are not mere decorative rhetoric, but an often
effective means of giving a clearer explanation of the facts described.
This task, at which he worked with great speed, take shape on paper and
in his mind like the foundations, the main walls, the bases of arches in a
great edifice. Everything speaks to him of Florence: the books and
papers which he peruses, the Palace where he goes to do his duty as a
citizen or to talk to his friend the Gonfalonier, the enchanting view of
the city which he sees from his hillside.

In the study therefore the pile of notebooks grows in which he drafts
these *Cose fiorentine*. From time to time for a change he turns to another
work: a secret book, indeed the secret book *par excellence*, which costs
him less labour and which he loves better. These are the *Ricordi*,[8]
where throughout his 'active life' in the labour of business or in brief
moments of rest he distilled the essence of his experience, his thoughts,
his feelings. It is not true that such origins lend to these fragments merely
personal and local value.[9] They date from different times and occasions
and circumstances, while the spirit informing them is always the same:
this little book of the *Ricordi* is a mirror of many facets which reflect
differently but faithfully the same image.

And this is the image which we have perceived in other works of his,
in his correspondence, his actions, in the portrait painted by Bugiardini
and in that composed by an anonymous astrologer: 'acute investigator
of facts', impassive in his reasoning, always and at all costs objective. In
these *Ricordi*, to which their brevity gives greater force, the writer
sometimes gives the impression of an anatomist seeking with his knife,
among nerves and muscles, the secret of the human soul. Under that
knife Guicciardini the man, and mankind itself as seen by him, appear
more moral and at the same time more limited than Machiavelli the
man, or than Man seen through his eyes. Honest and incorruptible himself, sincere and open, when it is not absolutely necessary to dissimulate,
greedy of honour rather than money, yet giving to money an importance which has appeared excessive both to moralists and romantics;
courageous but not more so than may be compatible with prudence and
reason; hating the vices of priests so that he could have 'loved Martin

Luther as himself', but not to the point of abandoning the service of priests. Like Machiavelli he believes that 'too much religion ruins the world because it makes men effeminate', but as for himself in spite of that and in spite of that hatred, he is religious and catholic to the marrow of his bones, both by education and tradition.

This, therefore, is the Guicciardini whom we have come to know day by day, page by page; but there is one thing we did not know about him. Quite unexpectedly we observe in some of the axioms a secret melancholy. Here indeed *sunt lacrimae rerum*: it is the lament which arises from the reality of things, as it appears to the inexorable realist shut within the bounds of his desolate horizon. It is no longer the 'deep sorrow' of the *Consolatoria*, fallen upon him without warning with misfortune; it is a general melancholy which also pervades certain thoughts set down at the time of his 'great and perpetual good fortune'. He keeps it hidden, and comments: 'To give rein sometimes to one's feelings of pleasure or displeasure is a thing of great comfort, but it is harmful; hence it is wise to abstain.'[10] He abstains therefore with nature's help, but what we glimpse between the chinks of his armour, leads us to imagine a suffering all the more painful because more reserved and enclosed. As when, in that letter to his brother Luigi, moderate as always, we suddenly find a few simple words on his little daughter's death that are more moving than a great lamentation: 'How unexpected a misfortune!'

There is in this little book not only the melancholy which stems from the unhappiness which inevitably accompanies even the least unfortunate conditions of life, there is also that more subtle and final disquiet which emerges from the vanity of all things: vanity of the most sought after honours and gains, vanity of generous actions done in the cause of one's country's liberty, vanity even of his own maxims and the experience they embody of many particular events, 'and what these events may be, cannot be understood from any rule, nor is there any book to teach them'. All the three hopes he placed at the summit of his thoughts were to prove vain. 'Three things I wish to see before I die, but I doubt that I shall see any of them even if I live a long time: in our city the life of a well-ordered republic, Italy freed from all barbarians, and the whole world set free from the tyranny of these wicked priests.'[11]

He therefore collects these *Ricordi* from the notebooks and papers in which they are dispersed, he chooses them, polishes them, and re-arranges some of them,[12] so that a collection of them is made 'at the

beginning of the year 1528 in that period of complete leisure I had';
and he added a further ten in April the same year. Then, occupied as he
is with the *Cose fiorentine* he has just begun, he puts them away, and the
biographer must do likewise until Guicciardini takes them up again to
rework them in a new form.

Among those ten axioms added in April three bear a very painful and
contemporary significance. They tell us, better than a long speech, what
he thought of the popular government. In the *Consolatoria* he had tried
to comfort himself with the thought that the men in power would not
continue to reject him always, but would one day regret 'not having
taken advantage in times of much difficulty of *his* ability and experience'. But that April as things had not changed except for the
worse, he noted contemptuously: 'When the wicked and the ignorant
govern, it is not surprising that virtue and goodness are not valued, for
the former hate these qualities and the latter do not know them.'[13]
Shortly after, he observed that the Medici had made a mistake in
wishing to govern a tyrannical state according to the rules of a free one.
The free state in turn erred in trying to run itself like a tyranny, excluding from power so large a part of the citizens. He pleads his own
cause, but it is heartfelt. Even more so are these other words: 'You fall
all the more into that extreme you wish to escape, the more you withdraw to the other extreme to avoid it, being unable to hold the mean; so
popular governments, the more they approach license to avoid tyranny,
the more they fall into tyranny; but our Florentine people do not
understand this reasoning.'[14]

Indeed they did not. The *Arrabbiati* did all they could to irritate the
Pope, which was a stupid thing to do, and to damage his former
supporters in Florence, which was perhaps even more stupid, as it
alienated from the popular government even those who, because they
had favoured that change or for other reasons, would have supported it
gladly. This quite apart from the fact that no wise and temperate person
could be pleased, as Guicciardini's axiom says, to see a tyranny changed
into a worse one. An unimpeachable witness to this was the good
republican and supporter of the popular government, Donato Giannotti,
when he expressed the wish that anger and jealousy might be abandoned
and they might at last live with 'a true liberty'.[15]

One of the Pope's first thoughts, as soon as he had escaped from the
claws of the Spaniards, had been to send an ambassador to Florence,
since the city would send none to him. He had therefore sent the

Florentine bishop Antonio Bonsi with moderate instructions to 'persuade . . . that nothing was further from his thoughts' than regaining power, 'and that he desired only that that republic should recognize him as Pope . . . and that in private matters they should not persecute his people, nor the honour, arms and ornaments of his family'.[16] They did not even allow his ambassador to enter the city.[17]

At that time some of the more trouble seeking of the *Arrabbiati*, going to the church of the Annunziata, had thrown down and broken the statues of Clement VII and Leo X. Immediately after, a public ban made compulsory the removal of Medici arms and symbols wherever they might be. As though this were not enough, in defiance of canon law and without seeking permission, the Florentines imposed levies and taxes on the clergy, thus openly defying not merely the former master of Florence but the Roman Pontiff himself. It was a case for excommunication, and to avert this, in April 1528 Capponi sent to the Pope a friar of St Mark's, as he could not send an ambassador without the consent of the city. And Clement, who asked nothing better, did him honour.[18]

It was the worthy Gonfalonier's daily task to mend the pots broken by those madmen and avert worse damage. Guicciardini was still the most faithful counsellor of his wise and moderate policies, particularly since family bonds had strengthened those of kindred minds. Without the assistance of the mob, and even in spite of the mob they did their best to bring the threatened ship of the Republic into port. Of course, as is only human, each of these men endeavoured to save also the cargo of his own private interests. The Gonfalonier knew that in time of need he would not find a better advocate with the Pope than his former Lieutenant. The latter knew he had no other defence against the levies and severity of the *Arrabbiati* than the Gonfalonier.[19]

We have few letters and little information about Guicciardini while he is working on the *Cose fiorentine* in his villa, but that little we have shows him solidly in support of his country and prepared to respect, according to his principles, the government in power that he disliked. Indeed a letter to his brother Luigi in May 1528 shows him quite otherwise than inclined to a return of the Medici, and it is a document far more worthy of belief than the mistrustful commentaries of an *arrabbiato* historian.[20] Furthermore, from the beginning of that year the Pope having sought the consent privately of the Signoria for his former Lieutenant to return to him, this had not been permitted;[21] but as the request was probably made to Capponi, I am convinced that

Guicciardini himself was a party to that refusal. The *Arrabbiati* at that time would gladly have got rid of him.

In fact he preferred his country to money and honour which he would not have gone short of even serving a bankrupt Pope (as Clement used to describe himself). For this reason, that is to enjoy its amenities, to continue to help it at Capponi's side, he was resigned to listen in the Grand Council to certain foolish speeches which would have sufficed to make him change his mind (if there had been any need) about the advantages of majority rule over an oligarchy. He put up with the forced loans which flayed him alive;[22] he put up with the suspicious looks of the *Arrabbiati*. They, however, managed to prevent the Gonfalonier from calling Guicciardini and other former Medici supporters to the small councils. After which, Capponi continued as before to take advantage of Guicciardini's advice, having him come privately to his chamber.[23]

Meanwhile Capponi had been re-elected at the end of the first thirteen months of his office. It seemed, and it was, a victory for moderate policies clearly preferred by the majority. A pyrrhic victory, for the majority gave way more every day, as it commonly does to the violence of the minority. 'During the whole of his term in office Niccolò had two prime objects: to defend from fresh jealousy those who had been favoured by the Medici, and ensure that honours and public councils should come their way as to other citizens; and to avoid irritating the Pope over matters not of real importance to liberty.'[24] But we have already seen his success in not estranging from the State so great a part of the best citizens: among them Guicciardini alone through his relationship with the Gonfalonier, did better than the others.[25] As for his negotiations, through Iacopo Salviati, with the Pope who had returned to Rome meanwhile, he was at last forbidden to continue with them or to treat of affairs of state without the concurrence of the Ten.

Thus, diminished in power, almost a prisoner in the Palace of a guard consisting for the most part of *Arrabbiati*, the Gonfalonier's lot was far from happy; a letter of the Este representative shows him in a pathetic state of fatigue and agitation.[26] Yet with patient obstinacy he waited for the vetoes to be relaxed and began again to try and pick up the threads. In those Roman negotiations Serragli acted as his mediator. We do not find that Guicciardini ever intervened in them, though with his links with both Capponi and the Pope he seemed the person best qualified to conduct them. One must suppose that either he stood apart from them entirely, or that he employed extraordinary prudence and astuteness. It is true that he was once seen to write a letter in lemon juice in the house of Baccio Valori;[27] but this evidence is vague, for we do not know the date or anything else about it. Not in lemon juice, unfortunately, but in all too clear ink was written a letter from Serragli to Capponi, which fell into the hands of the *Arrabbiati* one April day in 1529. A bad day for the Gonfalonier who was deposed, but afterwards escorted to his house by almost the entire population as a mark of respect; an even worse day for the Republic, which needed as never before his moderating and conciliatory efforts.

For the armies of the League commanded by Lautrec, after driving the Spanish to extremity and forcing them to die in Naples of hunger and plague, had themselves been beaten not by the enemy but by that terrible disease. Charles's final victory, again in the fields of Lombardy, removed for ever from Clement after so many years the embarrassment of choice between the two great rivals. Therefore, on the 29th June he made with Charles the treaty of Barcelona, and in that treaty was one article which obliged the Emperor to put the Medici back into Florence. When in August there followed the Peace of Cambrai between the Emperor and the King of France, the Florentine Republic remained alone against the Pope whom she had reviled in so many ways, defied and outraged. Something could still be saved, if not as much as Capponi might have saved in his time, but the *Arrabbiati* who were now masters of the city, hoping for who knows what, continued their mad career. Having succeeded Capponi, their leader Francesco Carducci sat in the highest seat of the Republic. He was a good popular leader, who perhaps deserved the posthumous angry contempt of Guicciardini for his qualities of mind, not for those of spirit.

They had always refused to send ambassadors to Clement as though he were the offending party not the offended, a mere secular prince not the supreme Pontiff, and so they continued now he had them at his mercy. An embassy to the victorious Emperor might have helped, but when with the greatest difficulty they decided to send one, they were told: 'You come too late and in an ill hour', and that they should do their best with the Pope. The city now was condemned, and to carry out their sentence the Pope sent into Tuscany the Prince of Orange with a formidable army which was the secular arm placed at his disposal by the Emperor. On the 14th September he crossed the boundaries of the Republic and laid siege to Cortona.

With that dagger at its throat the Florentine government called on the 15th and 16th a council to which were summoned the best qualified citizens, not excluding this time the friends of the former government. It was decided in the end to send ambassadors to the Pope; a tardy provision, and one rendered more useless by the restrictions with which their commissions were surrounded. The ambassadors were Pierfrancesco Portinari, Andreuolo Niccolini, Francesco Vettori, Iacopo Guicciardini. Francesco's brother and substitute had been (as may perhaps be remembered) a supporter of liberty since the time of Pope Leo. Francesco Guicciardini is supposed, according to contemporary witness, also to have taken part in that council.[28] If this were true, which I have good reason to doubt, it would be the last time he sat in a republican council.

His last hopes disappointed by the fall of Capponi, he had withdrawn to the solitude of his villa of Santa Margherita; the plague which kept him away from the city this time was of quite a different nature, and his consolatory work was called *Cose fiorentine*. The proof of his complete isolation is the lack of correspondence or any mention of him in documents of this period.[29] In the end when the papal imperial army had moved on Tuscany, he retreated to Finocchieto to remove himself from the sight of his enemies, and get nearer the border. He did not wish to remain prisoner of a maddened and hostile mob in that ship which was heading for destruction. Nor was it a matter of metaphorical imprisonment, for in the government committees and councils they had talked of locking him up together with other leaders with Medici sympathies.[30] They had also decided to 'publish him as a rebel and outlaw', and had withdrawn this only because their recent decision to send an embassy to the Pope would hardly have harmonized with the banishment of his Lieutenant. Thus, learning on the 19th of the loss of Cortona, he set off from Finocchieto with Alessandro Pazzi and Giovanni Corsi on the way to the Casentino.[31]

From there he wrote to his brothers Luigi and Iacopo a very respectful letter, which could be shown to the magistrates, to justify his flight and show him to be a good citizen, protesting that if he had thought 'that staying in Florence would do any good at all to the city and its liberty', he would gladly have risked his life for it. This letter is of the 20th September;[32] but on the 25th, having meanwhile crossed the boundaries of the Republic and taken refuge in Spinello, a castle of Count Ramberto Malatesta, he wrote to Giovan Battista Sanga the papal secretary, another letter on the subject which shows the reverse of the medal, overflowing with hatred for those who wanted to 'banish him as a rebel', urging the Pope to revenge, boasting of what he had done to persuade other rich citizens to flee so that the city should lack money for its defence.[33] One can understand in the first letter his legitimate desire to avert the danger of banishment and confiscation, one can understand in the second his just resentment against those who had ill-treated him without any fault of his own. Understanding which, we can also understand his duplicity; but we would have preferred to see a noble sorrow and reserve in the place of that resentful persecution of his fellow countrymen.

In the first letter, written to his brothers and more to the magistrates than to the brothers, he says he is determined 'not to leave Florentine territory, nor go to any place which might arouse suspicion'; but in the second written immediately afterwards, having already left the dominion, he expresses his intention of going to the very place which could give the Florentines most cause for mistrust, that is to the Pope. And as the Pope was about to move on to Bologna, where according to what seemed to have become a habit with the Medici popes he went to receive and crown his conqueror, Guicciardini prepared to meet him on the road.

Meanwhile in Florence, after so long deluding themselves with false hopes, after having attempted to delude with words and gifts the Prince of Orange now encamped with his army between Figline and Incisa, they had made up their minds to make a virtue of necessity. On the 28th September a great meeting to take a final decision had resolved to defend liberty at all costs, to engage their lives and their wealth, to burn the city or lay it in ruins rather than surrender it to the Pope. As a start, for a mile and a half from the walls they destroyed all the churches, all the villas with their famous gardens, the delight and the pride of the city. With unbelievable enthusiasm those Florentines, regarded as so avaricious, so sceptical, so corrupted by their own cleverness and culture, could be seen destroying with their own hands so much beauty and wealth – they who were so keenly sensitive to beauty. And they sang:

> Deh, quanto è gran dolore
> ruinar di nostre mani
> l'arche de' padri nostri,
> le case de' cristiani!

Deh, quanto è gran dolore
pensar che a tal destino
mena la madre patria
un papa, un cittadino!

Ma di tener Fiorenza
non avrai, Papa, il vanto
o tu l'avrai morente
per darle l'Olio santo.

[Alas, what grief to ruin with our own hands the tombs of our fathers, the houses of Christians! Alas, what sorrow to think that a Pope, her own citizen, drives the mother country to such a fate. But, Pope, you will never boast of holding Florence or you will have her dying to give her holy unction.]

The last delays over, on the 12th October the enemy appeared at the pass of Apparita, an outpost of Florence, where the Spaniards are supposed to have raised their famous cry: 'Get out your brocades, Florence, for we are coming to measure them with our pikestaffs.' Thus began the memorable defence by which the nation renowned for its culture, showed to the world unexpected valour. Made for the arts of peace, they became noble in war; famous for the subtlety of their politics, after pursuing a policy which was madness, they retrieved themselves by the impetuous deeds of romantic courage. Those heedless men, made obstinate by the hopelessness of their case, could be numbered among those whom Guicciardini in his *Ricordi* calls madmen. Yet there is a point, hard to define, at which 'madmen' become heroes.

Useless to ask oneself whether the 'wise' Guicciardini might have been on the side of the defenders of Florence if they had not done everything possible to anger and make an enemy of him. Certainly he would not have lacked courage nor firm resolution, but he was body and soul on the other side of the fence; nor should one forget that Clement VII was not a foreign enemy but a Florentine, the head of a faction to which messer Francesco, even if he did not greatly love it, was fatally bound. And as he liked to say, 'volentes fata ducunt, nolentes trahunt'. Besides he was too 'wise' to involve himself in a war which was lost in advance, having once lost a war which had appeared to be won before it started: 'Pray God not to find yourself on the losing side.'[34]

Chapter 19

EXILE. THE 'CONSIDERAZIONI' AND THE 'RICORDI'

◇◇

W HILE the armies were encamped around Florence and the
Prince of Orange went to lodge at Santa Margherita in
Guicciardini's very own villa, the latter was consumed
with impatience, 'idle' and anxiously waiting in the dominions of
Malatesta.[1] He remained there twenty-two days,[2] but on the 19th
October the Pope, leaving the road to Tuscany where such fires were
burning on his account, went to Rimini, and Guicciardini, who was at
Sogliano only ten miles away, went to present himself.[3] Immediately he
was approached by the Florentine ambassadors, first of all by his
brother Iacopo, who had sadly followed the papal cortège from Rome.
No one better than the former Lieutenant could present to the angry
Pope the case of their city and its nomadic orators. It was unhoped for
assistance.

It was indeed like the touch of a magic wand. Messer Francesco spoke
the same evening to the Pope. The following day the ambassadors, who
had pursued him so far in vain, were received in Cesena with sudden
kindness, and heard conditions proposed which they could not have
dreamed of obtaining before.[4] He only wanted his family to return to
Florence as private citizens, and he was even willing that the Great
Council should be kept, though with some reforms. These conditions,
perfected and polished the following day in Forlì, were carried in all
haste to Florence by Anton Francesco Nori, assistant ambassador, but

the government at home did not believe them to be sincerely meant, and so that the people's resolution should not be weakened by sweet hopes of peace, they forbade Nori to reveal their terms: for men who constantly had the word liberty on their lips it was certainly a tyrannical proceeding. Contrary to the belief of some authorities[5] I can now affirm that Guicciardini really did succeed in obtaining those conditions from the Pope, though of course one cannot be sure that the Pope had any intention of honouring them: I would not put my hand in the fire for that, nor do I believe Guicciardini would have done so at any time.

Having achieved this miracle, Guicciardini said he wanted to ask leave to depart for Ancona, but his brother and the other Florentine ambassadors, who now regarded him as their patron saint, begged him so hard to go with them as far as Bologna that he went there; and everything leads us to believe that he would have gone even if they had not asked him.[6] He stayed on there after all attempts at an agreement had been broken off, with one final episode in which his brother Iacopo is supposed to have spoken very sharply to poor Clement. Possibly this has been exaggerated.

The eyes of the world were then fixed upon Bologna. After the Pope's triumphal entry Guicciardini was able to enjoy the much more splendid one of Charles V, and the shows of mutual affection between the Pope who had raised so great a war against the Emperor, and the Emperor who had punished the Pope with the sack of Rome and imprisonment. It was written that they blamed their ministers for these mutual offences. One would like to have seen Guicciardini's face when he heard that.[7] I do not know how much good it may have done him, but during those days in Bologna there was nothing but festivity. While Florence was besieged, its country districts devastated by the armies, 'things (he writes to his brother Luigi) to break the heart of anyone born in that city',[8] he saw triumphant a foreign Emperor whom he had wished to drive out of Italy, and who was now virtually the ruler of Italy and the world; nor do I believe that those thoughts and that spectacle could rejoice his heart, though it never occurred to him to reproach God, as one poet was later to do, for not having brought the Garisenda down in ruins 'upon Charles V and Clement VII'.

And then he had the worry of his family, of his possessions left behind without much hope of seeing them again. His anxiety became anguish when at the beginning of December his brother Iacopo informed him that, as a reward for having obtained for the city these unexpected terms of agreement, the Otto di Guardia had accused him of having plotted against the State.[9] It was a case for the Quarantìa, but this time he did not feel any desire to compose an *Accusatoria* and a *Defensoria* as he had when the prosecution was only imaginary. Iacopo and Niccolò di Braccio Guicciardini who were the *Popolani* or supporters of the popular party, of the family – indeed the latter was an *Arrabbiato* – begged him to present himself in Florence 'because the case was without foundation', or wished that he would at least remove himself from the shadow of the Pope and transfer to Lucca where his contumacy would appear less serious. They begged in vain. He would never have agreed to the first proposal, the second he might have adopted unwillingly and then only to please Iacopo. Indeed it seemed to him a manoeuvre little likely to impress the Florentine judges, and he would be sorry 'not to improve things there and spoil them here':[10] that is, lose the Pope's favour. Quite apart from the fact that he had better quarters in Bologna on which the flower of the world had descended. It seemed better to temporize.

On the 12th December, therefore, he wrote a fine letter to the Eight, in which he avoided giving a straight answer as far as putting in an appearance went, and even as regards removing to a less suspect place; however, it was very effective in refuting the accusations, where he had ability and reason on his side. The prosecution in fact was under three headings: the first which accused him of having left Florence in defiance of the ban was quite true, but he offered acceptable excuses to justify his action. As to the second, which charged him with having gone to Bologna with the Pope, he could answer easily by calling to witness the Florentine ambassadors. As to the third heading which reproached him with having sent to Florence letters against the State, it was enough to list the few letters he had written, which indeed had all fallen into the hands of the Eight.[11] He would not have shown such certainty if he had been afraid that some intercepted letter might have given him the lie. He did not know that the calumny came from near-by Ferrara, saying that he was going to see the Pope twice a day to read him secret reports from Florence.[12] A ridiculous calumny, since the Florentine Pope had no lack of men or means to obtain information directly on the affairs of the city, and Guicciardini was not likely, watched and distrusted as he was, to involve himself in such dangerous proceedings.

Finally, on Christmas Eve, after having delayed and wriggled as much as possible,[13] he resigned himself to leave Bologna just when things were at their best,[14] and go to Lucca where he had sent his wife and daughters some days before. But that departure, his letter to the Eight, and Iacopo's representations, only served to win a postponement of a fortnight of the date stated for him to appear, then a further one of ten days: his situation had not improved.

Were we to conjecture how he spent his time in the bitter idleness of Lucca, we might imagine him thinking of the interrupted *Cose fiorentine*, as no one would believe that he could have taken with him in his flight the great tomes which contain them and the materials he needed to continue his work. However, in one of his notebooks, obviously one he used in travel, we find something better than conjectures. In fact, not many pages away from the notes made at Bologna for the letter to the Eight of which we have just spoken, there is an extract made at Lucca of the well-known Epistola of Lapo Castiglionchio.[15] The author was thinking of using it, having just reached the point in his work where messer Lapo is banished by the fury of the unchained mob. And was not he, Francesco Guicciardini, a doctor and professor of law like Lapo, like him noble, in danger of suffering the ban of rebellion from a popular government? He then wrote straight off in these same pages, anticipating its chronological place in the account, the very fine discourse to be placed in the mouth of messer Donato Barbadori, who had also been prosecuted by the popular government.[16] (To think that some people would like to consider literary works entirely on their own merits detached from the circumstances which produced them!) In the discourse he sets forth the city's ingratitude towards its greatest sons, beginning with Dante himself. Nor is there any doubt that as he wrote, the historian was thinking of his own case. One would only need to change a few names and a few details to turn it into an apology for Guicciardini, another eloquent *Defensoria*, an outburst of the soul in those anxious and unhappy times:

'If this [innocence] does not suffice to save me, I should not feel any surprise, for we are born of a city where it has always been natural to hate the virtues of the citizens, to be jealous of their glory and persecute those who have brought her honour and benefits. . . . The man who openly and to his own peril defended the cause of this city before Pope Gregory in the presence of the whole court of Rome . . . who never spared his own labour or danger in the service of this Republic, always absolutely faithful to the Palace, loyal to your city, now as a reward for his good deeds, on the outcry of the ignorant populace roused by the iniquity of a few wicked citizens, your officials prevailed upon by force, the sacred authority of justice violated, he is led forth in infamy like a public thief, an assassin. . . . We go to satisfy the rage of our enemies, to offer an example that in ill-governed cities virtue and innocence do not suffice to defend good men. I hope nevertheless that God, a just judge, will bring retribution to the authors of such wickedness. But upon you, ignorant and ungrateful people, I invoke no other revenge than that you should never know or enjoy true liberty, but that living always either under a tyrannical government, or, while appearing to be free, with a disordered licence, you may suffer in misery and torment a constant longing for liberty since you are incapable either of knowing or using it.'[17]

He too, like Barbadori, felt a symbolical (but he could not be sure how far it was so) sword hanging over him. And the sword was raised threateningly on the 7th March, when, as he continued defiant, his case was sent to the Quarantìa.[18] Asked to do so by his brother Iacopo who sent a messenger on purpose the same day,[19] he wrote a second letter of excuses to the Eight very like the first;[20] and so that it should not appear to have been written under that threat, after a few curious alterations which can be read through the erasures of the draft, he backdated it to the 2nd March.[21]

The letter did him no good, neither did the prayers which, the Quarantìa meeting on the 17th, the worthy Iacopo had offered in the convents of the Murate, of Santa Chiara, of San Marco (charging his brother, though, with the respective alms);[22] nor was his brother's courageous defence any use. After various votes were taken with some opposition, he was condemned to banishment as a rebel and confiscation of his property with a much shorter and much less eloquent accusation than the imaginary one he had composed, though it was no less dramatic: 'There should be no such difference of opinion. I should like to know who does not believe messer Francesco has erred, what they would wish him to have done to commit such offence, and what greater injury our city could have received apart from its destruction. Would you wait to punish him until he assaults you with fire and sword? Yet I hope in Christ's name that you and he may be punished first. . . .'[23] Useless now the resource of donations and trusts for his family which he had adopted when the storm was drawing near: all his goods were seized, his possessions sold: his library consisting of 'books of law in a hundred and ten bound volumes and twenty-four unbound, and a number of literary works and others', was bought in by Iacopo to save them, at the modest price of ten florins or slightly more.[24]

Guicciardini did not wait for his brother to send news of the sentence. Either he had immediate news of it from another source, or, while still without information, he had no illusion about the clemency of his judges in the fiery atmosphere of Florence under siege,[25] considering how little he had gained by that sojourn in Lucca, he was not willing to remain there one day longer to die of boredom and spleen, and with the further danger of losing the Pope's favour. Thus on the 18th he set off for Rome. He told Iacopo, who had written to him the same day, that he had left Lucca 'to go to Loreto to fulfil a long-standing vow'. See how devout messer Francesco had become! But, as we know, this business of the vow to Our Lady of Loreto was an old Florentine expedient. His brother kept writing to him in vain to persuade him to return under safe conduct; yet with a thousand considerate expressions and evasions he allowed him to understand that he would not set foot in Florence until its government were changed.[26]

So he had burnt his boats. He would never have gone, as Baccio Valori did, to be commissioner of the armies besieging the city; indeed even after his sentence, he showed formal respect for the laws and the magistrature, and I marvel at the scholars who have expressed surprise at this,[27] since it is entirely in keeping with his character and since he had no reason to exacerbate the magistrates while there were still pending his appeals against the confiscation of the trusts and his wife's dowry and maintenance for his daughters.[28]

Writing to Iacopo he justified his move to Rome by the need to obtain some governorship from the Pope to keep himself, after being so cruelly despoiled of everything by the confiscations;[29] but he did not forget that Iacopo was on the other side, and we must not forget it either. At this period, unlike so many other Florentines on the Medici side, and certainly by his own express desire, we do not find him employed by the Pope in any way against his native land.[30] Let us see, therefore, what he was doing in Rome during the months he was there, which certainly hung heavy for those who like him spent them full of anxiety.

Meanwhile the famous *Considerations on the Discourses of Machiavelli*, written in the same travelling notebook, are undoubtedly of this period.[31] The words of the text which permit us to give it a date, would not prevent us from fixing its composition a few months earlier, but although it seems probable that among his 'works of literature' there was also this work by his friend, I do not think it very likely that he carried it with him in his flight through the mountains of the Casentino. That Guicciardini kept the *Discourses* as his bedside book would be a fascinating hypothesis, but it is, alas, entirely improbable, nor does it seem any more likely, as the work had so little circulation, that he would immediately have found a manuscript copy at Bologna or Lucca. In Rome, on the other hand, at the house of Cardinal Gaddi there was then being prepared the first edition which came out the following year, and that was based on the autograph preserved in the famous library of Cardinal Ridolfi. Indeed, since messer Francesco was in close contact with both these prelates who were his fellow citizens, (though with one more than the other), one does not really require a great deal of imagination to conceive how the *Considerations* came to be written.[32]

In these, to pick out the few points which are relevant to a biography, we find certain aspects of Guicciardini's intolerance, in a more acute form than elsewhere: intolerance for theory, for Machiavelli's tendency to move from the particular to the general, whereas he himself liked to go from the general to the particular, and this empiricism clipped his wings for any flight of speculation; intolerance towards Machiavelli's constant references to antiquity, failing to understand what the author brought out of it that was new and inspired and beyond practical ends, which were all that Guicciardini would consider. His critical remarks, nearly all correct, rarely miss the target. But he who knew how to see his friend's weak points with such marvellous acuity, had not observed that all those errors are merely rough stones on the surface of new roads opened up by his thought. To insist as he does on certain particular confutations would seem a pointless pedantry if one could not discern in it an irresistible aversion from everything which departs in the very slightest from truth and reality. We have already noted in these pages Guicciardini's secret admiration for Machiavelli's intellect, which he yet felt to be so unlike himself, so far away from his own solid realism; and the combination of these contrasting feelings in a spirit like his was bound (I believe) to generate that affectionate acerbity which he had professed for him in his lifetime and which he again expressed in the *Considerations* written after his death.

The work remained unfinished, as is well known. The author had written on as many blank sheets the consecutive numbers of the *Discourses* of Machiavelli which he was proposing to discuss. Having glossed thirty-eight, he left the next twenty pages blank, and it would be impossible to say if the observations, which had arisen in his mind while reading, became fewer when he came to write, or whether as the work grew he felt a certain weariness in it, or if quite simply he lacked time to finish it.

However, he had time to attend to a new version of the *Ricordi*.[33] He began it towards the middle of May when the Florentines had 'defended their walls from the enemy armies for seven months when one would not have expected them to resist for seven days'.[34] For the first passage of this new version is dedicated to the prowess of his fellow citizens, and one feels in it, together with irritation at their courageous folly, a touch of admiration. Perhaps a similar feeling was aroused in him sometimes by Machiavelli's ardour. Used to put reason before faith, he must yet recognize in this *ricordo*, inspired by the defenders of Florence, that faith can sometimes do greater things than reason; thus (even if afterwards analysing it, he seeks to give a materialistic explanation) he suddenly discovers it to be true 'what religious people say, that a man with faith may achieve great things, and as the Gospels say . . . faith will move mountains'. If I am not mistaken, in this 'discovery' of his declining years there is a shadow of weary sadness.

These new *Ricordi*, those, that is, which appear for the first time in the new version, are even more shot through with melancholy than the earlier ones which appear with some revision. There is a more desolate pessimism, a more subtle melancholy. 'An intelligence above the average is given to men for their sorrow and torment':[35] *expertus loquitur*. And then: 'It is a great misfortune to be in a position where you cannot have the good without first suffering the bad.'[36] Considering all the things which must combine to produce them, nothing astonishes him more than 'an old man, a fertile year'.[37] Now, as though to correct a previous axiom, he observes that there are 'more bad men than good';[38] now barely stifled by the usual practical considerations, this sigh escapes him: 'I despised when young, music, dancing, singing, and such frivolities. Also I despised fine writing, horsemanship, the art of dressing well . . . but later I regretted it. . . .'[39]

Guicciardini was melancholy in his Roman exile in the decline of his life. He was forty-seven and beginning to find the lees in the bottom of his cup. Concluding these *Ricordi*, he observed: 'It sometimes happens that fools achieve more than wise men . . . The wise men of Florence would have given way to the present storm; the fools who insisted on putting up a fight against all reason, have achieved up to now what no one could have believed our city at all capable of. . . .'[40] At that age he, as a wise man, had unwillingly to observe the miracles achieved by 'fools'. And previously he had written: 'having against all reason set themselves to await war with the Pope and the Emperor, without any hope of support from others . . . they have . . . achieved a position such that no one would be astonished if they were victorious'.[41]

For Florentine arms had indeed risen to these heights. The attack of the night of San Martino having been repulsed with great bloodshed, they had moved from defence to attack with courageous sorties, several times endangering and almost routing the enormously strong papal and imperial armies, in vain supplied with fresh reinforcements. At the end of April Ferrucci recaptured Volterra, holding it against overwhelming enemy strength. Shortly after, on the 5th May, a sortie by Malatesta had sown destruction in the camp besieging Florence. Stefano Colonna did likewise on the 10th June; but the fortunes of the besieged did not prosper after that point when Guicciardini would not have been surprised by their victory: the city was short of all supplies, then plague came to join hunger. There remained a last throw, to call in Ferrucci and with their joint forces assault the enemy camp, to conquer or die. But Malatesta, thinking it better for the city and particularly for himself to come to an agreement with the Pope, refused the easy task of attacking the enemy camp which had been weakened in order to move against Ferrucci. Meanwhile Ferrucci himself fell at Gavinana, after defeating and killing the Prince of Orange. Yielding to necessity and treachery, the city therefore had to capitulate on the 12th August, but under conditions as honourable as its defence had been: 'agreeing that their liberties should always be safe . . . and that the Pope pardoned injuries received from all citizens'. Such conditions made the surrender hardly less than a victory, but those who arranged them did so without difficulty knowing that Clement would not honour them. Thus the unhappy city was again betrayed. The Florentines were to have only the meagre satisfaction of renaming the victor Pope Che-mente (the lying Pope).

In less than a week the main square was occupied by Malatesta's troops and the usual comedy of the parliament was put on: the same evening the Signoria was deposed and another elected, in which the Gonfalonier was that Giovanni Corsi who followed Guicciardini in the Spanish legation and fled with him into Casentino before the siege. He came from Rome, having grown in favour in the shadow of the Pope. But the Signoria itself was no longer anything but a shadow: only Baccio Valori, commissioner general, and the traitor Malatesta were all powerful. The city had first of all to be freed, through further exactions, of the troops which were draining her life blood; revenge and reform were to follow at once.

To carry these out, Guicciardini was sent by the Pope.[42] He had spent the last few months of the siege in unspeakable anxiety and wretchedness. Seeing that the defenders' morale did not weaken with the diminishing of their forces, and the danger therefore growing that the city might be moving towards ultimate destruction, he had first inspired Clement to seek an agreement;[43] and being unable to approach the Florentines, he had collected in one of his discourses the reasons which should have persuaded them to a settlement.[44] Then he had set all his hopes on negotiations between Malatesta and the Prince of Orange; finally that slender thread too being broken, he did not know what more to do, seeing the Florentines more resolute than ever, 'as though they were about to achieve victory, which is indeed an extraordinary thing'.[45] Sometimes he was prepared to believe that they were expecting assistance other than that heavenly kind promised them by fra Girolamo. And in the meantime, with the news of ever greater destruction and devastation, he wrote to his brother Luigi: 'Our misfortune has led us to see so great a ruin through the fault of a few wicked men.'[46]

Those words tell us with what feelings he returned to Florence, and with what attitude towards its defenders. When he arrived on the 24th September after a hard journey 'full of a thousand accidents and fears', the ruin seemed to him greater than he could have imagined. 'The people and their resources exhausted, all the houses around Florence destroyed for many miles and in many towns of the Florentine dominion, the peasant population immeasurably decreased, the common folk disappeared almost entirely.' To these public disasters might be added his own private ones, which, even if they did not grieve him more than the others, he felt perpetually weighing upon him 'Poppiano . . . entirely destroyed and virtually razed to the ground; Santa Margherita likewise in a very bad state'. They had sold up 'even his chairs', and those were so many and of such good quality that (as he remarked with a touch of pride), 'although they were sold in May – a time when things were virtually being given away', the Commune had made 700 ducats from their sale.[47]

With these things before his eyes he was consumed with anger and long nourished rancour, while he addressed himself to his unpleasant task. Not for nothing does the astrologer present him in that youthful portrait as a 'man who remembers the injuries done to him and exacts revenge for them'. Elected immediately to the Otto di Pratica, 'who ruled everything', he united in his own person the great authority of that office to that which came to him directly from the Pope. On the 17th October he wrote: 'We have made a good beginning, having detained all those rogues, and begun to examine Carduccio, and thus we shall continue, for indeed if one wishes to put this state on a proper footing, mild measures are useless.'[48]

And the defenders of Florence certainly did not receive mild treatment. Guicciardini had shown in his governorships his desire to distinguish common crime from misdeeds committed out of partisan passions, nor was any other fault to be found in the defenders of Florence, as he himself confessed: 'Although Carduccio said something of importance, yet apart from their perverse obstinacy through which they have destroyed this city, the reports do not reveal any of those frightful crimes which were suspected.'[49] And yet without regard for the terms of the capitulation, on this occasion he worked more than any other member of the commission to ensure that punishment should be merciless. Carducci and others were, after torture, beheaded. The Gonfalonier Girolami, through the intercession of Ferrante Gonzaga, had the death sentence changed to one of perpetual imprisonment, during which he died. Then the proscriptions began. Among them in an endless and painful list was the flower of intellect and ability: the historian Iacopo Nardi, the jurist Salvestro Aldobrandini, and Donato Giannotti, the theoretician of Venetian and Florentine government who had held with honour the secretariat of the Ten which had once been Machiavelli's.

In the proscriptions too Guicciardini was merciless beyond all others. In Florence they called him ser Cerrettieri, who had been the headsman and executioner of the Duke of Athens,[50] and it will never be possible to lift the shame of this from him. Moreover, to increase this infamy, the hatred of the Florentine writers of the time, and the noble sentiments inspired in all ages by the defenders of Florentine liberty, have seen to it that the burden of other men's guilt has all been laid on him. He well knew this when he wrote: 'We preferred to draw upon ourselves all this burden so that by friends and enemies alike all is attributed to us.'[51]

One must take account of all these things if one wishes to retain one's equanimity, but there still remain that zeal, that exceptional rigour shown by him beyond all others who fulfilled this wretched function with him: he protested that Girolami's sentence was commuted;[52] he complained that on the protests of the imperial ambassador 'enthusiasm had cooled off' in Rome in the matter of sentences and proscriptions.[53] He stood fast on the letter of the law to have citizens proscribed whom others would have liked to save.[54] Such harshness in a hard but just man, who on other occasions had shown himself not averse from mercy, reveals that he had suffered in his deepest feelings more than one could have guessed during his exile, or it may be merely that he placed before anything else the iron necessity of state.

Furthermore it is curious to note that his good qualities contributed to this stain on him no less than his faults; indeed his coherence, his rigorous observing of decisions once taken, his integrity and honesty, no less than his inflexibility, his revengeful anger, his touchy pride, all tended to it. It is not surprising that the Florentines preferred to Guicciardini's inflexibility the easy ways of Baccio Valori, so much less exemplary a character, but for that very reason more humane, more inclined to indulgence and mercy, sometimes out of pity, sometimes for friendship's sake, sometimes for gifts or money or to attract followers.

Guicciardini's rigidity was soon to come into conflict with this yielding habit of Valori's.[55] But, in addition to their differences of character, even certain common characteristics set the two men against one another. Baccio was also ambitious and greedy for honours and power; as the Pope's commissioner general and virtual lieutenant, he had immediately taken up his lodging in the Medici palace and went about the city with a train of guards and citizens: things which messer Francesco did not like to see in anyone but himself. In a letter to his friend Lanfredini, the Pope's treasurer, but written more for the Pope's benefit than Lanfredini's, he cries out against Baccio and his behaviour, disgusted to 'see one of ourselves in a position to give orders to all the others, so that they have to address him cap in hand, with a court and a following always around him like Duke Lorenzo had or Cardinal de' Medici'.[56]

So he did not get on with Valori, but what was worse at this period he did not even get on with the Pope. What led to this was not only his continual disagreements with the commissioner, but also a general difference of views on the government of Florence and the economic revival of the city. The Pope, for example, would have liked to extract money from that bloodless corpse by levies, and Guicciardini on the other hand wanted to save some money on the transactions of the Monte. He was made Officer of the Monte, but this job, which also carried with it a salary, was later taken away from him by Rome, not without displeasure and resentment on his part.[57] Thus his desire grew to get away from Florence where he had little stipend and others had all the honour. He had to pay more attention than ever to the financial aspect, since he had spent or lost nearly all his money and had his property returned to him sucked dry.

On his departure from Rome he had been promised his beloved Presidency of Romagna,[58] and from the first moment when he had tasted the bitterness of Florence, he had never failed to close his frequent letters to Lanfredini without begging him to remind the Pope of that old promise and his present need. Though unwillingly, on a suggestion from Rome, he also procured that complaints against their present governor should come from Romagna. Nevertheless, when he had done that and the present incumbent had been deprived of the Presidency, it was given instead to Valori. Guicciardini wrote bitterly to Rome that he had done 'like Virgil when he hung up those three lines which begin: *sic vos non vobis*'.[59]

In exchange he was promised the governorship of Bologna which might have been even more honourable because of the power and importance of the city. Yet having tasted the fat income and small labour of the Presidency, he was less satisfied 'as Bologna is a place where, having due regard to the quality of the city . . . one cannot live without much ceremony and very heavy expenses', particularly if he had to take his wife and daughters, 'who in such a place can only be kept in luxurious circumstances'. They should therefore send Valori 'by nature fitted to enjoy the pomps of the government of Bologna', and much better suited than he to such an office, 'for there it is very important to know how to entertain and flatter the nobles of that city, which I do not well know how to do, and he is extremely good at it, and he will also be equipped with the other qualities needed for government, which do not require you to be clever'.[60]

Later however, seeing he could not avoid it, he decided to take what was being offered, flattered perhaps by the urgings and offers of Cardinal Cybo, the Legate of Bologna, whose Vice-Legate he was to be. This too, as on previous occasions, was a sudden decision: on the 18th day of the New Year 1531, although on the very day before he had shown himself still undecided, he wrote impetuously that he accepted Bologna and wanted to be off; the sooner the better. Instead this affair too dragged on, as the Protonotary Uberto Gambara who was governor there, happened to be at the Imperial court on behalf of the Pope, who did not wish to give someone else his job in his absence. To remove this obstacle and hasten his departure, moved by the desire for gain and the fear of seeing this other prize evade him, Guicciardini wrote, wrote again, stormed and at last went to Rome.[61] But having returned on the 14th May with orders to leave within a few days, on the 18th a letter sent after him ordered him to delay his departure until St John's day. The things he wrote to Rome in his terrible rage add greatly to our picture of Guicciardini: '. . . I thought it would have sufficed him [the Pope] to have taken away from me the office of the Monte with as much dishonour as if I had murdered the entire commune, to have treated me over the Presidency of Romagna as you well know how, after forcing me against my will to have the grievances of the Romagnoli brought up in Rome, and so made a fool of me, without now doing this further thing to me, which in the space of four months would be too much for any base fellow. I am determined to complete my arrangements to take the governorship and quite decided that any end to this affair will be better than going on like this. And if His Holiness thinks otherwise, I will send the brief and the patents to Cybo at once, and will take what resolve for myself God inspires me with. I will not do this out of pride or anger nor because I am unaware of the gravity of such an action and the consequences it must have. But although I value His Holiness's good graces at their true worth, and my service in his house, yet in all my actions I have always valued and will always value my own honour more than any other consideration, and with this style and manner of living I shall go on until my death, come what may. And I commend myself to you praying you to show this to His Holiness.'[62]

When Lanfredini, who acted as spokesman, read this letter, he thought the judicious Guicciardini was 'going out of his mind';[63] and even the choleric Governor, once his rage had passed, admitted that he had gone too far 'inasmuch as a master's wishes must be borne and further should be shown to be borne with more patience'. He therefore armed himself with patience and took up negotiations directly with Gambara who was passing through Florence. Then one fine day, the 20th June, after a trip to Massa to visit Cardinal Cybo, he at last set off.

Chapter 20

GOVERNOR AND VICE-LEGATE
OF BOLOGNA

A REPUTATION for fearsomeness had preceded Guicciardini to Bologna. As soon as the Pope's intentions were known, the Bolognese had done all they could to evade the yoke. First they explained they regretted being governed by a layman, contrary to the usual custom; the city was, at least for this occasion, especially 'fond of the Bishop's rochet'.[1] Then they discovered that they were extremely attached to their Governor, the protonotary Uberto da Gambara, and begged not to be deprived of so great a blessing. But when their ambassador presented the petition, Pope Clement, perhaps remembering some old complaints, replied that 'they used to speak in quite another tone',[2] and for once he stood firm. The same ambassador, having visited Guicciardini in Rome when he went there fearing that someone else might snap up this job also, was able to quote his reassuring words, which however did not suffice to reassure the unfortunate Bolognese: 'He had heard that in our city the view was widely held that he was very terrible, and he had no doubt . . . that their ideas would change, because outside the dignity of his office . . . in everything else they would find him full of courtesy and kindness, and so straight and without bias towards any one side, and so jealous for justice and equity, that all our city would be happy and satisfied.'[3]

Thus between Governor and subjects there was tension, but it relaxed to the relief of both sides after their first contacts, so that

Guicciardini wrote, two days later, very pleased: 'I have been looked upon kindly, and honoured too in the usual manner, and I have found no bears and shall not be a bear myself.'[4] The Bolognese were very mild people for Romagna. Otetea describes them as 'gentler';[5] perhaps the Rumanian scholar had in mind the 'singolare dolcezza del sangue bolognese' [singular sweetness of Bolognese blood], that Boccaccio praised in their women, 'quick to surrender to amorous desires',[6] but I am not sure that the men were quite so loving. At any rate they seemed all honey to one used to the ferocious ghibellines of Forlì and Bertinoro. Certainly Guicciardini was comfortable there and his correspondence at Bologna abounds in unusual convivial good humour.[7]

Four months later he wrote: 'Now I have got everything under control, I can tell you that the government is splendid, magnificent, and as honourable as may be.' However, there was a reverse even to that medal, because the cost of living there was extremely high and his expenses would have increased if he had had his family come there. Therefore he had to do his accounts carefully: 'Between auditors, chancery clerks, the train of women and my ordinary servants I shall have perpetually at my expense more than forty mouths not counting the horses, and I cannot economize on a single one of them.'[8] The Governor's ordinary salary was a hundred ducats as at Modena and Reggio, but the Pope had added a further seventy out of the judicial income. In this way he received more than the hundred and sixty he had when he was Governor of Modena and Reggio together, but it was hard to forget the great salary of the Presidency, and when his memory of it was refreshed by the ostentation displayed in Romagna by the man who had taken it from him, he noted acidly: 'He seems more like a prince than a president, and we a mayor rather than a governor.'[9] In conclusion he asked the Pope for a further supplement of seventy ducats to be given privately and without the knowledge of the Legate, and the Pope reluctantly gave him a part of it.'[10]

The Legate of Bologna was, as we know, Cardinal Cybo, but fortunately he was hardly ever there and disdained to lower his purple to common administrative tasks.[11] The Governor was also Vice-Legate, and before then, as the office had always been held by an ecclesiastic, his powers had also extended over the clergy: Guicciardini a layman, was given a chancellor in orders, Martino Agrippa, senior canon of San Petronio, who was to be the Legate's lieutenant for spiritual affairs. At first this annoyed Guicciardini as it seemed to his umbrageous nature that there would be two Vice-Legates, and Martino would be a 'half governor', but he calmed down when Cybo said that Martino would be 'the writer' and Guicciardini 'the spirit';[12] and subsequently he did not have anything to complain of for the whole period of his governorship.

In this he always had a lot of business, but none of great moment: he who, as we know, enjoyed talking about himself, found nothing to say about this period in his *History of Italy*. We have up to now searched closely into his times in office to find the man in them; the vice-legation at Bologna, that others have judged as 'of little importance',[13] and which adds little to our research, we shall pass over rapidly; it shall be a labour reserved for a young scholar now working in this field.[14] It will suffice for us to touch briefly on Guicciardini's main tasks both routine and exceptional.

As an example of the unusual, in the first months of his governorship he had to work on an affair which at the time was more important than the rest put together, and would be more important now if it were possible to reconstruct some of the 'ifs' of history. There were still the remains of the old quarrels with the Duke of Ferrara. The Pope, who had not been willing to ratify the arbitration of the Emperor to whom the disputes had been referred, was ever more embittered against the Duke, and 'intent on defeating him by cunning'.[15] To these few words of the *Storia d'Italia* Guicciardini was to reduce, after their failure, all the long story of those manoeuvres and his voluminous correspondence with Iacopo Salviati who managed the affair in Rome for the Pope.

As usual it was a question of having one of the gates of Ferrara opened, and putting in a troop of lances in a suprise attack. Guicciardini was to collect this armed band and prepare the *coup de main* with such secrecy that nothing should transpire. Early in July everything was ready and the order came from Rome to make the attack if he judged it 'eighteen per cent likely to succeed'. He could not stand things like that. He replied: 'I am not on any account prepared to take this responsibility, nor can I calculate this eighteen per cent, or count in such a way as to make myself judge of what I am obliged to execute.'[16]

In Rome they could not make up their minds, and the affair dragged on all summer. Guicciardini was ill with his usual Romagna fever and had to seek healthier air in the convent of San Michele in Bosco, abandoning all business other than the conspiracy.[17] Finally in mid-September the affair came to the ears of the Duke, whose remonstrances found Guicciardini astonished and indignant, ready to retort that 'he has always been in the habit of proceeding with these arts and finding every day fantastic charges to accuse His Holiness of'.[18] Right or wrong, the affair had to be covered up; to make sure of the discretion of two men who had managed the affair, the hasty Governor would actually have liked to put them into 'a dungeon'.[19] The lances were dispersed on the quiet, the last threads were cut and no more would have been said if at the beginning of the new year the Duke had not laid hands, in his own city of Ferrara, on one of the accomplices. Then all was buried with that unfortunate creature, and the affairs of government returned to their normal paths.

Usually indeed there was nothing of importance. The city was governed by the forty *Riformatori* with some degree of autonomy in the more or less accepted shadow of the Legate and his Vice-Legate. The latter was certainly involved in a lot of work with the administration of justice, but it was not a great worry. Within the city the rivalry between the powerful families of the Malvezzi and the Pepoli had not been without danger of some severe disorder, since, obliged as they were to keep their houses full of armed men, any spark might set off a great blaze, but the new Governor had at once increased the authority of the government to such an extent that, if hatred had not been abandoned, their arms at least had been laid down. Guicciardini displayed his usual impartiality among these rival contenders. If anything, running through his letters we may feel that he inclines towards the Pepoli, and it might have seemed so to others, for even at that time there was talk of a marriage between one of the Pepoli and a daughter of his. Nevertheless it was the Pepoli who were to conceive a deadly hatred for him.[20] The conditions in the Montagna were worse, where as men were wilder and offences committed between parties more heinous, while the government had not sufficient power to put down their disputes with a strong hand, Guicciardini sought to improve matters by means of agreements and truces.[21]

While in Bologna he was handling these minor everyday affairs, his thoughts were turned towards the affairs of Florence which at that time was being completely transformed. Clement had decided to remove the city's last shadow of freedom and give it as a princely state to the young Alessandro, officially the son of Duke Lorenzo, but his own son as was then said by the malicious, and is now thought to be the truth.[22] Hence, having bought him the duchy of Penne, he had got the Emperor to give him his daughter Margherita as his wife, and finally to clear the way he had made Ippolito a cardinal – for whom the overlordship of Florence had at first seemed destined. The city was so reduced and laid low that it might now be coerced into anything. Nevertheless, as the poison was so strong, the Pope wished to administer it in small doses and contrive according to his nature that the citizens themselves should bear the responsibility. Allowing something of his wishes to be glimpsed by those in his confidence, and then drawing back while the arbitration was delayed, which Caesar was to have published on the terms of the capitulation, he caused the Balìa to enable Alessandro to sit in all the councils with the title of provost; and as the latter was delayed by his imperial father-in-law, the Pope sent Archbishop Schönberg to rule the city meanwhile, with the pious hope that he might afterwards be able to manage the young Duke too. Thus from the outset, in spite of the terms of the capitulation, the government went back to what it had been after the Medici return in 1512, but with a new severity, and a people more downtrodden and hopeless.

These things had happened before Guicciardini left for Bologna. Not long after his departure, Alessandro arrived in Florence, and Muscettola, the imperial ambassador, who also reached the city at that time, solemnly promulgated the imperial rescript which provided that the magistrates were to be elected as they had been before 1527, and the form of the state was to be a republic of which Alessandro was to be the head and his succession in the male line. If this failed, other members of the Medici family should succeed. But this was not what Clement wanted; not for this had he suffered and dissembled, or besieged and almost ruined his native land, opened between himself and his fellow citizens a great gulf of hatred.

Concealing therefore his surreptitious manoeuvres, he would allow his principal adherents to understand something, and then withdraw till another time if they objected. Francesco Vettori wavered as usual, but he would have liked at least to save republican appearances. Iacopo Salviati demanded safeguards with more courageous firmness. Only Roberto Acciaiuoli and Luigi Guicciardini, thinking only of their own interests, gave way to the Pope's wishes. The latter, though entirely resolved, continued to hear opinions from everyone with the hope of finding what he wanted. Through Schönberg he also sought Francesco Guicciardini's opinion, and the latter at different times sent or included in his papers no less than five.[23] These writings all advised against the princely state, except, say, 'at the end of fifty or a hundred years'; and it is no wonder they did not please the Pope.[24] They are also all dominated by a painful reality and iron necessity: 'We have as our enemy an entire people . . . so that we are forced to desire any solution which may ensure our power in the State, of whatever kind it may be.'[25]

With that conviction rooted in his soul, he was certainly not one uselessly to jeopardize his 'personal profit' in order to dissuade the Pontiff from his intentions. With that conviction, in spite of his attachment to republican institutions, which is also shown in the above-mentioned opinions, forms in the end could make little difference: everything had to give way to necessity dictated by a 'private interest' common to the Medici and to each of their followers. Thus, when in mid-April of that year 1532 he was called to Florence to establish, together with eleven others chosen to carry out that bitter task, a government according to papal wishes, he could only measure by the yardstick of that necessity decisions which on the whole were already irreversible. The principal of them were these: destruction of the Signoria, transformation of the Balìa into the council of the Two Hundred, creation of the limited senate of the Forty-Eight, who were to elect from their number four Councillors presided over by the Duke or his Lieutenant. Thus ended the glorious forms of the Republic and even the name of Florentine liberties.

Returning to Bologna early in May, he decided to send to Clement through the usual channel of Lanfredini the truth about the contriving of that reform, and the thoughts it had aroused in him. Among the twelve of them there had been no differences of opinion nor any opposition to what had been 'indicated' to them, but he added: 'If you were to ask me whether this action pleased all of them, and also the others, so that they would have carried it out if they had believed that it depended simply on their own views, and not put forward as something which had to be done, I must tell you that it would not, for in fact in all the city there can be but few whom it can have pleased.' It had been unwelcome not only to the enemies of the Medici state, but to its friends (as he went on), 'to remove the Signoria which has existed for nearly three hundred years, and close the Palace which has been for so long, one might say, venerated'.[26]

In the meantime, to distract his mind from these troubled thoughts of Florence, he had worries in Bologna. He had left the management of affairs at an inconvenient moment, and in the twenty days he had been away the threads of not a few matters had been tangled or broken. There was the raising of an extraordinary tribute demanded by the Pope and laboriously negotiated by the Governor between the exhausted city and the hungry Roman wolf.[27] There were the usual quarrels between Pepoli and Malvezzi, now marked with bloodshed.[28] There was a truce between opposing factions in the Montagna, which he had at last arranged two days before his departure for Florence but not yet properly settled, which during the absence of its chief architect had got into difficulties and broken down. Seeing no way of getting it going again, he endeavoured with the factious parties 'to use them to beat one another, making no difference between them, but just as opportunity might arise'. The supreme opportunity (as he wrote complacently) arose at that very time. 'An armed band of the adherents of the Tanari was put to flight, and Camillo de' Sacchi, the most important and factious person of the Montagna, was penned in a house together with fourteen or sixteen companions; they were burnt inside the house, since they could not otherwise be got out: which was a great beginning towards pacifying the country.'[29]

Then things resumed their usual course. Only a part of the levy was paid and the usurers advanced the rest as usual. Counterfeiters were caught and tried. Cardinal Ippolito de' Medici passed through Bologna, sent by the Pope to Hungary against the Turks to remove him from any temptations in Florence where he had made a lightning trip before Alessandro was installed, more to alarm the Pope than attempting to do anything in his own cause. At Bologna he was honoured and given hospitality by the Governor in his palace.[30] There also passed through the notorious historian Paolo Giovio, but he found a Guicciardini much less attentive and hospitable, who wrote humorously about him: 'And if I do not now figure in his histories, I shall be able to bear it.'[31] Indeed that was his fate.

In August Clement fell ill and Guicciardini held his breath. At the first news he wrote to Lanfredini: 'Since yesterday evening I feel my spirits fail me at every hour.'[32] And it is hardly credible that words so unusual for him were written as a pure form. We know that sincere affection bound him to that unlovable Pope, and there was something in it perhaps of that feeling which the strong cherish for the weak; but above all, as we know, and he knew it much better, Clement was for him the source of honour and wealth. He applied to him again to help marry off his remaining daughters Laudomina and Lisabetta. Those daughters were a trial to him. It seems that they were not models of beauty, and they had a father who was hard to please and measured out their dowries with a miserly hand while his ambition for them was ampler. He sought for them none other than Lorenzo di Pierfrancesco de' Medici, to whom the succession would pass if Duke Alessandro died without male heirs, and a son of Filippo Strozzi,[33] the richest man in Italy, a close relation of the Pope – a Pope who had ties of marriage with the Emperor and was at that time endeavouring to form them with the King of France.

It was perhaps this marriage being negotiated between Pope and King which more than anything else inspired Charles V to seek a fresh meeting with Clement VII. The place chosen for it was again Bologna, but this time Guicciardini was not there, as he previously was, as a fugitive; he was the Governor. On his shoulders therefore weighed a thousand cares: to feed in a lean year two courts with their trains of courtiers, all people with hearty appetites, each with his own little court. Then he had to think about ceremonies and shows, although the citizens had conveyed to him that, 'in order not to burden the exchequer . . . which was very poor, if they thought it possible, they would rather do less than more'.[34] But first he had had to calm the fears of the Bolognese and explain to the people at Rome that they should persuade the Emperor not to come there with too many soldiers.

On the 8th December the Pope made his entry and on the 13th the Emperor, and it was Guicciardini himself, more solemn and pompous than ever, who went to hold his bridle. Who would have thought it while he was raising the League against the Emperor? Receptions, ceremonies, demonstrations between Charles and Clement were all the warmer on the surface in that they had to disguise the coldness within. The former was displeased by that French marriage, the latter dissatisfied by the protection given to Ferrara and the unwelcome things the Emperor had come to ask for.

To discuss these matters the Emperor nominated his celebrated ministers Cobos, Granvela and Tara. For the Pope were Cardinal Ippolito de' Medici, Iacopo Salviati and our Governor, who was the only one capable of standing up to the three Spanish foxes. There is a legend (and it is appropriate to quote it here) that Charles V once said: 'In one hour I can make a hundred grandees of Spain, but in twenty years I could not make a man as great as Guicciardini.'[35]

223

In those difficult negotiations the Emperor demanded the calling of a Consilium 'for the peace and satisfaction of Germany', a fresh general confederation, the marriage of the young Caterina de' Medici, last legitimate offspring of the descendants of Lorenzo the Magnificent, with Duke Francesco Sforza. It was a marriage sought less for love of the Duke than to upset any plan for a marriage between Catherine and the second son of the King of France. As none of these things were to the Pope's liking, after two months' skirmishing, those acting for him gave way on the matter which both sides cared about least: the confederation.[36] This was contracted on the 24th February 1533 and Charles left the following day, not much satisfied. A few days later Clement left Bologna. And on that occasion too the Garisenda stood firm.

Chapter 21

THE MEETING AT MARSEILLES.
END OF GUICCIARDINI'S CAREER
AS GOVERNOR

HE Bologna meeting had ended only by promoting those
French marriage ties and the Pope's meeting with the King of
France which it had been intended by Charles to avert.
Clement then prepared to go to Nice as had been promised in Bologna
to the French cardinals sent by the King. He did not want to go without
Guicciardini, and in May of that same year 1533 he gave him some hint
of it. In fact Guicciardini did not like the idea of that meeting at all: he
feared they might be embarking again on the kind of manoeuvres
which had brought Italy to its present condition. He sighed: 'May it
please God so to enlighten His Holiness that we shall not soon have to
see the ruin of the world starting again.'[1] But as for accompanying the
Pope, he showed himself quite ready, though requesting permission to go
overland as he felt the sea 'as badly as possible';[2] 'I fear the sea excessively' he repeated some time later.[3] Not even that was he to be spared.

That long voyage of the Pope's, particularly if he were to be away
several months as it was rumoured, aroused fears that 'the greater part of
the states of the Church might be thrown into confusion',[4] but as far as
Bologna went, Guicciardini felt confident, and he was not put off by
the catastrophic forecasts of the astrologers. Indeed, while continuing to
seek their views with interest, he protested that he liked them because

the opposite of what they said always happened.[5] We would like to know whether, when he thus maligned the scrutinizers of the stars, he included the author of his famous horoscope, since in these later years he could several times have found it in error. Beware lest one day it take its revenge!

Where he feared some great disorder might indeed occur because of this journey of the Pope's, and perhaps even without it, was in Romagna itself. To hold that country down they needed someone better than Baccio Valori. Indeed, when it was hinted in Rome that even there they thought so, his appetite for the Presidency was again whetted, and we find him making a thousand plans for it. He could give up Nice, and I believe he would have done so gladly, or he would go to Nice and send his brother Luigi to Romagna, where the wolves would become lambs when they realized who was behind Luigi.[6] But then he realized that these were dreams, and for the first time he allows a sigh of weariness to escape him: 'I have no more ambition, and, though not entirely exhausted, my love of affairs has cooled off. I am more inclined to peace than to labour.'[7]

One of his private worries meanwhile ceased when he married Laudomina, his youngest daughter but one, to that good fellow Pandolfo Pucci, son of his friend Roberto. For this occasion, lacking a sufficiently solemn style or patience to describe such events, I shall hand over to a chronicler of the place and time: 'On the 12th August were celebrated the sumptuous nuptials, and a superb supper was held in the Palace in the great hall hung with noble tapestries. The bridegroom was at the head of the table, then the Governor and the Gonfalonier of Justice, who was messer Giulio Cesare Guidotti, facing one another, next the bride, with fifty honourable gentlewomen of the city, and no other men, and all the halbardiers of the Guard; then the hall was full of people watching the solemn banquet; also there were musicians with different instruments and the singing of most beautiful choral music. The meal began at twenty-three hours and continued until two at night. Then, the table rising, they went on to dance until midnight. Every man might dance without hindrance. The feast was free and peaceful.'[8]

As the time drew near for his departure for Nice which had been put off several times, Guicciardini asked permission to have his brother Girolamo take his place (there could be no mention of Iacopo now in disgrace) to make sure that the Cardinal Legate, or rather his secretary, should not meddle in the government to the detriment of the jealous Vice-Legate. But all his thoughts were now set on that great journey. He asked Rome 'whether a great number of courtiers will be going, what number of servants they will take and what effort the court will make to go with all honourable ornaments so as not to appear entirely thread-bare in that *mare magnum* of the court of France'.[9] He asked for an estimate of the duration of the meeting and particularly for the date of departure so that he might set out in time and avoid the bitter experience of sea travel. However, this possibility drew nearer when there began to be talk of Marseilles instead of Nice. Then still more when the papal cavalcade was already on its way to Tuscany to embark and he fell ill with kidney trouble, and his wife too was ill, I do not know from what cause. Thus delayed, to the ruin of all his plans, he had to fall back upon a sea journey, and he applied to his friend Lanfredini: 'I do not know what diligence one must use to have one of the less uncomfortable places in the galley, which indeed, anyone who suffers at sea as I shall, would deserve more than a man who does not fear the sea. I beg you to remember to put me on the list too.'[10] The die having been cast, on the 22nd September he reached Pistoia, and on the 24th in Pisa he joined the papal cortège to embark on the 4th October at Porto Pisano.

At this point, swallowed up by the hated galley, Guicciardini disappears, first out to sea and then after a few days of a 'quite good journey',[11] he disappears into what he had called the *mare magnum* of the French court. And as we are to lose sight of him, there is little impor-ance for us in the celebration of the marriage, the festivities and even the meeting between Pope and King in which Guicciardini took little part. He himself tells us that there were very great demonstrations of affec-tion, confidence, agreement, but no actual and genuine political negotiation, still less the rumoured secret pacts on the duchy of Milan which was said to have been promised to the Duke of Orleans, the bridegroom, virtually as an addition to the dowry of the young Catherine. But this jewel from the dowry was seen to shine only in a joke made by Filippo Strozzi to the royal treasurers; and although one illustrious scholar puts it differently, I prefer to believe Guicciardini who certainly knew more about it, and denied the tale expressly when he had no longer any reason to keep the secret, rather the contrary.[12]

In short, at Marseilles he was not entrusted as at Bologna with political negotiations but rather with juridical ones. He was not this time Clement's minister of foreign affairs but his lawyer. He drafted or at least revised, corrected, altered the marriage contracts and other documents connected with the marriage. And of all these we have minutes corrected and annotated in his own hand, among which the only really political document is an instruction to the Spanish nuncio to allay the jealousy and suspicion of Charles V.[13]

The meeting and the festivities lasted little more than a month. Then while the Pope was preparing to embark, Guicciardini took at his ease the land route, delighted to travel on solid ground which he liked in fact as well as metaphorically; he was even more pleased when he learnt that this time the sea had not been kind to the return of Clement.[14] Then he had only to worry over the fate of his possessions, most of which had been sent by sea, and of which there was still no news after a month. He feared it was all lost, and with it all that he had earned by that journey. Of course it grieved him, but even more he was oppressed by a more general feeling which caused him to sigh: 'Even my stars do not permit me to rise or fall, but wish to keep me between rich and poor.' He was in fact rich already, and this complaint sounds very characteristic to me.[15]

Having reached Bologna on the first day of December, he found the city quiet and orderly as he had left it. Famine, the sad heritage of war, was that year plaguing even the rich lands of Emilia. The Bolognese had been energetic in importing large quantities of grain and the city would not have suffered if the Legate of the Marches had not kept back in Ancona two ships, one after another. He said it was to feed his own people, but in fact it was to profiteer with it. This Legate was no less a person than the famous Benedetto Accolti, Cardinal of Ravenna, nick-named 'Unico' like his uncle, though the name would not appear capable of such a plural use.

Guicciardini, however, when it was necessary, had small respect for the purple and still less for literature, and at once asked them at Rome to 'pull his ears', adding: 'Anyone with the time could compose the best comedy ever seen on the subject of that most reverend Legate . . . for if you put together all the Uniques and all the Accolti who ever lived they would not make up a third part of this one.'[16] It may partly have been because the Bolognese were in danger of starving as he said, but partly it was out of pique. The question of the grain was for a long time the principal subject of his letters to Lanfredini, while the latter did nothing but request money for the empty papal coffers. So that Guicciardini wrote to him in fun: 'Anyone who looks at our letters will think that I never have any bread for my supper, and yours show that you never have any money to pay your bill at the tavern.'[17]

He had no affair of greater importance than this on his hands. Early in the New Year 1534 Count Guido Rangoni conveyed to him that he had a good plan against the Duke of Ferrara, but at Rome they let the matter drop.[18] The time was no longer ripe and Clement had other things to think of. Returning from France with foreboding of death, after having had 'the ring made and all the vestments usual for Popes at their burial', and quietly announced to those about him his early demise, he indeed fell so ill that all thought his words prophetic.

That very long illness, between times when it grew worse and brought him to the point of death, followed by miraculous improvement, was a period of torture for Guicciardini. After having felt his 'flesh creep' at the end of May, we find him lively and restored as a young cockerel in mid-July when the doctors say his Pope is cured. Guicciardini advises that they should move him from Rome 'leaving in the bad air those who are hoping to be Pope, whose joy will (thank God) have been turned to bitterness in these recent days. They will be comforted the more if new promotions are made, which will compel them to make fresh calculations.'[19]

That was an old plan of his: to make a large batch of cardinals which would ensure for the young Ippolito a devoted majority in future conclaves and make the papacy safe for him. Messer Francesco had acquired a taste for it: after Leo and Clement he would have liked St Peter's chair to become hereditary in the Medici family. But it was he who had to make fresh calculations. That sickness with its ups and downs caused him to hope and despair for the beloved Pope all through August, 'fearing that even the birds may carry him away'.[20] He consulted doctors, he even sent some on, though sharing the sick man's lack of confidence in them: 'If he has lost faith in doctors, he has every reason, for indeed in this matter those err least who never had any faith in them.'[21] Who knows whether the Pope, like last time, did not renew a vow like that of the verses by Berni:

> Quest'è un voto che papa Clemente
> a questa Nostra Donna ha soddisfatto
> perchè di man d'otto medici un tratto
> lo liberò miracolosamente.

[This is a vow which Pope Clement fulfilled to Our Lady, for she by a miracle freed him from the hands of eight doctors at once.]

As that dizzy see-saw went on, in the letters of 24th August 'he received extreme unction'; on the 7th September a 'great hope' arose and was immediately extinguished on the 11th; 'returned from death to life' on the 15th, on the 28th Guicciardini died again with the news of the Pope's death. He knew it was the end of his tenure as Governor, and wrote at once: 'I will make my arrangements here and will try to manage things in such a way that when the new pope comes in, I shall maintain my honour, and for the rest we shall leave it to the priests whose business it is.'[22]

In fact he had begun to make his arrangements in August. When Clement's illness had got worse recently, he had reinforced the garrison with a few hundred soldiers, and he had been very annoyed that the Bolognese agent in Rome had been going around saying that the Governor had decided to abandon the city if the Pope died. As the thing was neither true nor even likely, nor at all like him or any of his actions during his terms of office, Guicciardini wrote to Rome an angry letter attacking the incautious agent and promising to 'show him up in so many ways . . . as to lay bare his roguery'.[23] These were the penalties of his profession. One cannot govern for so many years with such severity without gathering a harvest of rancour and hatred, nor did our Governor suffer any shortage of such troubles even in Bologna. Hatred is in the very ink of the letters written to Rome by those powerful lords, of the bad sonnets put about by their creatures:

'Guizardino Francesco, Francescazzo . . .'

and of the city chronicles which are far from kind to him. All behind his back however.[24] For meanwhile even those rebellious nobles had to be satisfied with a 'bergamasque sneer'. Common people and feudal lords, great and small alike, feared the claws of the old lion.[25]

He was not a novice at vacant sees but a veteran of such challenges. This time there were no enemy armies at the gates, and yet he felt more fearful, almost cowardly; the enemy was within the walls, in the streets, in every house; the multitude of a great city with its impetuous mob, its overbearing nobles.[26] At that very moment two of them had returned: Girolamo Pepoli and Galeazzo da Castello, who having left the city the year before out of hatred for him, had conspired in Modena with Florentine exiles to assassinate him;[27] and now he watched them not without anger and suspicion, arriving with the storm, joyfully visited by their followers.[28] And they had not come alone: armed exiles and gallows birds roamed the city. The Governor showed more patience than on other occasions, and yet before the game was over the gallows received a couple of those men.

In Bologna the Pepoli 'were accustomed to live like princes at any time when the See was vacant', but a Guicciardini would not stand for it and lowered their pride. Having consulted and agreed with the magistrates, he sought and obtained that the city should be governed as in normal times, properly, with order and with just severity. He wrote to Cardinal Cybo: 'if this were not done ... I should increase the insolence of those who are misbehaving; I should frighten not only their rivals but all those who desire to live well; and whereas it has happened that many, though in error, have regarded me as being more favourable to the Pepoli than to the others, I should have confirmed this false belief at a time when it would have been extremely damaging if the rest of the city did not regard me as neutral, as it is my duty to be'.[29]

On the 14th October news came of the election to the papacy of old Cardinal Farnese, who became Paul III. Although he was not one of those whom Guicciardini would most have wished to succeed, he was glad just the same to be released from uncertainty. He knew that there was no longer any room for a lay governor in Bologna; he knew that the profitable times for the Florentines were over, but a last hope reminding him that he had once been confirmed in his post by Pope Adrian, a foreigner, inspired him to write a handsome letter to Pope Paul. And he dropped a few grains of incense into it.[30]

Meanwhile it was no longer to his advantage to remain there with the Pepoli cutting the ground from under his feet, as they had not been able to dig his grave; and with the winds now blowing from Rome, he felt he was 'diminishing from captain to light horseman',[31] or at least 'from governor to mayor'.[32] Then he wrote to the Pope another letter which has not survived but of which we have certain knowledge: like so many others he had sent in happier days from Modena, from Reggio, from Parma, it seems to have asked for complete authority or permission to return home.[33] But the times were no longer right for such letters: there was a Pope at Rome who certainly did not venerate the relics of his predecessor, and who was saying that the Florentines 'had enjoyed too much [of the spoils]'. So Cybo wrote that 'the Pope had graciously replied that He was pleased to replace him': to take his place Giovan Maria del Monte would come, who was Archbishop of Manfredonia.[34] The attempt had failed: never mind! He took comfort with Lanfredini who like himself had lost his job, urging him to return quickly to Florence to enjoy their home together and 'speak ill of the priests, that is, the living not the dead'.[35]

He therefore prepared to await the arrival of the Archbishop without impatience when at the beginning of November he learnt that the new Pope wished to investigate all the ministers of his predecessor. Worse still when he learnt that one of the investigators was Cardinal Lorenzo Campeggi who had never forgiven his rivalry with his brother Tommaso for the governorship of Parma. To be thus 'pushed around' was unbearable to his pride. 'Full of bitterness', he later informed the Pope that he was prepared to give a financial account down to the last penny but not an account of his administration.[36] Meanwhile, resolved to leave without awaiting the convenience of the new Governor, 'so that no one might hold him so cheap',[37] he sought leave from Cybo. Indeed, as he had put it in a recent letter, to that city from now on he was only 'stuck with wax'.[38]

The thoughts that may have passed through his mind while he was getting ready to leave Bologna, I think one can divine from what has been said already: perhaps a mixture of regret and resentment, something like that of sincere feeling and irony in a letter he wrote to Guiducci, Cybo's secretary, after a memorable farewell supper. During it 'no one thought about investigations or melancholy things, but all was joy and merriment except at the end when some people were staggering and others falling down and we sang the Lamentations of Jeremiah at having to leave Bologna, so gracious a city, so pleasing, so beautiful, the first city in the world, storehouse of all fine arts, a city so grateful to those who confer benefits upon her, hating fortune and flattery, where yea is really yea and nay nay, where despite Accurtius and all glosses men have in their mouths what they have in their hearts, where there is no vainglory nor ostentation, where every man is the enemy of idleness, where the good days are not wasted, a city which is mother of letters, of arms, and of all virtues . . . a city which beyond all others has learnt the Greek proverb which says one should know one-self, for they know very well that in all the world there is only one Bologna, and that those who have once tasted of this place cannot leave it without the deepest regret. Here the women are delightful, the young men handsome and affable, the wines and all food most excellent. . . .' But this was how the dinner ended, this is how the account ends which the solemn governor wrote the following day: 'Count Ottavio made a speech and at the end of the leave-takings he made everyone cry with tender feeling, so that we recovered partly from the wine we had drunk by weeping. The rest went in sleep and today in fasting, and I can still feel it in my head . . .'[39]

On the evening of the 23rd November the Cardinal Legate's reply arrived, not only giving him the leave he sought, but actually 'urging him to depart at the earliest moment in his own best interests'.[40] This may have been a kindly warning or a stratagem to get rid of the intractable Governor. Either Guicciardini was convinced by it or he was stung, but he did not wait to hear it twice. The following morning the Forty were called into his presence and he informed them abruptly that he had decided to depart 'without fail or delay'.[41] Suiting the action to the word and leaving his wife with his daughter Laudomina, who was married to Pandolfo Pucci and expecting a child, at eight o'clock that evening he mounted his horse. But this departure was well in keeping with the traditions of his governorships. For he would not depart by secret byways at an unfrequented hour; but in broad daylight he was pleased to ride escorted by his guard of halbardiers and crossbowmen, past the houses of the Pepoli who had sworn to take his life.[42] Thus it pleased him to do, thus we see him leave the stage, defying those arrogant enemies, with a clattering of hooves, a jingling of arms and the gleaming of armour.

Chapter 22

THE COMMENTARIES OF THE LIEUTENANCY. ADVOCATE OF DUKE ALESSANDRO

⋄⋄⋄

IT WAS now twenty-three years since he had left for the legation to Spain. From that date on, excepting for the bitter period of idleness *post res perditas*, he had lived almost entirely outside Florence and had become accustomed to ideas, manners, customs, so remote from civic Florentine simplicity, that he seemed to his fellow Florentines 'a foreigner'.[1] Yet perhaps, as in honours and all else, he had found in the end 'they had not in them that satisfaction he had hoped for'; at Bologna during the closing days of his governorship his only thought was to 'lay down all this pomp', to 'enjoy the pleasures of Santa Margherita'.[2] In that bitterness and fatigue, in the decline of his life, he was perhaps sincere.

So he is now at Santa Margherita. And this idleness has a different feeling from last time when he returned from the Lieutenancy, with less fear for the present in the friendly shadow of the Medici, protected by the far greater imperial shadow, but seven years older, seven heavy years. In the rediscovered pleasures of country life, accepting some vegetable seeds, he writes with melancholy that it seems to him 'more appropriate to [his] age and to [his] not having sons, to plant cabbages and lettuce than pines and fir trees'.[3]

Among the things which give man the pious illusion of surviving,

the hope of male issue had vanished some time before (a great disappointment for him), and now he even feels too old to plant trees. But
the greatest hope remains: to write the book which will give him a life
'as long as the world'. And he sets his hand to it in the very days while
the tedious structure of the ecclesiastical commission was collapsing;[4]
at this same time he is sowing in his notebooks the seed of a plant far
greater than pines and firs.

On returning to Florence after his exile he had again taken up the
Cose fiorentine, and brought it on, with many gaps which betray the
author's impatience and fatigue, to a point well on in the third book.
Then impatience and weariness had grown: running ahead of the
narrative by about four years, he had also written in the middle of the
mass of material collected for the fourth volume two imaginary speeches.
Then, as he continued his work on extracts from the archives, he had to
pack up his notebooks and leave for Bologna.[5] On his return more than
three years later he took them up again, but only to copy out those
speeches again, abandoning the rest as a dry skeleton.[6] Begun in misfortune, dragged on and interrupted over so many years, that
history of the dead republic seemed to him a dead thing. Another
history which was alive, other events, in which he himself had been not
a spectator but an actor, had tempted him for some time. In 1528 we
find him telling the historian Iacopo Nardi that he wished to write the
commentaries of his Lieutenancy.[7] The death of Clement VII, which
consigned these events to history, had closed a period in his life and
gave him the necessary leisure to write about them.[8]

For such a work, as it took shape in the first plan, he did not even
need any other information than that amply provided in his own papers,
where all the things he wanted to describe were written. He therefore
worked rapidly, though the revisions of the autograph reveal great
application and a certain difficulty involved in this new undertaking,
due also perhaps to his search for a style. Having begun to write, without
any hint of a title or any divisions in the text, from the 'battle of Pavia',
he probably intended to go on as far as the capture and sack of Rome,
perhaps dividing the work into four books. He ended the first with the
liberation of the King of France; but having written under the heading
'second book' only a few pages, in which he concluded the League of
Cognac and followed the Lieutenant as far as Piacenza, he had to break
off his work to get his new master out of difficulties.[9]

Duke Alessandro had inherited the legacy of hatred incurred in

Florence by Pope Clement, and had further increased it by his natural traits, his intemperate behaviour, his cruel government. Even the oldest and best tried friends of the Medici, those who had received most benefits and had been most compromised, and even his few remaining relatives had nearly all been alienated by him during Clement's lifetime. When the Pope was dead, this hatred became at once more bitter and open, since the Duke had lost that last restraint, and the friends and relatives of the Pope the last respect they had enjoyed. The greatest among his relatives were Filippo Strozzi, whose wife was Clarice the sister of Lorenzo Duke of Urbino, Cardinal Giovanni Salviati and Cardinal Niccolò Ridolfi, the sons of two sisters of Leo X. These men, regarding themselves as more legitimate heirs of that glorious branch of the Medici tree which Cosimo *pater patriae*, Lorenzo the Magnificent and Pope Leo had raised to such eminence, objected to Florence being held and abused by this bastard, quite apart from the fact that he had treated them and continued to do so in a very insolent manner.

They therefore roused against Alessandro the man who had been driven out by him, Cardinal Ippolito, a bastard too, but at least the son of a gentlewoman and not of a maidservant like the other one, and legitimated by the dignity of the purple, by the urbanity of his manners, by a truly medicean liberality. Around these men, great by birth, by authority, by wealth, was at once gathered the doleful band of Florentine exiles. Those guilty of having so vigorously defended their nations' freedom in the memorable siege, after having been proscribed in defiance of the terms of the capitulation, had after the three years of their sentence were up, been again exiled in wild and unhealthy places.

Having decided to send ambassadors to the Emperor to protest against the failure to observe the capitulation and to complain of the Duke's tyrannical government, two different embassies went to Barcelona: one for the Cardinals and for Strozzi, the other for the exiles. They had a good reception and kind words but nothing else. As His Majesty was on the point of embarking for the expedition against Tunis, they were told, it would be better discussed at Naples where Charles planned to stop on his return. Impatiently Ippolito then decided to go to meet him in Africa, but while he was waiting for the ships to embark in, he died suddenly in Itri of a disease which scholars now describe as malaria and which was then invariably called poison. We cannot be sure, however, that the terms should not sometimes be reversed.[10]

On Ippolito's death the Cardinals Ridolfi and Salviati remained with

Strozzi to support the cause of the exiles and of freedom, and later they were joined by Cardinal Niccolò Gaddi, with less authority and no title other than his Florentine nationality. They had collected in Rome at their own expense a large number of exiles who, though with a wide and discordant variety of opinions covered by the changing mantle of patriotism, followed them with high hopes. Such magnanimity and magnificence added fresh grandeur to these last medicean relics: I think this is what was meant by Lorenzo Ridolfi, the Cardinal's brother, 'then a young man, great and illustrious by wealth and noble blood',[11] when at the table of Raffaello da Sommaia he announced that in Florence 'there were no noble houses other than Strozzi, Salviati and Ridolfi'; whereupon Giuliano Gondi said indignantly 'So the rest of us are rubbish', and left the table.[12]

But already, Charles having returned with his African laurels, Duke Alessandro was preparing to appear with arrogant pomp in Naples to receive the imperial judgement. Indeed he had nothing to fear but Spanish greed, particularly when one considers that Charles was his father-in-law at least on paper, and that the state of Florence was safely in his hands and it would not have been easy to take it away from him. At all events for safety he took with him an advocate named Francesco Guicciardini.

From the time when he had been raised to his present state, perhaps on the Pope's advice, he had always held Guicciardini in great esteem. Even while Guicciardini was in Bologna, he had not failed to write to him often to seek his advice with expressions of extraordinary esteem. On his return he was shown great favour and given employment; 'he took more heed of him than of anyone else'. Immediately appointed one of the Four Councillors, then Lieutenant or 'vice-duca' as it was at first called, messer Francesco could be seen 'almost every morning with the Duke'.[13] He negotiated with the Imperial representatives the renewal of the treaty of Bologna of 1533,[14] and we know from those near him that at that time 'he was in very good spirits'.[15] He was quite right to be satisfied.

Alessandro with his tyrannical ways and intemperate nature could certainly not be pleasing to Guicciardini, but if the Duke was a man who wished to follow his own inclinations in managing internal affairs of state, he was not clever enough to manoeuvre on his own in foreign matters, and this was all Guicciardini asked for: a prince who would allow himself to be managed by him. And then, according to an old axiom of his, he regarded it as 'the office of good citizens, when their country falls into the hands of tyrants, to try to gain influence with them to persuade them to do good and hate evil'; and again: 'it is in the interests of the city that at all times men of quality should hold authority'.[16] Nor, great realist that he was, could he close his eyes to the realities of Italian politics. Since Charles V had triumphed, and her misfortunes under the shadow of Clement VII had bound Florence to the victor's chariot, any movement, any adventurous innovation could provoke a worse disaster. For Guicciardini the Duke was a good means of consolidating the ground.

All these were general convictions, ideas deeply rooted in Guicciardini. But in every man when thoughts and general ideas are woven together and become identified with personal interests, then they really become unshakeable. So from the moment when, in the middle of the previous November in Bologna, he had received news of the first actions of the exiles, he had hastened to ask Duke Alessandro for a copy of the treaty made in 1530, well aware that this was their strong point; and writing of it to his brother Luigi he ended with notable lack of scruple: 'In all reason our course must be to run in all and for all with the Duke, and I for my part am quite decided, both on account of my obligations towards his house, and for my own interests, for I know I cannot trust those rogues, nor could anything ever persuade me of the contrary, for I know they hold me in the utmost hatred.'[17] Could he have expected them to love him? 'Quite determined', therefore, on the 21st December he took the road to Naples with Alessandro and the great ducal cavalcade. When they arrived, the Emperor had already received the Cardinals, heard the fiery protest uttered by Iacopo Nardi on behalf of the *émigrés*, and given to all kind but general words: 'The Duke will come here and we will do what is just.' There walked through that city eyeing one another askance old friends like Filippo Strozzi and Francesco Vettori; Lorenzo Ridolfi and Bernardo Salviati supporters of the exiles' cause, Luigi Ridolfi and Alamanno Salviati their brothers, partisans of the Duke. Needless to say Guicciardini was looked at askance; his old odious nickname 'ser Cerrettieri' was heard.[18] As the Duke's advocate he met in Naples in judge's garb the great imperial ministers with whom he had for three months negotiated in Bologna the affairs of the Pope and of Italy. It was another point in his favour and hence also for Alessandro.

When asked to do so, the exiles presented their grievances in writing.

These briefly and in substance asked the Emperor to observe the capitulation of 1530 signed for him by Don Ferrante Gonzaga and later ratified by him containing 'in primis . . . that liberty shall be preserved'. They went on to relate how and by what means liberty had on the contrary been at once extinguished; how the Imperial judgement promulgated in 1531 had been evaded and set aside; how not even the promise to pardon all injuries had been observed, of which the eloquent proof was that very multitude of émigrés; how finally the tyrannical government introduced by Pope Clement was exercised with unbearable cruelty and arbitrariness by Duke Alessandro. And here the complaints went on to give details of many particular outrages and dishonest practices: unjust and disproportionate sentences, overbearing behaviour by ducal ministers and hired ruffians, murders carried out by the Duke's own hand when he took pleasure in going out at night to hunt Florentines; other more pleasurable chases of gentlewomen in their own homes and of nuns in their convents were covered by a decent veil of general terms.

These complaints were conveyed to Alessandro by the Imperial ministers within four days, and a week later the Duke's reply was received. He, although he had brought to Naples men like Francesco Vettori, Roberto Acciaiouli, Matteo Strozzi and Baccio Valori, 'nevertheless did everything with the advice of messer Francesco Guicciardini, and it was he who was the head, the author and the counsellor for everything; et hoc ad perpetuam memoriam'. This is told us with indignation by a narrator of these affairs who was procurator for the émigrés;[19] but there was no need for him to say so, for in this Defence Guicciardini's style can be smelt a thousand miles away.[20]

Extremely clever but captious and false, he begins with a distinction: if the complaints originated with those who 'not of necessity but voluntarily' had embarked on the course of opposing the Duke, that is, the Cardinals and Strozzi, they had no grounds for complaint, having at one time consented to or taken part in the actions now imputed to the Duke. If on the other hand they were brought by those who had been banned and exiled, those could not be heard, since they had been justly and legitimately deprived of their rights, on account of their misdeeds. Indeed, but it was precisely the justice and legitimacy of that deprivation which were contested by the plaintiffs. After which, coming to the first point of the accusations, Guicciardini's defence interprets in an unheard-of manner that clause of the capitulation: 'understanding always that l iberty be preserved'. It meant according to him that the city was not to be placed under foreign rule nor deprived of its privileges. This would take one's breath away, but immediately following this Guicciardini gives us a brief account of Florentine history *ad usum Caesaris* which would shock one even more if one did not know that it is not the historian who speaks but the lawyer. Lucky for him that his works were not published, otherwise it would have been a fine game for the exiles to show their pages to the imperial ministers and give him the lie with his own words.

From this point on nothing can further astonish us. The parliament called immediately after the surrender under the threat of the victorious troops, was absolutely legitimate; so too the reform of the government introduced in contradiction to the forms laid down in the imperial edict, because 'as a free city . . . there is no doubt that it can freely dispose of all matters pertaining to government at its own good pleasure'. How freely it had disposed of them, we have seen, though in a more decent form, in one of Guicciardini's own letters. It would certainly be amusing to go from one subtlety to another, from sophism to sophism through the whole of this *Defence* refuting it with words from his own works, from his letters, from contemporary witnesses; but this could be done only in a special monograph. In these pages the little we have already said will suffice to give an idea of it. And yet I cannot resist the final shot, where endeavouring to force them too far, the words themselves force the defender's hand: 'One cannot reply in detail to the charges about women, rape and similar calumnies uttered in general; but His Excellency's virtue, his fame, the opinion of him held throughout the city, of his prudence and his virtuous habits, are a sufficient reply, since his proceedings are so laudable that the calumnies of wicked men do not suffice to obscure them.' In fact, as a contemporary noted sarcastically, 'he concludes that the morals of Duke Alessandro are most saintly and his government free and merciful. *Laus Deo*'.[21]

At that time Guicciardini's *Defence* was judged 'silly and wicked'[22] by those who supported the exiles, perhaps also by those who supported neither party. I would not describe it as silly since the too evident falsehoods and obvious distortions of which it is full, were laid before foreign judges who might accept them as true and indeed wished for nothing better; so that Guicciardini was telling them what they wanted to hear and what the interests of his patron required. Certainly it is not pleasant to read such things, but without remaining open mouthed before them as Rossi does in his apologia,[23] one cannot be scandalized either. We must again remind ourselves that Guicciardini was the Duke's advocate; in that ill-famed defence at Naples he was only exercising his profession like any other lawyer since the beginning of the world. It was his misfortune that in defending an unjust and objectionable cause and a shady client he earned a further odium to add to that he had earned already.

Be that as it may, the imperial ministers deprived the *émigrés* of an easy triumph when they commanded them not to refute in any manner this reply of the Duke's but to state merely in what respects they held the city to be oppressed, and the manner of remedying it.[24] They added, however, that the Emperor wished in no way to alter his arbitration of 1531 nor to abandon the promises made at Barcelona, namely that Alessandro should be his son-in-law and head of the Florentine Republic. Hearing this and seeing the affair turned to ridicule, the exiles meant to depart at once leaving all unfinished, then on maturer reflection they replied verbally that, as for his daughter, His Majesty could give her to whoever he liked; as for the government of the city, since His Majesty had prejudged the affair, they asked in writing on the 16th January that the authority conceded to Alessandro should at least be personal only and should not be handed down by succession, and that he should not be able by his intervention in the councils 'to prevent on his own authority what had been legitimately decided by others, but let his vote be only that of a legitimate head in any free city'; and that of the public revenue he should have no more than a fixed share, etc.[25]

These requests, though very far from the early hopes conceived by the Florentine exiles, would have reduced Alessandro to the mere shadow of a duke. Nor did a free Florence and a son-in-law in such minor and temporary authority suit the Emperor. They were rejected therefore by the Duke in a short and brusque refusal, to which however Granvela had his friend Guicciardini add a postscript in which the pardon of the *émigrés* was agreed to.[26] Finally an imperial oblation was published in Spanish proposing this same pardon and the restitution of property, without at all touching on the reform of the government.[27] The exiles were shocked, and assuming (which was not far from the truth) that this was the Emperor's final decision, setting aside all respect, they delivered the stunning reply which begins: 'We did not come here to ask His Majesty under what conditions we should serve Duke Alessandro, nor through His Majesty to beg from him a pardon for what we voluntarily did in justice and duty, nor so that through the restitution of our property we might return as slaves to that city which we left as free men. . . .'[28]

This noble protest gave great pleasure and was much approved throughout Italy: a clear indication that the 'mad' on that occasion too, did much better than the 'wise'. However, Charles V was not at all pleased by it, 'as it seemed that the *émigrés* wished to imply that he had failed to keep faith with them'. So that they should not depart too dissatisfied by imperial justice, he caused them to be given verbally greater hopes for a time when the war clouds already threatening over France should have dispersed, while in writing he had a general reply given to them, defending the published oblation and admonishing them to rely on His Majesty.[29]

The Duke's reply to this oblation was given verbally by his defender and has remained unknown until the present. I have found an autograph summary of it among Guicciardini's papers.[30] In their turn the exiles presented fresh proposals according to which Caesar should 'within three months order and establish in Florence a free form of government'.[31] These proposals were rejected on the Duke's side with an indignant reply 'that Granvela would not accept', as we are informed in a note added by Guicciardini.[32] It was then that Alessandro, losing patience and the little sense God had given him, wished in his turn to depart abruptly; and it was then that Guicciardini saved him by dissuading him from that act of folly,[33] and presenting another reply in which it was requested that the delay within which Caesar was to reform the government should be extended from three months to a year.[34]

It was not three months nor a year. As we said, Alessandro was more important to Caesar than the exiles were. He had promised him his daughter, he held the government of Florence, from him he could extract the moneys of which he had the usual urgent need. While feeding the exiles' hopes he had grilled him on a slow fire and made him disposed to greater sacrifices. When Alessandro opened his purse or rather that of his subjects, he renounced the dowry promised at Barcelona, and concluded in secret from Guicciardini, who had advised him against becoming a feudatory of the Empire,[35] an agreement which mortgaged to the Emperor all the fortresses of the State: the long skirmish was over.[36]

After so many proposals and replies Caesar's final judgement went no further than that oblation which conceded to the emigrés the remission of their punishment. And there were no further documents other than those pertaining to the marriage with all the negotiations and papers connected with it, which still gave Guicciardini a great deal of work, as is shown in many minutes corrected and annotated in his hand.[37] Finally on the 26th February 1536 Alessandro gave the ring to his bride and held a great party at which there sat Caesar and those great ministers of his who had lately been sitting in judgement. Nor could the defending counsel be absent from the feast. Meanwhile the Florentine exiles were scattering along the roads of Italy. None of them had wished to accept Caesar's grace; all preferred poverty and exile.[38]

Then the festivities were transferred from Naples to Florence, where on the 29th April Charles V entered with great pomp on his white horse, and as usual Francesco Guicciardini walked at its head dressed in purple velvet;[39] even though he was not sitting in the office of the Lieutenant, he was really henceforth the Vice-Duke. The Emperor remained in Florence a week. Father- and son-in-law hid their mutual irritation under good appearances, resentments brought all the way from that litigation at Naples, one because he had not had everything he wanted, the other smarting at having been skinned alive. Nor did the feasts end there, since on the father-in-law's departure, the bride arriving shortly afterward, the marriage was celebrated and so festivities went on until mid-June.

Meanwhile Charles had gone with a formidable army and even more ferocious intentions to compass the destruction of his perpetual enemy who had suddenly occupied the duchy of Savoy. Having entered Piedmont, Charles carried the war into French territory, relying on fortune which was always kind to him, more than on his captains and counsellors. According to malicious tongues Pope Paul was not displeased by that war beyond the mountains which brought Italy peace. However, wishing to fill the role of good shepherd, he intervened with the two great rivals, exhorting both sides to lay down their arms. He sent to the King of France Cardinal Agostino Trivulzio, and to Charles V at Aix the famous Giovanni Guidiccioni, Bishop of Fossombrone, and with him, according to the historians, but for what reason I do not know, he is said to have sent Guicciardini.[40] One cannot understand what might have induced the Pontiff, when he already had with Caesar someone dealing with that affair, to send someone else as well, a layman

243

without any connection with his court, seeking him moreover among the counsellors of the loathed Duke of Florence.

In fact there are in print from the sixteenth century some letters to Cardinal Trivulzio and the Grand Master Montmorency, written from Aix and from the Imperial camp between the 15th August and the 7th September 1536[41] and signed by Guicciardini. But a careful examination of these letters and comparison of them with others written at the same time to the same people, and published with Guicciardini's signature in the same collection, arouse in me the strongest perplexity and reveal even greater singularities than any I have remarked on just now apropos of this mysterious Guicciardini legation.[42] And however hard one may try, one can find no hint in the papers of the time, no confirmation in the abundant family archives. Quite apart from the fact that the style of all the letters seems to me more like Guidiccioni's than Guicciardini's. I would not be at all surprised if the similarity of the names had not led someone astray, who then dragged with him into error, on the authority of those letters published in the sixteenth century, eminent historians and diligent scholars. The author is sorry to be the first to cast doubt upon, indeed to deny completely, this most notable Guicciardinian expedition.

Meanwhile Charles V found the small remains of his great army was melting like snow in that summer on the plains of burning Provence; so that, if they were not all to die of hunger and plague, they had ingloriously to depart. In mid-October he finally moved to Genoa, and Guicciardini was undoubtedly there if not at Aix. He was in the train of Duke Alessandro,[43] who, having gone to do honour to his imperial father-in-law, remained there until mid-November, returning then to Florence to enjoy his last days.

They were Guicciardini's last political joys. I would not like to do him the injustice of believing that he repeated to Alessandro what, according to one historian Charles V is one day supposed to have said to Guicciardini: *Inveni hominem secundum cor meum.* (According to someone else, he said it more appropriately to Andrea Doria, but it may be he was in the habit of saying it to anybody!) It is, however, true that Guicciardini was never so honoured and consulted in Florence as he was under Alessandro; and this meant a great deal to a man like him: even the most intemperate of his apologists recognizes it.[44] One is sorry to have to say this, but a good few of the Duke's numerous vices served Guicciardini's ambition: his thirst for honours, for authority, for power.

He was, therefore, as a friend says, 'in good spirits' when on the eve of Twelfth Night 1537 his satisfaction was cut short with the life of Alessandro, by the dagger of Lorenzino. That very Lorenzo di Pierfrancesco de 'Medici, to whom not long ago he had dreamed of marrying one of his daughters, had to do a thing like that to him! But the Duke had given the nickname 'the philosopher' to Lorenzo, with his melancholy face, his ambiguous smile, his clever remarks, and, as we know, Guicciardini had never expected anything good of philosophers.

Chapter 23

THE ELECTION OF COSIMO:
THE 'HISTORY OF ITALY'

◇◇

L ORENZINO had the courage to kill Duke Alessandro and thereby win eternal fame with a fine humanist tyrannicide, showing himself a 'man of honour' as he had promised Piero Strozzi, and giving Benvenuto the reverse of the medal they had joked about [Cellini, *Vita*, I, 81]; but he had not enough courage to revive Florentine liberty. Instead of rousing the people, he preferred to mount his horse and ride to safety, carrying with him the key of the room where he had left the Duke's body. He thus had ample time to get over the frontier, but deprived the people of the opportunity to rise at once while government supporters were still ignorant, unprovided and unarmed.

Cardinal Innocenzo Cybo was in Florence at that time, and Alessandro had given him the regency of the city when he went to Bologna in 1533 and later to Naples. Astute, ambitious, entirely devoted to the interests of and pleasing to the Emperor, he possessed every quality and condition to grow in the Duke's favour, not excepting his morals. It was therefore to him that the dead man's faithful guards, having fruitlessly searched for their master even through the convents, carried their first suspicions. It was them who, before Alessandro's death was known for certain, took the necessary measures. The first of these was to deceive the city with some pretext so that nothing should be suspected, 'as they were without arms and the populace most hostile',[1] then to find arms. He also conveyed the matter to Guicciardini, asking what should be done if the Duke could not be found, to which Guicciardini, thinking it an odd question, replied that they should look for him better and then they would discuss it.[2] To find him all they needed was the courage to open that room.

Meanwhile it was late on Twelfth Night which that year fell on Saturday, but it seemed a good thing to go on concealing the incident and the Duke's body. On Sunday, when something began to leak out among the partisans of liberty, instead of rising at once, some of them wanted first to win over the principal men of the city; but having spoken of it to Vettori, he with devilish cunning praised, encouraged and promised his help, then going immediately to find Guicciardini, he had little difficulty in persuading him of the danger they were in and the measures that were needed.[3]

For the Duke's death must have thrown messer Francesco into great dismay. He was bound to him by ambition more or less satisfied and by the hope of its future satisfaction, but much more by fear of a popular state. That fear, which in 1532 had caused him to accept against his real feelings as a sad necessity the end of republican forms, had grown with reason after the defence and offences of Naples where the abyss dividing him from the exiles had widened. He could not hope that they, with their powerful patrons outside Florence and their many followers within, would allow that wonderful opportunity to escape. According to Varchi, all that was wanted in order to raise a revolt was for one man to start: 'so that Guicciardini, who without any doubt was the leader of all the *palleschi*, and even more so the Cardinal and all the courtiers trembled with fright'.[4] Tremble may be an unkind exaggeration of Varchi's, but the fear was there, and no other voice was listened to as Guicciardini's was in the consultations which took place in those days.

The Forty-Eight met on Monday morning, but the senators agreed only on rejecting the succession of the four-year-old Giulio, the dead man's natural son, favoured by Cardinal Cybo who had ambitions to be regent. He got the regency but only until a successor could be found. To find one, that very evening Guicciardini and the other three Medici leaders, Vettori, Acciaiuoli and Matteo Strozzi, met secretly with Ottaviano de' Medici, the Cardinal, and Alessandro Vitelli, the captain of the ducal guard, sent for in furious haste from Città di Castello. There were seven of them. Cybo then gave up his ambitions and the others their differences, and they agreed among themselves to elect Cosimo de' Medici, the young son of the famous ser Giovanni,[5] whom Guicciardini had already sent to fetch from Trebbio.[6]

It was written that Guicciardini plumped for that election for two reasons: one, the youth's lack of years, which led him to hope that he would take his counsel as he was doing at that moment in an important civil action; secondly, that he had already planned to give him his last marriageable daughter, Lisabetta.[7] In truth, of the two reasons offered by a contemporary who was a distant relation I believe mainly the first. However, one or both ideas, together with their distant relationship through the Salviatis, may well have led him to attempt to diminish the authority of the new master and make him tamer and more manageable.

The election of Cosimo having been decided by these few men, they needed to have it confirmed by all the senators. Here Vitelli entered the game: recovering from the first shock and holding the armed forces and the fortress, he then felt himself master of the city and indeed showed it all too clearly. The Forty-Eight having met again the following morning, Tuesday 9th January 1537, their deliberations were accompanied by the shouting of soldiers and clash of arms, much more eloquent than the little speech prepared by Cybo, and Guicciardini's arguments, 'who in fact managed it all'.[8] But opinions still differed, and Palla Rucellai courageously showed his adverse vote, saying: 'here is my vote and here is my head'. Whereupon Guicciardini withdrew with his collaborators and Matteo Niccolini into another room and together they fixed the conditions of which it seems a draft had already been prepared by Guicciardini.[9] The principal of these were that signor Cosimo should be called not Duke but head of the Florentine Republic; that he should while abroad leave a Florentine and not a foreigner as his lieutenant; he should be paid twelve thousand florins a year and no more: at this point in his reading Guicciardini 'lowered his head and raised his eyes, saying twelve thousand florins is a lot to spend'.[10] One can almost see him.

Having returned to the hall, the altercations continued with Palla exclaiming: 'If you had consulted among yourselves and decided what to do, there was no need to call me.' Finally Vitelli, seeing things dragging on, caused a fight between soldiers to be started under the windows. Immediately afterwards was heard a great clattering of arms in the yard, and behind the door of the hall a voice saying to hurry up because the soldiers could not be held any longer.[11] With this compelling argument agreement was reached and the game won.

Thus Cosimo de' Medici was elected; thus Florence, freed from one master, immediately got another one: *'uno avulso non deficit alter'*, said Cybo that morning with the humanist erudition appropriate to a Medici cardinal, while Guicciardini would have said more concisely in the vulgar tongue: 'Murder princes, others will arise at once.'[12] That election was learned of in the city with the greatest regret, except by the lowest classes.[13] 'They particularly blamed and cursed Guicciardini.'[14] He must have been used to it by now.

Those who would have liked to go back to the Gonfalonier or even the Grand Council as had been suggested that morning, were right to curse him. But he, besides the overwhelming reasons of fear and 'private interest', knew that one cannot stop history, still less turn it back. Rather it was surprising, and still is so, that acute realist though he was, he should have been so grossly deceived over the limitation which he thought to impose upon the young Cosimo, not without hope of holding the reins himself. He was reproached for this by serious contemporary historians, by Vettori that same morning,[15] and by Cellini who with his artist's wit at once turned the idea to ridicule: 'They have mounted a young man upon a wonderful horse – then they told him he must not pass certain defined limits; now tell me who is going to be able to hold him when he wants to go beyond them? Laws cannot be imposed on one who is their master.'[16] One asks oneself how it was possible that the earthy common sense of the goldsmith should see further on this occasion than the great politician.

I have been asking myself that question for forty years and I concluded in the end that Guicciardini must have set those limits with no greater illusions than those of Benvenuto. But convinced again that he must accept princely rule, both in the general and in his own particular interest, he wished to make the attempt to contain the Prince's authority, as one makes emergency repairs and dykes even without hope that they will hold. This effort, however, besides being unsuccessful, had little effect upon the hatred of his fellow citizens and aroused the resentment of Cosimo. Likewise one might say that the keen-eyed messer Francesco made a mistake in supporting one who in a lowlier state had some respect for him and some debt of gratitude. All the worse if (though I do not believe it) words or actually letters had passed between them on the subject of marriage. After being raised to the princely state, those former ties would divide rather than unite them. But at least he felt he ought to try.

Whatever his illusions may have been, we cannot say with certainty when disillusion set in. Perhaps early on in small doses, but not in the first few days, when the young Prince needed everyone and all were either his enemies, or unreliable and greedy friends like the imperial agents, Cybo and Vitelli; when the throne, reduced by Guicciardini's efforts to little more than a bench, was tottering in an alarming way. Vitelli's forces would keep the helpless city down, but outside there were the exiles supported by the authority of the Cardinals Salviati and Ridolfi, by the wealth of Strozzi, by the disfavour of Pope Paul towards the Medici state. Alessandro's death had raised their spirits and revived their hopes. Cosimo's election had grieved them unspeakably but also encouraged them to do what their oppressed fellow citizens had not dared to do.

They had already set out from Rome in the train of the Cardinals, who were on their way with about two thousand men between foot and horse, while from the opposite side of the ecclesiastical State in Bologna, Filippo Strozzi had given money to Count Girolamo Pepoli, Guicciardini's old enemy, to raise a further three thousand soldiers and descend on Florence with them. Caught thus between two fires, the Medici galley barely launched would have been sunk entirely if by a miracle there had not arrived at Spezia three thousand Spanish infantry, and if the bold resolution and resource of the defenders had not been met by the *naïveté*, weakness and indecision of the attackers. The Cardinals, convinced partly by kind words and promises, partly by their fear of the Spaniards, provided the latter did not advance, not only agreed to come to Florence without troops, but also wrote to Strozzi to dismiss his men. The latter, who grudged the expense, asked nothing better. Thus ensnared they entered the city without arms or power; all they had for them were their ingenuous hopes of a people which still believed in liberty.

It was not enough to have to deal with unscrupulous men who were well armed; meanwhile those Spanish infantry were coming on by forced marches. 'The method of negotiation was simply this: that signor Alessandro fully armed in the midst of many of his soldiers and with his page always before him carrying a huge shield . . . accompanied messer Francesco Guicciardini to the Salviati house where he went in and out several times in the day.'[17] Therefore it was still he, the old politician, negotiating for the new prince; yet probably the fact that Salviati was his cousin, was no less a factor than his own still intact authority in causing him to be chosen for these negotiations. These followed the only course possible: 'Those of the government standing firm on not changing anything; on the other side Cardinal Ridolfi and Baccio Valori refusing to agree to anything until the city were again free.'[18] Salviati showed himself less inflexible: according to malicious report, seeing the State going to Cosimo his nephew, he had become pacific and accommodating.

As the Spanish continued to advance, the Cardinals were on the point of departing in confusion. 'Then signor Alessandro Vitelli appeared with a large number of guards, and with him messer Francesco Guicciardini ... and they resumed their discussions trying to reach an agreement.'[19] The agreement was reached, but it was yet another trap: the Spaniards were to be sent back while the Cardinals dismissed their men, which they did promptly, while the Spaniards came on as before. Thus Cosimo won the game and the Cardinals had to depart without having obtained anything except the pardon of the exiles to which they found Guicciardini very favourable. He will appear henceforth much gentler towards the exiles, almost remorseful,[20] hoping perhaps to win back the friendship of his fellow citizens and certainly better disposed to listen to them. But he had gone too far in alienating them, and for a reconciliation not even the execution of the loathed ser Maurizio would suffice – this was the real ser Cerrettieri of Duke Alessandro – which he carried out as 'head of the Otto della Pratica' during that month of April.[21]

Up to that point, therefore, his authority had remained as before, nor did it seem any less when on the 11th May the Conde de Cifuentes, the Imperial ambassador, came to Florence and Guicciardini was at once chosen to negotiate with him together with Cosimo himself, Vitelli, the faithful Ottaviano, and Acciaiulo.[22] The commission was renewed twelve days later for the city by the Forty-Eight. But henceforth they were no longer forty-eight, there was only one man in command. Cosimo daily emancipated himself from them and from his powerful electors. Some private letters show us at this period for the first time a strangely helpless Guicciardini, in the dark over the matters dealt with between his young master and Cifuentes. Until, on the 4th June, he confesses openly: 'I know very little about it.'[23]

Then on the 25th bitterness spills over: 'We hear that signor Cosimo has again reached some understanding with these imperials. The details are not known to the rest of us, but from what is believed to be true I fear they are matters little pleasing to us ... we cannot provide against them because we are not consulted and enjoy no confidence whatever; but the trouble is that ruin will be common to all.'[24]

He enjoyed no confidence; it had come to that! We cannot safely conjecture whether in the dealings with the Cardinals there had begun to arise resentments and conflicts between him and Cosimo. But the negotiations with the Imperial envoys were matters which might well exacerbate differences and distrust. Guicciardini had awaited them with anxiety, 'because of the difficulties and evils which any decision must involve',[25] as he was at least as jealous of Florentine independence as Cosimo was greedy for absolute power even at the cost of some diminishing of that independence. It is probable therefore that such negotiations would have occasioned from the very first approaches a silent conflict. Unless Cosimo, knowing Guicciardini's attitude, preferred to negotiate alone with Cifuentes or with the assistance of more compliant counsellors like Campana or those entirely devoted to the Emperor such as Vitelli and Cybo. In any case he was already champing at the bit, impatient at the tutelage of those great citizens who in his eyes stood as the last relics of the free city.

Nor was the result of the negotiations such as to sweeten for Guicciardini the extreme bitterness of having been excluded from them. Apart from the usual imperial exactions which sucked the city still further dry, Cifuentes obtained the fortresses of Florence, Pisa and Leghorn. A hateful and heavy yoke upon the Florentines! Shut out from the secret deliberations, Guicciardini had only been able to oppose it 'strongly' in the public councils,[26] with the sole effect of rendering him even more suspect to Cosimo and his imperial tutors. When it was done he concluded: 'It is said the Count will depart and leave us in the state in which he found us, but without the fortresses and with less reputation and hope.'[27] These words, spoken for the whole city, were also very relevant to his own 'private interest'.

Cosimo meanwhile by the sacrifice of the fortresses had bought the ratification of his election, the Emperor's protection, and the title of 'duke', despite Guicciardini's limitations. The forces of the exiles having been defeated shortly after at Montemurlo, Baccio Valori and others decapitated, Filippo Strozzi dying in prison, Francesco Vettori a prisoner of his own despair, it was really an end in Florence of the last traces of the idea expressed in those words: *Libertas aut potius* αριστοχρατία which Chirico Strozzi wrote at the head of one of his letters,[28] and which could have been set as the inscription on Guicciardini's dialogue on the *Reggimento di Firenze*.

Guicciardini had loved that ideal all his life, but he had to suppress it for Clement and Alessandro and bury it altogether with the election of Cosimo. And here he is, repentant and regretful, vainly attempting to restrain the man he had placed upon a 'wonderful horse', attempting first to dispose him towards clemency towards the exiles, then for those defeated at Montemurlo.[29] Here he is (as he was shown by a historian who was a distant relation, before the documentary evidence was discovered) 'despairing' at having been mistaken, 'at having placed a prince in power',[30] hated on those grounds by his fellow citizens, 'put aside' by the man who owed him his position.[31] This is Guicciardini's tragedy.

He was mortally wounded, and in spite of his reserved nature the humours of that wound had to discharge. It was at that point that Pope Paul III offered him a governorship in the States of the Church.[32] He did so through Roberto Pucci who in past years, with his nephew Raffaello Pucci, had on several occasions carried to the Pope the greetings and respects of that old minister of Popes, receiving each time in reply words of the highest esteem.[33] He was far from being partial to Florentines, an enemy of the new master as he had been of the former one; I do not think Pope Paul would have gone to choose a governor among Cosimo's ministers if he had not known, perhaps from Pucci himself, of the disfavour into which Guicciardini had fallen and of his discontent.

This was most soothing to Guicciardini's sore spirit. Someone still held him in esteem, a prince of quite other power and possessions than that presumptuous youth. The way to honours was again open before him and would have taken him away from Florence where there was now no more he could do. Years and troubles were beginning to weigh upon him, yet the temptation to set out again upon that road was great. And great must have been his satisfaction on the day when he could tell the Duke of the situation offered him, and could ask his permission to accept it. He was so afraid that he would refuse, but instead to his astonishment he agreed at once.[34] Perhaps Cosimo's indifference somewhat diminished the pleasure of his revenge and the desire to go, though his disgust may have increased it.

He therefore replied to Pucci not only to thank him but also in effect to accept. Only one thing left his acceptance somewhat in suspense, the negotiations for the marriage of his last born, Lisabetta. He did not wish to lose such an opportunity on this account. On the other hand he was compelled by 'honour, love and fatherly duty'. He hoped to discharge this obligation by the end of February and present himself to the Pope at Bologna or wherever he might then be. Then, if he did not succeed in placing his daughter, he did not promise but he did not exclude the possibility of his going. And, as in the great days of Pope Clement, virtually in the same manner though more wearily, the pursuit of honour and wealth was beginning again. Honour, 'praiseworthy in all men', was what moved him to leave his country where he could have 'remained in great comfort'; he protested one need not speak of money, as all the reward he needed was the great honour done him by His Holiness; however in the end he spoke of it just the same and asked how much His Holiness would give him.[35]

He remained 'very comfortably' at home. And we do not know if this was because the money did not seem to be enough, or as has been conjectured, Cosimo had second thoughts, or whether in the end his solicitude for his daughter, who did in fact marry Alessandro Capponi the following year,[36] caused him to lose his opportunity; she was the last daughter he had to provide for, but it was also his last chance to rise or rise again.   Of all these reasons the first is perhaps the right one, added to weariness of body and soul.[37] Perhaps there also contributed to it a growing interest in a great work he had lately undertaken. But as this will seem a most unusual reason for Guicciardini, we must show first that in this work the interest of the author was also exceptionally strong.

We left him at grips with the commentaries on that cursed war, origin of all evils including his own; but they were pages which seemed ill-starred like the events they described. On his return from Naples instead of taking up the narrative where he had left it, as though the better to pick up the threads he recopied in his own hand the first version, but not without correcting and reworking it all with infinite care. However, a short way past the point where he had broken off, he stopped again. He then began a third time, again from the beginning, dictating to his secretary, and the third time again (it seemed like a spell) he stopped with the army of the League before reaching Marignano.[38]

There is no doubt that a secret difficulty held him up. There could be none in narrating things he had described day by day in his minute books after having lived and suffered them hour by hour. But in the tormented beginning of the first version, on the same copybook which he had before him to dictate the third version, he had written 'No battle in Italy since through the imprudence of princes and her own ill fortune the foreigners from beyond the mountains entered the country ...'.[39] These words, which are not crossed out like other tentative beginnings but underlined and left there for a new version, fascinated him. And more and more the composition he had planned, to which he had returned a third time, shrank before his eyes. It appeared to him as a mere detail of the great fresco which was unfolding itself in his troubled mind and tempted him more and more; that war, which he had begun to describe, being merely the lamentable conclusion of the upheavals begun in Italy 'from the time when through the imprudence of the princes ... the foreigners entered the country'. Thus he had already 'decided to write ... the things which happened in Italy since the arms of the French, called in by our own princes, began with great conflicts to disturb it'.[40] The *Storia d'Italia* which had sprung from that seed, was already spreading its great branches in his mind.[41]

Only municipal histories had been known in Italy until then. Those which had come out of the cities were either bare summaries or fat compilations or rather pamphlets than books. His was to be the first history of a geographical unity,[42] divided, as Italy was, into multiple and discordant political units. A bold concept, a great enterprise, but much greater and bolder if it were carried out as the author proposed, as he envisaged it already: to seek the evident or secret causes of all events and their ultimate consequences. And the search was to be conducted among papers, in books continually compared and evaluated, and in that secret book which is the human soul, upon which he had all his life fixed his attention.

The unfinished *Cose fiorentine* had been as it were a model for the *Storia d'Italia*, smaller than life size in a lowlier and easier worked material.[43] On that old sketch the artist would base his masterpiece both for the collection and use of sources and in the classic annalistic form and the eloquent speeches, the one cleverly freed from its major defects, the other turned into a useful instrument for the narrator. Everything about the model was to be proportioned and equalled to the scale and dignity of the new work. In those ten years his thought had still further matured, his art had become more finely tempered; disappointments, bitterness, sadness had better prepared him to compose, with the quiet anguish of an ancient drama, the tragedy of Italy.

Chapter 24

DEATH WHILE WORKING ON
HIS MASTERPIECE

BEHIND the cover of honourable appearances his private drama
continued. As Commissioner of Pistoia, where after the death of
Duke Alessandro the fury of the factions had been unleashed, he
did not however move from Florence. His brother Luigi went to
Pistoia instead. He was a member of the Forty-Eight for life, as we
know; he belonged in 1539 to the Councillors, to the Otto di Pratica
and to the Council of State. He did not in fact lack the authority of
the highest positions in the magistrature; it was the offices which had
lost their authority, 'for not the State nor the Forty-Eight nor the
Councillors in particular but Cosimo governed all. Nor was anything
done or said either great or small to which he did not give his approval.'[1]
Others might be satisfied with the position and glory of being councillor to a prince who kept his own counsel, but not Guicciardini.

He had henceforth adjusted to reality; sometimes, if it happened that
his opinions found the Duke in disagreement, he did not insist or
attempt to get him to change his mind.[2] But resentment, I might even
say contempt, simmered within him. In his private letters something of
this shows through if one knows how to read between the lines, though
these were things to be expressed verbally rather than written, or even
more by silence and gestures; unfortunately these are impalpable things
particularly for posterity. And yet I have been able to find evidence
even of those. A precious unpublished letter shows us Guicciardini to

257

the life wishing to give an interlocutor to understand what he felt about the Duke, and he makes him understand very well with half words, with 'frequent shrugs and silences', in such a way, however, as to let it seem 'that he said more by his silence than if he had spoken'.[3]

The biographer has to listen to silences and understand them no less than words, even though a keener ear is required. In 1538, which was the year of the great refusal of the offer of Paul III, Guicciardini actually seems to draw aside, to shut himself up in a silent and diligent retreat. Even his letters, which great good fortune has preserved for us in extraordinary abundance, suddenly become scarce. Of that year we have only three letters. Thus we saw him disappear in the same way when he was in the first flush of the *Cose fiorentine*, but the withdrawal and silence in which he is hidden seem more complete this time, the sea into which he had ventured being so much more vast. One does not know of any other possible reason for his silence, and the fact of its happening a second time at such a juncture leads one to think that there is a patron saint for biographers. On the other hand, it is enough to look at the great pile of original manuscript from which issued after great labour the twenty books of the *Storia d'Italia*, and add to it the materials collected by the historian for its composition, and then to consider the incredibly short time in which the great work was finished. Anyone must think it a miracle, and even more of a miracle any private or public matter which the historian found time to transact in addition, every scrap of a letter he contrived to write.

To broaden as far as possible these too brief limits, it seems permissible to conjecture that the collection, ordering and a first digest of the material may have been begun at the end of 1536. In this labour he was greatly assisted by an extremely curious circumstance which has hitherto escaped students of Guicciardini and historians of archives: the author, when he came to Florence after the siege to act as the instrument of Clement VII's revenge and his own private one, had taken and carried home with him nothing less than the entire archives of the Ten.[4] He did not lack the authority to carry out such an abuse. The reason given, if he gave one, must have been that he needed those papers to examine the accounts of the popular government before settling them in the manner we know of; but I think that his proposals as a historian had something to do with it even then. Otherwise he would not also have taken possession of other correspondence so much earlier in date than that which could possibly have formed a basis for his inquiry.

Thus, without leaving his study, he had under his hand that fabulous mine of information constituted by (and even more so before the dispersal of a part of it) the foreign correspondence of the Florentine Republic, present everywhere in the world through its ambassadors, its envoys, its merchants. Guicciardini was certainly not the first historian to build his work on a basis of archive materials. In Florence itself Bruni had used them; for him as Chancellor of the Republic with the papers always under his hand it would have been less difficult to use them than not to. In the *Storia d'Italia* Guicciardini used documents with a method more rigorous than any had done before him and few did after.

Many of his notebooks and extracts have survived, and in them we can be present (as if we could see him) at the work of composition.[5] The historian ran rapidly through the papers which he needed, and dictated to his secretary more or less brief summaries or extracts headed with the date and an indication of the source. More rarely, when his secretary was not there or had something else to do, he took up the pen and wrote in his own hand. This first series of extracts, disordered and rough, he later worked over in order of time and place in a second version. Finally he co-ordinated and put together his material in a third redaction which is already more than a mere mass of information.[6] In other books he made notes from the historians such as Biondo, Borgia, Capella, Commines, Giovio, Platina, Rucellai, Sabellico, Vegio; while on loose leaves or in the margins of the notebooks he noted various things seen or heard by him during a lifetime lived entirely among great personages and great negotiations: for instance, certain curious details he had from Cardinal Cybo on the delays of Lautrec in Lombardy in 1528. For the *Storia d'Italia* would not be what it is either in content or in style if he had not been something more than a writer, if some of the things he narrated he had not handled himself or at least observed in person and considered from a position of power among men of power. Not only did he thus have information of many things that the papers would not have told him, but his narrative took from it that momentum which was his alone.

When he had all that material before him, he began the writing of the work, going back to the point which had obsessed him while he was writing the commentaries of the Lieutenancy, that is to the descent of Charles VIII or rather the events which prepared the way for it. This may have been in spring 1537. He wrote that part of the text which in the final version occupies the first book, then, without going any further, he dictated to his secretary a new version to which he added, part in dictation and part in his own hand, the second book. Thereafter, hesitating for a while and dictating yet a further version of that difficult beginning, he then resolutely set off and moved rapidly to the end of the fifteenth book (in the final numbering), at which point he incorporated in the text the first and second books of those commentaries which had been the first root of the works, and they thus became the sixteenth and seventeenth books of the final division. When he got to the point where all the versions of the commentaries had stopped as though held by a spell, this time he did not halt but drove safely on to the goal: the death of Clement VII and the election of Paul III.[7]

He thus had a first draft of the whole work, but considering the dissatisfaction of the historian and the artist, I would say that the greater part of the work was still to be done. Indeed doubts of all kinds arose in his mind at the first reading and he filled page upon page with them in an endless list. Just to mention one of them, with one 'Note of the things of which the truth has to be investigated concerning the battle of Vaila', he filled a good three sides.[8] But after these scruples which are not surprising in so scrupulous a searcher after truth, others arose which would cause us astonishment in any writer of the times and which are amazing in him who had always had so little fondness for literature. Indeed he became involved in diligent linguistic and orthographical studies; nor was it enough for him to make notes on the *Volgar Lingua* of Bembo; the extremely powerful influences of Latin and the scholarly vulgar tongue conflicted in his mind with the idiomatic forms of Florentine, graphic with phonetic forms, raising in a mind acute and original as his, questions most singular for those times.[9]

Meanwhile the prospect of the long road ahead drove him on. He ordered his usual secretary to make a copy of that part of the text which corresponds to the first five books of the present text, and corrected it in his own hand, then he divided up the whole work in a new form. The ten books of excessive length into which it had before been divided, he now made into nineteen. Finally he had a fair copy made of the whole. This was perhaps late autumn 1538.[10] While the amanuensis completes this long labour in two or three months, the writer dwells on a more exact research into the truth of certain contradictory sources. He extracts sayings, phrases, words, idioms from Livy to adorn his work; he pursues his studies for that orthographical revision of the text which fate was to prevent him ever making.

If other witness were lacking of the extreme importance which Guicciardini attached to the *Storia*, and also other evidence of his intention of publishing it, this care and these unusual studies would be a sufficient proof. But there is further proof. Of all his other works written only for his own satisfaction or amusement or to clarify his thoughts on some subject, not one did he show to another living soul, none ever escaped from the secrecy of his study: instead he chose to submit the *Storia d'Italia* to the correction and judgement of the most learned of his friends of the 'ancient circle': that Giovanni Corsi whom, when he took his place in the mission to Spain, he teased with the Castilian proverb 'madder than a man of letters'[11]; and he had fled with him through the mountains of Casentino before the siege of Florence, and had afterwards shared with him misfortune and disappointment.

To him, therefore, he began to send the great notebooks of the new copy as soon as they issued beautifully written from the secretary's hands. They returned with certain small sheets of notes which suggested additions and corrections. The additions mostly concerned things dealt with by Corsi in Spain. The corrections were either mere slips of the pen or words and expressions of the spoken language which offended the critic's ear. He further advised him to divide the work into twenty books instead of nineteen, 'as a more perfect number'.[12] Guicciardini paid a certain amount of attention to these suggestions. He accepted and at once carried out the one of dividing it into twenty books, redistributing the material of the first eleven books among twelve. He corrected the errors; he rightly altered some words, and even more rightly left alone those judged by Corsi to be 'too Florentine'. In this too is shown the difference in intellect between the cultured rhetorician and the great writer. Nor did he include the additions which would have upset the text too much. Either he did not think them necessary or he never had time.

In short, this revision did the book some good and also benefited the author, and that done to the author was also reaped by the book in the form of a keener solicitude and more loving care. For any author at a certain point of his labour may be elated or depressed over any opinion that is offered, and the judgement of Corsi, whom Guicciardini must have valued as being more learned and literary than himself, was in the end positively enthusiastic. Already in returning the last book to him, he had written flatteringly to say he was sorry the misfortunes of Italy had ended, because they afforded him such pleasure in reading them. Later he sent him, like a good humanist, a fine Latin epistle containing a general opinion on the work, which does not lack subtle and acute observations among its rhetorical and scholastic flourishes. In letters of this kind, as we well know, flattery was handed out rather freely, but how can those praises be called flattery which any modern critic would support? He compared the *Storia* to an astonishing woman, without jewels, without rich clothes, and yet more beautiful than any other: for a thousand years Italy had seen nothing like it! And in this book Guicciardini seemed to him superior to any others who ever wrote histories because of his most exact knowledge of the facts; then the style always seemed to him solemn, always cultivated, always the same, always his own. [13]

Would that this critic, who was sometimes so acute and shrewd, had observed, besides the speeches *'efficaces et historiam hanc maxime illustrantes'*, the wonderful portraits and the supreme art shown by the narrator in leaving, picking up and elegantly weaving the threads of his narrative among such a multiplicity of things, persons and places, while always observing the sequence of events: an art which reminded Ranke of Ariosto (a happy thought among so many of his unfortunate judgements and so many distorted prejudices!). It is also the mastery we admire in the marvellous architecture of Guicciardini's periods, full of substance and well organised.[14] Another modern critic was quite right when he wrote that reading the *Storia d'Italia* 'is one of the greatest satisfactions in life'.[15] It is only for the strong, certainly. A famous critic, no more favourably disposed than Ranke, actually opined: 'From the point of view of intellectual power it is the most important work ever to come from an Italian mind.'[16]

It was not just a 'fable', as the author had modestly described it in sending it to Corsi. It can hardly have been a perfectly sincere modesty, for the expectations already aroused by the work, not only in Florence,[17] reveal that he had discussed it with relatives and friends, which was also a new and unusual thing for him. But there is also a more decisive proof, that is touching evidence of the extraordinary importance which the author attached to the *Storia*: the first words of the work which appear in the portrait of him which Bugiardini was painting at the time. No one but he could have told the painter to put them in.[18] Furthermore, there is the fact that he had mercilessly pillaged the manuscript of the *Ricordi* to adorn the object of his last great love: it was completely looted, signifying in a sense the author's intention to sacrifice that little work which must yet have been dear to him.

When the revision by his friend the critic was finished at the end of 1538 or the beginning of 1539, Guicciardini began his own, in which he intended to give the work its final perfection of form.[19] He worked on it all through the spring and part of the summer with the greatest diligence, now retouching, now crossing out and even rewriting whole pages several times. In July he was working on the twenty-first of the twenty-eight books which contain this version of the *Storia*;[20] he had revised a good bit more than half, filling the wide margins with additions and corrections, with rewritings and notes, when he fell seriously ill. One cannot gather with any certainty what his illness was; from the little information we have, it does not seem however that it was an apoplectic fit, as an error in reading by Otetea had led us to believe, and still less that it was gout as he wrongly affirmed.[21] We can only say that from the beginning of July he was 'shut up at home', kept in by his illness and its treatment. Shortly after, his condition having grown worse as the result of a stroke, he wrote: 'Because of the douches I am not able to write as much as I would like, and because of a stroke which has affected my tongue I am not able to dictate.'[22]

Thus a cruel destiny struck him down so near his goal. Then, rather than continue with it as best and as quickly as he might, as anyone would expect, he broke off his work of correction abruptly, and without even bringing it up to chapter fifteen, which was so well within reach,[23] he ordered his secretary to make a final clean copy of the entire work (for some parts of the text it was the seventh redaction!), including the last five books which had remained intact and without corrections in his notebooks just as illness had taken him.

These tormented volumes, from which we have already perceived many unwritten facts about the work, therefore speak to us of the author's love for his masterpiece. Feeling the end draw near and despairing henceforth of being able to give it the desired perfection, he was seized with a great anxiety to leave it at least neat and in good order, if as yet incomplete.[24] Indeed there were still some descriptions of cities to be written, which he always did very well, the speech of Niccolò Capponi, the end of the fifteenth book, and other things. Parts of the last four books were left barely sketched out. It was a pathetic renunciation. While the faithful scribe, writing against time, covered the pages, the sick man wrote in a shaky hand the last notes on the last copybooks. Later, however, he seemed to improve.

He could still enjoy the good things of the country; at Santa Margherita and Poppiano he was able to find consolation. And here we find in nearly every letter a Guicciardini unwontedly georgic in mood, 'among tree grafts and artichokes' and cherry trees: 'This year I have so given myself up to agriculture that, if I go on like this, I am sure that next year I shall have become a complete countryman, and willingly so, for I see no art which pleases me more.'[25] But that recreation too ended with the first cold of winter. On the 27th October he wrote: 'After this week we shall all go back to the shop and attend to business with less neglectfulness, and it will truly be time. No more cherry trees, no more, no more!'[26]

And he could still, 'back at the shop', attend to those unimportant affairs and swallow his bitterness in those councils imperiously dominated by the terrible Duke. Coolly treated though with honour, consulted little on important affairs, and not always asked about lesser ones, he repaid the Duke as we have described. Juan de Luna who had succeeded Vitelli, now in disgrace no less than Cybo, was one day to reveal that Cosimo had no greater enemy than Guicciardini.[27] And yet, while all intrigued against Cosimo, and not only the *émigrés* but also certain great 'imperials', more imperialist than Caesar, like Cardinal Cybo, don Juan de Luna, the Spanish ambassador at Rome, all secretly concerted by the quietly implacable Cardinal Ridolfi,[28] Francesco Guicciardini, faithful to himself, consistent with the view expressed in the *Ricordi*, was a true realist, never conspired against the hated legitimate Prince or against the State. If I were asked to choose one trait which of itself would express and represent this man, I could not find one better than this.

It is understandable that he could not be in favour with a prince who on one occasion – among many – praising a secretary of his because he had roughly reminded the Councillors of their subjection, commanded him to inform one of them that his opinions were orders and that he regarded as an adversary anyone who opposed him.[29] To this were the highest offices of the State reduced! For all that, Guicciardini, in an exemplary manner, never failed to sit on them whenever he was not confined to the house.[30] But he had had to drink too much bitterness from that cup, and his soul was flowing over. In a letter of 29th November 1539 to Roberto Pucci, who had spoken to him of events in the world such as the League against the Turk and an agreement between the Emperor and the King of France, he expressed his feelings thus: 'For myself I do not contribute to these things, and whether it be the result of age or because fortune has removed me from public affairs, I certainly feel that I forget more every day. Hence not without cause I have begun to abstain from discussion, leaving that to you and others whose minds may rise to such heights. And though the others are lost, as I am, in this extraordinary state of things, it appears to me that our age is beginning to be a happy one, for it is freed of the necessity to extend its thoughts further than from day to day; if this is a personal experience of my own, I must call it a private piece of luck.'[31]

Such outbursts were rare. His unhappiness was the greater in that it was secret. He had to suffer it all himself, bear it all without sharing it with others. It was given to him, as a wonderful privilege, to express it in his writings, and in that manner to communicate not only with relatives, friends or fellow citizens, but with all countries and all ages. Lately he had begun to build a bridge between himself and other men over the incomprehension created by his own faults and theirs, by their misunderstanding and his own rebarbative greatness. But now this bridge was endangered by misfortune. Nor, more detached and lacking his former confidence, did the little improvements he made here and there to the great work on the fair copy finally prepared by his secretary have any great importance for him.[32]

The year 1539 ended in this crepuscular melancholy. Perhaps on the threshold of each new year which according to Florentine usage began on the 25th March, partly for fun, partly from superstition, messer Francesco may have looked at the horoscope in which year by year all his life was described. That he did look at it is revealed by the notes written here and there in his own hand to decipher with curiosity the astrological signs.[33] The year just ended had been forecast as 'of little joy, dangerous to life', and that devil of an astrologer had guessed right! For 1540, the fifty-ninth year of his life (according to the horoscope which starts at 1482), he read: 'But the fifty-ninth year will be much more dangerous to life.'[34] And the worst of it was that at this very moment with some very general words, very confused, very awkwardly expressed, the astrologer dried up; beyond that 'much more dangerous' fifty-ninth year there was nothing more, as if it were to be his last. All that remained was for him to read in another part of the book, where nothing was forgotten, the description of his own funeral.[35] Nor perhaps was he able to throw off that lugubrious melancholy by the consideration noted in the *Ricordi* 'that astrologers are right only by chance'. Chance or no, he was right about the previous year. If on the 25th March 1540 he looked at the horoscope, he certainly had no cause to rejoice.

And before even two months had passed he fell ill again and suddenly grew worse, so that on the 21st May he made his last will, *cogitans dubium mortis eventum*;[36] this time, alas, the legal formula could be taken at the letter. Then, as he read, the dying man was asked what his intentions were for the History he had so greatly laboured on, upon which, until the last, he had written some few weary words. 'Burn it,' he is said to have replied.[37] The incident is told by someone who had it from his heirs, and who did not lack means of knowing the truth. Whether it is true we do not know; we could wish it were not, that the object of so much labour, so much love, such hopes, had not at the last hour received, like everything else, the leaden seal of Guicciardini's pessimism. It is unfortunately necessary to say that that word of despair well expresses the man's sovereign hopelessness.

The following day, 22nd May, Duke Cosimo, whom a ridiculous rumour was to accuse of having poisoned him,[38] shed a crocodile tear: 'This evening messer Francesco *laborat in extremis*, a thing which could not displease us more because of his good qualities and the loss not only to myself but to all this city.'[39] In fact he died that same evening.[40] He was buried the following day in Santa Felicita, the old church of his family, 'buried honourably with monks and priests and candles, but without any special honours from canons or citizens'.[41] The man who had once lived with such splendour, had wished to go in that way, 'without any worldly ceremony', to his last dwelling, 'in the tomb of his forefathers'.[42]

A fourteenth-century tombstone covered his remains, and for nearly two centuries, beautiful in its bare simplicity, it bore only a name that was not his own: that of an ancestor whom he had described in his *Memorie* as 'openly infamous and a usurer'.[43] Nor did the brothers who had inherited his wealth, nor the city, nor later the Italian nation so prodigal in monuments to the mediocre, take the trouble to give this great man a tomb of his own. Yet perhaps it was better. That monument suffices which he himself had prepared when he felt death approaching, and which his heirs, merrily employed in selling his possessions, melting down silver, making inventories and valuing everything,[44] did not forget to mention, though not including it in their accounts since it could not be given a value in florins: 'The History with his other writings and books put together with good care' in the keeping of madonna Maria.[45]

Chapter 25

LIFE AFTER DEATH

'MESSER FRANCESCO, besides his rank, his wealth, his doctor's degree, his having been Governor and Lieutenant for the Pope, was further remarkable and enjoyed an extraordinary reputation, not only for his knowledge but for his great experience of the affairs of the world and of men, on which he discoursed and commented wonderfully well; but he did not apply these powers as he might, for apart from the fact that he was extremely proud and intemperate, often ambition and avarice drove him to actions far beyond what was fitting for a modest and civil man.'[1] Thus Varchi wrote, and the antipathy which shows in these words did not prevent him from perceiving Guicciardini's greatness and placing him 'among the wisest heads in Italy'.[2] And in truth, as far as one can see and know, the majority of those who had to do with him did not judge him otherwise. Was Guicciardini therefore really like that?

The anonymous astrologer drew his portrait on the verge of maturity before he had proved himself in any great affair; without love or hate he portrayed the man as he was in his private life, not the Governor nor the author like those who saw him only in the seat of government or in his study. This portrait which is therefore by far the most valuable, placed beside the one barely sketched by Varchi and others, differs from it only by its far greater wealth of detail, and merely as two drawings of the same subject may differ where one is a kindly likeness and the other a cruel one. In any case, we have added certain touches to that youthful portrait, page by page, which make it more complete. Now we can say: here is the man.

The avarice of which Varchi accuses him should not be understood as common meanness. The astrologer did well, in making a single package of his cupidity, to describe him as avid 'for honours, wealth and possessions'; for the appetite for riches was inspired in him, as he confesses in the *Ricordi*, by his lust for greatness: 'Greed for money would be a mark of baseness, if it arose only from the desire to enjoy it; but corrupt as our life is in this world, anyone who desires reputation is forced to desire wealth, for it gives lustre to our virtues and causes them to be appreciated.'[3] Despising prodigality in others, he was equally averse from vulgar parsimony. He showed himself generous and openhanded on many occasions; in his governorships he avoided the meanness and grasping habits of other ecclesiastical governors, particularly as regards the poor.[4]

He was certainly an egoist, and such egoism grafted by nature upon such a mind could not fail to bear fruits which to most people seemed sharp. Certainly he was arrogant, and it would be surprising if a man of his nature were not. Joined with certain faults which won him hatred, certain qualities which no one could call faults, also won him hatred. Likewise, when Guicciardini the thinker and writer is blamed for possessing a mind so practical and positive that it may sometimes appear pedestrian, for aversion for ideas that are too bold, for 'vain cogitations', for speculation and abstraction, people forget that these 'faults' of his are the basis of certain qualities as a politician and a historian which are most characteristic of him and most admired. But I do not wish to repeat things which are already in these pages.

I also wrote at the beginning that Machiavelli would help us to understand Guicciardini, and I think we have not lacked some assistance in that quarter. Generous, warm, impetuous, the Secretary unfortunately had other friends who were selfish, cold and cautious, all for themselves as much as Machiavelli was all for his friends. The first who comes to mind is Francesco Vettori, also a man of intelligence and taste in matters of writing. Neither of him nor of anyone else did Machiavelli ever dream of saying what he said about Guicciardini, placing him on a level with his own country: 'I love messer Francesco Guicciardini, and I love my country more than my own soul.' He would not have spoken such words of a man who beneath his pride and egoism had nothing but intellect. He had opened doors which kept the secret of that reserved man, his hidden qualities and his too obvious faults: that secret which I do not know whether any member of his family or any of his brothers knew, but which Machiavelli had fathomed, akin to him as he was in greatness.

There was one therefore who loved Guicciardini and loved him more than his soul. Those words are a revelation and a testimony; for the biographer a confirmation of everything he may have been able to read between the lines of some personal letters: more often in those to Machiavelli himself, but also in a few to Sigismondo Santi and others. Anyone capable and worthy of going beyond the locked doors would have found beneath the haughty reserve, together with the noble moral qualities already glimpsed, the friendliness already noted by our astrologer and the human feelings which poor Sigismondo's widow had come to know, forgotten as she was by all others.[5] Under that armour which must have weighed on him and hurt him as it commonly does upon reserved souls, there was even (who would have thought it?) a facetious and pleasure-loving humour; under that unpleasing hardness there was something of 'an amiable epicurean'.[6] These are the words of De Sanctis, who used them in a more general sense, but understood in this particular way there is some truth in them.

Nor was Guicciardini incapable of generous manners and impulses: he was only incapable of detaching himself from the present reality of things. We have seen his generous ardour in action and word at the time of *his* League and *his* war, when it seemed realistic to be so. But he suffered a disappointment and a punishment for it, which long weighed heavily upon his spirit and were no good specific against his scepticism.

It is natural that men of perhaps slightly less egoism but certainly much less genius should have been offended by Guicciardini's egoism when it was also joined with such a mind and character. Likewise, a great idealist like Machiavelli could understand and perhaps admire Guicciardini's practical realism. Lesser idealists were not able to understand him, and thought his realism discreditable. It was said that he worshipped expediency as well as his own ego.[7] I do not think he was a polytheist, or at least I would argue, if so, that the two cults were perfectly balanced in him.

As Guicciardini was, it was inevitable that those who knew him only from outside should not like him. Those loved him least who had to suffer, in addition to his faults, the consequences of certain good qualities to which I have already referred: captains of armies, more or less rebellious subjects, feudal lords competing with him in arrogance. If his fellow citizens disliked him, not caring to be over-whelmed by his grandeurs, among them the supporters of the free republic had better cause to hate him, and more so those who suffered his worst rigours for their sincere love of liberty. One finds that history is never written by the vanquished; and yet with few exceptions it was the vanquished republicans who in Florence wrote the history of those times, and it is not therefore surprising that Guicciardini was maltreated in them. Varchi in particular, although he had later hung on to the victor's chariot, freely expressed all the old bitterness when it did not displease the person paying him. Nor were his imitators any kinder, like Iacopo Pitti who particularly in the *Apologia dei Cappucci*, seeking to discredit Guicciardini, only discredited himself.[8]

His own generation passed with its burden of hatred, but the writings remained. Only other writings much greater than those, only his own works could overcome them and win over to him future genera-tions. But he had published nothing in his lifetime as we know. Indeed he had shut away his writing no less than his thoughts and his feelings. As for his brothers, his heirs, all they cared for was to pocket those thousands of ducats. Only a nephew, in rivalry with another, decided to publish the *Storia d'Italia* twenty-one years after the author's death.[9] It was almost by chance and through a manuscript copy given by a great-nephew that later still, and without the family's knowledge there appeared – I am not sure whether to say 'redone or undone' – the *Ricordi*.

Not even then was peace made between Guicciardini and his fellow men. The History gave offence to many, biting, as the shameless Giovio said, 'too freely those who deserve it'.[10] Indeed some were indignant not just at what was said but at what was not said.[11] The *Ricordi*, on the other hand, on their first appearance entitled *Avverti-menti*, although they were very much read and reprinted, made little noise[12] by comparison with the reverberations of the *Storia*, whose editions and translations came thick and fast;[13] but they too attracted a few more or less poisoned shafts. The *Ricordi* were later to be the favourite target of moralists. Meanwhile all the blows fell on the *Storia*. Montaigne's remark on 'son Guichardin' and the opinions expressed on that opinion are too well known to need further comment.

But where, on the subject of his pessimism about the motives of human actions, he writes 'peut estre advenu qu' il ait estimé d'autruy selon soy',[14] it is appropriate to remark that if this is in a sense true, that mirror seems to have enabled him to see 'the world and its princes not as they should be but as they are',[15] in fact as he, a historian and not a moralist, needed to see and depict them.

But here we do not want to pass in revue the fortunes of Guicciardini over the centuries, and still less those which concern merely his reputation as a historian and a writer, which would be not a proper theme for a biography; not to mention the fact that it would be pointless to summarize in a few brief pages what has been so well done by Luciani in a large volume. Here we have wished merely to hint at this second life of Guicciardini, not without hope that some light might be reflected on his own life.

One might say paradoxically that a third life began for Guicciardini when between 1857 and 1867 the ten volumes of his *Opere Inedite* came out. From the hidden papers of so secret a writer only those two works had appeared and only several decades after his death when Guicciardini was known only as a statesman and man of many affairs. But here after a further three centuries the coffers were opened and further riches appeared: the youthful *Storia fiorentina*, the *Reggimento di Firenze*, the autobiographical writings, the *Considerazioni sopra i discorsi del Machiavelli* (Considerations on the Discourses of Machiavelli), the *Political Discourses*, and all the rest. Among these the letters were of prime importance, though chosen without much intelligence and barbarously edited, and a more authentic text of the *Ricordi*. Indeed, among such discoveries of unpublished material one might say that this latter text was the most important and destined even to take pride of place over the *Storia*.

As was written by the greatest Italian critic of the age and among the greatest of all time, 'the publication of the *Opere Inedite* of Guicciardini should have given a great forward impulse to our historical studies; they are the kind of discovery which would suffice in themselves to create a whole body of historical criticism'.[16] In fact they gave it a good push; but if it increased the reputation of the author, who until now had been overshadowed by Machiavelli as in his lifetime Machiavelli had stood in the shadow of Guicciardini, it did not help the reputation of the man himself.

The *Opere inedite* came to light just when Italy was achieving national unity. It was the hour of Machiavelli and the *Prince*, and a bad time for Guicciardini. In the first dawn of our Risorgimento he had been reproached with having adhered to the reality of his own times, with not having been a forerunner of the future, with being a realist as his character demanded, and not a prophet. Everyone attacked the destroyer of liberty, the minister and defender of tyrants. 'He was pilloried, covered again with infamy'.[17] In the studies of tribunes, poets, novelists, even of critics the inflammatory days of the siege of Florence and the election of Cosimo were relived. Down with ser Cerrettieri!

But the greatest reproach came from De Sanctis in a famous essay of 1869;[18] for him Guicciardini became only the man of 'personal interest'. In that phrase were included or implied all the base and mean acts, but not among other things that highest sense of honour, which does not seem entirely despicable and which was really at the bottom of that 'personal interest';[19] while outside it stood things that are not at all 'wretched', such as devotion to duty, impeccable honesty, and the concept of justice. The great critic's password was Guicciardini's 'moral weakness'.

Guicciardini's realism is partly responsible for that famous 'self-interest'. Still young in years he observes on looking round him: 'personal interest is the mistress who drives all men; these are no longer the days of the Romans and the Greeks nor those generous spirits all aspiring to glory'.[20] And being a sceptical realist and not a reformer, nor wishing to resign himself to being the earthen pot between the brass ones, it is not surprising if he 'quietly adapts himself to this world he esteems so little'.[21]

After such accusations, before which Guicciardini's own *Accusatoria* pales, defences could not fail to appear; and it would have been remarkable if some of them had not gone too far like the accusers. But from the collision of arguments came the first sparks of truth. Greater light came later with a new enthusiasm for Guicciardini studies. The *Opere inedite* were not something that could be digested in a mere generation or two. In this renaissance, where there matured among other things the excellent monograph of Otetea, the Palmarocchi editions of the *Opere* and the correspondence, the celebration of the centenary (the fourth since the historian's death, but the first to be honoured in any way)[22] – in all this the late Paolo Guicciardini had a great share, for he had the archives in which the papers of his great ancestor are kept, reorganized and opened to the public. He endowed it with useful indexes, and put together an extremely rich Guicciardini library, edited texts and documents, promoted studies, encouraged and supported scholars.[23]

At that time and in that climate the author of this Life had the singular good fortune of discovering, seventy years after the publication of the *Opere inedite*, so many other unpublished works and writings of Guicciardini, that two further volumes besides the original ten would hardly suffice to hold them. From the first literary compositions of adolescence, through the extremely valuable writings concerning his work for the Pope, to that second Florentine History, which much more than the first, through its method, its structure, its careful composition, prepared and matured the author for the *Storia d'Italia*.[24] And for these further discoveries too a whole generation could not suffice to digest them.

Since then thirty years have gone by. Before ending this Life, which brings to a close these thirty years of study, and perhaps all my studies; rising one day for the last time from the papers of messer Francesco, I went back to the near-by church of Santa Felicita to see his tomb. I went to take leave of him, but also as one returns to certain pages one has read to seek a better understanding of them.

It was a melancholy parting, even more so than partings generally are at my age in which man begins to die away. And on that marble at the foot of the high altar in the ancient romanesque church, I at last understood why Guicciardini, rich and without male children, who had lived more as a great nobleman and a great master than as a private citizen, proud, greedy for honours and to be distinguished among his fellows, should have wished to disappear like this, and leave his bones and his name unmarked by any stone in his family grave. Always true to himself, the great realist merely consented to the disconsolate reality of death.

BIBLIOGRAPHICAL NOTE

Abbreviations of principal editions and works cited in the footnotes

Carteggi=FRANCESCO GUICCIARDINI, *Carteggi* ('Fonti per la Storia d'Italia'), Rome, Istituto Storico Italiano, 1938. . . . This edition may be considered to consist of two series of volumes clearly distinguished by a fundamental change of method: vols. I–IV (1499–1521), edited by Roberto Palmarocchi, are an ambitious but premature attempt at a complete edition of Guicciardini's correspondence, including his letters and their replies; the following vols. V–X (1522–6) so far published (up to 1964), are confined to a more modest edition (prepared by Pier Giorgio Ricci) of Guicciardini's letters alone. See the review by ROBERTO RIDOLFI in *Archivio Storico Italiano*, CXIII, 1955, pp. 419 ff.

Carteggi A.S.I.=*Alcune lettere inedite di Francesco Guicciardini degli anni 1518–1523*, edited by Fernanda Lanzi Burani, in *Archivio Storico Italiano* (which I abbreviate as *A.S.I.* in my notes), CX, 1952, pp. 53–85. No less than 58 letters – an indication of the incompleteness of Palmarocchi's edition quoted above.

Cose fiorentine=FRANCESCO GUICCIARDINI, *Le cose fiorentine*, published for the first time by ROBERTO RIDOLFI, Florence, Leo S. Olschki, 1945.

Lettere al Lanfredini=FRANCESCO GUICCIARDINI, *Dall'assedio di Firenze al secondo convegno di Clemente VII e Carlo V: Lettere inedite a Bartolomeo Lanfredini*, edited by ANDRÉ OTETEA, Aquila, Vecchioni, 1927

MACHIAVELLI, *Lett. fam.*=NICCOLÒ MACHIAVELLI, *Lettere familiari*, edited by EDUARDO ALVISI, Florence, Sansoni, 1883.

Opp.=FRANCESCO GUICCIARDINI, *Opere* ('Scrittori d'Italia'), Bari, Laterza, 1929–36, 9 vols.: I–V, *Storia d'Italia*, edited by COSTANTINO PANIGADA; VI–IX, edited by ROBERTO PALMAROCCHI.

Opp. in.=FRANCESCO GUICCIARDINI, *Opere inedite*, with notes, etc., by GIUSEPPE CANESTRINI, edited by Counts Luigi and Piero Guicciardini, Florence, 1857–67. 10 vols.

OTETEA=ANDRÉ OTETEA, *François Guichardin, sa vie publique et sa pensée politique*, Paris, Librairie Picart, 1926.

Quarto centenario=*Francesco Guicciardini nel IV centenario della morte (1540–1940)*. Supplement n. I to *Rinascita*, Centro Nazionale di Studi sul Rinascimento Florence (1940).

Ricordi=FRANCESCO GUICCIARDINI, *Ricordi*. Critical edition by RAFFAELE SPONGANO, Florence, Sansoni, 1951. On those occasions only when it is necessary to distinguish between the redactions *B* and *C* (for which see ch. XVIII, n. 8), I quote Palmarocchi's edition in *Opp.*, vol. VIII, pp. 241–336.

RIDOLFI, *Genesi*=ROBERTO RIDOLFI, *Genesi della 'Storia d'Italia' guicciardiniana*, Florence, Leo S. Olschki, 1939.

RIDOLFI, *Machiavelli²*=ROBERTO RIDOLFI, *Vita di Niccolò Machiavelli*, 2nd revised edition, Rome, Belardetti, 1954.

RIDOLFI, *Noterella guicciardiniana*, in *La Bibliofilia*, LXVIII, 1966, pp. 77 ff.

RIDOLFI, *Opuscoli*=ROBERTO RIDOLFI, *Opuscoli di storia letteraria e di erudizione: Savonarola, Machiavelli, Guicciardini, Giannotti*, Florence, 'Bibliopolis' (Leo S. Olschki), 1942.

ROSSI=AGOSTINO ROSSI, *Francesco Guicciardini e il governo fiorentino dal 1527 al 1540*, con nuovi documenti, Bologna, Zanichelli, 1896–9. 2 vols.

Scritti inediti=FRANCESCO GUICCIARDINI, *Scritti inediti sopra la politica di Clemente VII dopo la battaglia di Pavia*, edited by PAOLO GUICCIARDINI, Florence, Leo S. Olschki, 1940.

Storia d'Italia=FRANCESCO GUICCIARDINI, *La Storia d'Italia*, edited from the original MSS. by ALESSANDRO GHERARDI, Florence, Sansoni, 1919. 4 vols. This edition is unfortunately very rare because of the partial destruction of it ordered *in extremis* for religious scruples by Count Francesco Guicciardini who had promoted and published it at great expense; but it is preferable to that of C. Panigada in *Opp.*, vols. I–V. On the other hand this latter edition was able to incorporate some important amendments proposed by Plinio Carli in his fine review of Gherardi's publication, in *Giornale Storico della Letteratura Italiana*, LXXVI, 1920. My reasons for preferring Gherardi are the same as those indicated in kindly fashion by A. LUZIO, *La 'Storia d'Italia' del Guicciardini nell'edizione Laterza*, in *Atti della R. Acc. delle Scienze di Torino*, LXV, 1930, pp. 231–48.

TOMMASINI, *Machiavelli*=ORESTE TOMMASINI, *La vita e gli scritti di Niccolò Machiavelli*, Rome, Loescher, 1893–1911. 2 vols. (the second vol. in 2 parts).

VILLARI, *Machiavelli²*=PASQUALE VILLARI, *Niccolò Machiavelli e i suoi tempi*, with new documents; 2nd ed. revised by the author, Milan, Hoepli, 1895–7. 3 vols.

ABBREVIATIONS:
LIBRARIES AND ARCHIVES

A.G.F.=Archivio Guicciardini, Florence.
A.S.F.=Archivio di Stato, Florence.
A.S.M.=Archivio di Stato, Modena.
A.S.P.=Archivio di Stato, Parma.
B.E.M.=Biblioteca Estense, Modena.
B.L.F.=Biblioteca Medicea Laurenziana, Florence.
B.M.F.=Biblioteca Marucelliana, Florence.
B.N.F.=Biblioteca Nazionale, Florence.
B.R.F.=Biblioteca Riccardiana, Florence.

NOTE ON SOME
BIBLIOGRAPHICAL AIDS

A complete Guicciardini bibliography is lacking. There are errors and omissions in the bibliography of editions of the *Storia d'Italia* published by E. Rostagno at the beginning of Gherardi's edition of the *Storia*, pp. clxviii–clxxxv (cf. P. GUICCIARDINI, *Contributo alla bibliografia di Francesco Guicciardini*, Florence, Tip. Giuntina, 1946, and idem, *La Storia guicciardiniana* . . ., Florence, Olschki, 1948: two essays originally published in part in *La Bibliofilia*, XLVI and XLIX). My great friend the late Count Paolo Guicciardini had been engaged on a Guicciardini bibliography for many years, assisted by his faithful librarian–archivist Antonio Gigli; and when he too died, it was taken on by the librarian Dott. Giuseppe Sergio Martini using material left by Count Paolo, but since he moved to the United States I fear he has abandoned the project.

Fortunately, however, at least as regards the vast literature on Guicciardini, we are very well served by VINCENT LUCIANI, *Francesco Guicciardini and his European Reputation*, New York, Karl Otto, 1936, in which all the works concerning Guicciardini are spread out before us and given due relief like on some great map. It is better to consult this work in the Italian edition: V. LUCIANI, *Francesco Guicciardini e la fortuna dell'opera sua*, Florence, Olschki, 1949; it was revised and improved not only by its author, but also by Count Paolo Guicciardini who edited the volume for the press; it naturally absorbs Luciani's earlier essay: *Recent Guicciardini Studies*, in *Italica*, XXVII, 1950, pp. 109–27.

NOTE ON GUICCIARDINI'S PAPERS

'The *History* with his other writings and books put together with good care' under the care of Maria after the death of Francesco (see p. 267 of this volume) were later divided among the heirs, Luigi, Girolamo, Iacopo and Bongianni, each of whom would certainly have wished to have something of their great brother's writings. Indeed, among the admittedly not very plausible reasons given at the time for the long delay in publishing the *Storia d'Italia* was the fact that the manuscripts were 'in the hands of several co-heirs' (R. RIDOLFI, *Documenti sulle prime stampe della 'Storia d'Italia' guicciardiniana*, in *La Bibliofilia*, LXI, 1959, p. 51). Fortunately, however, those precious manuscripts were once more brought together in the hands of Girolamo, or rather of his son Agnolo, who undertook publication of the *Storia*; and it is the line descended from Agnolo di Girolamo which, surviving all the others, still flourishes today and has preserved with such rare and exemplary diligence the papers of Francesco Guicciardini. I know of no other writer of that age who has been so fortunate.

Some few of Francesco's papers must, however, have remained in the hands of other co-heirs – certainly with the eldest Luigi. But luck would have it that when his line died out in 1625, his papers did not share the fate of so many others which ended up by being destroyed or used as wrappings; they passed to that great collector, Carlo Strozzi. So they too were saved and are preserved in the Carte Strozziane in the Archivio di Stato, Florence (for the history of this extraordinary miscellany see C. GUASTI, *Le Carte Strozziane del R. Archivio di Stato in Firenze. Inventario,* Florence, 1884–91).

The bulk of Guicciardini's papers, apart from some minor items given to the Grandducal Biblioteca Palatina, thus remained in the library of the descendants of Girolamo, and they were re-ordered and provided with a summary inventory by the abbott D. M. Gallizioli in 1755. This was the situation until the late Count Paolo Guicciardini had them arranged in the family archive which he generously opened to scholars. Under this new arrangement the *Carte di Francesco Guicciardini* formed a separate series consisting of 27 parts accommodated in 37 large boxes. They were summarily catalogued, with many errors and omissions, by OTETEA, pp. XI–XIX, and subsequently more thoroughly described by R. RIDOLFI, *L' Archivio della famiglia Guicciardini*, Florence, Olschki, 1931, pp. 55–100 (republished with minor corrections in R. RIDOLFI, *Gli Archivi delle famiglie fiorentine*, vol. I (no further vols. published), Florence, Olschki, 1934, pp. 95–210). A few years later some other papers of Francesco were found in the family library (i.e., in the main library as opposed to the Guicciardini library organized by Count Paolo). These too were arranged in the Archive, together with others from different sources, and placed in three boxes forming a new series of *Accessions*. It is on my conscience that I have so far not fulfilled my promise to my late friend to catalogue these accessions in an appendix to my earlier publication.

While speaking here of the Guicciardini Archive, so rich for me in memories as well as in documents, I should like to take the opportunity to thank the present archivist Dott. Gino Corti and Prof. Pier Giorgio Ricci who more than any other scholar has worked there recently for the edition of Guicciardini's correspondence. They have assisted me often and in many ways in my work.

NOTES

CHAPTER I

¹ *Memorie di famiglia*, in *Opp.*, vol. IX, p. 3.

² P. GUICCIARDINI, *Alcune notizie sulla famiglia Guicciardini ricavate da una pergamena del 1199*, Florence, Tip. Ariani, 1928; R. DAVIDSOHN, *Geschichte von Florenz*, Berlin, E. S. Mittler, 1896–1927, vol. I, p. 343.

³ *Opp.*, vol. IX, p. 4.

⁴ *Opp.*, vol. IX, p. 5.

⁵ *Opp.*, vol. IX, p. 11.

⁶ *Opp.*, vol. IX, p. 31.

⁷ *Opp.*, vol. IX, p. 37; see also pp. 21, 23, 26.

⁸ R. RIDOLFI, *Gli archivi delle private famiglie fiorentine*, Florence, Olschki, 1936, pp. 122, 133; cf. *Opp.*, vol. IX, p. 36.

⁹ *Lettere inedite del Senatore Carlo Strozzi*, etc., ed. G. Gargani, Florence, 1859, p. 54.

¹⁰ P. GUICCIARDINI – E. DORI, *Le antiche case e il palazzo dei Guicciardini in Firenze*, Florence, Olschki, 1952, pp. 32, 116. They make abundantly clear the character of the 'big house' where Francesco was born and brought up in his early years, a house very different from the present Guicciardini palace. It consisted of a 'tower residence' with later extensions, 'developed almost entirely in depth . . . with narrow frontage on the street and little daylight'. All of which justifies my describing it as 'gloomy'; and it seemed to me worth noting as a factor possibly influencing the character of Guicciardini.

¹¹ *Ricordanze* of Iacopo Guicciardini, A.G.F., *Libri di Amministrazione*, 13, p. 185.

¹² Simona outlived her husband many years. We find her mentioned many times up to 1529 in correspondence and elsewhere (A.G.F., *Libri di Amministrazione*, 15, p. 7), as well as in the will Francesco made on 15 April, 1531 (see p. 316, n. 63). She died shortly before 25 January, 1533. On this date there is an entry in the *Libro di possessioni* of Iacopo di Piero Guicciardini regarding certain monies 'given to charity for a mass for our mother madonna Simona': A.G.F., *Libri di Amministrazione*, 22, p. 128.

¹³ *Opp.*, vol. IX, p. 72.

¹⁴ *Opp.*, vol. IX, p. 71.

¹⁵ *Opp.*, vol. IX, p. 53. Piero Guicciardini was one of the three Peters to whom Ficino addressed his well-known *Apologia*, published at the end of his three books *De Vita*. Cf. A. DELLA TORRE, *Storia dell'Accademia Platonica di Firenze*, Florence, 1904, p. 727 ff.; P. O. KRISTELLER, *Supplementum Ficinianum*, Florence, Olschki, 1937, vol. II, p. 344.

¹⁶ *Opp.*, vol. IX, p. 42.

¹⁷ *Opp.*, vol. VIII, p. 311, ric. 125; *Ricordi*, p. 136

¹⁸ They are Guicciardini's own words in the exhortation 'to himself' written in Spain in 1513, *Opp.*, vol. IX, p. 99.

¹⁹ *Oratio defensoria*, in *Opp.*, vol. IX, p. 280

²⁰ *Opp.*, vol. IX, p. 60. The education of children 'at home . . . under the care of a private tutor' was considered inadvisable by Maffeo Vegio: E. GARIN, *Il pensiero pedagogico dello Umanesimo*, Florence, Coedizioni Giuntine-Sansoni, 1958, p. 180.

²¹ *Cose fiorentine*, pp. 6 ff. But cf. R. SABBADINI, *La scoperta dei codici latini e greci ne' secoli XIV e XV*, vol. II, pp. 224, 254. It is curious to note that the *De aquaeductibus* of Frontinus was in fact discovered by Poggio (1429) to whom Guicciardini believed it to be unknown. But in the margin he noted with characteristic scruple: 'find out when Frontinus lived and when his work was discovered'.

[22] L. MALAGOLI, *Guicciardini*, Florence, La Nuova Italia, 1939.

[23] *Opp.*, vol. IX, pp. 53 ff.

[24] This group of unknown and unpublished letters, the only ones extant of Guicciardini's youth and early studies, were discovered by me in a Magliabechi MS., and published by P. GUICCIARDINI, *Lettere giovanili inedite di Francesco Guicciardini*, in *Rivista storica degli archivi toscani*, vol. V, 1933, pp. 205-19. The letters, addressed to Alessio Lapaccini, were then republished in *Carteggi*, vol. I, pp. 5-9.

[25] *Opp.*, vol. IX, pp. 53 ff.

[26] Guicciardini himself tells us this in his *Oratio accusatoria*, in *Opp.*, vol. IX, pp. 211 ff. One might object that this speech put in the mouth of a hypothetical accuser, was merely a calumny declaimed with excess of rhetorical elaboration, especially as it is later repudiated to a large extent in the *Oratio defensoria*; but it must be said that the accusation, for all its rhetoric, has a greater ring of sincerity than the defence, which in the end does little more than claim lack of proof – whereas the accusation quoted the evidence of contemporaries ('of our companions there are many alive on whose word one can rely') – and moreover seeks to pass over lightly these 'childish matters'. This piece of evidence is accepted as true by the most serious scholars like Chabod.

[27] G. MASI, *Il Guicciardini e la giurisprudenza del suo tempo*, in *Quarto centenario*, pp. 117-39. The words quoted in the text are on p. 120. This study is useful for an account of Guicciardini's career as a professional lawyer, rather than for information on his studies and legal training. For the latter see also P. ROSSI, *Guicciardini criminalista*, Milan, Fratelli Bocca, 1943.

[28] For these and all subsequent details about Francesco's university studies see his *Ricordanze*, in *Opp.*, vol. IX, pp. 54-7.

[29] *Carteggi*, vol. I, p. 8; see n. 21.

[30] Letter from Cardinal Giovanni de' Medici, 16 Nov. 1509, in P. DELPHINUS, *Epistolae*, Venice, Bernardino Benali, 1524, lib. IX, ep. 43.

[31] *Opp.*, vol. IX, p. 54. A. VISCONTI, *La storia dell'Università di Ferrara*, Bologna, Zanichelli, 1950, p. 25, refers to the poverty continually suffered by the University from its foundation. For the particular conditions obtaining in Guicciardini's time see p. 44.

[32] *Opp.*, vol. IX, pp. 55 ff.; cf. pp. 44 ff.

[33] See the third sermon *On the Psalms*, and the eleventh *On Amos*: SAVONAROLA, *Prediche italiane ai fiorentini*, Florence, La Nuova Italia, vol. II, p. 40; vol. III, 1, p. 260.

[34] *Opp.*, vol. IX, p. 56.

[35] We have a document of Guicciardini's legal studies at this time in Vatican MS. Lat. 4605 written in his own hand. It is a *Repertorium in jure canonico*, with the following inscription: 'This book belongs to me Francesco Guicciardini, and I wrote it with my own hand.' On f. 136 is the date: Padua, 25 March 1505.

[36] *Opp.*, vol. IX, p. 56.

[37] *Opp.*, vol. IX, p. 57.

[38] *Ibidem.*

CHAPTER 2

[1] *Opp.*, vol. VIII, p. 287.

[2] *Opp.*, vol. IX, pp. 24, 27.

[3] *Opp.*, vol. IX, pp. 28-44.

[4] These are Savonarola's own words at his first cross-examination, P. VILLARI, II², p. cviii.

[5] Letter from Francesco Tranchedino to the Duke of Milan, 12 April 1498, published by VILLARI, II², p. cii.

[6] Guicciardini tells us this in his *Storia fiorentina*, in *Opp.*, vol. VI, p. 240; cf. G. CAPPONI, *Storia della Repubblica fiorentina*, 2nd ed. revised by the author, Florence, Barbèra, 1876, vol. III, pp. 86 ff.

[7] GUICCIARDINI, *Storia fiorentina*, in *Opp.*, vol. VI, pp. 297-302.

[8] RIDOLFI, *Machiavelli²*, pp. 168 ff., 422 ff.

[9] E. CASANOVA in his justly severe (indeed not severe enough) review of E. ZANONI, *Vita pubblica di F. Guicciardini*, Bologna, Zanichelli, 1896, in *A.S.I.*, 4th ser., vol. XVIII, 1896, pp. 437 ff.

[10] We have letters of his about the countryside. Typical, among others, is the philosophical

letter published by C. GUASTI, *Le Carte Strozziane*, cit. sup., vol. I, pp. 342 ff.; cf. ibid. the letter on p. 329.

11 We may note in passing, as we shall have occasion later on to mention Iacopo merely as the affectionate and assiduous correspondent of Francesco, as his lieutenant in times of good fortune and his defender in times of adversity, that it was he who brought back from Ferrara, where he had gone as Florentine ambassador, certain youthful writings of Savonarola which he then made known in Florence; among them the famous letter to his father. He could only have obtained these documents from members of Savonarola's family. Cf. R. RIDOLFI, *Studi Savonaroliani*, Florence, Olschki, 1935, pp. 26 ff., 33. See also the passage in a Latin letter of his about Luther in C. GUASTI, *Le Carte Strozziane*, cit., p. 583. Further detailed information about Iacopo, which confirms this impression of his excellent qualities, may be found in P. GUICCIARDINI, *Cusona*, Florence, Rinascimento del Libro, 1939, vol. I, pp. 152 ff.

12 E. CASANOVA, op. and loc. cit.

13 VARCHI, *Storia fiorentina*, ed. L. Arbib, Florence, 1838–41, vol. II, p. 518.

14 *Opp.*, vol. IX, p. 75. Cf. also *Carteggi*, passim.

15 A complete edition of his dialogue *Del Savonarola*, hitherto known only in extracts, has recently been published by Bono Simonetta, Florence, Olschki, 1959. The dialogue is supposed to take place in Pisa after the battle of Gavinana, between Francesco Zati and Pieradovardo Giachinotti, whom the author had beheaded after tortures which even to contemporaries accustomed to such pleasantries, seemed 'excessive and horrible'. The edition contains a good deal of information about Luigi, indeed a biographical study which by its completeness absolves me from giving more details here. Another of Luigi's dialogues was also published not long ago by R. VON ALBERTINI as an appendix to his excellent volume, *Das florentinische Staatsbewusstsein im Übergang von der Republik zum Prinzipat*, Berne, Francke, pp. 413–21, where the reader will find useful information and views about Francesco's brothers. Unlike Simonetta, whose approach is somewhat apologetic, Albertini stresses the courtly and opportunist character of Luigi, as on pp. 261, 272, where he speaks of the 'tiefe Verbeugungen' to Cosimo in the dedication of his *Comparazione del giuoco degli Scacchi* and his *Sacco di Roma*. The latter and the *Discorso al Duca Alessandro* are too well known to need comment here; in any event, B. Simonetta, op. cit., considers at length these and other (mostly unfinished) writings of Luigi's.

16 *Opp.*, vol. IX, p. 71.

17 VARCHI, ed. cit., vol. I, p. 140. R. VON ALBERTINI, op. cit., attempted a reassessment of Niccolò, and published one of his discourses (pp. 377–404). Some of his correspondence was published by C. GUASTI, *Le Carte Strozziane*, cit.; among which note the greedy letters to his father about his uncle's estate.

CHAPTER 3

1 See above, chap. I, n. 24. We have some documents of Guicciardini's professional career as a lawyer, written opinions and submissions for defence, which are quoted by G. MASI, op. cit., pp. 129, n. 134 ff.

2 For the bodies which elected Guicciardini as their advocate see his *Ricordanze*, in *Opp.*, vol. IX, pp. 57, 60, 62–6, 68, 70, 73–5, 78.

3 *Opp.*, vol. IX, p. 69.

4 *Opp.*, vol. IX, p. 58.

5 *Ibidem.*

6 *Opp.*, vol. IX, p. 60.

7 *Opp.*, vol. IX, p. 58.

8 *Oratio Accusatoria*, in *Opp.*, vol. IX, p. 213.

9 *Opp.*, vol. IX, p. 64.

10 *Opp.*, vol. IX, pp. 65 ff.

11 *Opp.*, vol. IX, p. 66. Via di San Procolo was even at that time also known as Via de' Pandolfini, as this family had its oldest houses in the street just beside the church of San Procolo. In the Archivio Salviati, Pisa, *Libri di commercio*, series II, 49, f. 10, there is a document regarding the tenancy of this house which Francesco occupied from 1508 till his death (and I am indebted to Prof. Gino

Corti for pointing it out to me): it reads: 'MDXXVI. Messer Francesco di Piero Guicciardini owes us on 21 May 1534 fl. 690, for the rent of our house in Via de' Pandolfini for 17 years and 3 months from 1 November 1508 to 21 January 1527 at fl. 40 a year.'

[12] Ibidem.

[13] F. GUICCIARDINI, *Storia fiorentina*, in *Opp. in.*, vol III. I quote, however, from the more recent and more accurate edition of R. Palmarocchi with the title *Storie fiorentine*, in *Opp.*, vol. VI. Though I cannot accept all the arguments and conclusions of V. DE CAPRARIIS, *Francesco Guicciardini dalla politica alla storia*, Bari, Laterza, 1950, pp. 27–62, who calls the *Storie fiorentine* 'a great political *pamphlet*' (p. 104), I do agree with him that political interest is the guiding motive in this work. But it is ingenuous to argue (p. 61) that Guicciardini 'preferred to leave it without title, perhaps foreseeing that some other future work of his might more justifiably aspire to that description (i.e., a history), or else aware in his own mind that this youthful composition did not deserve such a name'. (It is worth recalling that the *Cose fiorentine* too, and even the *Storia d'Italia* were left without title by the author: cf. chap. 23, n. 41 of this volume.) On the sources of the *Storie fiorentine* – which, in accord with the character and limits of the work, do not go beyond the papers in the family archive and his own or his father's experience – see N. RUBINSTEIN, *The 'Storie fiorentine'*, etc., in *Rinascimento*, IV, 1953, pp. 171–225.

[14] *Storie fiorentine*, in *Opp.*, vol. VI, p. 8.

[15] The autograph original has no divisions into chapters; but I think Canestrini, who introduced such divisions for the first time, did better when he closed the first chapter at 1454 than Palmarocchi who ends it some years later at the death of Cosimo.

[16] See preceding note, and cf. E. FUETER, *Storia della storiografia moderna* (Ital. translation by A. Spinelli), Naples, Ricciardi, 1943, vol. I, p. 88. But it is clear that a division into books would have remedied this defect at least in part; and the first book might have covered, as a kind of preface, the period which is more summarily described.

[17] For this embassy see, besides the more general works already quoted, the special study by R. PALMAROCCHI, *L'ambasceria del G. in Spagna*, in *A.S.I.*, XCVII, vol. I, pp. 145–69, and republished in R. PALMAROCCHI, *Studi guicciardiniani*, Florence, Macrì, 1947, pp. 59–85.

[18] *Opp.*, vol. IX, pp. 70, 80.

[19] *Opp.*, vol. IX, pp. 69 ff.

[20] The reason for the choice of Guicciardini is certainly not the very odd one suggested by Palmarocchi, op. cit., pp. 146 ff., viz. that his youth would render him less suspect to the King of France! The real reason must lie in a compromise between the Optimates, who had supported the proposed embassy and wanted to send one of themselves, and Soderini, who having opposed it, did not wish any of the leaders of the opposite faction to go. Soderini could expect the young Guicciardini to be moderate as the respectful son of Piero, who was himself moderate, good, and the least hostile of the Optimates. In fact the whole thing was a compromise, both embassy and ambassador.

[21] *Storia d'Italia*, vol. II, p. 402.

[22] These instructions were published first by Rosini, then by Canestrini, in *Opp. in.*, vol. VI, pp. 3 ff., and republished in *Carteggi*, vol. I, pp. 24 ff.

[23] *Carteggi*, vol. I, p. 27.

[24] D. GIANNOTTI, *Discorso intorno alla forma della Repubblica di Firenze*, in *Opere politiche e letterarie*, Florence, Le Monnier, 1850, vol. I, p. 36.

CHAPTER 4

[1] F. BERNI, *Capitolo del prete di Povigliano*, v. 6. I think that the number of horses and horsemen was far greater than that supposed by P. Guicciardini in his comments to the edition of the *Diario* (p. 19) cited in the next note. Still less can I agree with my late friend about the speed of G.'s journey. But it is true that a commissioner and an ambassador travelled in different styles.

[2] R. RIDOLFI, *L'archivio della famiglia Guicciardini*, Florence, Olschki, 1931, p. 63; F. GUICCIARDINI, *Diario del viaggio in Spagna*, edited by P. Guicciardini, Florence, Le Monnier, 1932 (see p. 17 for information regarding its discovery). In the interests of uniformity and for ease of reference I shall quote from the second edition by Palmarocchi (*Opp.*, vol. IX, pp. 101–24). Although of a

much later date (1666), it is useful, or at least interesting, to compare it with the journey of a Lucchese ambassador published by A. PARDUCCI, *Diario del viaggio di Spagna di Francesco Spada*, in *Bollettino Storico lucchese*, vol. VII (1935).

³ *Opp.*, vol. IX, p. 104.

⁴ *Opp.*, vol. IX, p. 109.

⁵ *Opp.*, vol. IX, p. 110. Guicciardini calls it: *Abuois*.

⁶ *Opp.*, vol. IX, pp. 110–12.

⁷ *Carteggi*, vol. I, p. 30.

⁸ Letter to his brother Luigi, 2 April 1512, in *Carteggi*, vol. I, p. 57.

⁹ Letter from G. to the Ten, 2–3 April, in *Carteggi*, vol. I, pp. 33 ff. For information about Almazan, who died soon after G.'s embassy, see J. H. MARIÉJOL, *L' Espagne sous Ferdinand et Isabelle*, Paris, 1892, pp. 160 ff.

¹⁰ Letter from G. to the Ten, 15–21 April, in *Carteggi*, vol. I, pp. 38 ff.

¹¹ Letter of 4 May to his brothers Luigi and Iacopo, in *Carteggi*, vol. I, pp. 52 ff.

¹² Letter of 4 May, cit.

¹³ *Carteggi*, vol. I, p. 41.

¹⁴ Letter to his brother Luigi, 22 August 1512, in *Carteggi*, vol. I, p. 90.

¹⁵ Letter to his brothers Luigi and Iacopo, 4 May, in *Carteggi*, vol. I, p. 52.

¹⁶ Letter to his brothers Luigi and Iacopo, 13 May, in *Carteggi*, vol. I, p. 54.

¹⁷ Letter from Iacopo Guicciardini, 23 April, in *Carteggi*, vol. I, pp. 43 ff.

¹⁸ Letter to the Ten, 29 May, in *Carteggi*, vol. I, p. 59.

¹⁹ Letter from Piero Guicciardini, 3 June, in *Carteggi*, vol. I, pp. 63 ff.

²⁰ Letter from the Ten to G., 19 June, in *Carteggi*, vol. I, pp. 66 ff.

²¹ Letter from G. to the Ten, 18–22 July, in *Carteggi*, vol. I, pp. 76 ff.

²² *Ibidem.*

²³ Letter from G. to the Ten, 22–26 August, in *Carteggi*, vol. I, pp. 85 ff.

²⁴ Letter from G. to Piero, his father, 22–26 August, in *Carteggi*, vol. I, pp. 91 ff.

²⁵ *Storia d'Italia*, vol. III, p. 9.

²⁶ Letter from Iacopo Guicciardini to Francesco, in *Carteggi*, vol. I, p. 97.

²⁷ Letter from the Ten to G., 8 September, in *Carteggi*, vol. I, pp. 98 ff.

²⁸ Letter from the Ten to G., 24 September, in *Carteggi*, vol. I, pp. 103 ff.

²⁹ Letter from the Ten to Piero Guicciardini, 17 September, in *Carteggi*, vol. I, pp. 102 ff.

³⁰ Published by Canestrini in *Opp. in.*, vol. II, pp. 262–314, christened and regularly quoted by Otetea as the *Discorso di Logrogno*, and republished by Palmarocchi in *Opp.*, vol. VII, pp. 218–59. At the head of the original MS. there is the following note in the author's hand but in different ink: 'In Spain in 1512; and I was near the end when I had news that the Medici had entered Florence.' According to Palmarocchi this note is 'probably later'. He could have said without fear of contradiction, 'certainly much later', so much later in fact that when G. wrote it at the head, without looking at the date written at the end, his memory failed him.

CHAPTER 5

¹ Letter from G. to the Ten, 30 Sept. 1512, in *Carteggi*, vol. I, pp. 106 ff.

² Letter from G. to his brother Luigi, 26 Oct., in *Carteggi*, vol. I, p. 114.

³ Letter of 3–10 Nov., in *Carteggi*, vol. I, p. 117.

⁴ Letter of 14–17 Dec., in *Carteggi*, vol. I, p. 132.

⁵ *Carteggi*, vol. I, pp. 119 ff.

⁶ Letter from the Ten to G., 12 Nov., in *Carteggi*, vol. I, pp. 121 ff.

⁷ Reply from Niccolò Michelozzi to G. (G's letter is missing), in *Carteggi*, vol. I, pp. 202 ff. We only know of the letter to Giuliano from the reply, in *Carteggi*, vol. I, p. 146. The letter to Lorenzo de' Medici is in *Carteggi*, vol. I, pp. 221 ff.

⁸ Letter from G. to Leo X, 2 April 1513, in *Carteggi*, vol. I, pp. 161 ff.

⁹ Letter of 9 Jan. 1513, in *Carteggi*, vol. I, p. 138.

¹⁰ Letters to his brother Luigi, 30 March–12 April and 7–12 May, in *Carteggi*, vol. I, pp. 156 ff., 169 ff. In the B.R.F., *MSS. Palagi*, 405, ins. 3, n. 6, there is the copy of a letter without date

and without name of sender or addressee, but it was certainly sent to cardinal Giulio de' Medici by this exemplary secretary immediately after his inglorious return from Spain. Far from blaming Guicciardini, he sees fit to justify himself for his return: '. . . Paolo Vettori, who was here with Sig. Giuliano, Your Reverence's brother, sent for me and told me that you had asked him for information about my qualities, perhaps with the intention of giving me some employment, and that you had said you were happy about them except for the matter of my departure from Spain from messer Francesco Guicciardini. . . . Regarding which matter Your Reverence must know that I went there with him more for my own pleasure and to see the place than for any other reason, and without salary, thinking to stay a year at most; but when I had been there nearly two and felt like coming back for many reasons, especially too because of the happy repatriation of your illustrious family, from whom I hoped any good fortune I was destined to have in this world, and as our business was over and there was in the household one Gherardini doing practically the same work as me, he (i.e. Guicciardini), with great understanding, gave me free and gracious permission to go and sent me off well accompanied and at his own expense; and guarantee of this is the affection he bears me and would declare to all the world . . .' If we compare these words with the letters of G. cited above, the most reliable statement will appear to be that the ambassador 'sent him off well accompanied and at his own expense'! The rest of the letter seems to bear out the opinion of G. about its writer: 'He's one of the biggest liars I ever knew.' I say above that the addressee of the letter is Cardinal Giulio de' Medici; and this is certain, even though the words 'Sig. Giuliano, Your Reverence's brother' might suggest that it is Cardinal Giovanni de' Medici; for, when Bernardo returned to Florence, the latter had been Pope for several months. Of slightly more recent date was the nomination of Giulio as cardinal, and this is in fact referred to in the letter.

[11] Letter to his brother Iacopo, 14 March, in *Carteggi*, vol. I, pp. 155 ff. Note the Spanish word *loco* that G. makes play with. For some information about humanist studies under King Ferdinand, see J. H. MARIÉJOL, op. cit., pp. 309–32, and cf. the brief reference by G. in the *Relazione di Spagna*, in *Opp.*, vol. IX, p. 131.

[12] Letter of 17 June 1513, in *Carteggi*, vol. I, pp. 185 ff.

[13] Letter to his brother Luigi, 27 June–1 July, in *Carteggi*, vol. I, pp. 188 ff.

[14] Letter from G. to the Ten, 11 June, in *Carteggi*, vol. I, p. 182.

[15] Letter of 14 December 1512, in *Carteggi*, vol. I, p. 133.

[16] Letter to Iacopo Salviati, 4 July 1513, in *Carteggi*, vol. I, p. 194.

[17] Letter to Iacopo Salviati, 27 July, in *Carteggi*, vol. I, p. 198.

[18] *Ricordanze*, in *Opp.*, vol. IX, p. 73.

[19] *Ricordanze*, loc. cit.; cf. ibid., pp. 80, 81.

[20] Most directly in *Ricordi* 77, 105, 142, 144 (ed. Spongano).

[21] G. ROSINI, *Saggio sulle azioni e sulle opere di F.G.*, Pisa, Capurro, 1820, p. 10. (It is also at the end of Rosini's ed. of the *Storia d'Italia*, Pisa, Capurro, 1819–20, vol. X.)

[22] G. CAPPONI, *Storia della repubblica di Firenze*, ed. cit., vol. III, p. 192.

[23] Letter of 14–17 December 1512, in *Carteggi*, vol. I, p. 132.

[24] It is the discourse published in *Opp.*, vol. VII, pp. 260–66. It is certainly not of 1512 (otherwise he would not have written in the text 'the year 1512' but 'this year 1512'), and as G. used the Florentine style, it must be later than 25 March 1513. Indeed we are led to believe that it was after G.'s return to Florence by certain passages which would appear to be founded on direct observation rather than on scant information received by letter; e.g., 'now they openly give orders in all matters, great and small' (p. 262); 'the majority of the people is not happy with this government'; and he gives many details which it would be difficult for someone to know who had been away for two years.

[25] It is the third of the *Discorsi politici*, in *Opp.*, vol. VIII, pp. 80–88 (*Opere inedite*, vol. I, pp. 240 ff.).

[26] *Opp.*, vol. VIII, pp. 104–10. I cannot understand why Palmarocchi, who claims to have put these discourses into rigid chronological order, places these two after no. IV which was written several months later. They were written when the Grand Captain's coming to Italy was considered certain; but by September scarcely anyone mentions this any more.

[27] This is no. IV of the *Discorsi politici* in Palmarocchi's edition; but he put it out of order (it should have been no. VI: see preceding note); *Opp.*, vol. VIII, pp. 89–103.

[28] *Opp. in.*, vol. VI, pp. 271–97; *Opp.*, vol. IX, pp. 127–46.

[29] VILLARI, *Machiavelli²*, vol. II, pp. 253 ff.

[30] See the Reports of the Venetian ambassadors and J. H. MARIÉJOL, op. cit., pp. 233–45; also, and especially, V. LUCIANI, *Il Guicciardini e la Spagna*, in *Publications of the Mod. Language Assoc. of America*, vol. LVI, 1941, pp. 991–1006.

CHAPTER 6

[1] *Opp.*, vol. IX, p. 72.

[2] *Ibidem.*

[3] *Opp.*, vol. IX, p. 71; on p. 80, in the *Ricordanze* begun in 1527, G. noted that the night his father died he was 'on his way at San Giovanni in Moriana [Savoy]'; he had the news about twelve days later at Piacenza. In order to be able to recollect at some days' distance or even years after, where he was on that very night, it is likely he had also some diary of his return journey, now lost. P. GUICCIARDINI, *Ricordanze inedite di F.G.*, Florence, Le Monnier, 1930, p. 17, says that G. contradicts himself by writing in one place in the *Ricordanze* that he heard of his father's death at Piacenza and in another at S. Giovanni Moriana; but there is no contradiction; it is simply a question of interpreting the text correctly, as we have done here.

[4] *Opp.*, vol. IX, p. 74.

[5] *Opp.*, vol. IX, p. 73.

[6] *Opp.*, vol. IX, p. 80.

[7] *Opp.*, vol. IX, pp. 80 ff.; cf. p. 75. This division of the inheritance was completed by further transactions on 7 March 1524: cf. P. GUICCIARDINI, *Ricordanze inedite*, cit., p. 49. For the commercial enterprises (in silk, etc.) in which Francesco joined with his brothers, see *Opp.*, vol. IX, pp. 81, 82, 84, 90, 93.

[8] *Opp.*, vol. IX, pp. 73–4. G. also acquired many clients from Francesco Pepi who died at that time.

[9] The letter from Cardinal Giulio de' Medici is dated 25 Jan. 1514 (ordinary style); it was published in part by Rostagno in the Introduction to his ed. of the *Storia d'Italia*, cit., vol. I, p. cix, n.

[10] *Opp.*, vol. IX, pp. 75, 76. Worth noting is the letter from G. to Lorenzo de' Medici, dated 13 Oct. 1514, in which he commends to him his brother-in-law Giovanni Arigucci, 'who is just as much Your Magnificence's servant as the rest of us', asking for him to be included in the new Signoria: 'I will do in writing as I am accustomed to do when I am with Your Magnificence, that is ask you for what I need without ceremony . . .' This letter was published in *Carteggi*, vol. I, p. 228, from a rather corrupt modern copy; but the autograph of the original is in the Pierpont Morgan Library.

[11] *Carteggi*, vol. I, pp. 226, 236, 239, 242.

[12] Letter of 21 Nov. 1514, in *Carteggi*, vol. I, pp. 229 ff.

[13] The discourse *Del modo di assicurare lo stato ai Medici*, written at the beginning of 1516, in *Opp.*, vol. VII, pp. 267 ff.

[14] Letter from G. to his brother Luigi, 3 Jan. 1515, in *Carteggi*, vol. I, pp. 231 ff.

[15] Letter to his brother Luigi, 2 April 1515. The autograph is dated 2 April 1514, but it is a mistake easily explained by the fact that the old year, Florentine style, had only just ended; besides the correction is rendered necessary by the content. It is therefore surprising that the fact escaped the editor of *Carteggi*, vol. I, p. 226, where the letter bears the erroneous date and is out of place (it should have been n. 153, not n. 143) like a fish out of water.

[16] Letters of 3 Jan., 31 Jan., 21 Feb., and 2 April 1515 (the latter with the wrong date; see preceding note) in *Carteggi*, vol. I, pp. 229 ff., 231–38, 226. Things went so far that, in order to stem the tide of criticism of the Medici, someone had to be made an example of. Francesco, who was a member of the Eight at the time, found himself a party to this unpleasant task: 'I ceased to be a member of the Eight; and on the last day we admonished (i.e., deprived of office or the possibility of holding office) Bartolomeo Pandolfini for five years for having been so foolishly outspoken. It grieved me that such a thing should happen in our time, but, as it did, we had to put up with it and support the government; all the more so as, with all the rumours about the

French, the opposition had begun to get bold and speak out as usual, so it was decided that an example should be made of the first to pass the mark; and fate would have it that Pandolfini should be the one' (*Carteggi*, vol. I, p. 232).

17 *Ricordanze*, in *Opp.*, vol. IX, pp. 76 ff.

18 *Opp.*, vol. VII, pp. 267–81. See above, n. 13.

19 *Opp.*, vol. VII, p. 274.

20 Ibidem.

21 G. CAPPONI, op. and ed. cit, vol. III, p. 145, is wrong in assigning this discourse to the last years of Lorenzo (internal evidence indicates the beginning of 1516), and in saying that it was written for the information and even at the orders of the Pope and Cardinal Giulio de' Medici: G. wrote it, like most of his other things, merely for his own satisfaction; if he had not, he would not have used certain expressions that occur in the text.

22 L. STROZZI, *Le vite degli uomini illustri di Casa Strozzi . . .*, Florence, 1892, p. 114.

23 I refer to certain expressions of open discontent apparent here and there in his letters to his brother Luigi, and also in the Discourse cit. sup. in notes 13 and 21.

24 RIDOLFI, *Machiavelli*, pp. 239 ff.

25 Letter of 23 July 1515, in *Carteggi*, vol. I, p. 254.

26 Letters of 6 June, 4 July, 21 July, 23 July, in *Carteggi*, vol. I, pp. 247, 250, 253, 254.

27 Letter to his brother Luigi, 18 Aug. 1515, in *Carteggi*, vol. I, pp. 257 ff.

28 Letter of 18 Aug., cit.

29 Letter from G. to Luigi Guicciardini, 25 August, in *Carteggi*, vol. I, pp. 258 ff.

30 *Opp.*, vol. IX, p. 77.

31 Ibidem.

32 Letter from G. to his brother Luigi, 4 Sept., in *Carteggi*, vol. I, p. 259.

33 F. VETTORI, *Sommario della Storia d'Italia dal 1511 al 1526*, in *A.S.I.*, ser. I, vol. VI, 1848, p. 310. Villari is imagining things when he says that Lorenzo took umbrage at this order, 'all the more as he did not expect it from Francesco'!

34 Letter from G. to his brother Luigi, 28 Sept., in *Carteggi*, vol. I, p. 269.

35 G. had written on 4 July to his brother Luigi: 'Contessina died . . . just when life held the greatest happiness for her' (*Carteggi*, vol. I, p. 251).

36 CAMBI, *Istorie*, in *Delizie degli eruditi toscani*, vol. XXII, p. 87.

37 This draft, hitherto unknown and unpublished, is preserved in A.S.F., *Carte Strozziane*, ser. I, 136, ff. 205–206. After the attempt at a Latin version of the discourse to Leo X and Francis I (where the latter is compared to Godfrey of Boulogne, both French Kings, etc., and there is even a Virgilian *Arma virumque cano!*), G. tries various phrases for a fresh start, among which figure the words *Sunt mihi quattuor anni* repeated no less than seven times. What can he have meant? It was precisely four years since G. had set off for his embassy to Spain. For interest and by way of illustration I give below the uncorrected version of the unfinished discourse and the concluding verses (which, however, I think were jotted down there without any connection with the discourse), i.e., all the part written in Italian:

'Already, Most Blessed Father, already, Most Christian King, the Court of Rome and all the Christian flock, believing they see those things they have long desired but never so far hoped for, prepare their hearts and minds to follow such glorious and holy banners on an expedition full of just revenge, of piety and of religion. Not without such cause, Most Blessed Father, was your ascent to the Pontificate miraculous and divine; for no other purpose did God lead you into this Holy See in open day and by the great door: you did not enter furtively by night and by the windows; nor did God confer the Kingdom of France on you, Most Christian King, for whom at birth it did not seem destined, and at such prosperous age and with such favour and love of all men, for any other reason than that at last the city of the Holy Sepulchre and Constantinople, that other jewel of the Roman Empire, should be wrested from the hands of wretched wolves and dogs, and brought back to Christianity and to true obedience to the Holy Apostolic See. Why do you think, Most Christian King, that after so many favours, after so many honours conferred on your majesty, God in the first days (one might say) of your principality gave you the glorious possibility of conquering your enemies, and recuperating your inherited estates and those of your wife's dowry, were it not to bind you and fit you the more for an enterprise in which all Christians have placed their hopes? Why do you think, Most Blessed Father, that after so many other gifts and benefits, God has led to your holy feet with such reverence, charity and love, this your dearest son, if not to place in your hands an instrument fitted by goodness, prudence and power to help give effect to those holy thoughts of yours, to your noble and glorious intents? What a glorious and marvellous occasion never seen before in our day, when, even though all seemed disposed to peace, pernicious wars none the less have broken out! But today, when all the world rings with arms, and all kings and peoples are roused to war, suddenly, contrary to all belief, the light of salvation has appeared, a King of France is come in peace to revere and pay his respects to his Holy Pope. Today the Church has regained its right arm, today whole and united it may turn with all its might to works worthy of the Church and of the Pope. The matter is there; it remains only to give it form. You, Blessed Father and Most Christian King are sure of your purposes. Who doubts but that Caesar Maximilian, King of the Romans, seeing such an opportunity to realize a long-felt wish, will come to join you with all his might and forces? Ferrando, King of Aragon, though alone, has always fought the infidel; when he sees such powerful allies, all may imagine what he will do. The glorious King of England . . .

> In tutte le altre cose assai beata
> In una sola a me stessa dispiacqui
> Che in troppo humil terreno mi trovai nata.
>
> Duolmi ancora veramente che io non nacqui
> Un po' più presso al tuo fiorito nido
> Ma assai fu bel paese ove io ti piacqui.
>
> Che potea el cuore in che solo io mi fido
> Volgersi altrove, a te essendo ignota,
> Onde io fora meno chiara e di meno grido.
>
> No, risposi io, Madonna . . .

(There is one further line, illegible in the MS. Translation: 'Though very happy in all other things, I was only sorry that I was born on too humble soil. It grieves me too that I was not born a little nearer your illustrious nest, though it was a fine place where I pleased you. My heart, in which alone I trust, could have turned elsewhere, and I remained unknown to you, so that I should have been less distinguished and less celebrated. No, Madonna, I replied . . .' The subject of all but the last line is feminine.)

[38] *Opp.*, vol. IX, p. 78.
[39] The only historian who would have us believe in the civic inclination of Lorenzo is his great friend, courtier and companion in revelries (and so hardly reliable) Francesco Vettori (*Sommario*, cit., pp. 319, 328 ff.); but this was probably his way of trying to justify to his fellow citizens his intimacy with Lorenzo. Besides, even he admits that Lorenzo 'was not loved by the Florentines'.
[40] *Opp.*, vol. IX, p. 217.
[41] First published by OTETEA, p. 333, then in *Carteggi*, vol. I, p. 270, where Palmarocchi commits a gross error by adding, of his own invention, the place of destination as Modena. The address on the outside, which he omits in accordance with the principles he established for his edition, contains no indication whatever of place. It is difficult to understand why Palmarocchi did not realize that on 5 April, the date of the brief, G. could not have been in Modena, when he publishes scarcely two pp. later a letter in which G. says he made his first entry into Modena on 29 June! The original of the brief is in A.G.F., *Carte di F.G.*, XXIII, n. 167; as explained in the text, this gives G. no other title than Commissioner. In the later brief, on which G. himself wrote in his own hand: 'The authority to govern, 22 July' (A.G.F., *Carte di F.G.*, XXIII, n. 168), he is given the title of Governor.
[42] *Ricordanze*, in *Opp.*, vol. IX, p. 82.

CHAPTER 7

[1] *Oratio accusatoria*, in *Opp.*, vol. IX, pp. 209 ff.
[2] *Oratio defensoria*, in *Opp.*, vol. IX, p. 264.
[3] *Oratio accusatoria*, loc. cit.; cf. *Oratio defensoria*, loc. cit.

⁴ *Habent sua fata libelli*, and the fortunes of this MS. are perhaps worth recording for interest's sake. I discovered a large group of MSS., some with autograph notes by G. (cf. my introduction to the *Cose fiorentine*), not in the Archivio Guicciardini (though, despite the fact that it had been much worked over, I found there many unpublished documents), but in the main library of the family. Among them was the MS. mentioned in the text; but, as it nowhere bears the name of G., I did not at the time appreciate its contents and importance, and quoted it in my *Opuscoli di storia letteraria e di erudizione*, cit., pp. 118 ff., merely as proof of G.'s interest in astrology. Later on, my great friend Paolo Guicciardini gave me the MS. in recognition of my work on Guicciardini and for the inscription I devised for the restoration of the Guicciardini palace after it had been destroyed by German mines (it appears on the wall of the entrance and was published in P. GUICCIARDINI and E. DORI, *Le antiche case . . .*, cit., p. 99); and he then wrote on it a dedication which makes the MS. all the more precious to me. But not even then (to my shame) did I examine it very attentively, and it remained idle and almost forgotten on a shelf for many years, until one night as I was looking (as I often did) for some stimulus or pretext to get on with this biography which many people were encouraging me to write, I took it out and opened it casually, and there my eye fell on the date inscribed in the middle of the astrological drawing, and to my astonishment and excitement I read the year, day and hour of G.'s birth. What I had in my hand was his horoscope, with his own autograph notes! Discovered by me, then inadequately studied and quoted, it had come to seek me out in my own study, and had finally made itself heard. It is absolutely true: *habent sua fata libelli!*

⁵ MS. cit., f. 106v. On 21 Feb. 1516 Lodovico Alamanni, G.'s brother-in-law (he had married his sister Costanza), wrote to Luigi Guicciardini in Rome: '. . . I have discovered a great Hebrew astrologer, who has told me extraordinary things about myself, that is with marvellous accuracy, and similarly about other matters. If you want me to ask him any particular thing, write and tell me, for he is a very great friend of mine . . .' (A.S.F., *Carte Strozziane*, ser. I, 137, f. 150). The perfect coincidence of dates and his friendship with the brother-in-law suggest that the author of G.'s horoscope might well be this 'great Hebrew astrologer'. In this case the extraordinary knowledge of G.'s life and character would have been acquired indirectly, but none the less authentically, through his closest relatives. I have sought enlightenment in vain from the classic study of L. THORNDIKE, *A history of magic and experimental science*, New York, Macmillan, 1929–1958. One thing is absolutely clear: the dependence of the anonymous author on Arabic astrology, as is shown by his use of the terms *hileg* and *alcocodem*. Though he is not necessarily the same person as this astrologer, it is possible that Alamanni's 'Hebrew' might have been the famous Bonet de Lattes, though this would mean extending his life by at least a year, as he was believed to have died no later than 1515.

⁶ MS. cit., f. 106r.

⁷ MS. cit., f. 96v.

⁸ MS. cit., f. 106r.

⁹ MS. cit., f. 102v.

¹⁰ MS. cit., f. 105r.

¹¹ *Ricordi*, p. 223.

¹² *Ricordi*, pp. 66, 219.

¹³ *Cose fiorentine*, p. 283.

¹⁴ C. GUASTI, op. cit., vol. I, p. 319. Cf. R. RIDOLFI, *Opuscoli*, loc. cit.

¹⁵ *Ricordi*, p. 66.

¹⁶ VASARI, *Le vite*, Florence, Le Monnier, 1846–70, vol. X, p. 349. Cf. P. GUICCIARDINI, *Iconografia guicciardiniana*, in *Quarto centenario*, cit., pp. 107–15 (but it is better to consult this in the offprint made later which contains much more information, Florence, L'Arte della Stampa, 1940; the Bugiardini portrait is discussed on pp. 9 ff. and plate I gives an excellent reproduction). The original of the Bugiardini portrait is not, however, the one painted on canvas preserved in the Guicciardini palace, as was believed until quite recent times. The original, painted on a panel, was found in Vienna, whence it passed to the United States; Paolo Guicciardini tried in vain to get it back for Italy and his family house, but the traditional unenlightened meanness of the Ministry denied him the necessary foreign exchange to bring back into Italy this most authentic portrait of this great Italian. The premature statement, therefore, printed beneath plate I referred to above, that the original is in the Guicciardini collection, has to be corrected. The story is told

in detail in a rare appendix added to only 10 copies of the offprint quoted above, one of which is in my possession. There exist many copies of the Bugiardini portrait and others deriving from it: the one which was until recently believed by family tradition to be the original, is in fact a very late copy, possibly made for one of G.'s nephews. The original probably left the hands of the Guicciardini family, not for financial gain as the op. cit. suggests, but because of the extinction of the line of Francesco's eldest brother Luigi. Earlier and artistically superior to the copy mentioned, though different in many particulars, is the one attributed to Alessandro Allori, which is also preserved in the Guicciardini palace. According to Vasari, op. and loc. cit., the Bugiardini portrait was painted when 'messer Francesco Guicciardini . . . had come back from Bologna and was in his villa at Montici engaged in writing his *History*'. No one could say these words are inaccurate if the portrait was painted, not at the end of 1534 or the beginning of 1535, but four years later, which was in fact the case. In fact on the page which Francesco is writing in the portrait one can read the famous *incipit* of his *Storia*: 'I have decided to write about the events which have taken place in Italy within living memory since the time when the French armies called in by our own princes began to trouble her peace with great upheavals.' These words, if they were not put in after his death (and this could easily be checked by X-ray photography), besides bearing extraordinary witness to the importance given by Guicciardini to his masterpiece (for he alone could have been responsible for telling the painter to put them in), would also place the execution of the portrait in 1538 or 1539, because that *incipit*, as we know from the composition of the *Storia*, was not written until 1538 (cf. also RIDOLFI, *Opuscoli*, pp. 206 ff.). The earliest portrait of Francesco Guicciardini is therefore the medallion by a member of the Bolognese School, cast about 1533. For more complete information on these matters see P. GUICCIARDINI, op. cit.

The Guicciardini portrait attributed to Allori belonged, before it was inherited by Count Paolo Guicciardini, to the marchesi Torrigiani (formerly Guadagni) to whom it probably passed when Camilla di Angiolo Guicciardini married Vincenzo Guadagni. See P. GUICCIARDINI, *Il ritratto di Fr. Guicciardini della Galleria Torrigiani*, Florence, Tip. Giuntina, 1943.

The original of the Bugiardini portrait, whose wanderings are referred to above, passed into the Rabinowitz collection and subsequently to Yale University, New Haven. See L. VENTURI, *The Rabinowitz Collection*, New York, The Twin Editions, 1945, pp. 57 ff., plate XXVI; cf. figs. 15–17. This learned scholar does not, however, seem to have taken much trouble to study Guicciardini iconography and check his bibliography. He especially falls into a gross error by saying that the original came from 'the Medici collection', i.e., from the grand-ducal gallery where, according to him, it still remained until about 1740. Venturi was evidently misled by Franceschini's well-known engraving (based on the one by Giov. Michele Liotard) with the indication of derivation *Ex Museo Mediceo*. But this indication did not refer to the Bugiardini original, but to the copy of the Grand Duke, preserved in the Medici gallery; and it is from this that Liotard's engraving manifestly derives. [Plate I of this English edition shows the Bugiardini portrait as it now appears after cleaning in the Yale Art Gallery under the supervision of Prof. Chas. Seymour to whom thanks are due for the necessary photographic reproductions.]

[17] Suffice it here to say that the portrait of G. in the *Horoscope* is contained in the chapters *De phisionomia* (ff. 18a–20a) and *De spiritu et moribus* (ff. 19b–25a). I have summarized or paraphrased parts of these chapters; others I have quoted literally between inverted commas. L. MANZI in his recent study, *Un maestro dello Studio bolognese, medico di Fr. Guicciardini*, published extracts from two long letters written by the doctor, G. B. Teodosio, which have hitherto escaped the notice of Guicciardini scholars. They are replies to questions from G. after his departure from Bologna: one undated, the other of 4 April 1538 (IO. B. THEODOSIUS, *Medicinales epistolae LXVIII*, etc., Baslieae, apud Nicolaum Episcopium juniorem, 1553–4). Many details of the portrait sketched by the author of the *Horoscope* are confirmed by Teodosio, who also adds valuable information about G.'s habits and state of health. I am amused, like Manzi, by the concern with which the doctor, after referring to a certain corpulence of his client, hastens to correct the expression that might give offence, with a reference instead to his 'competens carnositas' (suitable covering of flesh). Unlike Manzi, however, I find no difficulty in reconciling the 'somewhat tortoise-like gait' of the *Horoscope* with the allusion to the long walks G. used to take ('excessive walking, in which almost all who accompany you become weary'). If G., wanting to slim or at least not get any fatter, took these exhausting walks (exercise was a concern common at that time to all stout people

of a certain age who were obliged to lead a largely sedentary existence), it does not necessarily mean he did not do them 'with a somewhat tortoise-like gait'.

¹⁸ *Opp.*, vol. IX, p. 99.

¹⁸ᵃ Dr. Teodosio (see 17 above) speaks of a 'maior coitus appetitus' mentioned by his client. Cf. L. MANZI, op. cit., p. 5.

¹⁹ *Opp.*, vol. IX, pp. 13, 41, 43.

²⁰ Instead of 'his father's teaching and the *piagnone* tradition', I might have written 'his *piagnone* education', and the contraction on the face of things at least would not have seemed overbold. See chap. I, pp. 5, 6, 12ff. The matter is of considerable importance for 'certain medievalistic religious motives which have probably been underrated by students of Guicciardini', of which F. CHABOD acutely writes in his fine article on G. in the *Enciclopedia Italiana*; also E. CECCHI, *Ritratti e profili*, Milan, Garzanti, 1957, p. 102.

²¹ The subject was treated, among others, by F. SARRI, *Il Guicciardini e la religione*, in *Quarto centenario*, cit., pp. 141–88, a careful and well-informed essay though not always convincing and not without some of the usual distortions and over-simplifications. No one could, however, be more ingenuous than A. LUZIO in his presentation of the '*Storia di Firenze' di F.G. nuovamente scoperta*, in *Atti della R. Accad. delle Scienze di Torino*, vol. LXVI, 1931, p. 78, where as proof of G.'s religious feeling he quotes no less than the title of the *Ricordanze*, which is merely based on the well-known formula of the time: 'In the name of Almighty God and His most glorious Mother and virgin St. Mary . . .' This is a bit much from such a distinguished historian, and worse still from such a famous archivist! For the varied opinions on G.'s religion, between the extremes of Sarri's essay, cit. sup., which comes near to sanctifying him, and that of G. ROVELLA who damns him completely (on the sole basis of the *Ricordi*), the reader is referred to the book by LUCIANI, cit., pp. 376 ff., 380 ff., 382 ff.; but we shall have other occasions to return to this subject later in this present biography.

²² MS. cit., f. 22b.

²³ MS. cit., f. 24b. The Horoscope is made up of 17 numbered chapters, followed by the annual tables and the chap. *De dispositione annorum* dealing year by year with G.'s past and future life; at the end a full index.

CHAPTER 8

¹ Brief dated 5 April 1516, cit., *Carteggi*, vol. I, pp. 270 ff.

² P. LITTA, *Famiglie celebri italiane*, Rangoni di Modena, tavv. III, VI; *Carteggi*, vol. I, p. 321.

³ LANCELLOTTI, *Cronaca modenese*, in *Monumenti di Storia patria delle provincie modenesi*, serie delle Cronache, vol. II, pp. 165 ff.; G. L. MONCALLERO, *Il cardinale Bernardo Dovizi da Bibbiena*, Florence, Olschki, 1953, pp. 435–7. For G.'s work in Modena see also T. SANDONNINI, *Modena sotto il governo dei papi*, Modena, 1879.

⁴ Letter from G. to Duke Lorenzo de' Medici, Modena, 30 June 1516, in *Carteggi*, vol. I, pp. 272 ff.

⁵ Letter from Cardinal Giulio de' Medici to G., in *Carteggi*, vol. I, p. 275.

⁶ Letter to Duke Lorenzo, 30 June, cit.

⁷ Letter to Duke Lorenzo, cit.

⁸ Letter to Duke Lorenzo, cit.

⁹ Letter to Luigi Guicciardini, 30 June, in *Carteggi*, vol. I, p. 274.

¹⁰ G. himself confesses this bluntly in a letter to Duke Lorenzo, 25 Aug. 1516, in *Carteggi*, vol. I, p. 296. In the A.G.F. *Carte di F.G.*, XXV, there is preserved the *Liber condemnationum civitatis Mutine* from 3 Feb. 1515 to 20 Dec. 1520; the MS. still has its original vellum binding with the arms of Leo X and Guicciardini on it.

¹¹ Letter to Duke Lorenzo, to whom he referred the case, 25 Sept. 1516, in *Carteggi*, vol. I, pp. 304 ff.

¹² Letter to Duke Lorenzo, 25 Aug. 1516, in *Carteggi*, vol. I, pp. 297 ff.

¹³ Letter to Duke Lorenzo, 1 July 1516, in *Carteggi*, vol. I, pp. 275 ff.

¹⁴ Letter to Duke Lorenzo, 26 Aug. 1516, in *Carteggi*, vol. I, p. 296.

¹⁵ Letter to Duke Lorenzo, 1 July 1516, in *Carteggi*, vol. I, p. 276.

¹⁶ Letters to Duke Lorenzo, 20 and 30 July 1516, in *Carteggi*, vol. I, pp. 285, 290 ff.

¹⁷ Published in *Carteggi*, vol. I, p. 287. It appears that Otetea, p. 82, did not know the brief, as it would seem from what he writes that G. did not get complete satisfaction; indeed, he implies the opposite.

¹⁸ *Carteggi*, vol. I, pp. 295, 297. OTETEA, loc. cit., quotes in support some words from G.'s *Oratio defensoria*: 'no enquiry was ever held into my administration, nor appeal granted against my decisions' (*Opp.*, vol. IX, p. 264); but this is clearly quite another matter.

¹⁹ Letter of 20 Nov. 1516 in *Carteggi*, vol. I, pp. 312 ff.; note in this letter the juridical argument according to which the Countess Diana would have no rights to legal privileges nor to the castles. Cf. the passage in the *Oratio defensoria* (*Opp.*, vol. IX, p. 265: 'Several were the occasions on which I was offered a thousand, three thousand, four, five thousand ducats . . .').

²⁰ Letter of Duke Lorenzo, 28 Aug. 1516, in *Carteggi*, vol. I, pp. 298 ff.

²¹ G. CAPPONI, *Storia della Repubblica di Firenze*, cit., vol. III, p. 192.

²² Letter of 31 Aug. 1516, in *Carteggi*, vol. I, p. 299.

²³ Letter of 1 Sept. 1516, in *Carteggi*, vol. I, p. 301.

²⁴ Letter from Iacopo Salviati in reply to one from G. of 30 June, in *Carteggi*, vol. I, p. 280.

²⁵ Letter of 3 Dec. 1516, in *Carteggi*, vol. I, pp. 318 ff.

²⁶ *Carteggi*, vol. I, pp. 319 ff., 322 ff.

²⁷ *Carteggi*, vol. I, pp. 324 ff.

²⁸ Letter to Gheri, 27 Dec. 1516: 'I should like it to be done before His Excellency the Duke leaves Rome' (*Carteggi*, vol. I, p. 237). On 16 Jan. 1517, having been assured by Gheri that Lorenzo had resolved 'at all costs' to give him the governorship of Reggio, G. asked him whether he should write to the Duke to thank him, and in any case he did write, enclosing the letter with the one sent to Gheri, cit. (*Carteggi*, vol. II, p. 5).

²⁹ The brief is in *Carteggi*, vol. I, p. 327. It was published earlier by OTETEA, p. 331, though I do not know how he came to state (p. 83 n.) that the brief was 'backdated'; it was held up for five months on account of the circumstances narrated in this chapter. Otetea also presents G.'s continual applications to obtain it, in a somewhat false light.

³⁰ *Opp.*, vol. IX, p. 83.

³¹ Letter from Luigi Guicciardini, 13 April 1517, *Carteggi*, vol. II, p. 84.

³² Letter of 16 Jan. 1517, in *Carteggi*, vol. II, pp. 8 ff. It is worth noting here that in the *Carteggi* the letter of 19 Jan. 1517 from Francesco and Luigi Guicciardini, in which information is given regarding military movements prior to the war of Urbino, has been inexplicably placed under the date 19 Jan. 1518 (vol. II, pp. 241 ff.) when it should have followed letter no. 13 on p. 15 of that volume. This is because Palmarocchi wrongly translated into Florentine style the date at the foot of the letter, no doubt misled by other letters from G. to his brother dated according to the Florentine style. It is not the only error of this nature made by Palmarocchi in the *Carteggi* (see chap. VI, n. 15, and cf. ibid. n. 40); and here too he could easily have avoided it by merely paying attention to the content of the letter.

³³ Letter to his brother Luigi, 10 Feb. 1517, in *Carteggi*, vol. II, p. 61.

³⁴ Letter to his brother Luigi, 21 April 1517, in *Carteggi*, vol. II, p. 90.

³⁵ *Carteggi*, vol. II, p. 77; cf. p. 67: 'I have nothing much to say about the governorship of Reggio, as I have kept quiet about it since these affairs began; but I do know from Rome and Reggio that Gozzadini, who is there on the spot and profoundly disturbed by them, now has had second thoughts about it; and I also know that the Pope and the Cardinal de' Medici are inclined, since these disturbances began, to take them seriously', etc.

³⁶ *Carteggi*, vol. II, p. 88. The Ferrarese ambassador in Rome also wrote to his Duke that it was rumoured at court that there was pressure on the Pope to give the Governor of Modena the rule of Reggio as well, but that the Pope had a weakness for Gozzadini (who was like himself much more interested in having a good time!). Cf. the monograph by L. CHIESI, cit., in the first note to the next chap., pp. 64 ff.

³⁷ *Carteggi*, loc. cit.

³⁸ Letter to his brother Luigi, 3 Dec. 1516, in *Carteggi*, vol. I, p. 318.

CHAPTER 9

¹ *Carteggi*, vol. II, p. 237. For Reggio under G.'s governorship, see also L. CHIESI, *Reggio nell'Emilia . . . e Fr. Guicciardini governatore della città*, Reggio Emilia, 1892, although several of the events narrated by the author are illuminated still further by G.'s correspondence which is now fully used for the first time in this biography. See also G. PANCIROLI, *Rerum historicarum patriae suae libri octo*, Reggio, 1847, of which bk. VII is almost entirely dedicated to G.'s governorship (pp. 461–508): the few quotations from this work are taken from this edition; the best MS. of it is in B.E.M.,a.X.1.8 =Lat. 468. There is also an Italian translation in print: *Storia della città di Reggio*, translated from Latin into Italian by P. Viani, Reggio, 1846–8, 2 vols.

² Letters from G. to Rosso Ridolfi, 30 June 1517; to Vincenzo Scaioli, 1 July; and to Goro Gheri, 2 July (*Carteggi*, vol. II, pp. 156–9).

³ Letters from G. to Cardinal Giulio de' Medici, 9 and 11 July, and to Goro Gheri, 25 July, in *Carteggi*, vol. II, pp. 168–70, 180.

⁴ Letter to Cardinal de' Medici, 17 July 1517, in *Carteggi*, vol. II, p. 173.

⁵ Letter to Cardinal de' Medici, 12 Aug. 1517, in *Carteggi*, vol. II, p. 188.

⁶ Letter to Cardinal de' Medici, 12 Aug., cit. Cf. also *Carteggi*, vol. II, pp. 173, 178, 221 and passim. On the subject see G. LIVI, *Il Guicciardini e Domenico d'Amorotto*, Reggio Emilia, 1875; but, as this book could only take slight advantage of G.'s correspondence and as it is partly based on the very inaccurate PANCIROLI, *Rerum historicarum*, cit., it is obviously for present purposes incomplete as well as defective. One point worth noting in it (curious rather than important) is the disquisition (p. 90 with facsimile) on the handwriting of Domenico, who was, however, completely unlettered (!) as is abundantly evident from a letter partly reproduced in the present chapter (*Carteggi*, III, pp. 205 ff.).

⁷ Letter to Cardinal de' Medici, 12 Aug., cit.

⁸ *Carteggi*, vol. II, p. 178.

⁹ Letter from G., 25 Nov. 1517, in *Carteggi*, vol. II, p. 220.

¹⁰ Information about this illness may be found in *Carteggi*, vol. II, pp. 187, 199, 200, 203, 216; G. PANCIROLI, op. cit., p. 466 calls it: 'ferme lethalem morbum', and tells with admiration of the indefatigable Governor's activities even during this grave infirmity. On p. 462 he writes that, unlike his predecessor, who always lived in the Palace, G. 'in arce . . . semper habitavit'.

¹¹ Letter of 17 Aug. 1518, in *Carteggi*, vol. II, pp. 315 ff.

¹² Letter of 13 March 1518, in *Carteggi*, vol. II, p. 262.

¹³ *Carteggi*, vol. II, pp. 303–306.

¹⁴ *Carteggi*, vol. II, pp. 290, 292, 294, 302, 306.

¹⁵ Letter from G. to the Cardinal and to Alfonsina de' Medici, 8 March 1518, in *Carteggi*, vol. II, pp. 260 ff.; cf. p. 27.

¹⁶ Letter of 6 Jan. 1517, in *Carteggi*, vol. II, p. 5.

¹⁷ Letter of 14 Feb. 1517, in *Carteggi*, vol. II, p. 63.

¹⁸ Letter from G. to Cardinal de' Medici, 29 March 1518, in *Carteggi*, vol. II, pp. 267 ff.

¹⁹ Letter of 4 April, in *Carteggi*, vol. II, pp. 271 ff.

²⁰ *Carteggi*, vol. II, pp. 258 ff.

²¹ At the end of October or the beginning of November the Elders of Reggio expressed their satisfaction to the Governor with the work of his brother Iacopo; G. thanked them on 2 November, and as for his indisposition he declared himself so far recovered as to expect to be rid of it very soon (*Carteggi*, A.S.I., p. 58).

²² Letter to Cardinal de' Medici, 21 Feb. 1519, in *Carteggi*, vol. III, pp. 9 ff. It must, however, be noted that G.'s letters do not agree about the date of the execution nor even with the calendar for 1519. See the letter of 7 February, in which there appears the first record of the deed, and those that follow down to the full account given in that of 10 March (*Carteggi*, vol. III, pp. 8–15).

²³ Letter of 2 April 1519 in *Carteggi*, vol. III, pp. 18 ff. As this was not the sort of subject suitable for record in the letter-book, G.'s letter to which this is the reply has not come down to us.

²⁴ Letter of 14 July 1519, in *Carteggi*, vol. III, p. 80. G. had always told the Cardinal little about the long negotiations for this peace, and for a long time he had not mentioned them at all, as he was encountering such difficulties as to lead him to expect 'their suspension rather than success'.

For more information about this peace and the 'small speech' G. made for the occasion, see L. CHIESI, op. cit., pp. 73–83.

25 Letter cit., in preceding note.

26 Less than eleven months before, on 24 Aug. 1518, G. wrote to the Cardinal: 'Two years have past since I was last in Florence, where I need to go for at least six or eight days for some private affairs of mine' (*Carteggi*, vol. II, p. 318); on 4 Sept. he thanked the Cardinal for giving him permission to go, but added that he would not take advantage of it until certain suspicions he had were cleared up (*Carteggi*, vol. II, p. 321). As far as one can see from his correspondence he did not take it up later.

27 Letter from Iacopo to G., 20 June 1519, in *Carteggi*, vol. III, p. 49.

28 Letter of 27 July 1519, in *Carteggi*, vol. III, p. 84.

29 In his letter of 20 June Iacopo wrote to him: 'I talked at length with your Maria and left her well content, as I have done on other occasions; but, what with her great desire to see you, and others interfering, she has not stayed that way.' From this one can conclude that the poor woman, who had not seen her husband for three years, was very unhappy, especially as others (perhaps some relative of hers) were fanning the flames of her discontent.

30 Brief of 18 May 1519, in *Carteggi*, vol. III, p. 25.

31 G. PANCIROLI, op. cit., p. 462, says that everywhere in Reggio were painted the arms of G. with the words: *Hoc duce parta quies.*

CHAPTER 10

1 Letter from Iacopo Guicciardini to Francesco, 20 June 1519, in *Carteggi*, vol. III, pp. 49 ff. This letter (cf. also the one from his more Medicean brother Luigi, in *Carteggi*, vol. III, pp. 46 ff.) adds several details to the better known historical sources, with which the only one to disagree (and, as I have said, for good reasons!) is Francesco Vettori's *Storia*, cit.

2 In G.'s minute book there is the following note in his own hand: 'Note that on 24 July 1519 I went to Florence and came back to Modena on the following 2 October; and my brother Iacopo stayed here in my place.'

3 Letter from G. to Cardinal de' Medici, 6 Oct. 1519, in *Carteggi*, vol. III, pp. 99 ff. As one can gather from the letter, it is merely to urge on a matter already begun in Florence. There is a further more urgent appeal on 31 October, in *Carteggi*, vol. III, p. 101.

4 Letter of 6 Nov. 1519 in *Carteggi*, vol. III, pp. 103 ff.

5 *Storia d'Italia*, vol. III, pp. 214 ff.

6 Letter from G. to Sigismondo Santi, 7 Jan. 1520, in *Carteggi*, vol. III, pp. 109 ff. This letter is an important and hitherto unnoticed gloss to that passage in the *Storia d'Italia*, vol. IV, p. 215, which sums up his disapproval and disappointment: 'especially as the neighbouring Governors of the Church were not informed of this matter and had no authorization, even had they known, to take any part in it'.

7 Letter of 3 July 1520, in *Carteggi*, vol. III, pp. 149 ff.

8 Letters from Iacopo Guicciardini to Francesco on 10, 13, 15, 17 Aug. 1520, in *Carteggi*, vol. III, pp. 181–7, 189–92.

9 Letter from Iacopo to Francesco, 19 Aug. 1520, in *Carteggi*, vol. III, pp. 194 ff.

10 Girolamo Camurana to G., 21 Aug. 1520, in *Carteggi*, vol. III, p. 205 ff.; cf. the letter written the same day by Iacopo to Francesco, in *Carteggi*, vol. III, p. 203.

11 See note 2 above. In the *Ricordanze* (*Opp.*, IX, p. 84) he noted: 'I record how on 28 Sept. 1519 as I had to return to Modena and Reggio from Florence, I made my will . . . and if she should have one or more sons, I made them my universal heirs . . . and my daughters were each to have as a dowry 2,000 florins, between what was in the *Monte*, what was in kind and ready money . . . However, if I died without sons, I made my universal heirs my brothers Luigi, Iacopo, Bongianni and Girolamo, and the sons of any of these who might then have died, *in stirpes* and not *in capita*.' This unpublished will has survived in the papers of Ser Pier Francesco Maccari, A.S.F., *Notarile Antecosimiano*, M.20, ff. 127–8 and 137. The notary signs himself *Ego Petrus Franciscus olim ser Macharii de Machariis*; G. calls him Pier Francesco di ser Maccallo.

12 *Carteggi*, vol. III, pp. 209, 211, 217, 240–45.

[13] Letters from G. to Cardinal de' Medici, 11 December 1520, and to the Governor of Bologna, 14 December, in *Carteggi*, vol. III, pp. 241 ff.

[14] *Carteggi*, vol. III, p. 245.

[15] *Carteggi*, vol. III, p. 250.

[16] *Carteggi*, vol. III, pp. 246, 250, 251, 252; vol. IV, pp. 5 ff.

[17] Letters of 14 Jan., 5, 6 and 18 Feb., in *Carteggi*, vol. IV, pp. 8 ff., 18 ff., 27 ff.

[18] *Carteggi*, vol. III, p. 234.

[19] The plot, initiated by Cardinal Ippolito on his return from Hungary and interrupted then by his death in Sept. 1520, was revealed by Conte Gaspare di Roio, the bad lot who had also informed about the conspiracy in Reggio; having at first been party to the affair, he then told all to G. (*Carteggi*, vol. III, p. 247).

[20] OTETEA, p. 95, who affirms that G. merely acted as intermediary in obedience to orders, without taking any responsibility in the matter; but he did not know of a letter to Giberti in which G. favours the enterprise and writes clearly that he had 'supported it strongly' (cf. *Carteggi*, vol. III, p. 234).

[21] Letter from G. to Giberti, 6 Nov. 1520, in *Carteggi*, vol. III, p. 233; the letter to Schönberg is dated 17 Oct., in *Carteggi*, vol. III, p. 227.

[22] Letter from G. to Cardinal de' Medici, 13 April 1521, in *Carteggi*, vol. IV, pp. 41 ff.

[23] *Carteggi*, vol. III, p. 233; vol. IV, pp. 29, 38–56, 64–71 passim.

[24] R. RIDOLFI, *Vita di N. Machiavelli*², cit., pp. 288, 299. In the second letter from G. to M. dated 18 May, after the reference to history repeating itself, see especially the words: '. . . you will use this example for some purpose, comparing or contrasting it with some one of those models of yours'.

[25] Almost a whole chapter is devoted to them in my *Vita di N. Machiavelli,* cit., pp. 280–92.

[26] *Carteggi*, vol. IV, p. 59. But it is preferable to read the text in P. VILLARI², op. cit., vol. III, p. 423, because Palmarocchi's is full of extraordinary mistakes. Cf. R. RIDOLFI, *Vita di N. Machiavelli*, cit., p. 452, n. 10. Even in the few words we quote from Machiavelli's letter, Palmarocchi managed to misread *guardonmi per ispirato* for *guardonmi per ispiritato!*

[27] *Carteggi*, vol. IV, pp. 61 ff. But the ordering of the letters is obviously mistaken; they should be re-ordered as follows: 72, 74, 73, 75, 76. Cf. R. RIDOLFI, op. cit., p. 452, n. 9.

[28] *Carteggi*, vol. IV, p. 63.

[29] G. CAPPONI, op. cit., vol. III, pp. 348–60. L. PASTOR, *Storia dei Papi*, Ital. translation by A. Mercati, Rome, Desclee, 1908–31, vol. IV, p. 136 ('with great skill the double-dealing Medici had once more succeeded in concluding agreements simultaneously with the two rivals').

[30] *Storia d'Italia*, vol. III, p. 232.

[31] *Storia d'Italia*, vol. III, pp. 233 ff.

[32] P. VILLARI, *Niccolò Machiavelli*, cit., vol. III, pp. 484 ff. G.'s letter to Cardinal de' Medici, with which Ranke thought to prove Villari patently wrong because there is no mention in it of the opportunity he had had to take Scudo prisoner, is the one published in *Opp. in.*, vol. VII, p. 281, republished in *Carteggi*, vol. IV, pp. 85 ff. But in the same letter-book there is a further letter immediately after it also written to the Cardinal and on the same day, which remained unknown to Ranke because it did not appear in Canestrini's selection. In this letter he wrote: 'If I had wished to deceive with an evil trick, I could have held Scudo prisoner, as he was inside the bridge with no one but Mons. della Motta.'

[33] See his letters from Bologna at this time, *Carteggi*, vol. IV, pp. 113–36.

[34] *Storia d'Italia*, vol. III, p. 339.

[35] *Opp.*, vol. IX, p. 87; for the expression of G.'s satisfaction to the Cardinal see *Carteggi*, vol. IV, p. 119.

[36] At Bologna G. developed a fever which at first made him fear the Cardinal might be obliged to appoint someone else in his stead; but it was a 'simple tertian', and he soon got rid of it. For the progress of his illness see the letters of 15, 16, 17 July, in *Carteggi*, vol. IV, pp. 121–6.

[37] *Carteggi*, vol. IV, pp. 132, 143.

[38] *Storia d'Italia*, vol. III, p. 243.

[39] *Storia d'Italia*, vol. III, pp. 249 ff.

[40] *Storia d'Italia*, vol. III, p. 251; letter to Cardinal de' Medici, 9–10 Sept. 1521, in *Carteggi*, vol. IV, pp. 218 ff.

⁴¹ The *Dialogo del reggimento di Firenze* (of which I shall speak at more length further on, when we find the author finishing it to his own satisfaction) was ascribed by its first editor, Canestrini (cf. BENOIST, p. 132), to the years 1527–9; and this dating was accepted and consecrated by all Guicciardini scholars and histories of literature. But Canestrini had not even bothered to read the second version of the proem, which the author rewrote three times, in which the work is dated with great precision: 'This work . . . which I began to write at the time of Leo X when I was his commissioner general for the Imperial and Papal armies . . . I have finished now that I have been appointed by Clement as Governor of all the cities of Romagna.' This version was published for the first time by OTETEA, pp. 369–73. Palmarocchi writing of the chronology in the critical note to his edition (*Opp.*, VII, p. 286), situates the beginning of the work between the early part of July and 1 December (death of Leo X). But G. did not have the briefs regarding his nomination as commissioner before 12 July, and for the whole of that month, busy as he was and in continual movement, he would certainly have thought of anything but writing a book. The beginning must therefore be placed between August and November; but for the reasons indicated in the text I would restrict it still further between 1 October (arrival of Cardinal de' Medici at the army) and 30 November. In my opinion it was after the Cardinal's arrival that G. spent his leisure time drafting the *Dialogo del reggimento*, rather than (to use his own words in which he recalls precisely those days) 'spend leisure and money on cards' in what he facetiously called the 'Marignano academy' – in which, among other courtiers of the Cardinal, was the Archbishop of Manfredonia, i.e., no other than the future Julius III. On the contents of the *Dialogo*, besides the relative pp. in Otetea's book, see the recent essay by F. FOCHER, *Il Dialogo del Reggimento di Firenze,* in *Critica storica,* vol. IV, 1966, pp. 504–38.

⁴² *Storia d'Italia,* vol. III, p. 258.

⁴³ G. PIERACCINI, *La stirpe de' Medici di Cafaggiolo,* Florence, Vallecchi, 1924–5, vol. III, pp. 209 ff. The distinguished writer gives a definitive account, historically and clinically complete, of the last days of Pope Leo.

CHAPTER 11

¹ *Opp.*, vol. IX, pp. 149 ff.; *Carteggi*, vol. IV, p. 255.

² This fine long letter is important because it confirms in detail the balanced account given in the *Relazione della difesa di Parma*; here, however, in the letter there is an immediacy and vitality dictated by the pressure of events. The autograph draft is in A.G.F., *Carte di F. G.,* VIII, ff. I–II; published in *Opp. in.*, vol. VIII, pp. 367 ff., but (*incredibile dictu*) omitted from the modern monumental edition of the *Carteggi* by Palmarocchi, even though this edition contains (vol. IV, p. 259) another letter to Iacopo of 21 December, in which this one is explicitly referred to ('I wrote you last night . . .').

³ Our account is based on that left by G. himself in his *Relazione della difesa di Parma,* in *Opp.*, vol. IX, pp. 149–61, and in *Storia d'Italia,* vol. III, pp. 271–6; but we have also used the *Carteggi,* vol. IV, pp. 259–66. The *Relazione* was written in the year after the event, as G. tells us at the beginning, probably in his spare time between Feb. and Oct. 1522 when he was left practically with Parma alone in his charge; in other words, between two and ten months after the event. U. BENASSI in his *Storia di Parma,* Parma, Tip. Adorni, 1899–1906, of which vol. IV is entirely dedicated to G.'s governorship, confirms the accuracy of the account in the *Relazione* with the aid of chronicles and contemporary documents. Benassi gives very detailed information about G.'s rule, and I am glad to refer the reader to his work for the kind of administrative detail which for Parma as for Reggio it would be unsuitable to include in these pages.

⁴ Letter to the Sacred College, 5 Feb. 1522, in *Carteggi,* vol. V, pp. 5 ff.

⁵ Letters to the Sacred College of 12, 15 and 18 Jan. 1522, in *Carteggi,* vol. V, pp. 7–10, 13 ff.; letter to Cardinal de' Medici, 29 Jan., in *Carteggi,* vol. V, pp. 14 ff. Cf. ibid. the letter, also of 29 Jan., to the Sacred College.

⁶ Letter of 2 Feb. 1522 (dated 2 Jan. in error), in *Carteggi,* vol. V, pp. 16 ff. Cf. also later letters to the Cardinal and Sacred College, ibid., pp. 20 ff. Unlike Rangoni and Pio, the Marquis of Mantua made no move to enter on the governorship of Parma; from his direction G.'s authority and self-esteem suffered no diminution. Cf. U. BENASSI, op. cit., pp. 84 ff.

[7] *Carteggi*, vol. V, pp. 24 ff. Paolo d'Arezzo was Paolo Valdambrini.

[8] See p. 96 and n. 41 to chap. X. I believe that a good part of the work was written at Parma where G., as he himself tells us, had little to do, though he was still Commissioner in fact, while only nominally Governor of Modena and Reggio until he had fresh confirmation of the appointment from the Pope. The first draft of the *Reggimento* was made in a miscellaneous notebook (A.G.F., *Carte di F.G.*, VIII), whose first pages (which are not numbered, but certainly belong to the original book, not added later, as is evident from the watermark) contain the draft of a letter to Iacopo written at Parma on the night of 20 Dec. 1521, a few hours before the enemy attack. The text of the *Dialogo* ends on f. 106a and on f. 106b begins the first redaction of the proem, which, like all his prefaces, was written after the work itself. Further on the MS. contains a group of discourses written while he was President of Romagna. In the very midst of these we find the famous discourses on the *Decima scalata* (*Opp.*, vol. VII, pp. 196–217) which Palmarocchi could not date, but which I think were written at the same time, not merely transcribed here then.

[9] Letter to Cardinal de' Medici, 19 February, in *Carteggi*, vol. V, pp. 27 ff. Cf. the dry reply to Alberto Pio when he wrote telling him of the commission he had been given, and cf. another answer to certain remonstrations by Pio in *Carteggi*, vol. V, pp. 20, 28 ff.

[10] Letter of 5 March, in *Carteggi*, vol. V, pp. 31 ff.

[11] U. BENASSI, op. cit., vol. IV, pp. 85–90.

[12] This Cesare Colombo, who was to become G.'s right arm, had been helped by G. from the first years of his governorship of Modena, when Leo X, who was always disposed to favour men of letters, ordered the Governor to restore to the Calcagnini the possession of a castle occupied by Cesare Colombo; but G. replied that he could not do this, as the Calcagnini had been dispossessed of the castle by Julius II, and Colombo had received it as an Imperial donation. Cf. *Carteggi*, vol. VI. p. 286. He was made a citizen of Parma for bravery in the defence of the city in G.'s time (U. BENASSI, op. cit., vol. IV, p. 56). From certain allusions it is possible to infer that G. paid him a salary of 50 ducats a month.

[13] Letter to Cesare Colombo, 19 Oct. 1522, in *Carteggi*, vol. V, pp. 73 ff.

[14] Letter to Cesare Colombo, 25 Oct. 1522, in *Carteggi*, vol. V, pp. 76 ff.

[15] Letter to C. Colombo, in *Carteggi*, vol. V, pp. 78 ff.

[16] *Carteggi*, vol. V, p. 81.

[17] Letter of 5 Nov., in *Carteggi*, vol. V, p. 82. The papal brief for Reggio is dated 13 November. There is a copy in the Archivio Comunale of Reggio; cf. G. LIVI, op. cit., p. 40.

[18] Letters to Cesare Colombo of 5 and 15 November; to Pope Adrian VI, 15 November; to Archbishop Niccolò Schönberg, 15 November, in *Carteggi*, vol. V, pp. 82–5. In his letter to Schönberg G. congratulates himself on having got thirty miles nearer Florence in coming to Modena.

[19] Letter to Cardinal de' Medici, 19 Nov., in *Carteggi*, vol. V, p. 86; L. CHIESI, op. cit., p. 110. As the citadel was occupied by Pio, G. took up quarters in the Palazzo.

[20] PANCIROLI, op. and ed. cit., p. 462.

[21] U. BENASSI, op. cit., vol. IV, pp. 96–104. Of particular importance, on pp. 117–20, the long report of the Ambassador Maestri to the commune of Parma, written on 7 Jan. from Reggio where he had had to take refuge to escape the revenge of the enraged Bishop of Feltre. We have taken from this report merely one sample of the exchanges between Maestri and Pope Adrian, which all together give a delightful picture of affairs.

[22] *Carteggi*, vol. V, pp. 117–20.

[23] *Carteggi*, vol. VI, p. 60.

[24] Letter to Cesare Colombo, 19 Jan. 1523, in *Carteggi*, vol. V, p. 141.

[25] Letter to Cesare Colombo, 8 Jan. 1523, in *Carteggi*, vol. V, pp. 130 ff.; and to Pope Adrian VI, 14 Jan., ibid., p. 137.

[26] U. BENASSI, op. cit., vol. IV, pp. 104–107.

[27] Letters to Pope Adrian, 13 Jan. 1523, in *Carteggi*, vol. V, pp. 133 ff.; letter to Archbishop Ruffo, ibid., p. 172. G. LIVI, op. cit., cart. n. 92 ff. published part of the instructions of the Elders of Reggio to an ambassador they sent to Rome to seek the restoration of the citadel to the Governor.

[28] Letter of 29 March, unpublished, in A.S.F., *Carte Strozziane*, ser. I, 129, f. 132. Also in a letter (also unpublished) from Iacopo Guicciardini to his brother Girolamo, of 3 April: 'Messer Francesco has asked the Pope's permission to return to Florence and leave his governorships; and

when he has it (as I believe he will), he will come home' (A.G.F., *Libri di amministrazione*, XXV f. 40a).

²⁹ *Carteggi*, vol. V, p. 177. As it had been suggested to him by Colombo, I do not know what other expedient, beyond the usual collection of signatures to a protest, would have met the case: 'I do not wish to be held a seditious or restless man, nor to beg governorships with wicked practices of this kind' (*Carteggi*, vol. V, p. 182).

³⁰ *Carteggi*, vol. V, p. 116.

³¹ *Carteggi*, vol. V, p. 178.

³² Letter to Cesare Colombo, 15 April, in *Carteggi*, vol. V, p. 181

³³ *Carteggi*, vol. V, p. 201.

³⁴ *Carteggi*, vol. V, p. 208; cf. p. 215.

³⁵ Letter to Cesare Colombo, 15 April, in *Carteggi*, vol. V, p. 181, VI, p. 68.

³⁶ Letter of 10 Sept., cit.

³⁷ Letter of 12 Sept., in *Carteggi*, vol. VI, p. 73.

³⁸ Letter to Paolo Vettori, 16 Sept., in *Carteggi*, vol. VI, p. 87.

CHAPTER 12

¹ Letter to the Otto di Pratica, 18 Sept. 1523, supported by a private letter, of the same date, to Roberto Acciaiuoli (where there is a characteristic remark by G. the Florentine about his fellow Florentines: '. . . these petty merchants of yours, for the sake of mean gold, should not ill-treat us as they do'); in *Carteggi*, vol. VI, pp. 96 ff.

² Letter to the Otto di Pratica, 25 Sept. 1523, in *Carteggi*, vol. VI, p. 110.

³ Letter to the Sacred College, 26 Sept. 1523, in *Carteggi*, vol. VI, pp. 118 ff.

⁴ Letters to the Otto di Pratica, 26 Sept., and to Cardinal de' Medici, 29 Sept., in *Carteggi*, vol. VI, pp. 119 ff., 126.

⁵ Letter to the Elders of Reggio, 25 Sept. 1523, in *Carteggi*, vol. VI, p. 108; cf. *Storia d'Italia*, vol. III, p. 325.

⁶ *Opp.*, vol. IX, p. 89. Some days later, when the danger was renewed, he wrote: 'I am determined, if I can and am in time, that my own downfall shall not accompany the loss of Modena. I am sure the Duke is very ill disposed towards me, for I believe the present affair awakens in his mind the memory of some past incident' (*Carteggi*, vol. VI, p. 187). By making this gift G. intended to remedy some omission in his will of 1519 which is explicitly referred to (see above, chap. X, n. 11). The document, drawn up by the Modenese notary Gio. Batt. da Festa or Festasi, and hitherto unknown, was discovered by me in A.S.M., *Notarile*, cass. 1567, n. 339, ff. 370–71, and published recently: R. RIDOLFI, *Un documento modenese del G.*, in *A.S.I.*, CXVII, 1959, pp. 379–84.

⁷ Letter of 28 Sept., in *Carteggi*, vol. VI, p. 123.

⁸ Letter to the Sacred College, 29 Sept., in *Carteggi*, vol. VI, pp. 123 ff.

⁹ Letter to the Sacred College, 30 Sept., in *Carteggi*, vol. VI, pp. 128 ff.

¹⁰ Letter to the Governor of Bologna, 8 Oct. 1523, in *Carteggi*, vol. VI, p. 155.

¹¹ 'If our guns and pikes were no more use to us than these papers will be, we should be in a bad way' (Letter to the Governor of Bologna, 9 Oct., in *Carteggi*, vol. VI, p. 156).

¹² *Storia d'Italia*, vol. III, pp. 325 ff.

¹³ *Storia d'Italia*, vol. III, p. 324, where (as in the pp. that follow) G. gives fine proof of his sincerity and objectivity, giving due credit to Rangoni for whom he certainly had no affection or esteem; *Carteggi*, vol. VI, passim.

¹⁴ *Storia d'Italia*, vol. III, pp. 330 ff.; *Carteggi*, vol. VI, pp. 190–232 and passim.

¹⁵ *Carteggi*, vol. VI, p. 244

¹⁶ Letter to Cesare Colombo, 21 Oct., in *Carteggi*, vol. VI, pp. 186 ff.

¹⁷ Letter of 22 Nov., in *Carteggi*, vol. VII, pp. 5 ff. One of the first briefs of the new Pope was one addressed to G. telling him to follow the instructions of Niccolò Schönberg, Archbishop of Capua; this brief, preserved in A.G.F., *Carte di F.G.*, was published by OTETEA, pp. 332 ff.

¹⁸ Letter of 1 Dec., in *Carteggi*, vol. VII, p. 18.

¹⁹ Letter to Cesare Colombo, 26 Dec., in *Carteggi*, vol. VII, p. 38.

²⁰ Letter to Cesare Colombo, 26 Dec., cit. Cf. the letters of 10 Dec. to Colombo and to Iacopo Salviati, in *Carteggi*, vol. VII, pp. 38 ff. Salviati, who was related both to G. and to the Pope, showed no keenness in the matter of these governorships, because the Legate under whom G. was refusing to serve, was probably going to be his son Cardinal Giovanni. G. tried hard to rouse him, bringing in his poor wife who was Iacopo's cousin: 'As I have been so long away from my wife, I am obliged either to go back home or bring her here with the rest of the family.'

²¹ Letter to Cesare Colombo, 1 Jan. 1524, in *Carteggi*, vol. VII, pp. 39 ff.

²² Letter of 1 Jan. 1524, cit.

²³ Letter of 2 Jan., in *Carteggi*, vol. VII, pp. 44 ff.

²⁴ Both these letters of 3 Jan. are in *Carteggi*, vol. VII, p. 46.

²⁵ Letter to Cesare Colombo, 18 Jan., in *Carteggi*, vol. VII, pp. 53 ff.

²⁶ *Carteggi*, vol. VII, pp. 56 ff.

²⁷ Letter to Cesare Colombo, 13 March, in *Carteggi*, vol. VII, pp. 70 ff.

²⁸ Letters to Cesare Colombo, 16 and 17 March, in *Carteggi*, vol. VII, pp. 72–4.

²⁹ It was published in part by OTETEA, pp. 333 ff.; cf. *Opp.*, vol. IX, p. 90. OTETEA also published in appendix a papal brief dated 6 April 1524, which gives G. authority to pardon certain exiles. I do not understand how Otetea can write (p. 109) that this is the brief nominating G. as President (I assumed that as a Sorbonne graduate he could read the Latin!).

³⁰ Letter of 2 May 1524, in *Carteggi*, vol. VII, pp. 74 ff.

³¹ In the next chapter we shall see that the task of going to see it and to report was given to Machiavelli. For the acquisition of properties see *Opp.*, vol. IX, pp. 85 ff., 88 ff., and also chap. XIII, n. 38 of the present volume.

³² *Opp.*, vol. IX, p. 90.

CHAPTER 13

¹ Canestrini (*Opp. in.*, vol. VIII, p. v), with excessive generosity, threw in also Piacenza, Modena and Parma! He also gave as G.'s predecessor a certain Niccolò Bonafede, who had been there earlier on, instead of the Bishop Bernardo Rossi. We still have copies of the brief nominating this Bishop and of the conditions offered to him; in their margins G. wrote in his own hand the conditions he himself expected: A.G.F., *Carte di F.G.*, XXIV, n. 2.

² *Carteggi*, vol. VII, pp. 74 ff.

³ Letter to Cesare Colombo, 20 May 1524, in *Carteggi*, vol. VII, pp. 76 ff.

⁴ Letter of 18 June, in *Carteggi*, vol. VII, p. 88.

⁵ Letter of 18 June, cit.

⁶ Letter of 18 June, cit.

⁷ VETTORI, *Storia d'Italia*, cit., loc. cit., p. 348.

⁸ Letter of 12 July, in *Carteggi*, vol. VII, p. 105.

⁹ *Istruzione delle cose di Romagna*, in *Opp. in.*, vol. VIII, p. 402.

¹⁰ Letter of 24 June, in *Carteggi*, vol. VII, p. 96.

¹¹ Letter of 28 June, in *Carteggi*, vol. VII, p. 97.

¹² Letter of 19 June, in *Carteggi*, vol. VII, p. 93.

¹³ Letter of 4 July, in *Carteggi*, vol. VII, p. 99.

¹⁴ Letter of 19 June, in *Carteggi*, vol. VII, pp. 92 ff.

¹⁵ Letter of 1 June, in *Carteggi*, vol. VII, pp. 80 ff.

¹⁶ Letter of 25 Sept., in *Carteggi*, vol. VII, pp. 141 ff.; cf., for the consequences, especially the letters of 26 and 30 Sept., pp. 143–5.

¹⁷ Letter of 9 Oct., in *Carteggi*, vol. VII, p. 155.

¹⁸ Letter of 12 Oct., in *Carteggi*, vol. VII, p. 162. This letter went with another to be shown, as usual, to the Pope, in which G. writes: 'I do not believe, however, that His Holiness could possibly form the impression that I am at all partial, for, besides having no interest in these people nor esteeming them one jot, my past conduct ought to guarantee the future. . . . You know how necessary it was to deal with Bertinoro . . .' (p. 161).

¹⁹ Letter of 13 Oct., in *Carteggi*, vol. VII, p. 166.

²⁰ Instructions to his brother Iacopo, in *Opp. in.*, vol. VIII, pp. 402 ff.

21 Letter of 26 Oct., in *Carteggi*, vol. VII, pp. 175 ff.

22 He was in Imola when the fort was attacked on the night of 5 January. It was repulsed, but to G.'s great disappointment, it was not possible to discover who was responsible for it. Letters of 5, 10, 19, 27 Jan. 1525, in *Carteggi*, vol. VII.

23 Letter from G. to Colombo, 27 Feb. 1525, in *Carteggi*, vol. VII, p. 221. The description of Antonio Numai quoted in the text is in *Carteggi*, vol. VIII, p. 144.

24 Letter of 27 Feb., cit.

25 Letter of 10 March, in *Carteggi*, vol. VIII, p. 5.

26 Letter of 19 April, in *Carteggi*, vol. VIII, pp. 20 ff.

27 Letter of 20 May, in *Carteggi*, vol. VIII, pp. 40 ff.; cf. p. 52.

28 Letter of 19 April, cit.; letters of 4 and 20 May, 7 and 28 June in *Carteggi*, vol. VIII, pp. 22 ff., 29 ff., 40 ff., 53 and elsewhere. The papal brief of absolution, dated 16 June 1525, preserved in A.G.F., *Carte di F.G.*, XXIII, n. 215, was published by OTETEA, pp. 334 ff. For the degradation of a friar whom he held prisoner, he realized that the brief of absolution he sought was not sufficient and special permission was necessary, but he added: 'If you see any difficulty in obtaining it, let me know, for I will do as in the past, as it does not offend His Holiness' (p. 72). 'As in the past' meant without permission of any kind!

29 Letter of 12 July, in *Carteggi*, vol. VIII, p. 81.

30 RIDOLFI, *Machiavelli*², p. 309.

31 RIDOLFI, op. cit., pp. 319 ff.

32 Letter of 18 June, in *Carteggi*, vol. VIII, p. 63.

33 Letter of 23 June, in *Carteggi*, vol. VIII, pp. 66 ff.

34 *Carteggi*, loc. cit.

35 *Carteggi*, vol. VIII, p. 78.

36 For this commission of Machiavelli see RIDOLFI, op. cit., pp. 320–24.

37 RIDOLFI, op. cit., p. 324.

38 RIDOLFI, op. cit., pp. 325 ff. The acquisition of Finocchieto was suggested to G. by his brother Iacopo (who had not seen it either!) in a letter dated 19 Feb. 1522–23: 'The one in the Mugello is called Finocchieto . . . The property, I hear, is very fine and useful, and there is a good house with it . . . The price will, I think, be 2,800 ducats . . .' (A.S.F., *Carte Strozziane*, 368, ff. 209 and 216). When the property had been bought, Iacopo wrote about it to his brother Girolamo in a letter of 3 April 1523 (A.G.F., *Libri di amministrazione*, XXV, f. 40b): 'I have bought recently for him (messer Francesco) a property in the Mugello with an income of 140 gold ducats, costing, with tax, 3,000 ducats, and it has a good house. . . .' One wonders what G.'s reaction was when, his enthusiasm aroused for that good house, he got Machiavelli's description of it.

39 *Opp. in.*, vol. X, pp. 100 ff. Cf. RIDOLFI, op. and loc. cit.

40 RIDOLFI, op. cit., p. 463. The complete text of the letter is in MACHIAVELLI, *Lett. fam.*, pp. 444 ff.

41 *Carteggi*, vol. VIII, p. 108.

42 Letter of 19 Sept., in *Carteggi*, vol. VIII, pp. 107–108.

43 News of these laborious negotiations, conducted however only with the guelphs, is scattered throughout the President's correspondence. See especially the letters of 5 Aug. 1525, 20 Sept., 22 Nov., 2 Dec., 24 Dec., in *Carteggi*, vol. VIII, pp. 89, 109, 133, 141, 152.

44 See above chap. X, n. 41, and chap. XI, n. 8. The new redaction composed during the Presidency is written in the hand of G.'s usual amanuensis, and was dictated, not copied, from the first autograph redaction from which it is significantly different. This final version is in A.G.F., *Carte di F.G.*, XXVII, which is not a miscellany like that containing the first version, but contains besides only the *Reggimento*.

45 *Opp.*, vol. VII, p. 5. This is what figures in the final version. In the second we read: 'written by me without thought of publication'; in the first this passage is missing, but he had written earlier in the proem that the dialogue could not have been published without danger. The first and second versions of the proem are in *Opp.*, vol. VII, pp. 295–301.

46 *Opp.*, vol. VII, p. 99.

47 OTETEA, p. 221. I am rather surprised to find this view shared by Chabod in the art. cit. in *Enciclopedia Italiana*, which I regard, despite its brevity, as the best thing written so far on G. The strange views of Otetea, who is inclined to attribute to the *Dialogo* an importance which in my opinion it does not have, were attacked by V. DE CAPRARIIS in his essay *Francesco Guicciardini*

dalla politica alla storia, cit., pp. 69 ff.; but I must say that I had made up my mind before he published these cogent arguments. In the passage cited in the text G. declares explicitly that he wrote the dialogue simply 'for his own pleasure and recreation'; beside which it is odd to find Otetea (misled by an earlier version) saying that 'the Dialogue is not . . . a recreational exercise'; but it is strange to find him citing as proof of his interpretation 'the fact that Guicciardini began to write his dialogue immediately after the death of Leo X'. As is known, the author himself says he began it when Leo was alive and his age certainly gave no cause to think of an early demise.

[48] BENOIST, p. 136, laments the lack in the *Reggimento* of these more lively, more Florentine expressions, but he would have been even more regretful if he had known that they abound in the first draft!

[49] G. TOFFANIN, *Il Cinquecento* (Storia letteraria d'Italia), Milan, Vallardi, 1929, p. 420.

[50] P. TREVES, *Il realismo politico di Fr. Guicciardini*, Florence, La Nuova Italia, 1931, p. 127.

CHAPTER 14

[1] *Carteggi*, vol. VIII, p. 123.

[2] *Carteggi*, vol. VIII, p. 126.

[3] This document to be shown to the Pope was enclosed with a letter to Colombo of 23 October (*Carteggi*, vol. VIII, pp. 122 ff.).

[4] I deduce this from the reply to Iacopo Salviati, 22 Oct., in *Carteggi*, vol. VIII, pp. 121 ff.

[5] Letter to Cesare Colombo, 26 Oct., in *Carteggi*, vol. VIII, pp. 125 ff.

[6] Letter of 24 Nov., in *Carteggi*, vol. VIII, pp. 134 ff.

[7] Letter of 4 Dec., in *Carteggi*, vol. VIII, pp. 143 ff.

[8] *Discorsi politici* X–XV, in *Opp. in.*, vol. I, pp. 302–378; *Opp.*, vol. VIII, pp. 136–197; Discourse XV in the Laterza edition (*Opp.*, vol. VIII, 198–211) is XVI in Canestrini's (*Opp. in.*, vol. I, 378–94), as Palmarocchi excluded Canestrini's XV on the basis of some questionable restrictive principle. Of these discourses Canestrini's XV is easily datable because it contains a particular reflection expressed in almost identical terms in a private letter to Machiavelli of 26 Dec. 1525, of which G. certainly would not have kept a copy. The others, judging by their position in the MS., must have been written shortly after the events they deal with, that is, within the last months of his Presidency. One must, however, consider the possibility that the MS. was bound together later on or that G. might have copied these discourses here from earlier drafts. OTETEA, p. 160, already observed that they contain forecasts of events which subsequently happened, so striking as to suggest prophecies *post eventum*; yet the one concerning the Colonnese offence to Clement VII had already been forecast, with reference to the same factors, by Machiavelli (*Lett. fam.*, p. 469) at the very same period when discourse XII seems to have been written. It is worth recalling that discourses X and XI were reworked and inserted in the first and second versions of that shorter *Storia d'Italia* from the battle of Pavia, which further on in this book I refer to as the 'Commentari della Luogotenenza'; but they were excluded from the later version. Not only for these two, but also for all the discourses in this group and in general for the speeches inserted in the *Storia d'Italia*, I refer the reader to my *Genesi*, cit., pp. 9 ff., 15–17, 27. Here I would merely add that the definitive text of discourses X and XI is that published by me in *Genesi*, pp. 95 ff., and not that published (in *Opp.*, vol. VIII, pp. 136–52) by Palmarocchi who did not know this final or the penultimate version.

[9] Letter to be shown to the Pope included in one of 24 Dec. to Cesare Colombo, in *Carteggi*, vol. VIII, p. 152 (see also, at the foot of the same page, the fuller and stronger version, on which G. made the marginal note: 'Not sent').

[10] Letter to Machiavelli, 26 Dec., in MACHIAVELLI, *Lett. fam.*, pp. 468 ff. As observed in n. 8 above, a part of this letter appears in almost identical form in discourse XV (Canestrini ed.).

[11] *Opp.*, vol. IX, pp. 82 ff., 85, 87, 93. The daughters who died at an early age were: Lisabetta I, Lisabetta II, Simona I, Maddalena. P. LITTA, *Famiglie celebri italiane*, Guicciardini family (prepared by L. Passerini), Table III, gives Francesco only three daughters: Simona (II), Laudomina, Lisabetta (III). Cf. P. GUICCIARDINI, *Ricordanze inedite di F.G.*, cit., p. 52.

[12] MACHIAVELLI, *Lett. fam.*, pp. 461–5 (end of Oct. 1525); 466–8 (19 Dec.); cf. pp. 452–4 (between 16 and 19 Aug. 1525).

¹³ RIDOLFI, *Machiavelli²*, pp. 333 ff.

¹⁴ Santi was going to France for the Pope (his instructions are in *Lettere di Principi*, vol. II, f. 85). G. lamented his death in the following words: 'I know no other friend whose loss could grieve me half as much, and I am not surprised at the sorrow of his master [Alberto Pio da Carpi] who will never have a minister like him' (*Carteggi*, vol. VIII, p. 142; cf. pp. 92, 100, 120). Secretary to an enemy of G. he had become his friend because of his personal and intellectual qualities. The little information about him given by OTETEA, pp. 140–41, is full of mistakes, starting from the form of his name and his relationship to Alberto Pio.

¹⁵ RIDOLFI, *Machiavelli²*, pp. 334 ff., 465 ff.

¹⁶ RIDOLFI, op. and loc. cit.

¹⁷ *Carteggi*, vol. VIII, pp. 158 ff.

¹⁸ *Carteggi*, vol. VIII, pp. 161 ff.

¹⁹ *Opp.*, vol. IX, p. 90.

²⁰ *Carteggi*, vol. VIII, p. 164.

²¹ *Opp.*, vol. IX, p. 91, where there is also a summary of the will. The deed, drawn up by G.'s usual notary, is also unpublished, in A.S.F., *Notarile Antecosimiano*, Rogiti di Pierfrancesco Maccari, M.20, ff. 129–130 and 135.

²² ARIOSTO, Satire VI (no. VII in the first ed. of 1534).

²³ They were later published by P. Guicciardini who writes with warm affection of this and my other discoveries in *Scritti inediti*, pp. 13 ff.

²⁴ Even where it was most difficult to omit some reference, that is, when he tells of his appointment as Lieutenant-General, he refers to himself as: 'President of Romagna at the time.' Perhaps it was the catastrophic ending of the enterprise, which was not his fault, that persuaded him to keep such a strange silence.

²⁵ In *Scritti inediti*, cit., P. Guicciardini dates this writing 'between 20 and 22 February', that is, before the departure of the envoy to France and after the arrival in Rome of the news of the King's liberation; but it is clear from the text that this liberation had not yet taken place (p. 47); the editor did not consider the fact that some of the conditions of the agreement had leaked out some time before and that the decision to send an envoy to France was also taken earlier than 20 February.

²⁶ *Scritti inediti*, cit., pp. 45–9.

²⁷ *Scritti inediti*, pp. 61–2. This too was wrongly dated and so wrongly ordered by P. Guicciardini. It was written before the news of the King's liberation reached Rome (20 Feb.), as is evident from the words quoted by me in the text and even more evident from the title given to it by the author: *Super litteris Legati usque ad 12 Ianuarii*, for the agreement was only concluded on the 14th. So this work is certainly not later than 19 Feb., and the ordering in the *Scritti inediti* needs correcting as follows: I, III, II.

²⁸ *Scritti inediti*, pp. 59 ff.

²⁹ *Scritti inediti*, pp. 61–72.

³⁰ *Storia d'Italia*, vol. III, p. 453.

³¹ *Scritti inediti*, p. 86.

³² All these drafts are in *Scritti inediti*, pp. 73–82, together with the summary of the earlier terms sent by the Emperor, the reply then given and the most recent terms come from Spain.

³³ The instructions *pro Roberto* are in *Scritti inediti*, pp. 94–7; those for Capino, pp. 101–105.

³⁴ *Scritti inediti*, pp. 105–113.

³⁵ MACHIAVELLI, *Lett. fam.*, pp. 476 ff.

³⁶ G.'s letter which initiated the matter, was dated 1 April and is now lost; Machiavelli's reply is dated 4 April, in *Lett. fam.*, pp. 485 ff.

³⁷ *Carteggi*, vol. VIII, pp. 164 ff. G. reproved Gambara severely when, outside the orders he had received, he tried to transfer the negotiations and settlement of the agreement from France to England; then in a postscript he apologized saying that he had had to write in this way to give vent to the Pope's anger. Or was it his own?

³⁸ *Carteggi*, vol. VIII, pp. 188 ff., 191.

³⁹ MACHIAVELLI, *Lett. fam.*, pp. 487 ff.

⁴⁰ Letters from G. to his brother Luigi, Rome, 4 and 22 May 1526, in A.S.F., *Carte Strozziane*, ser. I, 129, ff. 139, 142.

⁴¹ Letter to Roberto Acciaiuoli, Rome, 5 June, in *Carteggi*, vol. VIII, pp. 197 ff.; cf. the letter to Averoldi, same date, ibidem, pp. 195 ff.

⁴² Letter to Averoldi, 5 June, cit.

⁴³ *Opp.*, vol. IX, pp. 91 ff. The papal brief containing the nomination is in A.G.F., *Carte di F.G.*, XXIV, n. 24, and was published by OTETEA, pp. 335 ff.

⁴⁴ *Carteggi*, vol. VIII, pp. 185 ff., 188 ff.

⁴⁵ *Opp. in.*, vol. IV, p. 525.

⁴⁶ *Carteggi*, vol. VIII, p. 194.

⁴⁷ *Storia d'Italia*, vol. IV, p. 19.

⁴⁸ In a short letter to his brother Luigi, 6 June 1526, unpublished, in A.S.F., *Carte Strozziane*, ser. I, 129, f. 150: '. . . I am leaving tomorrow morning for Lombardy . . . I shall need various officers for victuals, sappers, and so on. I want you to think of someone suitable, that is, honest and capable.'

CHAPTER 15

¹ Letter to Count Guido Rangoni, 8 June 1526, in *Carteggi*, vol. VIII, p. 200. The Lieutenant's reply to the letter he had intercepted was approved by the Pope, on whose orders Giberti wrote to G.: 'In His Holiness's opinion, you replied admirably to Count Guido regarding whatever action he felt able to take' (A.G.F., *Carte di F.G.*, XXI, f. 130).

² Letter to Pope Clement VII, 12 June, in *Carteggi*, vol. VIII, pp. 204 ff.

³ Letter to Clement VII, cit., to which another of the same day to Iacopo Salviati (ibidem, pp. 205 ff.) provides a useful gloss.

⁴ Letter to Giberti, 14 June, in *Carteggi*, vol. VIII, p. 207.

⁵ *Carteggi*, vol. VIII, p. 213.

⁶ *Carteggi*, vol. VIII, pp. 221, 222 ff.

⁷ *Storia d'Italia*, vol. IV, p. 21; *Carteggi*, vol. VIII, p. 231.

⁸ *Carteggi*, vol. VIII, p. 238. Again on the attitude of the Venetians he wrote in a letter of 23 June: 'It seems to me they proceed in a high-handed manner in everything; and here, though they wish to persuade us to their views and needs, they do so more by authority than by argument and application . . . I felt I had to say this, not because it is the moment to enter into rivalry and competition, but because it is always as well to know about their odd behaviour' (ibidem, p. 255).

⁹ Letter of 24 June, in *Carteggi*, vol. VIII, pp. 258 ff.

¹⁰ Letter of 28 June, in *Carteggi*, vol. VIII, pp. 272 ff.

¹¹ *Carteggi*, vol. VIII, pp. 310 ff. In another letter, scarce two hours later (loc. cit., pp. 313 ff.) he writes with bitter irony: 'We have indeed been to Milan.' In a letter to his brother Luigi: 'The Duke of Urbino did not wish or did not know how to obtain victory; I do not know what we can expect from this leadership' (A.S.F., *Carte Strozziane*, ser. I, 139, f. 160).

¹² *Storia d'Italia*, vol. IV, p. 35; *Carteggi*, vol. VIII, pp. 313 ff., 325 ff. These and many other letters from G. to Giberti, first published in *Opp. in.*, vol. IV, were re-edited as though unpublished by TOMMASINI, vol. II, pp. 1194 ff.

¹³ R. RIDOLFI, *Machiavelli²*, pp. 344, 468.

¹⁴ Letter to Roberto Acciaiuoli, 18 July, A.G.F., *Carte di F.G.*, XX, iv, 4, n. 54. Up to now only Acciaiuoli's answer to this letter was known; cf. R. RIDOLFI, op. cit., p. 468.

¹⁵ Letter to his brother Luigi, 16 July 1526, in A.S.F., *Carte Strozziane*, ser. I, 139, f. 159. In the same letter Francesco writes that it is not 'appropriate' that the brothers should all be taxed the same amount (as he was richer than the others), and adds: 'For my part I shall never depart from what is appropriate.'

¹⁶ *Storia d'Italia*, vol. IV, p. 48; letter to Giberti, 20 July, in A.G.F., *Carte di F.G.*, XX, IV, 4, n. 64; cf. n. 66, on which the text of the *Storia* is evidently based.

¹⁷ Letter to Giberti, 27 July, in *Opp. in.*, vol. IV, pp. 119 ff.

¹⁸ *Opp. in.*, vol. IV, p. 162.

¹⁹ Letter to Giberti, 4 Aug., *Opp. in.*, vol. IV, pp. 170 ff.

²⁰ Letter to Giberti, 19 July, in A.G.F., *Carte di F.G.*, XX, IV, 4, n. 60.

[21] Letter of 6 Aug., in *Opp. in.*, vol. IV, p. 181. It is odd that in the *Storia d'Italia* (IV, p. 53) G., who is not usually averse to putting himself forward, says nothing of the part he played in persuading the Duke of Urbino; indeed he says explicitly that the attack on Cremona 'was decided on primarily on the advice of the Duke of Urbino'. The date of the letter cit. sup. (6 Aug.) reminds us of an affectionate letter written the same day to his sister Costanza who had lost her husband Lodovico Alamanni. It is in B.M.F., MS. B. III. 66, f. 28; as it is of a kind one would look for in vain in G.'s normal correspondence and shows us a very different Guicciardini (different, i.e. not from what he was but from the image we have formed of him from appearances and opinions based on appearances), I think it worthwhile to publish it here in full: 'My dearest Costanza. I have been as upset as you may imagine by the death of our Lodovico, especially hearing of it quite suddenly and completely unexpectedly. Indeed this loss is so grave in so many ways that I am at a loss to find words to comfort you; yet we must make peace with those things we cannot help; and I urge you to do so for your own good and that of the children and for the well-being of everyone of us; you could not do anything more pleasing than have us know you submit wisely and patiently to the will of God. I know it is unnecessary to offer you my services and my goods, as I think you know you can always rely on them as if they were your own. I am only sorry not to have been there to do what is needed; but I know our brothers will not have failed in their duty, and I shall certainly not fail you in whatever I hear will give you pleasure and assistance. I am at your disposal. May Christ protect you from evil. From the field, 6 Aug. 1526.'

[22] A letter to Luigi Guicciardini of 15 Sept. 1526, signed by Francesco but written entirely in Machiavelli's hand, was published by TOMMASINI, *Machiavelli*, vol. II, pp. 1249 ff., with facsimile. Nor is this letter unique of its kind. In another from G. to his brother Luigi, dated 21 Sept., he writes: 'I will get Machiavelli to send you the news' (A.S.F., *Carte Strozziane*, ser. I, 139, f. 164).

[23] Letter to Giberti, 24 Sept., in *Opp. in.*, vol. IV, pp. 393 ff.

[24] TOMMASINI, *Machiavelli*, II, p. 862; Tommasini, with his usual propensity for falling into traps, took these words literally, and stated that G. then ceased to be Lieutenant; he thereby aroused the just ire of OTETEA, p. 183 n.

CHAPTER 16

[1] See G.'s letters to the Datary, to Iacopo Salviati and Giovanni de' Medici, during the month of October up to the beginning of November (*Opp. in.*, vol. IV). Some difference arose between G. and Giovanni de' Medici when the latter suspected that a letter written to him by the Pope in his own hand had been forged by G. See G.'s letter to the Datary, 18 Oct. 1526, in *Opp. in.*, vol. IV, pp. 454 ff. He complained to Giovanni de' Medici that he should have thought him capable of forging letters, 'which in truth was never my custom, and least of all would I start it with Your Excellency' (*Opp. in.*, vol. IV, p. 458).

[2] Letter to Cesare Colombo, 27 Oct. 1526, in *Opp. in.*, vol. IV, p. 478. On 6 Aug. he had written: 'Sig. Giovanni is a man of great courage and tremendous vitality outside the actions of war; often there are disagreements between him and Count Guido. The Count perhaps sometimes gives him cause to get excited; but after that he behaves himself prudently . . . I temper their relations as far as I can, and if I had no other troubles than this, I could not say I had none at all' (*Opp. in.*, vol. IV, pp. 186 ff.).

[3] MACHIAVELLI, *Lett. fam.*, pp. 515 ff. Cf. the letters from G. to Machiavelli of 30 Oct. and 12 Nov., ibidem, pp. 513 ff., 518 ff,

[4] Letter from G. to Roberto Acciaiuoli, 22 Oct., in *Opp. in.*, vol. IV, p. 466.

[5] Instructions to Garimberto, in *Opp. in.*, vol. IV, pp. 544 ff.

[6] Letter from G. to Iacopo Salviati, 20 Nov., in A.G.F., *Carte de F.G.*, XX, VI, 3, n. 1.

[7] Letter to the Datary, 25 Nov., and to Iacopo Salviati, 26 Nov., in *Opp. in.*, vol. IV, pp. 376 ff., 583 ff.

[8] *Storia d'Italia*, vol. IV, pp. 34 ff.

[9] Letter to Giberti, 2 Aug. 1526, in *Opp. in.*, vol. IV, p. 159; after the passage quoted in the text the letter continues: 'I started to lecture him on the subject back in Bologna, but so much heat requires more water. I do wish His Holiness would tell him or write to him.' Two

days before, he had written: 'Sig. Giovanni is the very force and valour of this army and is considered such by friends and enemies alike' (ibidem, pp. 150 ff.).

[10] *Opp. in.*, vol. IV, p. 600.

[11] Letter to Bishop Altobello Averoldi, nuncio in Venice, 30 Nov., *Opp. in.*, vol. IV, pp. 597 ff.

[12] Letters to the Marquis of Saluzzo, 30 Nov. and 11 Dec., in *Opp. in.*, vol. IV, pp. 602 ff., vol. V, pp. 45 ff.

[13] The two letters from G. to Frundsberg, in *Opp. in.*, vol. V, pp. 50, 71. The word in inverted commas comes from a gloss to the Datary from G.

[14] *Storia d'Italia*, vol. IV, pp. 83 ff.

[15] *Opp.*, vol. IX, p. 95.

[16] Letter to Giberti, 6 Jan. 1527, in *Opp. in.*, vol. V, pp. 123 ff. Writing to Acciaiuolo after these negotiations G. numbers among the major errors of the Pope 'not agreeing with Ferrara and not making cardinals' (*Opp. in.*, vol. V, p. 145).

[17] R. RIDOLFI, *Machiavelli²*, p. 355.

[18] *Opp. in.*, vol. V, p. 211.

[19] Letter to the Cardinal of Cortona, 8 Feb. 1527, in *Opp. in.*, vol. V, pp. 214 ff.

[20] Letter of 28 Feb., in *Opp. in.*, vol. V, pp. 265 ff. For Cybo, see L. STAFFETTI, *Il cardinale Innocenzo Cybo*, Florence, Le Monnier, 1894.

[21] Letter to Giberti, 8 March, in *Opp. in.*, vol. V, pp. 294 ff.

[22] Letter of 18 March, in *Opp. in.*, vol. V, p. 333.

[23] *Opp. in.*, vol. V, p. 343.

[24] R. RIDOLFI, *Machiavelli²*, pp. 358 ff., 362 ff.

[25] *Opp. in.*, vol. V, pp. 399 ff. 'Anyone who believes this campaign can be sustained is gravely mistaken for it is in a state of complete collapse . . . So I urge you to make agreement if Bourbon's demands are such as to be acceptable . . .'

[26] Letter of 26 April, in *Opp. in.*, vol. V, p. 409.

[27] Ibidem.

[28] R. RIDOLFI, *Machiavelli²*, p. 364.

[29] Letter to Giberti, 24 April, in *Opp. in.*, vol. V, p. 417.

[30] VETTORI, *Sommario della Storia d'Italia*, cit., p. 378; NARDI, vol. II, pp. 142 ff.; GUICCIARDINI, *Storia d'Italia*, vol. IV, pp. 116 ff.; *Opp. in.*, vol. V, p. 421. For a critical review of the historical sources of what was termed the 'Friday riots', see the appendix 'Guicciardini and the *Tumulto del Venerdì*' in the excellent book by C. ROTH, *The last Florentine Republic*, London, Methuen, 1925, pp. 341–2; and cf. RIDOLFI, *Gli ultimi anni della Repubblica fiorentina*, in *A.S.I.*, ser. VII, vol. XII, pp. 267 ff.

[31] GUICCIARDINI, *Storia d'Italia*, vol. IV, pp. 118 ff.

[32] Letter to Giberti, 29 April, in *Opp. in.*, vol. V, pp. 423 ff.

[33] Letter to Giberti, 3 May, in *Opp. in.*, vol. V, pp. 434 ff.

[34] Letters to the Cardinal of Cortona and Guido Rangoni, 8 and 10 May, in *Opp. in.*, vol. V, pp. 436 ff.

[35] *Opp. in.*, vol. VI, p. 6.

[36] This collection of Savonarolan prophecies, autograph in A.G.F., *Carte di F.G.*, XIV, was published in Florence in 1863 and recently republished, in *Opp.*, IX, pp. 285–333, by Palmarocchi, who, having excluded from his edition of supposedly all G.'s writings quite a few original works, thought fit to include these Savonarola extracts – for reasons that are not at all clear. However, it is not such a bad thing, because at all events we now have a more accurate and orderly edition. The collection was made by G. who extracted passages from Savonarola's sermons on the Psalms, on Ruth and Michea, on Amos, on Ezechiel, and on Exodus. No small feat. One might be tempted to imagine it as a youthful compilation, but this is not the case. Those made from the sermons on the Psalms are enough to indicate they were made later than 1515, the year in which Fra Luca Bettini published them without leave after borrowing 'for a couple of days' from Lorenzo Violi the only surviving copy (RIDOLFI, *Savonarola*, vol. II, pp. 40, 138, 177). At a certain point in the collection (*Opp.*, IX, p. 318) G., who was prone to similar distractions, puts down a date 7 April 1528 instead of 1498 (it is very odd that Palmarocchi puts a question mark after this date when the passage relates to the famous exhortation pronounced before the ordeal by fire), and his error indicates without doubt therefore that 1528 was the date of the compilation

(R. RIDOLFI, op. cit., vol. II, p. 236). And so in the 'idleness' that followed the collapse of the campaign he had promoted, we find G. re-reading and making extracts from Savonarola's sermons!

CHAPTER 17

[1] Letter to the Otto di Pratica, 16 May 1527, in *Opp. in.*, vol. IX, pp. 3 ff.

[2] Letter to the Cardinal of Cortona, 18 May, in *Opp. in.*, vol. IX, pp. 10 ff.

[3] *Opp. in.*, vol. IX, pp. 11 ff. The letter goes on: 'If, on account of any difficulty in someone else coming here, you should propose to give me this charge, I am not only against accepting, but find it impossible to bear any longer, and for many reasons it would not be in your interests.'

[4] *Opp. in.*, vol. IX, p. 278. Cf. ROSSI, p. 79 (for the captains' hatred of G., see also p. 59).

[5] Letter to his brother Luigi, 26 May, in *Opp. in.*, vol. IX, pp. 18 ff.

[6] In the letter, cit. sup., of 27 April 1526, in which G. gave a full account to Giberti (i.e. to the Pope) of the behaviour of the Duke of Urbino (*Opp. in.*, vol. IV, p. 119).

[7] Letter to the Pope, 15 June 1527, in *Opp. in.*, vol. IX, p. 85.

[8] *Opp. in.*, vol. IX, pp. 31 ff.

[9] *Lamenti storici dei secc. XIV, XV, e XVI*, ed. by Antonio Medin and Ludovico Frati, Bologna, Romagnoli, 1887–90, vol. III, pp. 403–15.

[10] The person who most strenuously denied the attribution to G. was Pietro Fanfani who published it for the first time in 1879; but his denial was based on pure ignorance, for according to him, 'Guicciardini was always against the French and for the Imperialists'. For an earlier attempt to publish the *Supplicazione* see A. DE RUBERTIS, *Fr. Guicciardini e la Censura toscana*, in *La Bibliofilia*, vol. LI, 1949, pp. 86 ff. There is a good study of it by A. OTETEA, *La 'supplique' de Guichardin a François Ier*, in *Mélanges ... offerts a H. Hauvette*, Paris, 1934, pp. 260–68; there Otetea gave special attention to the matter of dating. As for its authenticity, no one has noticed that the copy of the *Supplicazione* in the *Carte Strozziane* (ser. I, 131, ff. 2–8) comes from the papers of Luigi Guicciardini (see the *Note on Guicciardini's Papers* in this vol., p. 279). It would be a great surprise to find this *Supplicazione* excluded from an edition of G.'s works like the 'Scrittori d'Italia' one, if there were not so many things left out of it already.

[11] Letter of 30 May, in *Opp. in.*, vol. IX, pp. 42 ff. This statement by G., which is far more explicit, firm and related to contemporary facts than the generic attitude expressed to Iacopo Nardi when the Pope was still lord of Florence, was missed by the usually careful ROSSI, vol. I, p. 68.

[12] Letter to Clementi VII, 15 June, cit.

[13] Letter of 20 June, in *Opp. in.*, vol. IX, pp. 94 ff.; cf. ibidem, pp. 95 ff., 98, the letters to the Ten and to Roberto Acciaiuoli ('His Holiness has declared himself content with the change of government and will not concern himself with these matters').

[14] Letter to Capponi, 9 June, in *Opp. in.*, vol. IX, pp. 61 ff.

[15] Letter to Capponi, 9 June, cit.

[16] Letter from Costabili, ambassador in Florence of the Duke of Ferrara, 31 May, cit. by ROSSI, vol. II, pp. 66 ff.; in it we read that in Florence they had 'a great desire to dispense with G.'s services'. In his *Ricordi autobiografici* G. wrote: 'I stayed with the army in the service of His Holiness until the end of May 1527 and after that I stayed unwillingly on behalf of the Ten until 29 June 1527' (*Opp.*, vol. IX, p. 92).

[17] VARCHI, *Storia fiorentina*, ed. cit., vol. I, p. 242.

[18] From Civitavecchia Machiavelli wrote to G. the last letter we have from his hand: R. RIDOLFI, *Machiavelli²*, pp. 372, 475 ff. Cf. R. RIDOLFI, *Spigolature machiavelliane*, in *La Bibliofilia*, LVII, 1955, p. 202.

[19] *Opp.*, vol. IX, p. 174.

[20] For the cessation of his office as Provveditore to the Hospital of S. Bonifacio and his 'dismissal' as advocate of the Arte di Calimala, see A. ROSSI, pp. 89–94. C. ROTH, *The Last Florentine Republic*, cit., pp. 89, 108, makes a mistake in saying that G. was repeatedly summoned before the Eight. It was Francesco di Giovanni Guicciardini, not our Francesco di Piero (A.S.F., *Otto di*

Guardia, 200, ff. 99b–100a), who was involved. This other Francesco, who is mentioned in LITTA, op. cit., held some minor offices in Florence, but was in no sense prominent. He outlived G. by many years. When he appeared before the Eight (16 Oct. 1527), it was for menaces and assault.

[21] VARCHI, op. and ed. cit., vol. I, p. 221. Cf. what G. himself wrote of these taxes in the *Consolatoria: Opp.*, vol. IX, pp. 166, 168.

[22] The letters which G. wrote to the Gonfalonier Capponi on 6 and 20 Aug. and 22 Oct. seeking clarification and accommodation in regard to these taxes, are still unpublished (A.S.F., *Signori, Carteggi, Responsive originali*, 43, ff. 69, 85, 470). They show how much confidence G. placed in the Gonfalonier, to whom he turned for help whenever the need arose.

[23] Letter to Clement VII, 15 June, cit.

[24] See the document published for the first time by ROSSI, vol. I, p. 84.

[25] *Opp. in.*, vol. X, pp. 134 ff. ROSSI, vol. I, p. 82.

[26] *Opp.*, vol. IX, p. 167.

[27] Ibidem, pp. 183 ff.

[28] Letter to Averoldi, nuncio in Venice, 2 July, in *Opp. in.*, vol. IX, pp. 111 ff.

[29] Letter to Averoldi, cit., and letter to Cardinal Salviati, 16 July, in *Opp. in.*, vol. IX, pp. 116 ff. For all the negotiations regarding the congregation of the Cardinals, see L. STAFFETTI, op. cit., pp. 74 ff.; on pp. 76 ff. an unpublished letter of Guicciardini.

[30] Autograph letter from G. to Capponi, unpublished, A.S.F., *Signori, Carteggi, Responsive originali*, 43, f. 110:

Magnificent Gonfalonier,

This morning one of my servants returning from Florence brought back the enclosed letter, from Mons. de Lautrec, which had been left at my house. I thought it best to send it to Your Excellency to ask your advice on what I should do about it, and whether I should reply and how. I think that, having no other way of communicating his desire to the Pope, it occurred to him to send to me because he knows I was in His Holiness's service in this war, and he believes I have some means of writing to him, which I have not. When you have read the letter or shown it to others if you think fit, please let me have it back. His plan would be good if it meant some rapid progress in Lombardy, but if there are difficulties there, I think it would be very bad for the general cause of the campaign and for our own interests. Perhaps it would not be a bad idea, to give him cause to haste, if I wrote and said that the Pope, after his arrival in Italy, had told me to tell him on his behalf to move quickly towards Rome while that army is in such disorder. But I will be guided by you. I commend myself to Your Excellency.

Finocchieto, 3 September 1527.

[31] See pp. 132 ff. in the present vol. It is strange to note that the only autograph copy known of the burlesque reply to Machiavelli about the Finocchieto property is in one of G.'s miscellaneous notebooks (A.G.F., *Carte di F.G.*, VIII, f. 213) between the *Consolatoria* and the *Accusatoria*; so it must have been written or transcribed there in Sept. 1527, i.e., two years after the letter which provoked it and three months after Machiavelli's death. The MS. is entirely original, without additions or interpolations, and the writing in question is in the last pages of a gathering containing the end of the *Consolatoria*. One might be tempted to assume that G. did not reply at once to his friend, and that he only got the desire to take up its defence when he had occasion to take up residence in the villa which Machiavelli had made fun of; but one would have to suppose, in view of the way he addresses Machiavelli and his Barbera, that, after all that time, he did not yet know of Machiavelli's death. As this seems highly unlikely, it is more probable to imagine that, while residing at Finocchieto, he felt the urge to transcribe from some other notebook the composition he had written earlier on about the villa. I confess that I have thought of the possibility that the unpublished verses here published on p. 289 belonged to a poem about Finocchieto; but then, as it seemed odd to me that G. should write them on a page full of rough drafts made a dozen years earlier, I reluctantly gave up the idea.

[32] *Opp. in.*, vol. IX, p. 116.

[33] *Opp. in.*, vol. IX, p. 119.

[34] *Opp.*, vol. IX, p. 92.

[35] *Opp.*, vol. IX, pp. 94 ff.; P. GUICCIARDINI, E. DORI, *Le antiche case ed il Palazzo dei Guicciardini*, cit., pp. 30, 114.

³⁶ *Opp.*, vol. IX, p. 93.

³⁷ Letter of 22 Oct., in *Opp. in.*, vol. IX, p. 13. Lucrezia died at Castrocaro while returning with her mother and sisters from Venice where he had sent them when Florence was threatened by the war. See p. 167 in this volume.

³⁸ At the head of the autograph (A.G.F., *Carte di F. G.*, VIII, ff. 198–212) G.wrote: 'Written in Sept. 1527 at Finocchieto, during the plague.' First published in *Opp. in.*, vol. X, pp. 103–33, then in *Opp.*, vol. IX, pp. 165–90.

³⁹ *Opp.*, vol. IX, pp. 170 ff.

⁴⁰ *Opp.*, vol. IX, pp. 176 ff.

⁴¹ *Ricordi*, p. 21; *Consolatoria*, in *Opp.*, vol. IX, p. 180.

⁴² *Ricordi*, p. 19; *Consolatoria*, in *Opp.*, vol. IX, p. 184.

⁴³ *Opp.*, vol. IX, p. 186. A little further on: 'You will therefore be idle, but with dignity . . . Nor will there be less praise in accommodating yourself well to this, than there was in a life of activity; indeed it seems to me that reputation requires, since you have shown your worth in affairs, that you have occasion to show you are able equally well to adapt yourself to not doing as to doing.'

⁴⁴ DE CAPRARIIS, op. cit., p. 20, writes of the *Consolatoria*: 'We are not interested in G.'s psychological reactions to this situation; what one might with some exaggeration call G.'s grief is of no concern. . . .' But I find it extremely interesting, no less than the maturing of his thought; and it is obvious that there must be some connection between the two. I do not say this out of a desire to interpret in a general sense a particular observation of this very good scholar, but because there are still people who, in particular and in general, think the same way.

⁴⁵ Certainly imaginary; though it is evident that as he wrote, G. saw this person clearly in his mind, and gave him the form of some particular adversary of his. Otherwise he would have been unlikely to adopt the useless fiction of certain details, such as the fact that he was a childhood companion of G., a friend of Filippo Strozzi and bound to him for some favour received, and so on.

⁴⁶ The *Accusatoria* and *Defensoria* (the original title is *Defensoria contra precedentem*), autograph in the same MS. as the *Consolatoria*, were first published in *Opp. in.*, vol. X, pp. 152–255, then in *Opp.*, vol. IX, pp. 193–281. Canestrini, *Opp. in.*, vol. X, p. 255, makes the strange conjecture that the *Defensoria* was not completed 'perhaps because in the meantime he had news of the sentence against him'; but he was grossly mistaken. In fact the *Accusatoria* and the *Defensoria*, composed in 1527 as their place in the autograph MS. shows, have nothing whatever to do with the sentence of 1530. As I said in the text, G. wrote them merely for his own amusement and satisfaction, pretending to be 'after the introduction of a new law . . . the first to be charged' before the Quarantia which had been set up immediately after the change of government (*Opp. in.*, vol. IX, p. 249). These words indicate clearly, even if we did not know from other sources that the first to be charged was not G., that the accusation is imagined as taking place in 1527 or at the beginning of 1528. Besides, the sentence of 1530 concerned quite other affairs; and G. himself says, when justifying himself to the Eight at the end of 1529 (*Opp. in.*, vol. X, pp. 134 ff.), that, when his accounts had been reviewed by the syndics, he had no further trouble in this sort of matter which had provided material for the *Accusatoria*. Misled by the first editor, P. ROSSI, op. cit., pp. 39–44, maintained that the *Accusatoria* and *Defensoria* had been written at the time of the trial which ended with G.'s conviction in 1529. Other more careful and better informed scholars, like OTETEA, p. 265, avoided this mistake and fell into the other of believing that G. had really been accused before the Quarantia and that he wrote these imaginary speeches for this trial. For the accusations supposedly made against G. by the Eight in 1527 (ROTH, op. cit., p. 98), see n. 20 supra.

⁴⁷ G. TOFFANIN, *Il Cinquecento*, cit., p. 433.

⁴⁸ E. BODRERO, *Fr. Guicciardini*, in *Quarto centenario*, pp. 29–48. See also D. BIANCHI, *Problematica e sofistica in Fr. Guicciardini*, in *Saggi di Umanismo Cristiano*, III, 1948, pp. 37–62 (especially pp. 58–61).

⁴⁹ *Opp.*, vol. IX, p. 240.

⁵⁰ *Opp.*, vol. IX, p. 211.

⁵¹ G. TOFFANIN, op. and loc. cit.

⁵² *Opp.*, vol. IX, pp. 240–42.

¹ Letter to his brother Luigi, 24 Nov. 1527, in *Opp. in.*, vol. IX, pp. 126 ff.

² Ibidem.

³ In the letter to the Eight, 12 Dec. 1529, G. boasts his good conduct as a citizen and recalls that he had 'often come to the Council' (*Opp. in.*, vol. X, pp. 133 ff.). Cf. *Opp.*, vol. IX, p. 200.

⁴ SEGNI, *Storie fiorentine*, Augusta (Florence), 1723, pp. 18 ff. *Vita di Niccolo Capponi*, which follows this ed., p. 18; A. ROSSI, op. cit., p. 100.

⁵ SEGNI, op. and ed. cit., p. 50; VARCHI, ed. cit., vol. I, p. 397. This family tie, which was kept secret during Capponi's period as Gonfalonier, was made only in writing at that time; cf. A. ROSSI, op. cit., vol. I, p. 98.

⁶ The autograph, lost and confused in the *mare magnum* of the material collected by G. for the compilation of the *Storia d'Italia*, was discovered and restored by me in 1928. News of this discovery was first given by the distinguished historian Alessandro Luzio who communicated a letter of mine to the Reale Accademia delle Scienze of Turin. This voluminous unpublished work, which has some very fine parts but is especially important for understanding G.'s evolution as a historian (I called it the 'dress rehearsal' for the *Storia d'Italia*), was not published until 1945 when no one was thinking about Italy and she had plenty to worry about other than books. For information concerning the edition, see my preface to the *Cose fiorentine*.

⁷ *Cose fiorentine*, pp. XVII–XXXVII, to which the reader is referred for further information regarding the date, the sources, the MSS. which contain the work and the extracts used for its compilation. I spoke of G.'s evolution as a historian in a lecture given in Oxford on 2 June 1962, which was published in almost complete form with the title *L'itinerario storiografico del G.*, in *Il Veltro*, 1961, fasc. 11–12, pp. 5–16 (the complete text was published separately in Rome, 1962).

⁸ In recent years there has been much controversy among editors and philologists about the text of the *Ricordi*. It was begun by M. BARBI, *Per una compiuta edizione dei 'Ricordi'. . .* in *Studi di Filologia italiana*, VIII, 1936, pp. 163–196. Among other things, Barbi pointed out that I had attributed to the sixteenth-century editor of the *Consigli e Avvertimenti* the function of 're-doing or undoing' G.'s *Ricordi*, and felt obliged to remind me of a piece of information, culled by Magliabechi from somewhere or other, according to which Piero Guicciardini, great-nephew of Francesco, gave a copy of the *Ricordi* to Fulvio Orsini. On the basis of this information, Barbi established, after examining various MSS., that the *Avvertimenti* published in 1576 are in fact a reproduction of the text which had been diffused in this way; this text, according to Barbi, was a more or less true copy or even the autograph of a redaction *A* made earlier than the text put together in 1528, *B* (we will talk of a third, later version, *C*, in due course). Against this theory, which at that time seemed rather hazardous, Palmarocchi (*Opp.*, vol. VIII, pp. 369–79) brought sound arguments; while in Barbi's defence came M. FUBINI, *Le quattro redazioni dei 'Ricordi'*, in *Civiltà Moderna*, XIII, 1941, pp. 105–24 and 247–71; followed, with a mass of fresh arguments, by Spongano in his fine edition of the *Ricordi*. Besides some not very conclusive arguments, Spongano adduced several really valid ones (pp. XXXV ff., XXXVIII ff.), especially that of certain cancelled readings in *B* which evidently derive from an earlier autograph redaction. Yet this observation, though decisive for some 'ricordi', does not prove that *all* the text of the *Avvertimenti* is authentic; still less that this collection was put together by G. himself, before *B* (in this case why would he have written that *B* was compiled by bringing together *ricordi* 'written before 1525, but in *other notebooks*'? He would have spoken of *one* notebook as he does about the collection made in 1528), and not by someone else, in those notebooks written before 1528. Barbi had to consider the possibility that Piero Guicciardini passed to Orsini 'a redaction put together by himself' (op. cit., p. 173). Indeed, why should this have not been so? Palmarocchi was therefore quite right when he said, in substance, 'show me the autograph'; and I was right to question whether the *Ricordi* in the 1576 edition had not been 'undone or re-done'. 'Undone' certainly in relation to the authentic definitive text. For, one may go on for ever developing theories, but the accurate collation of all the MSS. deriving from Piero Guicciardini's text can give us the perfect reconstruction of this text (and this is what Spongano has done admirably), but not the certainty of its complete authenticity and genuineness, still less of its derivation from a single autograph. Admitting, for purposes of argument, that the individual *ricordi* are all authentic and all more or less faithfully transcribed, was the collection put together by the author or by someone else? And in

this case, were they re-done or undone by Piero Guicciardini or by Corbinelli? Only the autograph of *A*, if it ever existed, could remove the doubts, though these are rendered less troublesome, at least for me, by the sound certainty of the two later autograph texts of the work.

⁹ E. CECCHI, *Ritratti e profili*, cit., pp. 102 ff.

¹⁰ *Opp.*, vol. VIII, p. 249, *ric.* 50.

¹¹ *Opp.*, vol. VIII, p. 243, *ric.* 14.

¹² See *ricordi* 41–43, in *Opp.*, vol. VIII, pp. 248 ff., in the third of which we read: 'I have put these *ricordi* together . . .'

¹³ *Opp.*, vol. VIII, p. 279, *ric.* 178.

¹⁴ *Opp.*, vol. VIII, p. 278.

¹⁵ RIDOLFI, *Opuscoli*, p. 88.

¹⁶ *Storia d'Italia*, vol. IV, p. 191. For the moderating role played by Capponi, see ROTH, op. cit., p. 356.

¹⁷ *Opp.*, vol. VIII, p. 213.

¹⁸ R. RIDOLFI, *Gli ultimi anni della Repubblica fiorentina*, cit., pp. 11–13.

¹⁹ *Vita di Niccolò Capponi*, cit., p. 26. NEARLI, *Commentari de' fatti civili occorsi dentro alla città di Firenze*, Augusta, 1728, p. 171. On the counterblows Capponi received from the Arrabbiati, Varchi (ed. cit., I, pp. 397 ff.) wrote: 'It did not help Niccolò to have contracted a family relationship with Guicciardini.' For the help G. had from the Gonfalonier, see chap. XVII, n. 22. To the letters there cited we may also add, for the date we have now reached, this other letter which is not without importance for the relations between G. and Capponi (A.S.F., *Signori, Carteggi, Responsive orig.*, 43, f. 293):

I shall be in Florence tonight and call on Your Excellency, who, I am sure, will be pleased to have the amount asked for reduced, and that I should not always be made the target for more than my resources justify; and meanwhile I will go on furnishing what I can and make an effort out of regard for Your Excellency, but I must be excused from the impossible. I commend myself to you.

Santa Margherita, 13 June 1528.

²⁰ *Opp. in.*, vol. IX, p. 133.

²¹ It is a letter from Orvieto, written in Jan. 1528, and published by Rossi, op. cit., vol. I, p. 131.

²² See note 19 above.

²³ SEGNI, ed. cit., p. 18: 'Soon afterwards he gave up summoning them any more, but he tried another way, and always had someone with him in his chamber with whom he discussed many matters of state.' A precise confirmation of these words is found in the correspondence of the Ferrarese ambassador, who reports this ban on meetings and tells of the Gonfalonier, 'shut up in his room with three or four friends, deciding matters'. Extracts from this correspondence were published by ROSSI, op. cit., p. 101.

²⁴ *Storia d'Italia*, vol. IV, p. 224.

²⁵ G. B. BUSINI, *Lettere*, etc., Florence, Le Monnier, 1861, pp. 37 ff.

²⁶ A. ROSSI, op. cit., vol. I, pp. 284 ff.

²⁷ BUSINI, ed. cit., p. 86. The information was repeated by VARCHI, vol. II, p. 183.

²⁸ Although the presence of G. at this meeting is twice affirmed by G. B. BUSINI (pp. 78, 102), and it is very difficult to think he was mistaken in such an unusual and consequently memorable affair, I do not know how one can reconcile it with the letter written by G. himself to his brothers Luigi and Iacopo from the Casentino on 20 September. It seems from this letter that G. had been out of Florence for some time (Busini and Varchi tell us where) and intended to return on 19 September as he had 'advised' on the Friday before; a glance at the calendar for 1529 shows that Friday was the 17th of the month, and therefore it does not appear likely that, having been at the meeting on the 15th or 16th, he would be writing from Finocchieto on the 17th to say he would be back in Florence on the 19th. So Busini must be wrong, unless one imagines that, after attending the meeting and before going back to Finocchieto, G. had told them verbally he would be back on the 19th. But this is a bit far-fetched and would involve stretching the meaning: instead of 'advised' (*avvisai*), he would have used 'said' (*dissi*). Besides it is noteworthy that VARCHI, vol. II, p. 160, as though correcting his source, names the principal Medici supporters invited to the meeting but does not include Guicciardini; indeed, after listing those he got from Busini, he immediately adds: 'M. Francesco Guicciardini . . . fled . . . as soon as Orange reached

311

the frontier.' NERLI, op. cit., p. 193, is still more explicit, and says that G. was not present, as he had already left Florence. It is clear, therefore, that he was invited (and this is what probably misled Busini), but he did not attend.

²⁹ The letter published in *Opp. in.*, IX, p. 134 under the date 19 Feb. 1529 (A.S.F., *Carte Strozziane*, ser. I, 129, c. 178) belongs in fact to 1521. This is something worse than a mere mis-reading: the text at a glance should have told anyone like Canestrini, who worked for more than ten years on Guicciardini's works and correspondence, that such a letter dated from Parma was written immediately after the memorable defence of the city, to which it contains a clear reference.

³⁰ BUSINI, ed. cit., p. 102 (see note 28 above).

³¹ Letter of 20 Sept. to his brothers Luigi and Iacopo, in *Opp. in.*, vol. IX, pp. 136 ff.

³² Letter cit. in preceding note.

³³ Letter to G. B. Sanga, dated 30 Sept. but not sent until 1 Oct., published by A. ROSSI, vol. I, pp. 286 ff.

³⁴ *Opp.*, vol. VIII, p. 270, ricordo 146.

CHAPTER 19

¹ Letters cit., of 25 and 30 Sept. 1529.

² Letter to the Eight (Otto di Guardia e Balìa), 12 Dec. 1529, in *Opp. in.*, vol. X, pp. 133 ff.; cf. his letter to the Eight of 2 March 1530, in *Opp. in.*, vol. X, pp. 141 ff., which tells us that meantime G. had moved from Spinello to Sogliano. The fiefs of Sogliano and Spinello were within the territory of the Presidency of Romagna, and G. had been on good terms with Malatesta who was guelph like his subjects. Cf. *Carteggi*, vol. VII, p. 184; vol. VIII, pp. 125, 132, etc.; *Opp. in.*, vol. VIII, p. 405.

³ Letters of 12 Dec. 1529 and 2 March 1530, cit.

⁴ In the letter to the Eight of 12 Dec. he writes: 'The Pope eventually agreed to some conditions of a kind he had not entertained before.' And in the letter to the Eight of 2 March 1530: 'The Pope gave up his earlier demands that the city should be handed over to him, and said he was willing to come to an agreement preserving the liberty of the people and the Great Council.' G.'s account is substantially confirmed by contemporary Florentine historians, or rather they are confirmed by his account, because G. could not tell the Eight a pack of lies.

⁵ C. ROTH, op. cit., pp. 237, 252, does not believe the conditions proposed by the Pope at Cesena and Forlì could be so advantageous, as otherwise they would not have been rejected. On this point my good friend is most certainly wrong, perhaps because he did not weigh G.'s evidence sufficiently well. Those conditions were rejected not because they were not good, but because they seemed too good to be sincerely offered. The Ferrarese ambassador, reporting to the Duke about Florentine reactions after Nasi's arrival, wrote on 30 Oct.: 'They all believe this is a trick on the part of the Pope' (A. ROSSI, op. cit., vol. I, pp. 291 ff.); cf. NERLI, *Commentari*, ed. cit., p. 204; SEGNI, *Storie fiorentine*, ed. cit., p. 92).

⁶ That G. had resolved some time before to remain with the Pope is evident from his letter to Sanga of 25 Sept., cit. But the persistent requests of the ambassadors and his own apparent reluctance were also true, if he could quote as unprejudiced witnesses Portinari and Niccolini, both of them 'popolani'.

⁷ G. GIORDANI, *Dellavenuta e dimora in Bologna del Sommo Pontefice Clemente VII* . . . Bologna, 1842, p. 40. Something can be gleaned from the vast agglomeration of information contained in this work; for instance, that G. then lodged in the Bottrigari house in the 'Middle Market' (p. 93).

⁸ Letter to his brother Luigi, 3/4 Dec. 1529, in *Opp. in.*, vol. IX, pp. 137 ff. On 5 December Iacopo Guicciardini wrote from Florence to his brother Luigi: 'Messer Francesco writes again to tell me he is coming to Lucca, and I reckon that, if he has not changed his mind, he should be there tomorrow or the day after; but I do not know what good this will do, unless he comes further, because, as you know, the Signoria has put out another proclamation; he might perhaps have defended himself before the Forty, but without coming back, I don't know how he can avoid the consequences of the proclamation (i.e., confiscation, etc.) . . . In the circumstances I am afraid he might run into serious trouble. Girolamo ought also to come back. . . .' This letter is in

A.S.F., *Dieci di Balia, Carteggi, Responsive*, 151, c. 111; which would appear to indicate that it was intercepted.

⁹ Letter to his brother Luigi, 3/4 Dec., cit.; letter to the Eight of 12 Dec., cit.

¹⁰ Letter to his brother Luigi of 3/4 Dec., cit.

¹¹ This information is contained in Iacopo's *Libro di amministrazione*, in A.G.F., *Libri di amministrazione*, 15, c. 110 v.

¹² C. ROTH, op. cit., pp. 242, 253.

¹³ Letters of 14 and 19 Dec. to his brother Luigi, in *Opp. in.*, vol. IX, pp. 142 ff., 144 ff.

¹⁴ We know this from the date of a letter, 25 Dec., from Imola, now lost but noted in Iacopo's *Libro*, cit.: 'his last letter was from Imola on 25 Dec. last, since when and up to the present (4 March 1529/30) I have had no more word from him at all'.

¹⁵ A.G.F., *Carte F.G.*, IX, c. 128.

¹⁶ A.G.F., *Carte F.G.*, IX, c. 127; cf. my introduction to the *Cose fiorentine*, p. xxiv.

¹⁷ I have followed the text of the first, though least polished, of the three versions of the discourse, namely the one written in Lucca: cf. *Cose fiorentine*, pp. 295 ff.; the second version, ibidem, pp. 296 ff.; the third, ibidem, pp. 79 ff.

¹⁸ The court of Forty (Quarantia) that was to try G., was chosen on 2 March. It met on 8 March, and having decided, according to its terms of reference, that the case concerned interests of state, it elected by lot eight examiners from among its own number: 'These examiners resolved on the said day to issue a proclamation to advise and request anyone who was able or willing to say anything either for or against the case and charges of the said messer Francesco Guicciardini and Giovanmaria Benintendi, pending before the members of the aforesaid court, to appear from now on up to and including the 13th before the said examiners in the palace of the Signoria, and before them state whatever he wishes to say or allege either for or against the aforementioned case; otherwise, at the expiry of this time, they will proceed according to the form of law governing the said court of Forty.' All these acts have remained unpublished and unknown to students of G., and are kept in A.S.F., *Signori e Collegi, Deliberazioni*, 132, cc. 173v, 182r.

¹⁹ See the entry in Iacopo's *Libro* for expenditure on 7 March 'to carry letters to Lucca to our brother Girolamo for messer Francesco, requesting him to write in his own justification a letter to the Eight'. A.G.F., *Libri di amministrazione*, 15, c. 110 v.

²⁰ *Opp. in.*, vol. X, pp. 141 ff.

²¹ Beneath the correction one can read the following succession of dates: 7, 5, 3 March! When he published the letter, Canestrini gave no indication of these alterations, which if nothing else, are an important witness to the true date of dispatch. This is also confirmed by the dispatch noted by Iacopo in his notebook and referred to above in n. 19. It is clear that his letter was requested by Iacopo on 7 March, and so it could not have been written before that date.

²² Iacopo's notebook, cit in n. 19.

²³ While wishing to keep to a minimum the baggage of erudition accompanying this biography, I consider it of interest and value to the work to give below the text of their deliberations and sentence, which has hitherto remained unknown to Guicciardini scholars. Of special interest are the opposition of a large number of the Forty to the condemnation, and the brief form of accusation in Italian which was finally carried (A.S.F., *Signori e Collegi, Deliberazioni*, 132, c. 197).

(in Latin)   17 March 1529

The Illustrious Gonfalonier of Justice of Florence, Dominus Raffaele de' Girolami, and . . . Dominus Francesco d' Antonio de' Giraldi . . . having met together with the Eight of the city of Florence and other members of the Forty elected as above to try Francesco di Piero Guicciardini and Giovanmaria di Lorenzo Benintendi, citizens of Florence, and being assembled in sufficient number according to law; having heard and seen the charge against them and various letters and witnesses examined by the Eight in this respect; and having seen the case drawn up by the Eight; and having seen their summons to appear before the court and their refusal to do so; and having heard the examiners of the Forty chosen on the 8th of the present month to investigate this case; and having seen various witnesses examined by the said examiners relating to these charges; and having heard Iacopo, brother of the aforesaid Francesco, and Nicolao, brother of the said Giovanmaria, and whatever they wished to state in regard to this matter; and having seen the law concerning the Forty and considered everything else that was necessary . . . the court wishing, therefore, to come to a decision, since today is the last day for judgement in this case, they took the oath . . . to give judgement according to their consciences; then, by the Gonfalonier and myself, the undersigned notary assigned to this case, the acquittal from the charges against Francesco and Giovanmaria was put to the vote twice according to the form of law governing the Forty. No majority was obtained in either vote.

Whereupon they resorted to proposal of motions. When the motions had been written, read and published, they voted three times, yet neither the first, nor the second nor the third was any decision obtained. Therefore they proceeded to yet a fourth motion. When this had been written, read and published and put to the vote, it was found that the following motion written upon one of the papers used for earlier voting, had been carried and had a larger number of black beans than the others, according to the procedure laid down for the Forty. The form of this motion or resolution is as follows:

(in Italian) 'Lord Jesus Christ and Saviour, can it be that we have all sworn before Your Majesty to do justice? By this oath we ought all to tend towards one end, and there should be no such difference of opinion. I should like to know who does not believe messer Francesco Guicciardini has erred, what he would wish him to have done to commit such offence, and what greater injury our city could have received apart from its destruction. Would you wait to punish him till he assaults you with fire (and sword)? Yet I hope in Christ's name that you and he may be punished first, and so I say that messer Francesco should tomorrow be declared a rebel with all the penalties applicable to rebels, and that he be given the possibility until the end of next April to present himself at the feet of our Magistrates and their Colleges to justify himself against these charges of error, and that if he should then have 32 beans in his favour he should be freed from this declaration of rebellion.

'As for Giovanni Benintendi, I move that, if he pay for the whole of this month the fine arising from the proclamation, he be allowed to return freely. None the less, he should be excluded from public office for three years to come. Should he not observe these terms, then he should be declared a rebel, with conditions as above.'

(in Latin) In the name of God they pronounced sentence in and for all these matters . . . witnessed and drawn up by

Dom. Alessio de' Lapaccini	⎫	Chancellors of the aforesaid Magistrates.
Dom Silvestro Aldobrandini	⎬	18 March, Domenico Mazzerio.
Dom. Jacopo Nardi	⎭	

[24] Iacopo's *Libro*, cit., I have been unable to find either the inventory or any of the volumes belonging to Guicciardini's library, except the *Horoscope*, from which I have already frequently quoted, and the Vatican MS. referred to above p. 282, n. 35.

[25] The first of these conjectures, viz. that he learned of the sentence immediately from other sources, seems by far the most likely; it is improbable that, hearing from Iacopo that the Forty would decide his case on the 17th, he left Lucca *on the day after judgement was made* without waiting to hear what it was.

[26] Letter to his brother Iacopo, Rome, 25 April 1530, in *Opp. in.*, vol. X, pp. 149 ff. In Iacopo's *Libro di amministrazione*, cit., there is a note about dispatch on 18 March of a letter to his brother Girolamo telling him of 'the judgement of the Forty regarding the charges against messer Francesco'. For safety's sake Iacopo wrote the letter to his brother Girolamo who had also fled to Lucca.

[27] A. ROSSI, op. cit., vol. I, pp. 156–9, writes at length about what appears to him 'considerable uncertainty of mind' on G.'s part, which would explain 'the incoherence of his behaviour'; but what seems to Rossi obscure is in fact perfectly clear. He is further still from the mark when, against all documentary evidence, he states that G. went to Lucca simply 'because his family was there', and maintains that 'one should reject completely the hypothesis that he went to Lucca to mitigate his apparent contempt of court' (p. 162).

[28] Iacopo's *Libro*, cit.

[29] Until now Guicciardini scholars have been unaware that he was charged a second time before the Forty in May 1530 together with Giovanni Tornabuoni and Francesco Vettori. Their judgement was promulgated on 9 June, and in conclusion, seeing that the accused had already been declared a rebel, 'left him with the same penalties stipulated by the said Forty'. The proceedings

relating to this second charge are in A.S.F., *Signori e Collegi, Deliberazioni*, 133, c. 20r, 24v, 33v, 45v.

[30] This does not mean that Clement VII did not make use in other matters of his old minister's counsels. We find, for instance, that G. translated from the Spanish Charles V's letter to the Pope about the Council he had in mind, and he also drafted the evasive reply dated 31 July 1530. See E. CASANOVA, in *A.S.I.*, ser. V, vol. VIII, 1891, pp. 126–38.

[31] A.G.F., *Carte di F.G.*, cc. 130–86. The *Considerations* were published in *Opp. in.*, vol. I, pp. 1–79; later in *Opp.*, vol. VIII, pp. 1–65.

[32] G. MAZZONI, *Sul testo dei 'Discorsi' del Machiavelli*, in *Rendiconti Acc. Naz. Lincei*, Classe di Scienze Morali, ser. VI, vol. IX (1933), pp. 41–82; cf. my observations on the *Discourses* and the *Considerations*, and especially on the dating of the latter, in my preface to the *Cose fiorentine*, pp. xxiii ff.

[33] This is version C (see chap. 18, note 8) published under the title 'Seconda serie' in *Opp.*, vol. VIII, pp. 281–336.

[34] *Opp.*, vol. VIII, p. 281.

[35] Ibidem, p. 297, *ricordo* 60.

[36] Ibidem, p. 317, *ric.* 146.

[37] Ibidem, p. 320, *ric.* 161

[38] Ibidem, p. 330, *ric.* 201.

[39] Ibidem, p. 324, *ric.* 179.

[40] Ibidem, p. 314, *ric.* 136.

[41] Ibidem, p. 281.

[42] 'Our Lord is sending Guicciardini to Florence to observe the state of affairs in the city and to apply what remedy is possible at present' (Francesco Gonzaga to the Duke of Mantua, 16 Sept. 1530, in A. ROSSI, op. cit., p. 208, n.).

[43] Letter to Luigi Guicciardini, Rome, 28 June 1530, in *Opp. in.*, vol. IX, p. 148.

[44] This discourse (*Opp.*, vol. VIII, pp. 212–19) can be dated precisely. As far as I know, no one has noticed the words: 'you lost Empoli, and Volterra has been wrested from you'. The Florentines lost Empoli on 29 May; but Volterra, heroically defended by Ferrucci, was not wrested from them, in spite of the violent and heavy attacks made by Maraldo and the Marquis of Vasto between 14 and 21 June. It would seem that when G. wrote this discourse, evidently between 16 and 23 June, he was taking for granted the seizure of Volterra by the overwhelming strength of the imperial forces, or perhaps there had reached Rome a false report of its capture after the breach made in the walls, which did in fact for a time persuade the assailants they had won a victory.

[45] Letters to his brother Luigi of 22 and 27 July, in *Opp. in.*, vol. IX, pp. 152–4. Guicciardini had news of the defeat and death of Ferrucci on 5 August at 8 p.m. (ibid., pp. 156 ff.).

[46] Letter of 30 July in *Opp. in.*, vol. IX, pp. 154 ff.

[47] *Lettere al Lanfredini*, pp. 3 ff. A resolution regarding all G.'s credits which had reverted to the Commune after confiscation, is published by BENOIST, op. cit., pp. 412 ff.

[48] *Lettere al Lanfredini*, pp. 10 ff.

[49] Letter to his brother Luigi, 30 Oct. 1530, in *Opp. in.*, vol. IX, pp. 157 ff.

[50] G. CAPPONI, op. cit., vol. III, pp. 308 ff.

[51] Letter of 6 Nov. 1530, in *Lettere al Lanfredini*, pp. 19 ff.; VARCHI, ed. cit., vol. II, p. 529; G. B. BUSINI, op. and ed, cit., p. 226.

[52] Letter of 17 November, in *Lettere al Lanfredini*, pp. 24 ff.

[53] Ibidem. See also the letter of 20 October on p. 12.

[54] G. especially wanted Niccolò Acciaiuoli's residence and movements restricted, but he never agreed to the execution of Niccolò di Braccio Guicciardini (G. B. BUSINI, op. and ed. cit., pp. 184, 185). See also following note.

[55] Letter to Lanfredini of 20 October, cit. Among other things he wrote: 'The commissioner . . . thought that it would be enough to cure this ill to stick a pin into the skins of 12 or 15 people.'

[56] Letter of 10 October, in *Lettere al Lanfredini*, pp. 6 ff.

[57] A. ROSSI, op. cit., vol. I, pp. 238 ff., 242–54; OTETEA, pp. 277–82. Shortly after his arrival in Florence G. was added to the 'inflated' *Balìa* (the Eight), and then made one of the *Accoppiatori* (controllers of elections).

[58] Letter to his brother Luigi, 30 October, in *Opp. in.*, vol. IX, p. 159; *Lettere al Lanfredini*, passim.

[59] *Lettere al Lanfredini*, p. 23.

[60] Letter to Lanfredini of 17 November, cit.

[61] *Lettere al Lanfredini*, pp. 59, 60.

[62] Letter of 19 May 1531, in *Lettere al Lanfredini*, pp. 61 ff. What worried G. most was that in Bologna, following a usage from which he himself had on other occasions benefited in Parmin, Modena and Reggio, they were making petitions to have the old governor remain in the city. Besides several of the letters to Lanfredini, see the documents quoted by ROSSI, op. cit., vol. I., pp. 272 ff.

[63] Letter of 27 May, in *Lettere al Lanfredini*, pp. 65 ff. Before leaving for Bologna G. made a new will dated 15 April 1531, which is unpublished; it is to be found among the papers of the notary Pier Francesco Maccari, in A.S.F., *Notarile Antecosimiano*, M. 20, cc. 131 and 134. There is also (on c. 132) a 'Short summary' in Italian of this will (which G. must have asked Maccari for when he wanted to change the conditions), followed by the notes that G. wrote or dictated to the notary so that he could give them proper legal form. This gives special interest to the document which I therefore publish here below:

Jesus

Short summary of the will of M(esser) F(rancesco), 1531, 15 April

To the distressed Poor, 200 gold florins to be distributed to poor persons according to the discretion of the officers of the said Company. To be paid within one year.

To Laudomina and Elisabetta, 2,000 gold florins (7 lire to the florin) in addition to the dowry in the Monte.

To your wife, 2,000 florins in cash and kind for her dowry;

and if she wish to remarry, 600 florins (7 lire to the florin) and all the rings you gave her;

and if she wish to remain a widow, she should have all her wardrobe and linen and in addition her widow's weeds, all the rings, belts, jewels, chains and every other thing for the adornment of her person and her chamber, all the effects in the country and in Florence existing in the properties left to her, the usufruct of the properties of Santa Margherita and San Miniato a Monte, her heirs to be deprived of the inheritance if they interfere in any way with that usufruct; in addition the usufruct of the farm you bought from the Galilei; and the heirs must once and for all time furnish those properties with all the necessary animals;

and 25 gold florins every year, payable in respect to half every six months;

and to this effect that she might have free use of these properties, all gifts respecting them made to your daughters are revoked.

To your brothers, the entire patrimony and all rights of legitime and trust dues (*trebellianica*) arising therefrom, and the farm bought from the Galilei on the expiry of mona Maria's tenure.

To the lay sisters, 12 yards of nuns' cloth and suitable material for veils.

There being no sons, the heirs shall be the daughters including any born after this date. Should any die minors or childless, or should any of them become a nun, half of their portion should go to the other surviving sisters and the children of any who had died before, and the other half to their brothers and to the children of any brothers who had predeceased them.

You provide what should go to daughters who wish to become nuns, and what should happen to the remainder of their portion.

Also you arranged guardians for your children.

To Laudomina all immoveable property and according to proper estimate; the monies to be invested in her name, and no rights to pass to her husband; her heirs to be her children and descendants in perpetuity with no right of alienation on pain of deprivation.

To Maria, 2,000 florins as in the will.

Also, 400 gold florins against the same sum loaned to make gifts (for her trousseau) to Elisabetta.

To the same, all the things purtaining to her chamber in the country and in Florence.

Also, apparel of all kinds for her use, jewels, rings, belts, chains and other objects of gold and silver that she has acquired at various times.

Also, she should have in her own right those of my other effects she pleases up to the value of 500 gold ducats according to estimate to be sought.

Also, to the same during her lifetime and not in any sense beyond, the house and farms of Santa Margherita, part of which is situated in the parish of S. Margherita and part in that of S. Miniato.

Also, my heirs should pay her every year, while mona Maria lives, besides the aforesaid, 200 gold flor:ns.

To my daughters, their proportion of gifts for their trousseau, and they should inherit one from the other (as necessary).

If Iacopo should be in my debt on account of the Presidency of Romagna, release him.

Release Luigi (from any debt arising) from the division of the house.

Heirs: Luigi, Iacopo, Bongianni and Gerolamo.

CHAPTER 20

[1] L. STAFFETTI, *Lettera faceta di Francesco Guicciardini in lode di Bologna*, in *A.S.I.*, ser. V, vol. XI (1893), pp. 387 ff.; see also the documents quoted by A. ROSSI, op. cit., vol. I, p. 274 n.

[2] Extracts from the petition and ambassador's correspondence published by A. ROSSI, op. cit., vol. I, pp. 272 ff.

[3] Letter of the Bolognese ambassador to the Forty, 27 April 1531, quoted by A. ROSSI, op. cit., vol. I, p. 274.

[4] Letter of 24 June in *Lettere al Lanfredini*, p. 76.

[5] OTETEA, p. 118.

[6] *Decameron*, VII, 7.

[7] *Opp. in.*, vol. IX, p. 225; L. STAFFETTI, *Lettera faceta*, cit., pp. 395 ff.; *Lettere al Lanfredini*, pp. 99, 167, 209 ('to get my own back for a bad dinner they gave me last Lent').

[8] Letter of 26 Oct. 1531, in *Lettere al Lanfredini*, pp. 95 ff.

[9] Letter of 6 Dec. 1531, in *Lettere al Lanfredini*, p. 102.

[10] Letter of 26 Oct., cit.; letters of 23 Nov., 6 and 13 Dec., in *Lettere al Lanfredini*, pp. 102 ff., 105.

[11] *Lettere al Lanfredini*, p. 136; L. STAFFETTI, *Il cardinale Innocenzo Cybo*, cit., passim.

[12] Letter of 17 June 1531, in *Lettere al Lanfredini*, pp. 70 ff. See the extract of the 'Authority in temporal affairs' of Cardinal Cybo, and the brief of Clement VII to G. with 'additional powers' in L. STAFFETTI, *Lettera faceta*, cit., pp. 388 ff.

[13] L. STAFFETTI, *Lettera faceta*, cit., p. 390.

[14] Mr. Alexander G. Mylonas, who is preparing a monograph on G.'s governorship of Bologna, which I hope soon to see published.

[15] *Storia d'Italia*, vol. IV, p. 269. On this dispute with the Duke of Ferrara see also the letter which G. wrote to Sanga on 15 June 1531 forwarding the letter of a person who, having been *podestà* (mayor) of Ferrara for ten years, stated that he had been obliged to authenticate false documents concerning the imperial investiture of Reggio. The letter was published by O. TOMMASINI, *Lettere inedite in un manoscritto dell'Archivio Vaticano*, in *Rendiconti della R. Accademia dei Lincei*, Classe di scienze morali, 1885, pp. 838 ff.

[16] G.'s letters to Salviati about this affair are in *Opp. in.*, vol. IX, pp. 163–201, 205–207, 210 ff., 213, 215–18, 225–30, 234–6, 239, 243 ff., 246 ff., 253. The letters containing the 'eighteen per cent' are in pp. 168 ff., 171 ff.

[17] Letters to Iacopo Salviati, 12 Sept., in *Opp. in.*, vol. IX, p. 192; *Lettere al Lanfredini*, pp. 85 ff. On 22 Aug. he no longer had a fever; on 3 Sept. he was 'free from the infection' but still too weak to attend properly to affairs; on 20 Sept. he wrote: 'I followed your advice to give up attending to business for a while, and if I had not done so I should never have thrown it off. I have been away several days now and still am, though I shall soon be back among the troubles again.' These words tell us what a sense of relief he enjoyed during his stay at San Michele in Bosco; later on he had as a gift from the friars of this convent the beautiful octagonal table decorated and inlaid with niello and enamel, which he became so fond of as to mention in his last will and testament, and which may still be admired in the Guicciardini palace in Florence. Yet in

this long illness, as we gather from his letter to Salviati, he never ceased to occupy himself with the plots against Ferrara.

[18] Letter to Iacopo Salviati, 15 Sept., in *Opp. in.*, vol. IX, p. 197.

[19] Letter to Iacopo Salviati, 30 Sept., in *Opp. in.*, vol. IX, pp. 206 ff.

[20] Letters of 30 April, 13 May and 9 July 1532, in *Lettere al Lanfredini*, pp. 144 ff., 146 ff., 152, 170 ff. For the rumours about a family connection with the Pepoli, ibidem, p. 153. G. himself confirms the existence of the view that he was 'more inclined towards the Pepoli', in a letter which I reproduce in part on p. 231 of this volume.

[21] Letter of 9 July, cit., in op. cit., pp. 146 ff. Elsewhere G. notes the relations between the factions in the hill areas around Bologna and those in similar parts near Modena. B.N.F., *Rari*, 67, cc. 42–3.

[22] G. PIERACCINI, *La stirpe de' Medici di Cafaggiolo*, cit., vol. I, pp. 398–403.

[23] The first four were published by Canestrini in *Opp. in.*, vol. II, pp. 354–82, as *Political Discourses* VII–IX (the title in this case is especially inappropriate). Although Palmarocchi excluded too many of G.'s writings from his edition, he at least did right not to include these among works of some literary dignity, as they are simply memoranda or notes G. gave or sent to Schönberg. For their chronology see the excellent article by F. GILBERT, *Alcuni discorsi di uomini politici fiorentini e la politica di Clemente VII per la restaurazione medicea*, in *A.S.I.*, XCIII (1935), vol. II, pp. 3–24. Yet the dating in some cases can be made even more precise: in fact the one published in *Opp. in.*, vol. II, pp. 368 ff., with the title *Discourse IX*, is later than 3 March 1531, as is evident from the reference to the new tax which was then 'published' (cf. *Lettere al Lanfredini*, p. 51); that published under the title of *Discourse X* (pp. 378 ff.) is later than the arrival of Cardinal Ippolito de' Medici in Florence, i.e., 20 April 1531. The fifth (republished by G. CAPPONI in *A.S.I.*, vol. I, 1842, pp. 453–8) was published in *Lettere ai principi*, etc., Venice, Francesco Ziletti, 1581, vol. III, p. 8v ff., together with the letter which accompanied it to Archbishop Schönberg dated 30 Jan. 1532; so that this sixteenth-century collection did not only contain the letter as Gilbert believed. In this same volume (p. 10 v) there is another letter of G. to the same archbishop dated 15 Feb. 1532, which it is interesting to compare with another of the same date and almost entirely identical, published in *Lettere al Lanfredini*, p. 122; it is probably the same letter, and the editor of the collection, Girolamo Ruscelli, made a mistake about the addressee. G. had written to Rome with high praise for Schönberg on the very day before his departure for Bologna: *Lettere al Lanfredini*, p. 72.

[24] Letter to Schönberg, 15 Feb. 1532, cit.

[25] *Lettere di principi*, cit., pp. 8 v ff.

[26] Letter of 13 May, in *Lettere al Lanfredini*, pp. 146 ff. Cf. the letter of the same day, pp. 150 ff. G. left Florence on 5 May: see his letter of 4 May to Lanfredini (pp. 145 ff.). It was the only occasion on which he came to Florence in this period; so I do not know how E. ZANONI, op. cit., p. 467, can affirm that 'he often left Bologna to hasten to Florence to organize the new régime'.

[27] The levy amounted to about 18,000 ducats. See *Lettere al Lanfredini*, pp. 114 ff., 120 ff., 121–9, and passim.

[28] Letters of 30 April, 13 and 16 May 1532, in *Lettere al Lanfredini*, pp. 144 ff., 146 ff., 152 ff.

[29] Letter of 9 July, cit.; cf. P. VIZZANI, *I due ultimi libri delle istorie della sua patria*, Bologna, Eredi di Giovanni Rossi, 1608.

[30] *Lettere al Lanfredini*, pp. 166, 174, 175.

[31] Letter of 21 July 1532, in *Lettere al Lanfredini*, p. 174.

[32] Letter of 2 August, in *Lettere al Lanfredini*, pp. 178 ff.

[33] Letter of 31 Oct. 1532, in *Lettere al Lanfredini*, pp. 210 ff.

[34] Letter of 12 Nov. 1532, in *Lettere al Lanfredini*, p. 216; for the request to Charles V, see the letter to Iacopo Salviati of 14 Nov., in *Opp. in.*, vol. IX, p. 255. For the composition of these private courts see F. PRISCIANESE, *Del governo della corte di un signore a Roma*, in the very rare edition of 1543 or in the quite rare reprint done in 1883 (Biblioteca de' Bibliofili).

[35] G. PAPINI, *L'imitazione del Padre*, Saggi sul Rinascimento, Florence, Le Monnier, 1942, p. 109.

[36] G., who was one of the protagonists, speaks at length of these negotiations in his *Storia d'Italia*, vol. IV, pp. 296 ff. For the celebrations in Bologna during the meeting, see P. VIZZANI, op. cit., pp. 5 ff. A draft of the conditions of the League negotiated by G., with many amendments in his own hand, is to be found in A.G.F., *Carte di F.G.*, XVI, n. 13.

CHAPTER 21

[1] Letter to Lanfredini, 11 May 1533, unpublished, in B.N.F., *Rari*, 67, c. 23 (an extract in A. ROSSI, vol. II, p. 55, n.). Cf. letter to Lanfredini of 15 May ('a return to arms would mean the ultimate ruin of everything') and 16 May to Iacopo Salviati ('I pray God will illumine the hearts of His Holiness and other princes so that there be no recourse to arms'): *Lettere di principi*, cit., vol. III, p. 23 r. Cf. also the letter from Filippo Strozzi, 23 May, quoted by A. ROSSI, vol. II, p. 53, in which it is said that G. 'condemned' the Pope's proposed journey.

[2] Letter to Iacopo Salviati, 21 July, in *Lettere di principi*, cit., p. 24 v. For the alacrity with which he accepted the invitation to accompany the Pope, see the letter of 1 June, ibid., p. 23 r.

[3] B.N.F., *Rari*, 67, c. 84.

[4] Letter to Lanfredini, 15 August, B.N.F., *Rari*, 67, cc. 74–5.

[5] Letter of 15 August, cit.

[6] See the long postscript in his own hand to the letter to Lanfredini, 18 Sept. 1533, published by A. ROSSI, vol. II, pp. 333 ff.

[7] Letter of 18 Sept., cit. in preceding note. For the negotiations about his temporary replacement, see letters of 31 July, 7 August and 2 September to Lanfredini, unpublished in B.N.F., *Rari*, 67, cc. 53, 67, 84.

[8] TOMMASO PIASI, *Cronaca*, contemporary MS. in the Malvezzi de' Medici Library in Bologna.

[9] Letter to Lanfredini, 21 July, B.N.F., *Rari*, 67, c. 51.

[10] Letter to Lanfredini, 12 Sept., unpublished in B.N.F., *Rari*, 67, c. 96.

[11] GUICCIARDINI, *Storia d'Italia*, vol. IV, p. 277.

[12] The scholar mentioned is G. DE LEVA, *Storia documentata di Carlo V in correlazione all'Italia*, Venice, Padua, Bologna, 1863–94, vol. III, pp. 112 ff.

[13] A.S.F., *Carte Strozziane*, ser. II, 148. Of these documents only the marriage agreement was published by A. REUMONT, *La gioventù di Caterina de' Medici*, transl. by S. Bianciardi, Florence, Le Monnier, 1858, pp. 189 ff. All the rest are unpublished. The 'Instruction to the Nuncio in Spain' (G. himself wrote this title) is intended to reassure Charles V concerning a clause in the marriage agreement relative to the wife's rights on the duchy of Urbino; as it is the most important, I give the text complete below, adding by the way that it contains many additions and corrections in G.'s own hand.

'The objections of the Count regarding the reserve of rights on the duchy of Urbino are twofold: first that, as His Holiness has come to an accord about that State, he has contravened the confederation of Bologna whereby it is forbidden to His Holiness and His Majesty to come to agreement with any prince without consultation one with the other, and His Holiness has not informed His Majesty of this agreement over Urbino. Second, it is scandalous to wish that through these rights the French should have title in Italy and cause to disturb her, and it would have been better to seek some means of removing them from the Duchess and transferring them to someone else.

'To the first the reply is that no accord whatever has been negotiated over the duchy of Urbino, as in the dowry agreement no fresh rights are stipulated regarding that State, nor does it contain any obligation or promise in this respect, but merely a reserve of rights if and as she possesses them, and a reserve by its nature does not determine anything. And even if this reserve had not been expressed, it would no less be implied; for, as these rights come to her by virtue of an investiture of Leo X made to her father Duke Lorenzo, and on his decease to his sons and descendants of either sex, it is certain that renouncement of the paternal inheritance would not remove them. The reserve was expressed not because it was necessary to do so, but to satisfy the opinion which for the sake of caution and open dealing required its inclusion. As it was not in itself of import, the request was not to be denied, especially as it was not possible to prove with the charter of investiture, which we did not have here, that she was there referred to as daughter and not as heir.

'To the second the answer is that His Holiness's intention never was to deprive his niece of any right she might possess, nor would it be fitting to take from her things which she had not received from His hands. It is clear that, if His Holiness has caused her to renounce her paternal inheritance, he has recompensed her with 30,000 scudi, which is more than that was worth. And if He did not wish Her Excellency to renounce in favour of his family without recompense, he would have had far less cause to do so in favour of others. And as His Holiness, in relation to his resources, took on considerable burden in respect of the 130,000 scudi, he could not shoulder still further charge to recompense her also, as the Count alleges, for the rights to Urbino, which have not been passed in this contract from His Holiness to Her Excellency, but continue to attach to her name such as they are. Furthermore, His Holiness, as appears from the contract, has not given them to her as dowry, but merely left them to her in her person in the terms in which they earlier were. And if the French have no other cause to upset Italy than these rights, we can promise ourselves a long peace, as that State (Urbino) is, among other things, so far from them that they would first have to get a foothold in Italy in a much stronger place.'

[14] *Storia d'Italia*, vol. IV, p. 278: 'in a very rough sea'.

[15] The trip to France was not without gain for G.; and the gain must have been considerable if he could express the fear that the loss of all his possessions sent by sea and the cost of the long journey back overland with a large company in attendance could come to that amount: this we learn from an unpublished letter of 25 Dec. to Lanfredini (B.N.F., *Rari*, 67, c. 138): 'I still have part of my things at sea, and have had no news of them whatever. Let me know if you have any information there, because if I lose them, between the expenses of the journey and the value of what I have on the ship, I shall just about break even: and none the less they will say the trip to Marseilles made me a rich man. I know you will laugh when you read this, and I can laugh about it no less than you. But I am really beginning to worry about something that concerns me more: my stars will not let me sink or rise, but insist I stay for ever between rich and poor.' The expression used in this letter 'sarebbe pareggiata la coppa' (lit. the cup would be equalled: transl. above as 'I shall . . . break even'), might suggest that G. was referring to a gold cup of great value given to him, as was the custom, by the King, especially since two cups estimated to be worth 1,200 ducats were found among his belongings after his death (A.S.F., *Carte Strozziane*, ser. I, 61, c. 121). But I think that *coppa* is used here in the sense of 'dish' in a pair of scales.

[16] Letters to Lanfredini of 9, 11, 23 Dec., in B.N.F., *Rari*, 67, cc. 126, 129–30, 135–6.

[17] Letter of 9 Dec., cit.

[18] Letter from G. to a Messer Cecco, 8 Jan. 1534, in *Opp. in.*, vol. IX, pp. 280 ff. An offer from certain adventurers to attack the Duke of Ferrara had been communicated by G. to Iacopo Salviati some months before (*Opp. in.*, vol. IX, pp. 270 ff.).

[19] Letter to Lanfredini, 20 July 1534, in B.N.F., *Rari*, 67, c. 203; *Opp. in.*, vol. IX, p. 301, where he repeats the same concern to ensure a majority for Ippolito in future conclaves.

[20] Letter to Lanfredini, 16 Aug. 1534, in B.N.F., *Rari*, 67, c. 220.

[21] Letter to Lanfredini, 23 July, in B.N.F., *Rari*, 67, c. 204.

[22] Letter to Lanfredini, 27 Sept. 1534, B.N.F., *Rari*, 67, c. 264.

[23] Letter of 17 August to Lanfredini, B.N.F., *Rari*, 67, c. 223. The rumours spread by the Bolognese agent were probably the source for some chroniclers hostile to G., like Muzzi, according to whom, for instance, the troops recruited by G. numbered not 400 (B.N.F., *Rari*, 67, c. 216) but 9,000! (see E. ZANONI, op. cit., p. 496).

[24] Chronicle of Tommaso Lancillotti, quoted by E. ZANONI, op. cit., pp. 504 ff.

[25] Such a grimace was made by Count Cornelio Pepoli when he went to intercede with the Governor, who 'within three or four days, that is in cold blood' had had 'a foreign soldier' hanged, and caused his palace to be entered by force and three of his ministers chastised; G. on this occasion told him that it would have been more just to punish him than them, and then turned his back on him (*Lettere al Lanfredini*, pp. 223 ff.).

[26] 'I know of no greater worry than to be in office when the see is vacant, especially in a powerful city like this one, where you have to proceed with infinite care' (B.N.F., *Rari*, 67, c. 218).

[27] BUSINI, op. and ed. cit., pp. 255 ff. (Busini, himself an exile, was partly responsible for the reconciliation of these two who were enemies of one another as well as of G.); VARCHI, ed. cit., vol. III, p. 14. For their return to Bologna, see P. VIZZANI, op. and loc. cit., and especially the letters from G., in *Opp. in.*, vol. IX, pp. 314 ff., 317 ff.

[28] P. VIZZANI, op. cit., p. 8.

[29] Letter of 14 Oct. 1534, in *Opp. in.*, vol. IX, pp. 317 ff.

[30] Published by C. GUASTI, *Le Carte Strozziane*, cit., vol. I, p. 543. The original is in the Biblioteca Comunale, Siena, and was recently discovered by Prof. Mario Martelli, to whom I am grateful for

this information. The Pope's brief sent in reply to G.'s letter, is dated 25 October; it was published by L. STAFFETTI, op. and loc. cit., p. 394.

³¹ In a letter to Roberto Pucci, *Opp. in.*, vol. IX, p. 326, he will later write, on the subject of the inquiry with which he was threatened: 'This matter originated there' (i.e., Bologna). For the reduction in his powers after the election of Paul III, see *Lettere al Lanfredini*, p. 230.

³² Letter to Lanfredini, B.N.F., *Rari*, 67, c. 292.

³³ In a letter written to Lanfredini on 27 Nov. 1534 immediately after leaving Bologna, G. says that he left 'for the reasons you will have seen from my letter to His Holiness . . . as it seemed to me completely unsuitable . . . to stay in a city with nothing but trouble and little standing which from day to day was being diminished by my superiors . . .' The letter to the Pope could not be the one of congratulations referred to above in n. 30, either for its date or its content. My own re-construction of the situation is confirmed by the words of Cybo's reply, cit., in following note 34: 'the Pope had graciously replied that he was agreeable to his being replaced' – a sure indication that G. had in fact asked for this, unless one supposes that he had got Cybo to ask on his behalf. The above-mentioned letter of 27 Nov. 1534 is unpublished, in B.N.F., *Rari*, 67, c. 292. A little before or a little later, he wrote to Cybo what he had written to the Pope: this appears from a letter to Lanfredini, that supports my conjectures: 'I become more and more determined to leave, and I have written at length on the matter to the Reverend Legate.' *Lettere al Lanfredini*, p. 230.

³⁴ Cybo's reply is quoted by G. in a letter to Lanfredini, 5 Nov., B.N.F., *Rari*, 67, c. 279. As we already know (see p. 164), the future Julius III had been with G. earlier on, for G. facetiously refers to him among the 'academicians' of Marignano.

³⁵ Letter of 17 Nov., B.N.F., *Rari*, 67, c. 285.

³⁶ Letter to Roberto Pucci, cit., in n. 31.

³⁷ Letter of 27 Nov., cit.

³⁸ Letter of 5 Nov. to Lanfredini, published by E. TEZA, *F. Guicciardini alla morte di Clemente VII*, in *Atti del R. Istituto Veneto*, ser. VI, vol. VII (1889), pp. 900 ff.

³⁹ L. STAFFETTI, *Lettera faceta*, cit., pp. 395 ff.

⁴⁰ Letter from the Forty to their ambassadors in Rome, 24 Nov. 1534, published by GIOSUÈ CARDUCCI, in *Lettere di Francesco Guicciardini*, in *Atti e Memorie della R. Deput. di Storia Patria per la Romagna*, IX (1870), pp. 86–7.

⁴¹ Letter from the Forty, cit.

⁴² *Life* of Guicciardini by Remigio (Nannini) Fiorentino, which precedes the text of the *Storia d'Italia* in the Venice ed., Gabriel Giolito de' Ferrari, 1567. The chronicler Tommaso Lancillotti (cit., above in n. 24), after saying that during his governorship G. had done 'extraordinary things, as if he were lord of the city', also produces the wonderful story that on his departure he gave as surety no less than 80,000 ducats!

CHAPTER 22

¹ BUSINI, op. cit., p. 209.

² *Lettere al Lanfredini*, pp. 229 ff.; cf. letter of 30 Sept., B.N.F., *Rari*, 67, c. 268.

³ Letter of 12 Feb. 1535, in *Lettere al Lanfredini*, pp. 235 ff.

⁴ OTETEA, p. 135. For the affair of the inquiry, see especially A. ROSSI vol. II. pp. 78 ff. On 9 Dec. he wrote to Lanfredini to ask him to have Cardinal Salviati recommend him to two of the Cardinals nominated for the inquiry, the third, that is Campeggi, being hostile (G. refers to his 'old differences with Campeggi' as early as 1525, in *Carteggi*, vol. VIII, n. 117): 'If possible I should like to settle this matter, though I am not worried about it except in as much as it would mean coming there and abasing myself by making up to the clerics of the Camera, and to have to do this would grieve me as much as all the harm that might come to me from the affair. For the rest, I care not a fig for them . . .' (*Lettere al Lanfredini*, p. 234). On 1 Jan. 1535, writing to his brother Luigi, Francesco was almost sure that the affair of the inquiry 'would dissolve into smoke . . . if there were not also involved the case of Bartolomeo Valori, regarded by the Pope with intense disfavour'. The same day he wrote: 'The Pope speaks well of me' (*Opp. in.*, vol. X, pp. 272 ff.). On 26 March he finally congratulated himself in a letter to Lanfredini that the affair had

'cooled off' (B.N.F., *Rari*, 67, c. 336). For his differences with Campeggi, see also p. 107 of this volume.

⁵ *Cose fiorentine*, pp. xxvi ff.

⁶ *Cose fiorentine*, pp. xxi, xxvii, xxxv.

⁷ RIDOLFI, *Genesi*, pp. 14 ff.

⁸ RIDOLFI, *Genesi*, p. 17. For reference purposes I use here for the first time, but with no intention of imposing it as a title, the term 'Commentaries'; it seems to me necessary to distinguish them from the *Storia d'Italia*, which later absorbed them, but this latter title would be totally unsuited to such a restricted narrative. Yet, whilst accepting this term 'Commentaries' – which (if it is true) Guicciardini himself is said to have used when speaking of the work to Nardi, and Nardi then passed it on to Sansovino – we must not take it to have a very precise sense. Not many years later Busini (op. cit., p. 275) called Nardi's *Istorie* 'a commentary'. Probably, too, G. intended in his 'Commentaries' – and the little we still have of book II (which is more detailed than XVII of the *Storia d'Italia*) appears to confirm this – to deal at greater length with the period of his Lieutenancy.

⁹ These 'Commentaries', which were the first seeds of the *Storia d'Italia* of which they later formed books XVI and XVII, escaped the notice even of the most recent and diligent students of Guicciardini's *magnum opus*. They were first considered by me in my *Genesi*, cit., where I also published (pp. 28-94) the complete text of the first version; on pp. 95-9 are two speeches taken from the text of the second version.

¹⁰ G. PIERACCINI, *La stirpe de' Medici di Cafaggiolo*, cit., vol. I, pp. 330-37. Under torture the Cardinal's groom several times confessed that he had put poison in his food; but he withdrew the confession when interrogated without torture.

¹¹ VARCHI, op. and ed. cit., vol. III, p. 85.

¹² BUSINI, op. cit., pp. 265 ff.

¹³ See the extracts published by A. ROSSI, vol. II, pp. 81-3.

¹⁴ A. ROSSI, vol. II, pp. 85-8. But neither Rossi nor Ferrai from whom he drew information, knew an important unpublished document, the draft, with corrections and additions by G. himself, of the instructions to Iacopo de' Medici who was sent to Antonio da Leyva for this affair of the League. It is in A.G.F., *Carte di F.G.*, XVII, cc. 134-7.

¹⁵ A. ROSSI, vol. II, p. 85, n.

¹⁶ *Ricordi*, p. 232.

¹⁷ Letter from Duke Alessandro de' Medici to G., 23 Nov. 1534, A.S.F., *Carte Strozziane*, ser. I, 16, c. 45 (*Opp. in.*, vol. X, p. 272). Letter from G. to his brother Luigi, 18 Nov. 1534, *Opp. in.*, vol. IX, p. 323.

¹⁸ SEGNI, op. cit., p. 190.

¹⁹ *Narrazione fatta per Galeotto Giugni del processo della causa agitata appresso la Cesarea Maestà . . . per li reverendissimi Cardinali Salviati e Ridolfi e fuorusciti fiorentini*, etc., published in appendix to I. NARDI, *Istorie della città di Firenze*, ed. cit., vol. II, pp. 335-74. The words quoted in the text are on p. 350.

²⁰ *Narrazione*, cit., pp. 350-63. For the documents of this case, and especially for the Duke's replies drawn up by G., it is better to consult the text published in *Opp. in.*, vol. IX, pp. 331-95, based on papers in the Guicciardini archive. The *Risposta per parte del Duca alle querele dei fuorusciti* (autograph title), referred to by scholars and also here by me under the title *Difesa*, may be read in *Opp. in.*, vol. IX, pp. 354-74.

²¹ BUSINI, op. cit., p. 220.

²² BUSINI, op. cit., p. 210.

²³ A. ROSSI, op. cit., vol. II, pp. 118-268, refers to the 'infamy' devolving on G., then embarks on a long defence of his Neapolitan *Difesa* that develops into a defence of Alessandro, in support of which he even has recourse to the much discredited apologetic pamphlet by Rastrelli, and even gives weight to the well-known popular *Laments*, so that in his enthusiasm he goes a good deal further than G. himself, with this important difference, that G. was the Duke's advocate and Rossi a historian.

²⁴ *Narrazione*, cit., loc. cit., pp. 363 ff.

²⁵ *Opp. in.*, vol. IX, pp. 375-8; *Narrazione*, cit., pp. 365-7.

²⁶ *Opp. in.*, vol. IX, pp. 378 ff. These documents of the case are not in Giugni's *Narrazione*, for

they were evidently not communicated to the exiles. Preserved among the Guicciardini papers, they represent an addition and clarification of considerable importance. The title (in G.'s own hand) of the second document is *Aggiunta fatta a istanza di Granvela alla risposta del signor Duca contro alla seconda dimanda de' fuorusciti* (addition made at the instance of Granvela to the Duke's reply to the second request of the exiles). In the first document, which is very brief, it simply says that to reform the government in the way proposed by the exiles would mean 'in substance placing it in the hands of the populace', which could not be done, adds G., concerned for his own interests, 'without putting in obvious danger all those who have followed Clement and the House of Medici'. Finally it does not omit to state what was perfectly true and very well understood by the imperial agents, that a popular régime would be wholeheartedly inclined to friendship with France, which was a particularly sore point at that time with Charles V. I do not understand how ZANONI, op. cit., p. 527, came to suggest that the two documents here referred to 'remained in draft form and were not communicated to the interested parties'. To the exiles certainly not, but to the Duke most definitely yes.

27 The original Spanish text from the Guicciardini Archive, is published in *Opp. in.*, vol. IX, p. 381. The *Narrazione*, pp. 368–70, gives an Italian version. According to NARDI, op. cit., vol. II, p. 268, Charles V later said to Cardinals Salviati and Ridolfi who were displeased with this answer, that it was simply 'una oblazione fatta da Alessandro e non sua deliberazione' (an oblation made by Alessandro and not his decision); but Nardi (who, however, was, together with Giugni, one of the agents of the exiles) either misheard or mistranscribed what he heard: he should have said: 'una oblazione fatta ad Alessandro' (an oblation made to Alessandro). This would in fact correspond with what I have reconstructed from the Guicciardini manuscripts, where it has the following original and revealing title: *Partito proposto al Signor Duca per parte di Cesare con istanza fussi accettato* (Decision proposed to the Duke by Caesar with the request that it be accepted).

28 *Narrazione*, cit., 370; *Opp. in.*, vol. IX, pp. 386–8.

29 *Narrazione*, cit., p. 372.

30 *Sommario della risposta facta per noi a bocca al partito proposto da Cesare* (Summary of the reply made verbally to the decision proposed by Caesar), in A.G.F., *Accessioni*, I, ins. 12, n. 1. In view of the importance of the document I publish it here below. Noteworthy, among other features, is the parting shot in which G. is at pains to convince that the city (which, apart from a few citizens like himself, greatly desired it) would never agree to the remission of the exiles.

Summary of the reply made verbally to the decision proposed by Caesar

No doubt about Caesar's desire for just solution, so encouraged to speak out being sure it would displease His Majesty if his proposal to achieve one end in fact achieved another quite different.

The exiles are of two sorts: those who were exiled and directed in 1530; the others voluntary exiles. Remission is useless; but if Caesar wants it, could more readily be agreed for the voluntary exiles, although they have offended the Duke more than others; with the other exiles the reverse is the case.

But to restore the former is harmful, as they were justly and solemnly condemned, and we would lose considerable reputation, especially as they are men of little worth: they are seditious and wicked, and would corrupt the rest. It would raise the credit and favour the Cardinals and Filippo, who will never change their views; lose confidence of friendly citizens gravely injured by them. Linked with Cardinals merely out of ambition, as not punished on their account, but before they were alienated from city.

Enough for their security the word of His Majesty given under the Duke's trust. Would only ask them why under cover of security they wish to obtain things against the Duke; and they too must give some surety, being men who, given the chance, will show no respect for His Majesty, to whom they had recourse after first trying all other means.

Remission cannot be agreed, nor demand just.

First because it is blameworthy and perhaps wholly unheard of that the leader should compromise his authority and his government, as the decision depends on the city which is not obliged to give remission to exiles, a very small and unworthy part of it.

It is not just to compromise issues already decided and a government which His Majesty has three times taken under his protection: in the league of Bologna; in the league constituted on the Pope's death, and when the Bishop of Iesi was in Madrid.

This would be the way to deprive the Duke of his state and authority, and to divide the citizens among themselves, for when they hear of the remission, not knowing His Majesty's purpose, some will begin to take heart, especially with the Cardinals and others giving encouragement, etc.; and so the way will be opened to disorders impossible to remedy without difficulties, and His Majesty will not thereby rid himself of the troubles of the exiles, they will merely increase from day to day.

The Duke cannot do this, even should he wish, because in so grave a matter the city will not cede to him, nor ever agree to give up its power or come into conflict with these exiles over a matter which pertains to the Republic and not to any private citizen. These exiles are not comparable in number or quality to those who remain in the city, who would rather die than consent to such an indignity. The Duke, if he should try to make them, will become hateful to them, and thus have lost his friends and made his enemies more powerful.

[31] The fresh proposal of the exiles are in *Opp. in.*, vol. IX, pp. 389–92.

[32] *Opp. in.*, vol. IX, pp. 392 ff.

[33] SEGNI, op. cit., p. 191; VARCHI, ed. cit., vol. III, pp. 202 ff.

[34] This reply, revised by G. and accepted by Granvela, is in *Opp. in.*, vol. IX, pp. 393 ff.

[35] VARCHI, ed. cit., vol. III, pp. 203 ff.

[36] ROSSI, vol. II, pp. 110–12.

[37] A.G.F., *Accessioni*, I, nn. 2–9. One of the major concerns of Alessandro, who needed to strengthen his reputation, was to be able to return to Florence bringing Charles's daughter with him. To this end he addressed several appeals to his father-in-law, that are preserved in Gs.' papers. In one of them (n. 8), when it had been agreed that he should have her in Florence in two months' time, he protests that to return without the Duchess would make his position so difficult that he would prefer to delay his departure for two months, in spite of the ruinous expense, rather than go back without her.

[38] For the background of the story I have followed primarily the histories of Varchi, Nardi and Segni.

[39] VARCHI, ed. cit., vol. III, p. 215.

[40] DE LEVA, op. cit., vol. III, pp. 170–74: in these pages of his classic work the author assigns to Guicciardini a very prominent part that must now be given back to Guidiccioni. BENOIST, op. cit., pp. 77 ff.; G. MOLINI, *Documenti di storia italiana*, etc., Florence, 1837, vol. II, p. 388; and especially A. ROSSI, vol. II, pp. 76 ff. and 271 ff., who was perhaps the one most convinced of G.'s part in this legation, and became involved in elaborate speculation on this account.

[41] *Lettere di principi*, cit., pp. 41 v–45 r; 47 v–50 r. The last three letters bear the date 7 November, which should obviously be corrected to September. This was pointed out by G. MOLINI, op. and loc. cit., who (or rather Gino Capponi who was responsible for the notes) did not, however, realize that the letter on p. 47 v with the signature of Guicciardini and the date 7 November, is exactly the same word for word as that published on p. 45 v with the signature of Guidiccioni and the date 7 September. Similarly the letter on 47 r signed by Guidiccioni is reprinted exactly the same on p. 49 v with the signature of Guicciardini.

[42] If Guicciardini and Guidiccioni had in fact negotiated with the same persons, at the same time and for the same purpose, it is impossible that one should not have spoken of the other in correspondence, that they should not at some time have mentioned one another's names. It is clear to me, therefore, as the style and language confirm, that all the letters, even those that have the signature of Guicciardini, belong to Guidiccioni. Highly revealing is the situation pointed out in the preceding note, where two of those letters are published twice, once with Guidiccioni's and again with Guicciardini's signature; and it also tells us how much trust we can place in Ruscelli who edited the collection (it is worth recalling the situation noted already in chapter 20, n. 22, where a letter published in the same collection as addressed to Iacopo Salviati is almost exactly the same as one to Lanfredini of which we possess the original). In fine – and I do not think these conjectures of mine are rash – one must read Guidiccioni in every instance in De Leva's book where Guicciardini's name is mentioned in connection with this legation; and this legation, as far as Guicciardini is concerned, should be expunged also from the relevant pages of the works, already quoted, of Gino Capponi, Benoist, Rossi, Zanoni (*Vita pubblica di F.G.*, cit., pp. 538 ff.). As I said above, one must render to Guidiccioni only those things that are Guidiccioni's. E. CHIORBOLI, *Giovanni Guidiccioni*, Iesi, 1907, pp. 114 ff., 123 ff., does not appear to have been

aware at all of this confusion. But the person who scented the truth was Carlo Minutoli, who in his fine edition of the works of Guidiccioni (Florence, Barbera, 1867, vol. II, p. 19) firmly ascribed to his author the letters which also appear over the signature of Guicciardini in the sixteenth-century collection. Unfortunately he did not support this with any proofs nor indeed with any discussion whatever, being content simply to observe that after the death of Clement VII Guicciardini 'held no office at the Court of Rome'. Too little evidence indeed to shake the established view. In fact, all students of Guicciardini, among them a man of De Leva's calibre, have continued to believe firmly in this ultramontane legation of the great Florentine politician.

[43] SEGNI, op. and ed. cit., p. 203.
[44] A. ROSSI, op. cit., vol. II, pp. 149, 271, 272.

CHAPTER 23

[1] VARCHI, ed. cit., vol. III, p. 240. For this chapter I have used R. RIDOLFI, *Diario fiorentino di Anonimo*, in *A.S.I.*, CXVI (1958), pp. 544–70. Also of importance is the letter from Francesco Vettori to Filippo Strozzi, 15 Jan. 1537, published among the documents that add value to the mediocre tragedy by G. B. NICCOLINI, *Filippo Strozzi*, Florence, Le Monnier, 1847, pp. 216 ff.

[2] VARCHI, vol. III, pp. 241 ff.
[3] SEGNI, ed. cit., p. 211.
[4] VARCHI, vol. III, p. 247.
[5] VARCHI, vol. III, pp. 248 ff.
[6] A. ROSSI, op. cit., vol. II, p. 275. But see especially, by the same author, *La elezione di Cosimo I Medici*, in *Atti del R. Istituto Veneto*, ser. VII, vol. I (1889–90), pp. 369–435. Cf. OTETEA, p. 304; AMMIRATO, *Opuscoli*, Florence, 1640, vol. III, pp. 218 ff.

[7] SEGNI, p. 217. I am obliged to modify somewhat the scepticism I expressed in the original Italian edition of this biography; because Segni's information is confirmed in greater detail by another hitherto unknown source: Lorenzo Poggi (see R. RIDOLFI, *Lorenzo Poggio e le sue sconosciute 'Istorie'*, in *La Bibliofilia*, LXV, 1963, pp. 189–94; and more recently R. RIDOLFI, *Fr. Guicciardini e Cosimo I*, in *A.S.I.* CXXII, 1964, pp. 567–606, dealing more fully with the relations between G. and Cosimo).

[8] VARCHI, vol. III, p. 255.
[9] SEGNI, p. 212.
[10] VARCHI, vol. III, p. 253.
[11] Pandolfo Pucci, G.'s son-in-law, in a well-known letter written from prison in 1559, boasted to Duke Cosimo that he had entered the hall of the Quarantotto (Forty-Eight) on the day of the election and threatened to kill his father-in-law if Cosimo were not immediately elected. But this fine boast, evidently written to gain the Duke's pardon, is in no sense true or probable, if for no other reason than because, as we have seen, Guicciardini had no need whatever to be persuaded in favour of this election. At most Pandolfo might have warned him of the danger he ran.

[12] VARCHI, vol. III, p. 251; SEGNI, p. 217.
[13] SEGNI, p. 217; VARCHI, vol. III, p. 254.
[14] SEGNI, loc. cit.
[15] SEGNI, p. 215.
[16] CELLINI, *Vita*, Florence, Le Monnier, 1866, p. 192. According to SEGNI, p. 215, Francesco Vettori reproached G. with very similar words: 'If you give him the guard, the arms and the fortress, why then ask that he should not go beyond a certain limit?'
[17] VARCHI, vol. III, p. 275.
[18] SEGNI, p. 219.
[19] R. RIDOLFI, *Diario fiorentino*, cit., loc. cit., p. 553.
[20] 'All the members of the Council and especially Guicciardini are resolved that the exiles should be recalled and restored': letter from Bernardo Sanzio quoted by A. ROSSI, vol. II, p. 291.
[21] See the extracts from documents published by C. PAOLI and E. CASANOVA, *Cosimo I de' Medici e i fuorusciti del 1537*, in *A.S.I.*, ser. V, vol. XI (1893), p. 313; also in appendix to G. B. NICCOLINI, *Filippo Strozzi*, cit., p. 250. For some details concerning the death of ser Maurizio, see R. RIDOLFI, *Diario fiorentino*, cit., loc. cit., p. 565.

[22] R. RIDOLFI, *Diario fiorentino*, cit., p. 567.

[23] Letter to his brother Luigi, 4 June 1537, in *Opp. in.*, vol. X, pp. 305 ff.; cf. the letter of 19 May to Roberto Pucci, *Opp. in.*, vol. X, p. 297.

[24] Letter to his brother Luigi, 25 June, in *Opp. in.*, vol. X, pp. 305-307.

[25] Letter to Roberto Pucci, 28 April, in *Opp. in.*, vol. X, p. 295.

[26] Letter from Filippo Strozzi to Bartolomeo Cavalcanti, cit., by A. ROSSI, vol. II, p. 308.

[27] Letter to his brother Luigi, 19 June, in *Opp. in.*, vol. X, pp. 304 ff.

[28] Published in appendix to G. B. NICCOLINI, op. cit., p. 213.

[29] A. ROSSI, vol. II, pp. 281-302.

[30] SEGNI, p. 428.

[31] 'Cosimo, confiding completely with the imperial agents, and excluding the best citizens, thought only of making himself absolute ruler.' Then later: 'Cosimo was disposed in all affairs to follow the Emperor's directions, though Guicciardini and Francesco Vettori wished it otherwise and would have preferred that like Duke Alessandro he should remain the friend but not the subject or vassall of Caesar.' SEGNI, pp. 223, 247.

[32] Letter from G. to Roberto Pucci, 2 Feb. 1538, in *Opp. in.*, vol. X, pp. 318 ff. What post was involved is not evident from this reply, but G. says it was an offer 'of considerable honour'.

[33] *Opp. in.*, vol. IX, pp. 324 ff.; vol. X, pp. 282, 287.

[34] Letter of 2 Feb., cit.

[35] Letter cit.

[36] P. LITTA, *Famiglie celebri italiane*, Famiglia Capponi, by L. Passerini, *tav.* XIII, does not indicate the date of the marriage, nor does it appear in the tables of the Guicciardini family. We know it from a letter from Niccolò Guicciardini to his father Luigi, Florence, 27 Nov. 1539: '. . . Messer Francesco's Lisabetta was married at Giuliano's house on Tuesday evening, the 25th. . . . There was a small supper which Caterina and I attended, and this morning there was a fine breakfast . . .' (A.S.F., *Carte Strozziane*, ser. I, 62, n. 56). Giuliano was the father of Alessandro Capponi, and the newly weds went to live in his house.

[37] Little known and in any case ignored by those who have tried to solve this minor mystery, is the explanation given by IACOPO PITTI, *Apologia de' Cappucci*, in *A.S.I.*, ser. I, vol. IV, pt. II (1853), p. 329, who refers to it as something well known at the time: 'If the controversy over the financial provision had not deterred him, he would have gone into the service of Paul III.' The *Apologia de' Cappucci* is a book swarming with errors and untruths to Guicciardini's detriment, but this small incidental detail I think one might accept as true. On the other hand, immediately after this passage one is forced to laugh at Pitti's saying: 'As soon as Duke Cosimo retired him . . . Guicciardini, in a fit of anger amended many parts of his *History*'; whereas the fact is that when Cosimo 'retired' him, he had hardly begun the work. A. ROSSI, op. cit., vol. II, p. 315, attributes G.'s refusal of the Pope's offer to consideration for Cosimo, but confesses it is merely a hypothesis. Remigio Fiorentino had also ascribed it to loyalty to Cosimo. OTETEA, p. 314, is undecided between the insufficiency of the salary and a veto from Cosimo; but the latter is absolutely at variance with the documentary evidence.

[38] A.G.F., *Carte di F.G.*, III. This third redaction was begun as a fair copy written with chancelleresque elegance in a nicely bound volume. Cf. R. RIDOLFI, *Genesi della 'Storia d'Italia'*, pp. 11 ff.

[39] A.G.F., *Carte di F.G.*, X, c. 41. Cf. RIDOLFI, *Genesi*, pp. 19, 28.

[40] *Storia d'Italia*, vol. I, p. 3.

[41] R. RIDOLFI, *Genesi*, p. 19. As far as I know, no one has hitherto considered that this title was not given to the work originally. G. TOFFANIN, op. cit., p. 425, writes: 'The title *Storia d'Italia* has in itself a deliberate greatness.' In fact, as I have already indicated (chap. 3, n. 13), this is not G.'s title, but a later addition: he gave it none at all.

[42] E. FUETER, *Storia della storiografia moderna*, cit., vol. I, pp. 91 ff.

[43] R. RIDOLFI, *Pagine inedite della seconda Storia di Firenze*, in *Quarto Centenario*, p. 10. Of the *Cose fiorentine* as the link between the *Storie fiorentine* and the *Storia d'Italia*, DE CAPRARIIS, op. cit., pp. 94-111, writes perceptively (though I do not agree entirely with him): 'The *Cose fiorentine* – unknown until a short time ago – add the document whose existence one might in the past have assumed without possessing it, the document which permits us to reconstruct completely the genesis of the *Storia d'Italia*.' Cf. R. RIDOLFI, *L'itinerario storiografico del Guicciardini*, cit. in n. 7 to chap. 18.

[1] VARCHI, op. and ed. cit., vol. III, p. 300.

[2] See the passages cited by A. ROSSI, op. cit., vol. II, p. 317.

[3] A.S.F., *Mediceo*, 345, cc. 270–72: Letter from Lorenzo Pagni to Ugolino Grifoni, 17 July 1540. Pagni tells Grifoni (like himself secretary to Duke Cosimo) of a long talk he had had with Giovanni di Luna who held the fortress of Florence for Charles V. The account could not have been intended to damage his relations with Cosimo, as G. had already been dead two months; so it is all the more worthy of credence.

[4] The important information comes from one best qualified to know it: Donato Giannotti, who, before being deprived of office and banished, was secretary to the Ten. He wrote to Varchi on 16 June 1547: 'I know that all the documents of that department came into the hands of Guicciardini, and they are probably among his effects.' And in fact some remain to this day in the Archivio Guicciardini. It is probable that their restitution was ordered by Duke Cosimo on information from Varchi, now his historian, who had it from this letter of Giannotti. Cf. R. RIDOLFI, *L'archivio della famiglia Guicciardini*, cit., p. 65.

[5] The greater part of this material is kept in four large files containing large notebooks and un-bound leaves, preserved in A.G.F., *Carte di F.G.*, XIV–XVII; some is scattered about in other parts of the Archivio, and some that accompanied the papers of Luigi Guicciardini (see p. 279 of this vol.) is among the *Carte Strozziane* (ser. I, f. 360, etc.); finally, as is evident from close examination of the extant papers, some has been lost.

[6] P. VILLARI, *Machiavelli*[2], vol. III, pp. 488–96, devoted a long note to these extracts and in general to the sources of the *Storia d'Italia*. GHERARDI, who knew the subject much better, studied them in his monumental ed. of the *Storia*, vol. I, pp. xlv–lix (published posthumously and unfortunately incomplete).

[7] This first draft of the complete *Storia* is in A.G.F., *Carte di F.G.*, VII. Cf. R. RIDOLFI, *Genesi*, cit., pp. 20 ff. A careful detailed review of the MSS. containing these and later redactions of the *Storia* (except for the first two of books XVI and XVII which he did not know) was done by E. ROSTAGNO in his introduction to the *Storia d'Italia*, vol. I, pp. lxiii–clxiii, completing the work by Gherardi (see preceding note).

[8] This note was published, as evidence of G.'s scrupulous pursuit of truth (a pity Ranke did not know of it!), by E. ROSTAGNO in the review of MSS. cit., in preceding note, pp. cxlvii ff. Another example, ibidem, p. xcix.

[9] The notes from Bembo and subjects for further research (in G.'s own hand) are in A.G.F., *Carte di F.G.*, XVII, n. 31. Samples of the latter were published in the introduction to the ed. cit. of the *Storia d'Italia*, vol. I, pp. xxxv–xxxvii. Stylistic extracts from Livy, which I mention a little further on in the text, are in A.G.F., *Carte di F.G.*, XVII, 29.

[10] Regarding the chronology of the *Storia d'Italia* critics and literary historians have expressed widely divergent and often erroneous views. Having established with certainty (in my *Genesi*, cit.) the dates of beginning and conclusion of its composition, I can now date fairly accurately also the various redactions. This is possible on the basis of four certain dates: the beginning of the *Commentaries* (later books XVI and XVII), Corsi's revision of which I will speak in a moment (see also below, n. 12), the illness and death of the Author. It is certainly surprising that a work of such size should have been composed in so short a time; all the more surprising when one considers the scrupulous care taken and the constant reworking of the text. But this is not the only instance we have, though it is the most remarkable, of what G. was capable of doing with what we have referred to as 'his tremendous capacity for work'.

This is also confirmed by Remigio Fiorentino in his *Life*, cit., written some twenty years after G.'s death, in which we find such accurate and by no means obvious details that can only have come from persons very close to Guicciardini, who were well acquainted with his papers and affairs: probably from Agnolo Guicciardini who is praised in this *Life* in such a way as to confirm our conjecture. Remigio writes: 'He was a strong man, but the strain of study and affairs wore him down; he was so attached to them and pursued them with such fervour that he often deprived himself of food and sleep, and his health suffered in consequence.'

[11] See p. 41 of this vol., and n. 11 to chap. 5.

[12] The MS. revised by Corsi, containing the second redaction of the complete *Storia*, is preserved

in A.G.F., *Carte di F.G.*, I. Of Corsi's observations there now remain only those to notebooks 22, 23, 28. None of these autograph pages, in spite of the epistolary formulae used at the end, bears a date, but a few words in the last one tell us that it was written at a time of intense cold. We may exclude the winter of 1537–8, as by then the redaction of the work could not have been so far advanced, and also the winter of 1539–40 as being too close to the author's death; then, taking into account the time needed for G. to go over the MS. revised by Corsi, and for the final copying of the whole work and later revision by the author (even if part of all this work could have been done simultaneously on different notebooks), there remains only the winter of 1538–9; so that this date must be regarded as certain. I take this opportunity to record a curious ambiguity arising from this revision by Corsi, which escaped the author's later emendations and gave rise to a strange reading that has since become fixed in the text of the *Storia*. At the end of book IV (vol. I, p. 306, 1, 2nd ed. Gherardi) G. had spoken of the old 'soggezione' of the Popes to the Emperors, and Corsi made a note on this word; so in the later version (*Carte di F.G.*, I, notebook 6) G. observed: 'suggectione non placet Cursio', and put down an alternative: 'o suggectione o dipendentia'; but as he did not eventually decide for one or the other, both these words remained in the next redaction, which he barely revised, and in all the editions. This ambiguity, together with the other no less curious instance indicated in my *Genesi*, p. 14, n., show how much should still be done to produce a true accurate text of the *Storia d'Italia*.

[13] Corsi's letter was published by Rostagno in his introduction to the *Storia*, cit., vol. I, pp. lxxiii ff. Ibidem, pp. lxix ff. some examples of Corsi's criticisms and evidence of what use G. made of them.

[14] E. FUETER, op. and ed. cit., vol. I, pp. 91–5; L. RANKE, *Zur Kritik neuerer Geschichtschreiber*, Leipzig, 1884, pp. 6 ff. On G.'s style see M. CERINI, *Lo stile della Storia guicciardiniana*, in *Civiltà Moderna*, 1930, pp. 984–91; U. OJETTI, *La prosa del Guicciardini*, in *Pegaso*, III (1931), pp. 613 ff.; G. PAPINI, *L'imitazione del Padre*, Saggi sul Rinascimento, Florence, Le Monnier, 1942, pp. 99 ff.

[15] P. LITTA, *Famiglie celebri italiane*, L. PASSERINI, Famiglia Guicciardini, *tav.* III.

[16] F. DE SANCTIS, *Storia della letteratura italiana*, Bari, Laterza, 1925, vol. II, p. 107.

[17] Of the great expectation of the *Storia* while it was still being written, we have the evidence of Corsi (*Storia d'Italia*, cit., vol. I, p. lxxiii); at that time Paul III spoke of it with Roberto Pucci. See R. RIDOLFI, *Fortune della 'Storia d'Italia' guicciardiniana prima della stampa*, in *La Rinascita*, II (1939), pp. 826 ff.; RIDOLFI, *Opuscoli*, p. 205.

[18] See chap. 8, n. 16. The *incipit* of the first draft of book I (*Carte di F.G.*, II,3) read: 'It is certainly true and agreed by all those who have knowledge of past events in Italy . . .' In the third version of this book, the first of the entire work, the *incipit* is altered to read: 'Known to all who have knowledge of past events are the atrocious calamities . . .'; then later in the partial reworking of this version (*Carte di F.G.*, V): 'The great wars and bitter events that have torn Italy in our time . . .' Only in a fifth version of books I–II (*Carte di F.G.*, IV, p. 146, which I was not aware of when I published the genealogical tree in *Genesi*, p. 20) did he write: 'Begin as follows: I have decided (in the interline: or, I have had the idea) to write of the events . . .'; and then, crossing out this and other *incipits*, he finally began: 'I have decided to write down the events that have taken place in Italy within our time . . .' This version, as I have said in the text, must be dated at the beginning of Autumn 1538.

[19] To this period, in which G.'s correspondence is remarkably slight, belongs a letter to Bembo, published in *Lettere volgari di diversi nobilissimi uomini et eccellentissimi ingegni . . . nuovamente ristampate da Paolo Manuzio*, Venice, Figliuoli di Aldo, 1545, vol. II, pp. 7b–8a. The letter bears no date in this edition, but it is easily datable because it was written to congratulate Bembo on his being made Cardinal. This was announced on 19 March 1539; so the letter must have been written at the end of that month. It is not without importance, not only because it helps to fill that gap in G.'s correspondence, but on account of the distinction of the person addressed and the way it is written. It is an elegant and spirited letter that shows the two must have been on good terms, though we have no other evidence of this; but, at that very time, G. was renewing his acquaintance, not with Bembo's person, but with his *Prose della Volgar Lingua*, which he carefully studied in order to revise the language of his *Storia d'Italia*.

[20] This date is suggested by the apparent coincidence of the interruption of the revision with his illness, and confirmed also by the tremulous uncertainty of the hand in some corrections.

[21] A. OTETEA, p. 315, publishing part of the letter of 19 July 1539 from G. to Lanfredini, reads:

'The *goccia* does not affect my hands, my head or my eyes sufficiently to prevent me from reading or writing'; and he thought *goccia* here meant gout, whereas it was a well-known term for a stroke. But Otetea was doubly mistaken, because his text contains a misreading: the autograph has 'doccia' (in fact, 'Doccia', with a capital), not 'goccia'. In view of the reserve of many people when they are ill, it is difficult to know whether G.'s right hand was affected by the treatment or by his illness.

22 Letter to Lanfredini, 24 July 1539, B.N.F., *Rari*, 67, c. 379. This was also published by OTETEA, who again read 'goccia' instead of 'doccia'. Clinical details about this and other earlier illnesses of G. are very few and do not permit certain diagnosis. As for the 'doccia' (for further information on this see the *Medicinales epistolae*, cit., of Dr. Teodosio, who treated G., and the full commentary by L. MANZI, *Un maestro dello Studio bolognese*, cit., sup., ch. 7. n. 17), G. had had recourse to this treatment in Bologna in 1534 (*Opp. in.*, vol. IX, pp. 295, 299, 312) for what appears to have been a form of sinusitis accompanied by infection of the eyes, as he talks about the 'endless powerful eyewashes' that were employed. Maybe it was the same trouble that affected him in 1539; though there are good reasons to believe that he was then afflicted also by a slight cerebral thrombosis. In fact, beside being impeded in his speech by 'a stroke affecting his tongue'. making it difficult for him to dictate, it seems he also suffered some impediment in his right arm. This suspicion is also confirmed by the tremulous handwriting in some letters and in corrections made in the *Storia* at this time; furthermore, dysarthria, arising from thrombosis in the left side of the brain, usually goes with paralysis of the right side of the body. As I said above, one must also take into account the reserve sick people often show, and from what we know of G.'s character, it would be all the more so in his case. We know almost nothing of the brief illness that led to his death. Segni, op. cit., p. 248, tells us it was 'at first very slight'; Remigio Fiorentino says he then developed 'a malignant fever'. This latter piece of information, besides being very vague, might seem to derive from a late and unreliable source; but see 10 above.

23 It thus remained incomplete, in fact with the last sentence unfinished.

24 R. RIDOLFI, *Genesi*, p. 23.

25 Letter to Lanfredini, 24 Oct. 1539, B.N.F., *Rari*, 67, c. 409. Cf. the letter of 19 Sept. on c. 396. After his illness G. began to go out of doors on 6 Aug. (A.S.F., *Carte Strozziane*, ser. I, 62, n. 1). Then in September and throughout the Autumn he made 'between Val di Pesa and Santa Margherita a long peregrination to the country', mostly in Val di Pesa, to Poppiano. But he came to Florence from Poppiano some times, once on 18 Sept. for the reason we learn from a curious letter from Niccolò Guicciardini to his father Luigi: 'Messer Francesco will be here this morning; he has been to Santa Margherita because they heard a ghost there; but they believe it has gone after the friars' benediction, because nothing has been heard for two days. Do not tell . . .' (A.S.F., *Carte Strozziane*, ser. I, 62, n. 10). See also n. 27 below.

26 Letter to Lanfredini, B.N.F., *Rari*, 67. c. 410.

27 Letter from Lorenzo Pagni to Ugolino Grifoni, 17 July 1540, cit. sup. in n. 3. Among the demonstrations of trust and esteem given by Cosimo to Guicciardini, if merely *pro forma*, is the request to be present at the trial of Biagio, a pharmacist, whom the Duke was supposed to have ordered to poison little Giulio, natural son of Alessandro. For this purpose G. came to Florence from Poppiano, where he was staying in the country, at the beginning of Oct. 1539. On 3 Oct. he wrote to his brother Luigi: 'It is best not to write you the details, but the upshot is that for the Duke and his family the case is wholly justified' (*Opp. in.*, vol. X, p. 323). The summary of Biagio's examination was published by FERRAI, op. cit., pp. 279–86. A clear account of this mysterious affair was done by the diligent and well-informed G. B. ADRIANI, *Istoria de' suoi tempi*, Florence, Giunti, 1582, pp. 62 ff. At the beginning of 1539 and then on 26 Feb. Guicciardini was summoned to the villa at Castello to appear as witness together with Cardinal Cybo, at the drawing up of the deed in which the Duke named messer Luigi Ridolfi and Iacopo de' Medici as his agents to make on his behalf the contract for his marriage to Eleanora di Toledo. Drawn by ser Bernardo Gambarelli, in A.S.F., *Notarile antecosimiano*, G. 77, n. 153.

28 R. RIDOLFI, *Opuscoli*, pp. 112 ff. A reader, led on by a quotation and the indication 'in the press' which appear in the monumental work of G. PIERACCINI, *La stirpe de' Medici di Cafaggiolo*, cit., pp. 292, 373, would be wasting his time looking for my *Life of Cardinal Niccolò Ridolfi* in which the intrigues against Cosimo were examined at length on the basis of unpublished documents. Written in the author's immature years and in a way that would only do him discredit,

it has remained happily unpublished; it would have gone into the fire if I had not continued, perhaps wrongly, to feel some affection for this first biographical work of mine. Pieraccini's reference way back in 1925, merely reflected the intentions of our common friend, the publisher Attilio Vallecchi.

29 G. PIERACCINI, op. cit., vol. II, p. 13.

30 The affairs with which G. was most concerned in these last years were the disturbances in Pistoia, of which many details are to be found in his letters to his brother Luigi and to Bartolomeo Lanfredini who was there as commissioner (following a decision taken by G. and Cardinal Cybo in the absence of the Duke, see G. B. ADRIANI, op. cit., p. 61). The last letter we have of G., dated 20 April 1540, deals also with the affairs of Pistoia, and has this humorous conclusion: 'Now that you are getting near the end of your term of office, you can give up showing off, for the peasants here say that since Zanobi Bartolini there never was a worse commissioner than you' (B.N.F., *Rari*, 67, c. 448).

31 *Opp. in.*, vol. X, pp. 324 ff.

32 This last and definitive version of the *Storia d'Italia* is preserved in B.L.F., *Cod. Mediceo Pal.* CLXVI; the edition of 1561 was based directly on this MS. Besides the few corrections made by the author it bears those of posthumous revisers and traces of its passage through the printer's hands.

33 See above p. 58 ff. and n. 4 to chap. 7.

34 Horoscope of F. G., cit., c. 113 v.

35 Horoscope of F. G., c. 73. The astrologer was right in foretelling that G. would die 'in some honourable office': in fact a few days before his death he had been made Lieutenant of the Duke. He was less correct in saying 'you will be honourably interred'.

36 The will, drawn up by ser Pier Francesco Maccari, the notary who did all the other Florentine wills of Francesco, was published by A. OTETEA, pp. 367–81, from a sixteenth-century copy preserved in the Guicciardini Archive. Reference to the original (A.S.F., *Notarile Antecosimiano*, M. 20, c. 122) permits correction of some mistakes which occur in the copy and the edition. For instance, where the latter reads (concerning the famous inlaid table adorned with a fine silver plaque bearing in enamel the Guicciardini and Salviati arms, which is still in the possession of the Guicciardini family): *illa mensa rotunda seu scannum donatum dicto testatori per fratres di Bononia vocati el populo di Moyse* (that round table or desk given to the said testator by the friars of Bologna called the people of Moses), it should read: *illa mensa rotunda . . . vocatum 'el tondo de moisa'* (that round table . . . called 'the mosaic *tondo*'). In this last will, unlike the two immediately preceding, in which he had named as his heirs his daughters and unborn children, G. makes ample provision for his daughters, leaves to his wife the usufruct of Santa Margherita and an income of 200 florins a year, then names his brothers as his heirs. See above, n. 62, chap. 19. But it is likely that the notes there published were not passed to the notary by the testator in his last hours nor perhaps even in the last days of his life.

37 Letter from Annibale Rucellai to Piero Vettori, which prefaces the text in the first edition of the *Latina monumenta* of Giovanni della Casa, Florence, 1564; cf. R. RIDOLFI, *Fortune della 'Storia d'Italia'*, etc., cit. p. 829 ff.

38 SEGNI, op. and ed. cit., p. 248, tells of the current rumour that G. had been poisoned by Girolamo degli Albizzi, without saying on who's behalf; but the dreaded name that is unspoken, is easy to imagine, also because Albizzi was notoriously a close follower of Cosimo. It is strange, however, that A. ROSSI, op. cit., pp. 320 ff., reproaches Benoist with interpreting in this obvious fashion the prudent silence of the Florentine historian. He could have reproached him not with the interpretation but with having believed in such an absurd calumny.

39 Part of a letter from Duke Cosimo to Pirro Musefilo, his agent with the Viceroy of Naples, 22 May 1540, published by A. ROSSI, op. cit., vol. II, pp. 336 ff.

40 A.S.F., *Medici e Speziali*, 250 (Libro dei Morti): May 1540, 'Messer Francesco di Piero Guicciardini, on the 23rd buried in Santa Felicita'.

41 Letter from Niccolò Guicciardini to Luigi Guicciardini, 24 May, published by C. GUASTI, *Le Carte Strozziane*, cit., vol. I, pp. 326 ff.

42 See his last testament, cit.: 'He elects to be buried in the church of Santa Felicita in the tomb of his ancestors, with such funeral expense as shall be seen to by the undermentioned heirs, provided that it be done without any worldly pomp or excessive cost.'

43 The tombstone, decorated simply with a fine black marble shield bearing the three white hunting horns of the Guicciardini family, was carved for Piero di Ghino Guicciardini, who died on 22 March 1369 (ab inc.). This Piero 'was a rich man and looked after affairs in Tuscany for messer Niccolò Acciaiuoli, Grand Seneschal of the Kingdom of Naples, and attended on his behalf to building at Certosa; and I can well believe, considering his other activities, that he made a lot of money out of it, as he was evidently a rogue and a usurer'. This is the way his great descendant Francesco writes of him, with his usual implacable objectivity (*Opp.*, vol. IX, p. 4); though it was Francesco's lot to end up beneath the marble slab bearing only that 'rogue's' name. Later on, unfortunately, there was added in 1727 the mediocre inscription recorded by G. RICHA, *Notizie storiche delle Chiese fiorentine*, etc., Florence, 1754–62, vol. IX, p. 297 (though the author is wrong in referring the reader for this Piero di Ghino to MANNI, *Sigilli*, IX, pp. 99–103, which deal in fact with Ghino). Another and more worthy inscription, written by Anton Maria Salvini but commemorating also the great-grandson Piero di Angelo, was put there a few years later *in cornu Evangelii* (on the Gospel side of the altar), and was also published by RICHA, op. cit., IX, p. 324. The ineffable E. ZANONI, op. cit., p. 584, published only the part concerning Francesco without mentioning any exclusion, at the same time affirming incorrectly that it was placed on his tomb. In this epitaph, which would not have displeased Francesco, Salvini, though he did not know the *Consolatoria*, seems to have divined the high ambition it expressed: 'Cuius negocium an ocium gloriosius incertum, Nisi ocii lumen negocii famam clariorem reddidisset.' (It would be difficult to know whether he was greater in affairs or in the pursuits of his leisure, had not the splendour of these rendered more illustrious his fame in affairs.)

44 Letter from Niccolò Guicciardini to Luigi Guicciardini, 8 June 1540, published by C. GUASTI, *Le Carte Strozziane*, cit., vol. I, p. 327.

45 Letter from Niccolò Guicciardini, cit., 8 June 1540. Madonna Maria lived on for a long time after her husband's death, and without being molested too much by the heirs, 'though she did have some trouble and displeasure' (C. GUASTI, op. and loc. cit.). In 1551 she was living in comfortable circumstances in Via de' Pandolfini, with two of her relatives (perhaps two of her daughters who were so unfortunate in the marriages for which Francesco had striven so hard), two manservants and four maids (B.N.F., ms. II. I. 120, *Descrizione dei fuochi*, c. 164 r). She died in 1559 and was buried in the Guicciardini tomb with the husband who had given her so much worry; she left 200 ducats to the nuns of the Monastery of S. Felicita for masses to be said for her soul every day in perpetuity at the high altar, below which the tomb stands (G. RICHA, op. cit., vol. IX, p. 298).

CHAPTER 25

1 VARCHI, op. and ed. cit., vol. I, p. 398.

2 VARCHI, op. cit., vol. I, p. 506.

3 *Ricordi*, p. 247.

4 See, for example, the following passage from his *Carteggi*, vol. VIII, p. 136, concerning the collection of duty on bread in Romagna: 'If the Reverend Armellino were prepared for them to close an eye or operate some limitation, that is, only make those pay who get above a certain sum at a time, the loss to the Camera would be minimal. . . . As it is, in some places on the borders the poor women take bread from one market to another to sell it outside Romagna: it seems wicked to be strict in matters of this kind.'

5 *Carteggi*, vol. VIII, p. 120; Guicciardini commended the children of Sigismondo Santi to his brother Iacopo in the directive he gave him on leaving the Presidency (*Opp. in.*, vol. VIII, p. 414).

6 F. DE SANCTIS, *Saggi critici*, ed. L. Russo, Bari, Laterza, 1957, vol. III, p. 17.

7 L. MALAGOLI, *Guicciardini*, cit., p. 18.

8 *A.S.I.*, ser. I, vol. IV, pt. II (1853), pp. 271–381; cf. LUCIANI, pp. 63 ff.

9 The circumstances which, after a long delay, hastened the publication of the *Storia d'Italia*, have recently been discussed, using hitherto unknown correspondence between Giovan Battista and Lodovico Guicciardini, by R. RIDOLFI, *Documenti sulle prime stampe della 'Storia d'Italia' guicciardiniana*, in *La Bibliofilia*, vol. LXI (1959), pp. 39–51; cf. R. RIDOLFI, *Fortune della 'Storia d'Italia' guicciardiniana prima della stampa*, cit., pp. 825–837; R. RIDOLFI, *Opuscoli*, pp. 203–217.

[10] GIOVIO, *Lettere volgari*, collected by Lodovico Domenichi, Venice, Sessa, 1560, p. 43 v.

[11] For instance, the Bolognese were annoyed (and their writers echo this feeling, sometimes even exacting revenge) that Guicciardini 'had hardly ever written about them' (P. VIZZANI, op. cit., p. 8).

[12] V. LUCIANI, op. and ed. cit., pp. 327 ff.

[13] P. GUICCIARDINI, *Le traduzioni francesi della Storia guicciardiniana*, Florence, Leo S. Olschki, 1950; id., *Le traduzioni inglesi della Storia guicciardiniana*, Florence, Leo S. Olschki, 1951. As is well known, the *Storia*, besides the famous sixteenth-century translations by Chomedy and Fenton, was also translated in that century into Latin, Spanish, German, Flemish, etc. In all, if I am not mistaken, the Italian editions, of the whole or part, number little short of a hundred.

[14] MONTAIGNE, *Essais*, II, 10.

[15] *Ricordi*, p. 191 (n. 179).

[16] F. DE SANCTIS, *Saggi critici*, ed. cit., p. 1. (It is the beginning of the famous essay entitled *L'uomo del Guicciardini*, published in *Nuova Antologia*, 1869.)

[17] See also V. LUCIANI, *Guicciardini and the 'Risorgimento'*, in *Italica*, XVIII (1941), pp. 186–92.

[18] In the essay cit., in n. 16 above, and in his *Storia della letteratura italiana*, Naples, 1870 (vol. II, which contains a chapter on Guicciardini, was in fact published in 1871). On the fortunes of G. and of De Sanctis's famous essay I can now add an article of mine which has appeared since the Italian edition of this book: *L'uomo Guicciardini cento anni dopo*, in *La Bibliofilia*, LXIII, 1961, pp. 227–37. This article (originally published in *Nuova Antologia* with an inaccurate title, as I was unable to see final proofs) refutes, *inter alia*, some strange views put forward by G. TROMBADORI, *Il giudizio del De Sanctis sul Guicciardini*, in *Nuova Antologia*, 1931, pp. 455 ff.

[19] N. SAPEGNO, *Disegno storico della letteratura italiana*, Florence, 'La Nuova Italia', 1950, p. 234.

[20] *Opp.*, vol. VII, p. 274; cf. p. 52 of this volume.

[21] B. CROCE, *Etica e Politica*, etc., 3rd revised ed. (*Saggi filosofici*, IV), Bari, Laterza, 1945, p. 252.

[22] Besides the centenary volume published by the Istituto Naz. per gli Studi sul Rinascimento frequently quoted in these pages with the title *Quarto Centenario*, see the catalogue of the *Mostra guicciardiniana* (Guicciardini exhibition) published by the B.N.F., Florence, 1940.

[23] *Per la inaugurazione di una sala di studio nell'Archivio Guicciardini* (Addresses by Count Paolo Guicciardini and Marquis Roberto Ridolfi to the Società Colombaria and the R. Deputazione Toscana di Storia Patria, at an extraordinary meeting held in that same reading-room (*sala di studio*) on 22 May 1930), Florence, 1930; cf. the obituary of my friend which I published in *La Bibliofilia*, LVII (1955), pp. 56 ff. To the patronage of Count Paolo Guicciardini we owe, among other things, the edition of the *Lettere al Lanfredini* done by Otetea, and the magnificent Italian edition of Luciani's work; he also made a monetary contribution to the resumption of the edition of the *Carteggi* published by the Istituto Storico Italiano and edited, in what is virtually a new series, by Pier Giorgio Ricci.

[24] For these discoveries of mine, see, besides the publication referred to at the beginning of the preceding note, the article by A. Luzio, cit. in n. 6 to chap. 18. My late friend Paolo Guicciardini also spoke of them every time he published texts I had found; and I also wrote about them at some length in my *Memorie di uno studioso*, Rome, Belardetti, 1956, pp. 80–88. On the *Cose fiorentine* see V. LUCIANI, *Recent Guicciardini studies (1945–8)*, in *Italica*, XXVII (1950), pp. 109–15, and before him, the splendid review by P. CARLI, in *G.S.L.I.*, CXXIV (1946), pp. 78–91. To conclude with a joke this biography of a man who (*pace* Remigio Fiorentino) was fond of jokes himself: when I was asked by some provincial newspaper full of praise for these and other discoveries of mine (two of which almost doubled the then known correspondence of Lorenzo de' Medici), whether I would compare myself with Angelo Mai, I replied at once: 'Mai' [never].

INDEX

INDEX